AMAZING

AMC MUSCLE

Complete development and racing history
of the cars from American Motors

Edrie J. Marquez

Motorbooks International
Publishers & Wholesalers Inc.
Osceola, Wisconsin 54020, USA   ®

First published in 1988 by Motorbooks International Publishers
& Wholesalers Inc, P O Box 2, 729 Prospect Avenue, Osceola,
WI 54020 USA

Library of Congress Cataloging-in-Publication Data
Marquez, Edrie, J.
    Amazing AMC muscle / Edrie J. Marquez.
        p.   cm.
    Includes index.
    ISBN 0-87938-300-3 (pbk.)
    1. American Motors automobiles—History.   2. Muscle cars—United
States—History.   3. Stock car racing—United States—History.
I. Title.
TL215.A44M37 1988
338.7′629222′097—dc19   88-4554
                                                                          CIP

On the cover: A 1969 AMX painted in Big Bad Orange. *Jerry
Heasley*
On the back cover: The Penske-Donohue racing Javelin in 1971
action.

Contents

To my wife Alice, my son Kevin and my daughter Kate

Acknowledgments

I am grateful to the following people for their invaluable assistance during the writing of this book.

Jane Barrett
Bruce A. Bender
Steve Collison
John A. Conde
Larry R. Daum
C. Barton Diehl
Paul Dunkerly

Richard D. Houtman
Ken Murray
Pat Murray
Philip J. Pinella
Darryl A. Salisbury
Robert C. J. Tuttle
Allan T. Yankielun

Special thanks to the following for providing photographs.

American Motors Corporation
The John A. Conde Collection
Larry R. Daum
Motor Trend magazine
Thomas P. Quinn
Rod and Custom magazine
Darryl A. Salisbury
Lt. Roy Smith, Alabama State Troopers
Super Stock & Drag Illustrated magazine

Introduction

AMC cars (or Ramblers or Nashes or whatever else they are called) are known as the underdogs of the American automotive world. At one time or another, most AMC owners and enthusiasts have taken abuse about their choice of wheels. I have been taking it since the fifties when my family owned not one, but two 1953 Nash Ambassadors. How many times have you heard, "But it's a Rambler," or "What on earth ever made you buy one of those things?" or "Don't you know those cars are nothing but trouble?"

In the mid-sixties when supercars were starting to proliferate, American Motors Corporation still stuck to the economy-minded ways of building and advertising cars that had made it so successful in the late fifties and early sixties. Company officials were quoted as saying, "The only race we care about is the human race." This slogan may have worked for a number of years, but as the sixties wore on it became apparent to AMC management that if an abrupt about-face in policy was not made soon, the company could very well become history within a few short years. AMC decided to take the big plunge, and was going full bore with various street and racing programs by 1970.

Although AMC was the last of the US manufacturers to recognize the supercar era, its high-performance contribution cannot be ignored. Many GM, Ford and Mopar enthusiasts would like to forget the times they were shut down by a friendly Kenosha giant killer on the streets and on the strip.

The high-performance 1957 Rambler Rebel 327 custom four-door hardtop V-8 was probably one of the most underrated cars of the fifties. The car was indeed a super street sleeper. Not until more than a decade later was the AMC sting felt again.

AMC recruited notable racers to represent and endorse its newly produced street candidates in the ever-growing muscle car field. Shirley Shahan, Craig Breedlove, Roger Penske, George Folmer and Mark Donohue were just a few who racked up victories in various types of motor sports while campaigning AMC products.

The prototype 1966 AMX was a preview of things to come. The 1966½ Rogue 290 was enough to whet the appetite. A well-prepped and good-running 1967 Rogue 343 made the competition take notice. AMC staked its street claim with the 1968 Javelin. The 1968½ AMX was AMC's way of saying, "We're here to stay." The mighty 1969½ Hurst SC/Rambler warded off any potential poachers with a stoplight Grand Prix shutdown signifying "Death by hanging." The 1970 Rebel Machine was an encore. Just when the muscle car era started to wind down, the potent 1971 Javelin 401 left just about everyone thinking. The 1971 Hornet SC/360 backed up AMC's high-performance commitment. The 1972 Gremlin 304 showed that even in the subcompact field AMC was thinking of performance. The 1972-73 Matador 401s and Hornet 360s still showed the Big Three (Ford, Chrysler and General Motors) that AMC was capable. Right up to 1974, a Javelin or Matador coupe equipped with the 401 V-8 could melt the asphalt.

The contributions and impressions AMC left behind during the supercar era cannot be ignored or overlooked. Now take a few steps back and see how those amazing American Motors muscle machines were able to meet the competition head-on with victorious results. Long live the underdog.

Chapter 1

Performance years 1957-67

In May 1954, the Nash Kelvinator Company merged with the Hudson Motor Car Company to form the American Motors Corporation. From the start, AMC was known as an economy-minded company that was not interested in performance. It built its reputation on economy and miles per gallon, something the Big Three almost always kept at the bottom of their priority lists.

This policy worked for AMC for a number of years, but then times changed. In the mid-fifties, during the height of the Detroit horsepower race, AMC found itself trying to push economical models when just about everyone else, including the other independents, was pushing performance.

In 1955, AMC still did not have its own V-8, so it purchased the Packard 320 ci engine and introduced it along with its new models. Although this engine had

only a Carter two-barrel carburetor, 7.8:1 compression and 208 bhp, it was good enough for the times.

It was nearly two years later, in mid-1956, when AMC finally came out with its own V-8—and even this was not an original design. When Kaiser-Willys moved to Argentina in 1955, one of its engineers, David Potter, came over to the newly formed American Motors Corporation. Potter brought all his engine designs, including an all-new aluminum V-8 he had been working on since 1951. His designs resulted in the new mid-1956 AMC 250 ci cast-iron V-8 with a two-barrel carburetor, 8.0:1 compression and 190 bhp. It was much more compact and lighter than the huge Packard engine.

Newer styling was also introduced on the 1956 models, and the Rambler was all new and bigger, but AMC still did not have a true performance model. The firm needed an image booster, even if only in styling—as its basic styling dated back to 1949.

The prototype 1956 Palm Beach was a joint effort between AMC and Pinin Farina of Italy. It could well have changed Rambler's image, but AMC ended the project before production could ever get off the ground.

The 1957 Rambler Rebel was AMC's first true high-performance domestic model. Although the AMA ban on racing put an end to its further development, production reached 1,500 units of this clean four-door hardtop sedan.

Rambler Palm Beach

The one-off prototype 1956 Rambler Palm Beach two-seater sports car could have turned the trick, but the project died as soon as the car appeared in the United States, after its tour of several major European auto shows. The car was designed and built by Pinin Farina of Italy, yet used a stock Rambler 172.6 ci L-head six-cylinder engine with a Weber sidedraft carburetor producing an anemic 82 bhp.

The chassis was a separate ladder type with box-section side-members. The wheelbase was 101.5 inches with a 54.5 inch front and a 53.5 inch rear wheel track. Most of the chassis and suspension components were stock Rambler. The car was light at an overall weight of 2,600 pounds, and an overall length of 176 inches.

The body was all steel with an oval nosepiece reminiscent of certain early-fifties Ferraris. The rear-end treatment, complete with outward-slanting fins and bright chrome back panel, was similar to that on the 1957-61 Studebaker Hawks. There was a unique twin-cowl treatment on the rear deck indicating the two-seater concept of the car. Two standard 1957 Rambler R badges were put on the nosepiece and the deck lid for easy identification. Palm Beach was spelled out on the deck lid and both quarter panels, and Pinin Farina spelled out with its insignia graced both fenders. Palm Beach was also spelled out inside the recessed oval grille.

The interior was well appointed. Deep-pile carpeting covered the floor and trunk area, and the two semibucket seats were covered in top-grain beige leather. A small between-the-seats bolster was used, similar to that in the 1954 Kaiser-Darrin. The engine instruments were gathered in two large round nacelles and included a tachometer; water temperature, oil pressure and manifold pressure gauges; odometer and a trip mileage recorder.

The steering wheel was telescopically adjustable and was a dual-spoke wood-rim type. Total turns were

The original 327 cubic inch V-8 for the Rebel was to use a Bendix electronic fuel injection system called the Electrojector. Engineering problems prevented its use, although two or three prototypes were built. A single Carter four-barrel carburetor was ultimately used for the production Rebels.

The elegant-looking 1964 Classic-based Typhoon two-door hardtop introduced AMC's new seven-main-bearing 232 cubic inch six-cylinder engine. Note the liberal use of blacked-out treatment on the grille and side spear. The hot 327 ci 270 hp V-8 would have been a natural for this model.

just three, lock-to-lock. (This steering wheel found its way almost unchanged onto the 1963 Studebaker Avanti.) The car had an awkward downward-angled, too-far-forward turn signal stalk, but a nice-looking floorshift for the standard three-speed manual Rambler transmission.

It is suggested that the Palm Beach was supposed to be the successor to the 1951-54 Nash Healeys, which were joint ventures between Pinin Farina and Donald Healey of Healey Motor Company. Evidence does point toward this in the building, styling and dimensions of the Palm Beach. For instance, its overall dimensions and wheelbase were just about the same as the Nash Healey's and its roof styling was nearly identical to that of the 1953-54 hardtop models. It was probably the last attempt by the regime of Nash president George Mason to continue building British-Italian-American sports cars.

New AMC president George Romney had other ideas based on what was said to be inside information (he was also the head of the Automobile Manufacturers Association, or AMA). In May 1957, the AMA announced that all factories were pulling out of racing and performance-related activities, but not before the midyear introduction of the new 1957 Rambler Rebel 327 V-8 custom four-door hardtop sedan.

V-8 power

Here at last was AMC's first true high-performance V-8-engine-equipped car. The engine was to have incorporated Bendix electronic fuel injection, called the Electrojector, a production car industry first. Nevertheless, only two or three prototypes were made with this system; the rest of the 1,500 cars built received a single Carter four-barrel, which, ironically, qualified them for NASCAR racing. Chrysler Corporation used a similar fuel injection system on fifteen or so 1958 models, but most were converted to carburetion owing to problems. Pontiac also tried fuel injection on some of its 1959 models, again with no success.

The fuel-injected Rebel engine was rated at 288 bhp and the four-barrel version produced 255 hp, both

at 4700 rpm. The new engine was a bored and stroked version of the previous year's 250 V-8 and had a 9.5:1 compression, solid lifters and a dual exhaust system. Torque was healthy, developing 345 pounds-feet at 2600 rpm. Only five more pounds-feet of torque was developed for the fuel-injected engine.

The Rebel was considered a compact car, having a wheelbase of 108 inches, a length of 191.14 inches, a width of 71.32 inches, a height of 58.4 inches, and front and rear tread dimensions of 57.75 and 58.0 inches, respectively. The overall shipping weight was a mere 3,353 pounds, which was light for the time. If the optional Continental tire was ordered, the overall length jumped to 198.89 inches. Tires were tall four-ply nylon whitewalls measuring 6.70x15. Standard transmission was a three-speed manual or three-speed with overdrive, and a 4.10:1 rear axle ratio, with a 4.44:1 optional. Another optional transmission was a Borg-Warner three-speed Hydra-matic having a 3.15:1 rear ratio.

To handle the extra power of the engine, the chassis and driveline were beefed up. A heavy-duty torque-tube driveline assembly and heavy-duty adjustable Gabriel shocks with heavy-duty springs were installed along with specially designed flanged brake drums to dissipate heat and maintain efficiency under hard usage. For added stability, a front stabilizer bar was incorporated into the front end. A vacuum booster with a high-output battery and generator was needed to operate the full complement of accessories.

Standard equipment was power steering and brakes, windshield washers, electric clock, radio and rear deck antenna, full-flowing oil filter and oil bath air cleaner, undercoating, Airliner reclining seats, foam cushions, padded sun visors and instrument panels, directional signals, back-up lights, Weather-Eye heating and special wheel discs. Options were limited to the overdrive or Flashaway three-speed Borg-Warner Hydra-matic transmissions and Continental spare tire. For the customer who wanted more, high-speed six-ply nylon blue-streak whitewalls, Solex glass, air conditioning and seatbelts could be ordered.

This clay model being sculptured by an AMC designer in the early sixties, showed that the company was serious about changing its image.

This early sketch was a bit radical, but typical of the automotive designers' dreams at the time. Many of its features would become reality in a few short years.

The interior seat upholstery was finished in special silver vinyl and silver-threaded black nylon fabric. A special perforated vinyl headliner and full floor carpets finished off the cabin.

The exterior was painted with a specially baked enamel finish in light metallic silver-gray with a bronze-gold anodized aluminum side panel. The combination was elegant.

Motor Trend magazine had a chance to road test a Rebel 327 V-8 and also to see what it could do on the sands of Daytona Beach in Florida. The model used was a prototype equipped with a four-barrel carburetor, three-speed overdrive and 4.10:1 rear axle ratio. On public roads on the way to Daytona, the Rebel was put through its paces. Zero-to-sixty times averaged out to 7.5 seconds (7.8 with three aboard) with overdrive locked out. Fifty-to-eighty in overdrive took just 7.2 seconds. A top speed of 110 mph was reached and the needle was still climbing. The fifteen members of the press crew all had a chance to quarter-mile drag the Rebel. The average speed was 87.5 mph, and the average elapsed time was 18.72 seconds. For a family sedan in the fifties, that was performance.

The car even boasted good gas mileage. With two aboard plus a full trunk and a rear passenger compartment loaded with luggage, and maintaining speeds of between 50 and 70 mph in overdrive, the car averaged 17.5 mpg. Handling, though not spectacular, was fine and firm, better than with a standard Rambler. Nose-diving, roll and bottoming were minimized with the heavy-duty suspension, but steering response was slow at almost four turns lock-to-lock. The flanged brakes with heat-dissipating drums were adequate, but

they could have used improvement, as was found out during repeated high-speed stops.

The Rebel was America's most powerful compact car. Its 0-60 time of 7.5 seconds was the fastest of any American production car with the exception of the 283 hp mechanical fuel injection 1957 Corvette, which could do 0-60 in seven seconds flat. The mighty Rebel 327's closest rivals were the Chrysler 300-C three-speed manual 392, which could do 0-60 in 7.6 seconds, and the Pontiac 347 Tri-Carb, which could do it in 7.9 seconds. All the other cars ran between eight and ten seconds. At a base price of $2,786, the Rebel was indeed a bargain performance car.

When the AMA banned all high-performance involvement and activities by car manufacturers, the red-hot Rambler Rebel 327 models were doomed. The idea of dropping a powerful big-block V-8 into a compact or intermediate lightweight body style was later revived by Pontiac Motor Division, however, which started the supercar era with the introduction of the legendary 1964 Pontiac GTO.

The Rebel was still continued for the 1958-60 model years but was limited to the 250 ci four-barrel V-8. The newer 270 hp 327 engine was reserved exclusively for the larger 117-inch-wheelbase Ambassador, which was a heavy luxury model.

Economy minded

When the recession hit in 1958, the United States became economy minded and AMC pulled another industry first. The economical 100-inch-wheelbase Nash Rambler had been laid to rest at the end of the 1955 model year because at that time performance was

The Tarpon show car, based on the 1964 Rambler American, was the forerunner of the 1965 Classic-based Marlin.

selling and economy was not. AMC still had all the tooling for the little economy champ. The Nash Rambler was resurrected and put back into production as the 1958 Rambler American. It was from one to two years before the others in the industry caught up and came out with their own compacts.

Studebaker was the first, coming out with the Lark for 1959. For 1960, Chevy came out with its radical rear-engine-design Corvair. Ford and Chrysler stayed with the conventional front engine layout, introducing the Falcon and Valiant, respectively. Mercury came out with its own Falcon-based version called the Comet in mid-1960. Dodge came out with the 1961 Lancer, which was a slightly restyled Valiant. Buick, Oldsmobile and Pontiac finally came out with their 1961 versions, called the Special, F-85 and Tempest, which would become intermediates on a larger wheelbase, for the 1964 model year.

From 1958 to 1963 it was as though AMC could do no wrong. Having built its reputation on economy, reliability and durability, its sales were strong, reaching their peak in 1961 when AMC placed third in the industry, ousting Plymouth from that position. In 1963, AMC received *Motor Trend* magazine's Car of the Year award. Ceramic-armored mufflers and tailpipes and AMC's Deep-Dip rust-proofing process were just a couple of the cars' unique features.

The Rambler Tarpon Showcar was unveiled at the SAE (Society of Automotive Engineers) convention in January 1964. This was a 1964 Rambler American with a fastback welded on. It sat on the American's 106 inch wheelbase but had a slightly longer overall length of 180 inches compared with the American's 177.25 inches. The Tarpon was quite attractive from any angle with its distinctive roofline, partly vinyl covered, and its large rectangular taillights with cross-pattern and integrated bull's-eye motif. Large one-piece front and rear bumperette bars were added on with rubber facings. The grille was a protruding convex six-piece

The 1965 Marlin blended a spacious interior with the growing popularity of the fastback roof-styling theme.

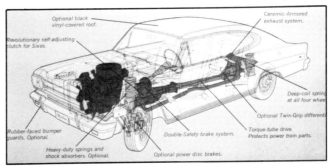

The 1966 Marlin was little changed from its 1965 counterpart.

vertical split type that would later appear on the production 1965 Rambler American in a slightly modified flush form.

Tarpon medallions were placed on the trunkless deck and on both fenders behind the wheels. A

The Rebel name returned to the classic series as that model's top of the line. A 327 four-barrel four-speed combination was available for this clean-cut hardtop.

11

chromed racing-style outside rearview mirror was added, along with special eight-slot chrome-plated wheels and three bar spinners. Tires were one-inch-thick whitewalls. Three chrome vertical bars were placed on each side of the fastback sail panels. The body was painted in a deep Candy Apple Red, with a fireflake metallic finish called Gold-Flecked Vermillion.

The interior was just as impressive. It was a four-passenger bucket seat type featuring hand-sewn leather upholstery and wood instrument panel trim. A padded-eyebrow-type dashboard was used, with speedometer, tachometer and a full set of gauges. A Mustang-like three-spoke sports steering wheel was used. The car was also equipped with a console and a stock production twin-stick overdrive transmission (one lever controlled the transmission while the other controlled the overdrive). The engine was the optional 196 ci ohv six-cylinder.

AMC produced a limited number of sporty looking 1964 Rambler Typhoon two-door hardtop models to introduce its new-design seven-main-bearing 232 ci six-cylinder engine, which was created by engineer David Potter. The Typhoon was introduced in April

1964. All of the 2,520 cars built were painted Solar Yellow with a black roof and featured a semiflat blacked-out grille and side spears. It was an attractive package. It is a shame AMC did not offer the 327 ci 270 hp V-8 engine as an option. With a shipping weight of approximately 2,800 pounds and a wheelbase of 112 inches, this car could have outdone and outperformed the 1957 327 Rambler Rebel.

Marlin pony car

About this time Ford Motor Company was getting ready to drop the bomb on the American auto industry. The Mustang, introduced on April 17, 1964, caught everyone off guard. Even Plymouth's Barracuda, introduced April 1 of the same year, came nowhere near the success of the elegant Mustang, which was the first and only automobile to be awarded the Tiffany Award by Tiffany and Company of Paris, for excellence in design.

The Mustang was an all-new design with Falcon-based mechanics; Barracuda was merely a Valiant with a fastback welded on. During its abbreviated 1964 model year, the Mustang broke all sales records and set new ones that still stand as of this writing. Its success, coupled with the fall 1963 introduction of the GTO option on the new intermediate 1964 Pontiac Tempest, heralded the birth of the new horsepower race coined as the supercar era.

AMC's first entry into the pony car field was the 1965 Rambler Marlin. Its production was finalized by two men: Richard A. (Dick) Teague, who had joined AMC in 1959 as assistant automotive design director and was named vice-president of styling on February 6, 1964, and Roy Abernethy, who had succeeded Romney as president of AMC in 1962.

The Marlin's original proposals were derived from the 1964 Rambler Tarpon Showcar. Abernethy disliked small cars, however, and thus approved the

The luxury Ambassador for 1966 was AMC's senior line. Shown is a 990 convertible V-8 model with crisp styling.

The Classic series was renamed Rebel for 1967 and received complete new styling. This SST convertible was one of the nicest looking cars ever put out by AMC.

112-inch-wheelbase Classic design model over the smaller American model. It has been said that the Tarpon might have been the better choice, since its fastback styling and compact Mustang dimensions were more tuned to the new wave of personal sporty cars.

The Marlin was introduced in February 1965 and was given the task of running against the Mustang until an all-new pony car could be developed. Unlike the Mustang but like the Barracuda, the Marlin was available in a fastback version only. It was also like the Barracuda in that it was simply a fastback added to an existing model—the Classic. Dodge did the same with the Charger, adding a fastback on the existing Coronet for 1966. The Marlin and Charger were based on intermediate-size body styles, unlike the Mustang and Barracuda which were based on compact car dimensions.

The Barracuda, Charger and Marlin came to bat with two strikes against them. The first strike was that they were merely cosmetically altered versions of existing body styles with the addition of a fastback. Their second strikes varied. The Charger was too heavy but could be moved along briskly with the right engine option. The Barracuda's huge rear glass area did not blend well with the rest of the body and its rear seat occupants fried at even the faintest hint of sun. The Marlin's second strike was by far the worst: the car had nothing new to offer in the performance department.

The top engine option in the Marlin was the 327 ci 270 hp V-8 that had been available, virtually unchanged, since 1957. Although the car came standard with power steering and power front disc brakes, it still retained the torque-tube driveline, and the 327 engine was equipped with a single exhaust and a three-speed manual or automatic transmission—no four-speed was offered yet.

All of Ford's competitors, including AMC, were building pseudo pony cars using existing models and off-the-shelf parts to try to keep up with the Mustang image until their own all-new versions could be developed. The Marlin came off with respectable but not supercarlike performance. AMC advertised that a 1966 Marlin equipped with the 270 hp engine could do 0-60 in ten seconds flat. No specific mention was made of which transmission or rear axle ratio was used to obtain that time.

The 1966 model was introduced in fall 1965 and was virtually identical to the 1965 version. There was a slight change in grille design, which was still basically the Classic grille. The base price of the car was reduced by almost $500 to $2,601 by making various standard components optional. The Marlin could be brought up to almost $5,000 for a super sport-luxury car with adequate performance. But the youth-oriented market demanded blistering performance in the form of cars such as the SS 396 Chevelle, Tri-Carb GTO, Olds 442, Hi-Po 289 Mustang and the like. There was no way the old-design V-8 driveline or suspension system could rival or even equal such fast acceleration.

Although the 1964 and 1965 compact Rambler American series was built to easily accommodate a V-8 engine, it did not receive one until mid-1966. The car's basic body construction type, new engine, driveline and suspension layout were the basis of most of the AMC supercars of 1968-74.

Model year 1966 saw the introduction of the advertising slogan, "The Friendly Giant Killers," and

Even the hardtop was an eye catcher. The 290 and 343 V-8s could be teamed to a new fully synchronized four-speed transmission with optional dash-mounted tachometer, as shown.

the revival of the Rambler Rebel 327, which became the top-of-the-line option on the Classic series. The engine could be had in a milder two-barrel carburetor, 250 hp version or the tried-and-true 270 hp, four-barrel version. This engine could also be ordered in the Marlin and the Ambassador series, and could be coupled, finally, to a four-speed Borg-Warner manual gearbox. Again, no dual exhaust was offered and the driveline and suspension were carried over from previous years. The Rebel 327 was also advertised as being able to do 0-60 in ten seconds flat. Although the 1966 Rebel two-door hardtop was an attractive package and could be ordered with just about any convenience and luxury option to satisfy the buyer, the most important option—performance—was still lacking.

The old fifties-style powerplant and mechanicals were gasping for air in the now-crowded supercar

The 1967 Ambassador featured one of the most comfortable and plush seats in the entire industry.

scene. The streets were being burned up with mighty 427s from Ford and Chevy, and the 426 Elephant Chrysler Street Hemi made its debut. So, 1966 was AMC's last year of holding on to the old battleship way of designing and motivation.

Performance plus

Model year 1967 finally saw AMC opening the right door into the performance arena. This was a prelude of bigger and better things to come. AMC would invest over $300 million in new and advanced design engines, bodies and plant facilities. In 1966, Robert B. Evans had been named chairman of the board and Roy D. Chapin, Jr., son of the founder of the Hudson Motor Car Company, had been named executive vice-president and general manager of the Automotive Division. Chapin became board chairman in 1967, and William V. Luneberg was named president. Victor G. Raviolo of road racing background came into engineering to oversee the new racing program, and Carl Chakmakian was put in charge of the new Performance Activities department as of September 1967. All were instrumental in the preparation of the new wave of 1967 models.

Another major advertising campaign was launched in 1967, proclaiming the cars to be "The Now Cars from the 1967 American Motors." The five-year or 50,000 mile warranty on the engine, drivetrain, suspension and steering together with the two-year or 24,000 mile warranty on the entire automobile were introduced. Gone were the old-design Classic, Marlin and Ambassador models. This also marked the first year AMC began to register some of its cars as individual makes, starting with the Marlin and the Ambassador. This trend continued for 1968 and on.

The 1967 Ambassador used vertical instead of horizontally placed headlights as on the Rebel. It too could be ordered with a host of high-performance items.

The Classic was now called the Rebel, with a top-of-the-line SST designation standing for Super Sport Touring, similar to Chevrolet's successful SS (Super Sport) models. The Rebel SST 343 was advertised as "The Excitement Machine," possibly a prelude to the 1970 Rebel machine. The Rebel also rode on a longer 114 inch wheelbase.

Although the Ambassador retained its name, it too had a new top-of-the-line model option, called the DPL, standing for Diplomat. Its wheelbase was also stretched, now sporting 118 inches, and was shared with the Marlin. The Marlin, now in its final year, was simply an Ambassador with a fastback. Grilles on both cars were identical, with vertically stacked quad headlights outside of a horizontal bar grille and integral rally lights. The rally lights were on the DPL version of the Ambassador only, and not on the two basic 880 and 990 models.

Body designs and overall styles of all the models except the American were totally new and pleasing to the eye. Another change that was badly needed occurred to the torque-tube drive and old suspension arrangement, which were finally deleted in favor of a new four-link trailing arm rear suspension design with front and rear coil springs—a la GM A-bodies, such as the Chevelle and Tempest. The American did keep its Hotchkiss rear-drive setup, however.

Probably the biggest and best news was that there was finally a new thin-wall block-casting-design compact V-8 engine that offered performance to match the new cars' looks. The new AMC V-8 sported one of the most compact exterior dimensions in the industry. It was called the Typhoon V-8, and was available in 290 and 343 ci versions to replace the old 287 and 327 engines. The 290 was roughly eighty-three pounds lighter than the old engines, and was available in a 200 hp, 9.0:1 compression two-barrel version and in a 225 hp, 10.0:1 compression four-barrel version. The 343 was rated at 235 hp for the 9.0:1 compression two-barrel and at 280 hp for the 10.2:1 compression four-barrel. Both new engines had the same stroke of 3.28 inches, but the 343 had a bore of 4.08 inches and the 290 had a bore of 3.75 inches. Valves on the 343 were larger, carrying 2.0 inch intakes and 1.625 inch exhausts. The 290 was set at 1.787 inch intakes and 1.406 inch exhausts.

Both Carter four-barrel engines required premium fuel. Heads were interchangeable, providing improved breathing for the smaller engine. A new aluminum timing case cover incorporated the distributor; fuel, oil and water pumps; and spin-on oil filter. Individual ball-stud rocker arms like those found on the small-block Chevy and Ford were also used. Rocker arm ratio was changed to 1.6:1 as opposed to the 1.5:1 used in the older mills. Net valve lift was increased from 0.375 to 0.425 and valve duration from 244 degrees to 266 degrees with forty-four degrees of overlap.

About the only undesirable feature of the new engine was the restrictive cast-log-type exhaust manifolds. A single exhaust system was standard, further restricting what was considered to be an otherwise free-breathing engine. Dual exhaust was listed as an option on the Rebel, but not on the American.

AMC made good use of existing tooling and parts in the development of the new V-8 engine. A number of components were interchangeable with the 232 ci six, such as the pistons, rings, piston pins, connecting rods (caps and bolts) and main bearing cap bolts. The 290 used the same valves, springs, spring retainers and locks. Miscellaneous pieces such as fan hubs, oil filters, rear main pan seals, thermostats, oil pump relief valve springs and water pump seals also interchanged.

All those specifications would have meant nothing if the performance hadn't been there—but it most definitely was there. The Rambler American, being the

The four-door 990 was a quiet and solidly built luxury cruiser. This model is powered by the smooth-running 232 six.

lightest car, produced the quickest 0-60 mph and quarter-mile times.

The hot setup in 1967 was the all-new inter-mediate-size Rebel SST equipped with the Carter four-barrel 280 hp 343 V-8. *Car Life* magazine road-tested a Rebel equipped with that engine coupled to a floor-shifted three-speed automatic transmission and twin-grip 3.15:1 rear. The car was also ordered with heavy-duty cooling, power front disc brakes and steering, heavy-duty electricals and various convenience items such as a clock, radio, headrests, sports steering wheel, light group, remote control outside rearview mirror, and electric windshield wipers and washers. The base price of the SST was $2,845, and $3,638 would purchase the car with all options.

With a curb weight of 3,560 pounds and a test weight of nearly 400 pounds more, times were not expected to be earth shattering. With a 0-60 time of nine seconds flat and a quarter-mile elapsed time of 16.9 seconds at 83 mph, performance was respectable and, more important, showed potential. *Popular Hot Rodding* was able to obtain a best elapsed time of 15.31 at 91 mph with the same engine and transmission combination.

The exhaust on this setup was restrictive, thus preventing the engine from breathing properly. The Rebel model chosen by most young buyers was equipped with the four-speed manual transmission and deeper 3.54:1 rear end gears. With the simple addition of a set of tuned headers and a free-flowing exhaust system, the car was capable of running the quarter mile in the low- to mid-fourteen-second range at over 95 mph. This car was in the supercar league practically right off the showroom floor. If the owner wanted to go further, the optional dealer-installed factory 4.44:1 rear end gearset and hi-po (high-power) cam and kit were available as of February 1967 under the Group 19 high-performance quipment. The Rebel could be turned into one mean street sleeper. An adventurous individual could even go drag racing if he

or she didn't mind competing way down in NHRA's (National Hot Rod Association's) I/Stock class, which is where the 343 Rebel was placed.

The newly styled Marlin could also hold its own with a little performance tuning. *Motor Trend* magazine road-tested a 343 four-barrel automatic transmission model and was able to obtain a 0-60 time of 9.6 seconds and a quarter-mile elapsed time of 17.6 seconds at 82 mph. The slower times (as compared with the Rebel's) were due to the Marlin's heavier weight. In a head-to-head road-test confrontation with the 1967 Dodge Charger, the Marlin's power was found to be theoretically equal to that of the Dodge 383 ci two-barrel 270 hp car (a four-barrel 325 hp model was actually tested).

A slightly reworked 343 Marlin could exceed the performance of a 440 ci 375 hp Charger and just about equal the performance of the 426 Hemi model. *Motor Trend* found that the 440 Charger could do 0-60 in eight seconds flat and the quarter-mile in 15.5 seconds at 93 mph—even the 343 Rebel could stay right with that one. The Hemi was able to do 0-60 in 7.6 seconds and the quarter-mile in 14.4 seconds at 100 mph.

Yes, AMC had finally showed the public that it could compete with the Big Three, and that it was totally committed to performance as well as to new styling. More evidence of this new focus appeared in AMC's forward thrust into the advanced styling concepts and cars of the Project IV Tour.

Dash-mounted tachs, woodgrain steering wheels, four-speed transmissions and modern design V-8 engines put the Marlin and AMC back on the high-performance trail for 1967 after an absence of nearly a decade.

The 1967 Marlin rode on the larger Ambassador platform. Its grille used running lights, as did the Ambassador DPL's.

Chapter 2

Project IV Tour 1966-67

American Motors was not only determined to shed its staid image regarding performance, but was also ready, willing and able to design bold new, crisply styled cars to match. And it had to do both, because since 1963 the company had been going downhill, and fast. With reported losses of $12,648,170 in 1966 and $75.8 million in 1967, there was no other road to take.

The Project IV Tour was developed to test the public's reaction to AMC's new wave of automotive designs. The four automobiles that made up the Project IV group were known as the AMX, AMX II, Cavalier and Vixen. Each car was designed for a specific market. The AMX (American Motors Experimental)

was the first of these designs to be unveiled, making its debut at the National SAE Convention in Detroit, in January 1966. The general public got a chance to get in on the action briefly during the AMX's dealer exhibition tours, by filling out a ballot to give the car a name of their choice. This first model, which now resides in the Crawford Museum in Cleveland, Ohio, was a non-operational plastic shell containing no engine, drivetrain or suspension, but its basic design suggested it could be modified for production.

The model sat on a ninety-eight-inch wheelbase and was forty-eight inches high, seventy-two inches wide and 179 inches long. It was built as a combination

The operational AMX was unique in every way. It was the model that spearheaded the Project IV Tour.

two-seater/four-seater with the rear seats being small jump seats. AMC also decided to resurrect a feature from the twenties and thirties in the form of a rumble, or mother-in-law, seat, which it chose to call a Ramble Seat. The rear deck was opened to provide for the back section of the seat. The rear window was designed to pivot upward to provide legroom for the passengers and to act as a windshield for their protection against the wind and the weather. This also allowed Ramble Seat passengers to converse with the front seat passengers.

The AMX incorporated many other unique features as well. The one most noticeable to the eye was the pillarless windshield butted tightly up against the immovable side windows. Whatever strength was lost there was compensated for in the roll bar that was built into the cantilever section of the roof itself. Its flying buttress roofline was very nicely blended into the quarter panels, which also contained gas filler neck lids on both sides.

The car also featured ribbed rocker panels with exhaust outlets at each end forward of the rear wheels and nicely designed flat machined five-spoke, fifteen-inch mag wheels with center caps on blue-streak tires. The taillights were a flush invisible wraparound type acting as side-marker lights. A silver mesh over the red lenses made them seemingly invisible in the daytime. With the stop- or taillights on, the mesh became transparent, and the red light spanned nearly the full width of the car for maximum visibility.

The rear bumper was integrated with the taillights and quarter panels and sat high at deck level. The front bumper was integrated into the fender contours, which also contained side-marker lights. Square single headlamps were used with round blinkers directly below, under the bumper. A V-shaped aluminum thin-bar horizontal recessed grille design finished off the front. AMX emblems were placed in the right side of the grille and on the right trailing edge of the deck lid. Flush door handles, twin racing-style outside rearview mirrors and a twin blister hood with eight leading-edge slots created a nice effect. The body was painted silver-blue metallic.

The interior of the car sported shell-type bucket seats finished in beige natural leather upholstery. Between the seats was a full-length center console.

Public reaction to the AMX was so favorable that an operational steel-bodied version was built roughly six months later under the direct supervision of Italian coachbuilder Vignale. (The Vignale AMX was later donated to the Wheels of Speed Museum.) The AMX was the only one of the four Project IV Tour cars that was made operational.

Changes made to the running model were few. The pillarless windshield design was achieved through the use of clear glass-to-glass vinyl seals, thus permitting optimum visibility for added safety. In the original design, the side windows were not operational; ventilation was achieved only through air entering the eight leading-edge hood slots and exiting a rear window outlet. In the production car, conventional ventilation could be achieved by closing the hood slots and rolling down the windows. This change was made because of the numerous drive-in establishments in existence at the time.

The hatch-type doors wrapped up into the roof for easy entry and exit, and were opened by a push bar mechanism. The flush door handles were eliminated and small vertical slots were cut into the quarter panels just behind the doors. The windshield wipers retracted into the cowl area and the Ramble Seat was activated by a push-button control inside the car. Blue body pinstriping was placed along the lower body sculpture. Fold-down rear seats were added, and these could be

The Vignale AMX was a further extension of the original mockup and operational AMXs. Here it stands poised at the Daytona Motor Speedway.

used when the Ramble Seat was not in use. A sports-type walnut-rimmed steering wheel added a nice competition flair. The only body dimension altered was the height, which was increased by one inch to forty-nine inches.

Power for the AMX was the all-new 290 ci 225 hp four-barrel V-8 with dual exhaust and Borg-Warner four-speed transmission.

On June 20, 1966, the Project IV cars were unveiled to the news media in New York. The operational AMX was chosen as the leader of the pack.

The AMX II was a modified version of the original AMX. This two-door hardtop sat on a slightly larger 110 inch wheelbase with an overall length of 187 inches. It had the same ribbed rocker panel treatment and mag wheels as the AMX, but had half-inch-thick white sidewall tires instead of the AMX's blue-streak type. A safety-conscious feature was the taillight assembly, which was made up of green, yellow and red lights. When the driver accelerated the green light shined; when he or she lifted off on the gas pedal the yellow light came on; and when the driver braked the red light was lit. The car had a unique V-shaped rear window that blended into the rear deck contours and carried out the fastback theme very well.

The AMX II was the forerunner of the production Javelin, whose target market was the pony car field for direct competition with the Mustang. The Javelin took about eighteen months from drawing board to final prototype, completed in April 1966. At one time in the Javelin's development a frameless fiberglass body was considered, and three such prototypes were made by Dow Smith, Incorporated, a firm specializing in automotive fiberglass components. The fiberglass body was considered to be unreliable strengthwise, however, and so the decision was made to produce a steel body. Although slight changes in the hood, grille, roofline and quarter panels were necessary when the change from glass to steel was made, ninety percent of the design characteristics were retained for the four-seater Javelin. The AMX II was finished off in a deep metallic green with gold pinstriping.

The Cavalier used numerous interchangeable components such as the doors, bumpers, hood and deck lid.

The four-door Cavalier was probably the most cost effective of the Project IV cars. Many body parts were interchangeable, thus keeping tooling down to a bare minimum. The right front fender and left rear fender were identical, as were the opposite panels. The left front and right rear doors were the same, as were the right front and left rear units. Hood and deck lids as well as the front and rear bumpers were also the same (as they were on the 1964-69 Rambler American and to a degree on the 1970-74 Hornet and Gremlin). Tooling savings were estimated to be twenty-five percent of the delivery price of the car, or $1,600, and this savings could be passed on to the customer.

The car had subcompactlike dimensions, sitting on a wheelbase of 108 inches (the same as the Chevrolet Corvair) and having an overall length of 175 inches. Like the AMX, the Cavalier featured a built-in roll bar. The same rear taillight treatment from the AMX II was used on the Cavalier.

The deck lid of the Cavalier featured scissor-type hinges, allowing the trunk to be opened in the usual manner or elevated to the roof's level if larger objects had to be loaded inside the compartment. Other fea-

The AMX II was a modified version of the AMX. It became the forerunner of the 1968 Javelin.

The Vixen gave a glimpse of the styling of the 1970 Hornet and Gremlin. It too used interchangeable body panels.

tures on the car were a vinyl-covered roof, SS chrome mag wheels and one-inch-thick white sidewall tires. The doors were the suicide-type opening common on cars of the thirties and forties.

The Cavalier was developed at the same time that new federal safety standards were to take effect beginning with the 1968 model year. In an open letter to the undersecretary of commerce, Abernethy explained that to force AMC into the upheaval of "Annual Model Changes" and forced obsolescence would preclude a car like the Cavalier from ever being produced. As it turned out, AMC was forced to change with the times.

The Vixen matched the looks of the 1970 production Hornet and Gremlin as the original AMX matched the production 1968 AMX. The Vixen was described as a sporty semifastback version of the Cavalier sharing the same interchangeability features rearranged in a cleaner body style.

The Vixen's wheelbase and overall length were the same as the Cavalier's, but the windshield was moved back a foot and the hoodline was extended an equal distance. The car also sported a deeply recessed concave window that blended in very well with the roofline. When this characteristic was coupled with the flat-black paint finish on the rear deck, it appeared as though the car had no rear window at all. The landau-styled roof with forty-five-degree canted vents in the rear roof panels increased visibility when the car was parked or being backed up. The vents also permitted flow-through ventilation regulated by the Vixen's sliding glass panels mounted in the interior.

The Vixen almost became the 1970 production Hornet, paralleling it closely in overall body design and dimensions. One feature on the Vixen that inspired later production designs was its functional raised-profile hood scoop. Modified versions of this hood scoop appeared on the 1969 SC/Rambler; 1970 AMX, Javelin and Rebel Machine; and 1971 Hornet SC/360.

The Project IV Tour was a complete success. It paved the way for AMC's new styling, which lasted over a decade, from the late sixties to the late seventies. More important, it showed that AMC could change with the times—that it could change for the better and could turn its image around in the crowded supercar era.

Vice President of Styling Richard A. Teague was the man most responsible for the design of the AMC models from 1964-85. Here he stands proudly next to the prototype 1966 AMX and a 1904 Rambler he owned at the time and still owns today.

Chapter 3

AMX 1968-70

From its introduction as a show car in 1966 to its showing as a production model ready for sale to the public in February 1968, at a press preview held at the Daytona International Speedway, the AMX created excitement. Here at last was a two-seater sports car American Motors could be proud to show off, and that's just what it did.

The AMX was introduced roughly six months after the Javelin, making its public debut at the Chicago Auto Show on February 23, 1968. The press and the public could not wait to get their hands on it, as indicated by the successful feedback AMC received from the Project IV Tour.

The factory brochure *The AMX Story* described the car as having an undefinable Italian look of "gentile masculinity." (Public relations representative John A. Conde spotted the "genteel" misspelling and all the literature was recalled and destroyed, but a few booklets survive with the mistake.)

Very seldom does a car look like its prototype or inherit most or all of its prototype's characteristics—but the production AMX came through with almost ninety percent of them. As is the case with any new car, existing tooling and off-the-shelf parts must be used whenever possible for the car to be cost-effective. Later changes could be made as mandated by federal standards, buyer criticism, acceptance and sales.

It has been said that the AMX was nothing but a Javelin with a foot cut out of its midsection. This is not entirely true. The two-seater AMX prototype preceded the modified four-seater AMX II prototype version that eventually became the Javelin. The production Javelin bowed in the fall of 1967 as a 1968 model and the production AMX made its debut in February 1968.

The AMX was a superbly styled car. The redline tires blended nicely with the optional all-chrome five-spoke wheels. This model is equipped with the popular 390 engine.

Both cars used modified versions of the existing Rambler American body and platform layout. When it came time to build the AMX, it was only logical to modify the existing American components to produce a two-seat configuration.

1968

The production AMX sat on a ninety-seven-inch wheelbase, and it had an overall length of 177.22 inches, width of 71.57 inches and height of 51.73 inches—just about the same as its prototype. Front tread was 58.36 inches, with the rear being slightly smaller at fifty-seven inches.

The car retained most of its show-car appearance. The cantilever-styled roof remained, as did the flying buttress roofline and sleek quarter panels with newly designed rear window. The nonfunctional hood blisters were slightly modified and the severely pointed hood was made a little more blunt. A large front bumper with a lower valance was used in place of the thin bumper. The grille and headlights were divided instead of being one piece, and standard round headlights replaced the square units. Ventless side windows were used, as on the original prototype. New flush door handles were designed, and these have been used on all AMC models up to the present.

Items that did not make it were the Ramble Seat and the built-in roll bar. (It is unusual that AMC chose to omit the roll bar, since Studebaker felt it was an important added feature and incorporated it into its beautifully designed Avanti. The roll bar was later incorporated into the production versions of the Matador coupe and Pacer.) The invisible silver mesh taillights were replaced with conventional wraparound red plastic lens taillights. And finally, the doors did not open up into the roof a la Corvette. The dual fuel filler necks and lids and the rear exhaust outlet rocker panel moldings were retained in nonoperational form only. All 1968-70 AMXs had simulated filler lids on the buttress panels in the form of chrome circles with AMX letters inside. A simulated side exhaust rocker panel molding was introduced with the 1969 midyear Big Bad or Mod Javelins and AMXs.

The AMX was a beautifully designed automobile, a fact echoed by the press and the buying public. Even when standing still it looked as though it were traveling 100 mph. The optional dual racing stripe over the hood, roof and deck enhanced this impression.

From its inception up to production, the AMX was designed as a supercar. AMC promoted its racy looks in three different painted posters showing the AMX at Monte Carlo, Elkhart Lake and the Nurburgring racetracks.

Just about all stops were pulled to make this car a performer from the start. No economy-minded engines for this car. *Acceleration* was the key word, and even handling was built in to control the power.

The optional over-the-top racing stripe indicated that the AMX was equipped with the Go Package. From any angle, the car was well proportioned.

The buyer could stick with the base engine or go two steps up to more power, while keeping luxury and cruising in mind. There were no "sissy" six-cylinder or two-barrel carburetor engines available and no single exhaust. All engines were V-8s equipped with Carter four-barrels and dual exhausts with chrome tips. The 290 produced 225 hp at 4700 rpm; the next step was the AMX 343 producing 280 hp at 4800 and the new AMX 390 pushing out 315 hp at 4600. The 390 was named after the car and was identified as such with red-white-blue decals on the air cleaner lid reading "AMX 390" regardless of the AMC car it was ordered in.

All the 1968 engines were painted a new medium shade of metallic blue as opposed to the bronze and copper colors of the previous year. To make the new 390 really stand out from the others, the valve covers, air cleaner lid and oil filler cap were chrome plated.

All engine ID emblems were placed at the rear section of the quarter panels, and each engine had its own distinctive plate.

The 290 and 343 V-8s were carryovers from 1967, and were rated at the same horsepower as previously. Even though the engines were now burdened with the new-for-1968 federally mandated smog emissions equipment (California had required such equipment since 1966), actual horsepower going to the rear wheels was not effected.

The new 390 engine was based on the two smaller engines and was an extension of the high-performance 343 four-barrel version. The first order of business was to beef up the block to handle more power and torque and to accept a larger bore and increased stroke. The block was stiffened at the pan rails and had thicker main bearing webs. The water jacket portion of the block was cast the same as for the 343 V-8. Bore and stroke were set at 4.17x3.57.

Although provisions were not made for four-bolt mains, it was possible to install them by modifying the bottom end. A forged-steel crankshaft and connecting rods were used instead of the cast nodular iron pieces on the smaller engines. A steel crank and set of rods could be ordered from the dealer under the Group 19 high-performance equipment for the 290 and 343. Tri-metal main and con rod bearings were used with special lightweight pistons, resulting in less reciprocating weight for the big incher.

The 390 used the big-valve 343's heads and shared its compression ratio of 10.2:1. Combustion chamber volume was reduced from 53 cc to a more efficient 51 cc. A new and more efficient intake manifold was designed with a slightly higher capacity cfm four-barrel carburetor, and larger exhaust manifolds were made for improved breathing.

All these modifications added up to only twenty-five pounds additional weight over the 343 four-barrel engine. Subsequently, the 390 AMX did not suffer from the dreaded nose-heavy syndrome that plagued most of the big-block supercars at the time.

The AMX engineers were able to give the car added power while retaining its excellent handling characteristics. This was a very important trait of the car.

Aftermarket speed equipment manufacturers and AMC found out that the new engines responded very

Even a stripped AMX with standard wheel covers and black-wall tires looked special. The 290 ci 225 hp V-8 was standard.

Another item introduced with the new 1968 AMX was the 390 ci, 315 hp V-8 with chrome-plated valve covers, air cleaner top and oil filler cap.

well to intake and exhaust manifold modifications. When these were coupled to a cam and valvetrain change, the engines were able to chop one to three seconds off 0-60 and quarter-mile elapsed times. The stock AMC cam had a 0.425 inch lift and a 266 degree duration with 44 degree overlap. The dealer-available hi-po cam had a 0.477 inch lift, a 302 degree duration and a healthy sixty-eight degrees of overlap.

Another important item made standard for the AMX was the new Borg-Warner 2.23 close-ratio T-10 V four-speed transmission. The Borg-Warner three-speed automatic was optional.

This emblem on the quarter panels meant the AMX was packing the high-torque big-displacement engine under the hood. It was the most popular engine option during its three-year availability in the little two-seater.

Other standard items included Goodyear E70x14 wide-profile fiberglass-belted black sidewall tires with collapsible space-saver spare, slim-shelled reclining bucket seats, padded aircraft-type instrument panel with recessed controls, 8000 rpm tachometer, heavy-duty springs and shocks, large-diameter front sway bar and rear traction bars that AMC called Torque Links.

At a base price of $3,245, it was quite a complete performance package.

All this looked good on paper and on the car itself, but the final test was what the car could do in 0-60 mph and in the quarter-mile. At the time, supercar buyers judged all cars on those merits alone.

At a curb weight of just over 3,000 pounds and depending on transmission and rear axle ratio, a 225 hp version could turn 0-60 times anywhere between eight and nine seconds. Quarter-mile times would come between sixteen and eighteen seconds at about 85 to 90 mph. These times were for a stone stock car, right off the showroom floor, with a tight engine and drivetrain. With a little performance tuning and prep, which was common practice with many magazine test cars, and a good break-in period, the times could be quickened.

Just about every magazine at the time road-tested the 390 version, with a couple of 343s thrown in for good measure. Most buyers were interested in the 390s as indicated by the number of those produced compared with the number of smaller versions made.

Road tests

Tom McCahill from *Mechanix Illustrated* magazine road-tested a 390 four-speed with a 3.15:1 twin-grip rear. His best 0-60 time was 7.1 seconds and the quarter-mile came in 15.4 seconds at about 93 mph. The 390 was a high-torque engine, producing 425 pounds-feet of torque at 3200 rpm. If care was not exercised, one could literally fry the tires. When that engine was coupled to the close-ratio gearbox, first

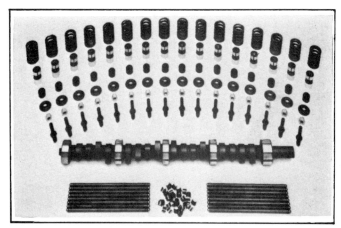

The hi-po cam and kit from the Group 19 parts bin could be ordered as a dealer-installed option to further enhance the car's performance. AMC V-8 engines responded very well to this change.

gear was almost useless, but it did help to launch the car hard. The times recorded by McCahill were very respectable for a showroom stocker. He was also able to top 120 mph.

AMC advertised in its factory literature and ads that "once the 390 was broken in, you could roll right onto a race track and be ready to do 130 mph, in pure stock form without special modifications." Raviolo called the AMX "A Walter Mitty Ferrari." Dick Teague called it "A hairy little brother to the Javelin."

AMC stated that the car was not designed to compete directly with the Corvette, but rather to fill in the present US personal/specialty car market—the void between pony cars and expensive foreign sports cars such as the Jaguar. Nevertheless, the AMX was often compared with the Corvette and did compete against the Corvette in a few races. On the other side of the coin, AMC was quick to point out that the AMX was priced between $1,500 and $2,000 less than a comparably equipped Corvette.

The AMX's dimensions closely paralleled those of the 1955 Ford Thunderbird, including curb weights. AMC decided to try what Ford had done back in the fifties, and went all out to make it last. The two-seater Ford Thunderbird was an attempt by that firm to combine luxury and comfort with the performance and handling of a sports car. In the mid-fifties, the Corvette and Thunderbird were going at it toe to toe in the marketplace, until in 1958, the Thunderbird went to a four-seater configuration as it lost ground to the Corvette, which continued right up to the current model as a performance car. And although the AMX was not intended to compete directly with the Corvette, AMC was willing to stake its reputation on making its own two-seater luxury-performance concept successful.

Road & Track was one of the many magazines to conduct a road test using the big 390. The car was also equipped with the four-speed but had a deeper-geared 3.54:1 twin-grip rear. It came up with a 0-60 time of 7.2 seconds and a quarter-mile time of 15.2 seconds at 90 mph. Not much different than McCahill's times. *Road & Track* also said the gear ratios were too close. Either the wide-ratio box used in 1966 and 1967 or the automatic transmission would be the better choice.

Car Life road-tested another 390 four-speed and came up with a 14.7 second time at 95 mph in the quarter-mile. *Car and Driver* tested a trio of AMXs, two with automatics and one with a four-speed. The automatic was able to rip off a 14.80 second time at 95.03 mph, and that was the car's first-ever run! At the hands of other experienced drivers, the four-speed cars turned low fourteen second times with terminal speeds approaching the century mark.

The 390 AMX was the hot setup, and it even proved to be quite competitive on the strip, where it competed in NHRA's E/Stock and Super F classes.

The various magazines that road-tested the AMX 390 praised its supercarlike performance. It was generally agreed that the best combination with the big engine was an automatic transmission and a twin-grip rear, although most buyers still opted for the four-speed. There was nothing like the sport of going up through the gears with the stick, even though the linkage was criticized for being too sloppy. That could be easily taken care of with an aftermarket Hurst Competition Plus shifter, which became standard on the AMX and Javelin in mid-1969.

The Jeffords AMX was extensively modified by Dave Puhl and his House of Kustoms. Note the large hood scoops. The R emblem on the sail panels stood for Ramble Seat.

The unique Ramble Seat was fully operational. This photo also shows the special Motorwheel Spyder wheels that are still on the car today.

It was also felt that the manual steering with a 19.3 overall ratio and four turns lock-to-lock had better road feel and response than the variable-ratio power steering. Finally, the car's braking power was superb when equipped with the optional front disc brakes.

Car and Driver had this to say about the car: "It looks too American (but good, but good), and its acceleration and top speed are too great to compare it to any similarly priced European sportscar."

Car Life was impressed with its handling: "For zipping through the countryside, over winding roads with sparse traffic, the AMX delivers the kind of enjoyment previously reserved for the very rich or the very spartan."

Road & Track liked the overall AMX package: "Typically American in its feel and performance, sporty in appearance, a comfortable long distance touring car for two only."

McCahill of *Mechanix Illustrated* praised the AMX's performance and handling: "In summing up, the AMX is the hottest thing to ever come out of Wisconsin and I forgot to tell you they have it suspended so that you can whip through corners and real hard bends better than with many out-and-out sports cars."

The AMX was truly an impressive car for its first time out.

Now that the AMX had proved it could perform, it had to prove it could offer convenience and luxury options to fit the tastes of just about any buyer—and it did. You could order your AMX in one of fourteen

A closer shot reveals the nice fit of the Ramble Seat with the body panels. The foot cutouts and kneepads prevented body and paint damage.

The grab-assist handles on the inside of the sail panels are visible. Note the different-styled tailpipe extensions as opposed to those on a stock AMX.

different triple-coated Lustre-Gard acrylic enamels. You could order reds, blues, yellows, whites, browns, metallics or whatever other color tickled your fancy. Interiors were restricted to three colors—tan, red or black.

The only colors for the dual over-the-top racing stripes were white or black. Whenever an AMX was seen with these stripes, it meant the car was equipped with the optional Go Package, which was available on the 343 or 390 only. This package included power front disc brakes, redline wide-profile tires, heavier-duty front and rear springs, specially calibrated heavy-duty front and rear shock absorbers, Twin-Grip rear and heavy-duty cooling system consisting of larger-capacity radiator, shroud and seven-blade Power-Flex fan. Some of these items were also available as separate options.

If you did not like to row the gears, you could order the only other transmission available, the three-speed automatic. Depending on transmission choice, rear axle ratios could be had in 2.87, 3.15 or 3.54 form, with optional dealer-installed ratios of 3.73, 3.91, 4.10 or 4.44.

To keep tabs on the engine's functions, a dealer accessory Rally-Pak was offered, consisting of oil pressure and ammeter gauges and clock (not available with air conditioning).

If the buyer wanted to go to the top of the dealer performance list, he or she could opt for the Typhoon hi-po camshaft and kit, which was made up of the 0.477 inch lift 302 degree duration cam, competition hydraulic anti-pump-up lifters and stronger valve springs with dampeners. Headers, which could be also ordered through the dealer, and dual exhausts were recommended with the cam and kit. The cold intake manifold conversion kit was a special heat-blocker metal gasket that increased power through greater density of the cooler fuel-air mixture.

Although performance was the name of the game, many buyers purchased AMXs for comfort or luxury cruising on the street. There was an array of creature conveniences to choose from. Automatic transmission, quick-ratio manual or power steering, power brakes, power front disc brakes, Twin-Grip rear, Adjust-O-Tilt steering wheel and all-season air conditioning were just a few of the more popular ones.

Heavy-duty batteries and alternators could be had. Visibility and light groups were made up of different-type mirrors and convenience lights. AM, AM/FM or eight-track stereo radios could be ordered with two rear speakers. Undercoating, rear bumper guards and even an engine-block heater appeared on the option list.

Buyers could also tailor their AMXs with several types of wheel covers, including the unique turbo-cast type or the chrome five-spoke mag.

Even a so-called stripped AMX was elegant, with its standard reclining bucket seats, carpeted floors and

Angela Dorian, 1968 Playmate of the Year, accepts her pink AMX from AMC vice-president of marketing services Roy W. McNealy.

rear storage or jump seat area. The console was a nice extension of the dashboard, which was padded with an injection-molded plastic instrument panel (first in the industry for the 1968 Javelin and AMX). The standard wood-grain sports steering wheel and wood-grain-trimmed door panels complemented the overall interior package very well.

AMC had hoped to build at least 10,000 AMXs in the first year, as stated in its factory brochure. The company also said, "We're even putting the production number on the dash—for collectors who want to prove they got in on a great car fast." As it turned out, only 6,725 were built in the abbreviated 1968 model year.

Factory records have shown that fifty to sixty AMXs were built in late 1967 with no dashboard ID number plaque on the glovebox. A few of these have surfaced as of this writing, proving their existence. The ID plaque was relocated to the center of the dash, just above the radio, in late 1968 and was carried over for 1969.

Specials

A few special edition or special interest AMXs also appeared in 1968, the most notable being the Jeffords AMX. The concept of this car came from Jim Jeffords, who managed the Trans-Am Javelin team for the 1968 racing season, and stylist Brook Stevens. Together, Jeffords and Stevens designed the car and laid out the suspension changes. Jeffords made an agreement with AMC for him to create the special AMX as a styling exercise for possible production of approximately 500 units per year.

The customizing of the car was handled by Dave Puhl of Palatine, Illinois, in his own shop. Puhl was the builder of the unique Phase II show car based on AMC mechanicals and discussed in the racing chapter.

When the car was completed, Jeffords attempted to get dealer support by showing it off at the various Trans-Am races during the season. He was not successful in convincing the dealers or AMC that production of the car would be another winning combination for the company, and he bitterly parted company with AMC.

The Jeffords AMX went into storage from 1968 through 1984, when it was donated to the Brooks-Stevens Museum and was brought to the 1984 AMO (American Motors Owners Association) national meet in Kenosha, Wisconsin, by museum representatives. In March 1985, the curator of the museum contacted Darryl A. Salisbury, president of the AMO, and informed him that the car was for sale for $15,000. A few months later Salisbury purchased the car. Salisbury noted that the car was heavily mildewed and in pretty bad shape cosmetically, but the odometer showed only 5,120 miles. The car is now being restored to its original condition.

The Jeffords AMX was a unique car from every point of its modifications. It incorporated the Ramble Seat, taken directly from the original AMX Project IV prototype. The new seat worked more or less like the earlier seat. When it was closed, or in its down position, the two lids were magnetically sealed to prevent them from popping up during normal vehicle motion. The seat could hold two adults or three small children comfortably. When the Ramble seatback was up, it was

necessary to disconnect the back-up lights by pulling out their sockets from the taillight assembly bosses and leaving them hanging.

A large seatbelt going completely across the Ramble Seat was provided for the occupants. There were two grab-assist bars inside the sail panels and two kneepads at the sides of the back portion of the Ramble Seat on the deck. Two indentations forward of the rear bumper on the quarter panels served as foot mounts to get into the seat.

JEFFORDS was spelled out on the red reflective taillight panel and on the forward side of both functional front-opening ram-air hood scoops. The three holes in the taillight panel where the stock letters AMX used to be were still visible after the JEFFORDS letters were put on.

The hood was custom-made of fiberglass with extended molded-in scoops and contained two flush-mounted hood locks. Special AMX R emblems, mounted on their own lids, appeared on both buttress stock locations and also appeared on the Ramble Seat back lid and on the hood between the hood scoops. These emblems and letters were all individually handmade of stainless steel and had threaded mounting studs with special nuts. The R in the emblems stood for Ramble Seat.

Richard Teague's personal AMX incorporated numerous unique features used for testing purposes for possible future use.

The car had special 15x6 Motorwheel Spyder wheels mounted on Goodyear F70x15 redline Polyglas tires.

The car that was used for the Jeffords AMX was a production model taken off the assembly line. It was originally painted Caravelle Blue and it did not have a dashboard identification plaque. The car was then painted Candy Apple Red with a gold underlay, and it was a "quickie job" as indicated by the engine compartment where the new paint was simply sprayed around the battery and windshield washer bag, so that removal of these two items revealed the Caravelle Blue color behind them.

The hood, fender tops, windshield trim, wiper blades and wiper arms were painted Shadow Mask or flat black. The black was divided from the body color by gold pinstriping. This black scheme, which also extended back into the quarter panels and indented roof sculptures, became an option on the 1970 production AMX models.

Modification was required to the backs of the front seats because of the Ramble Seat installation. The seats and interior were then covered with rolled black Naugahyde by Gene McCoughla.

The car had a stock 390 V-8, four-speed transmission and twin-grip rear. It was also equipped with power steering and power brakes.

Ronnie Kaplan of Kaplan Engineering lowered the body two inches to give the car a sleeker appearance and stiffened the suspension at the same time. It has been said that the entire project cost Jeffords over $60,000, although that figure may be exaggerated.

Another unique 1968 AMX that stood out was the pink model given to Angela Dorian, who was *Playboy*'s Playmate of the Year in 1968. Dorian was enamored with the car but not with the color—she hated pink. After almost a year of attracting attention anywhere she went with the car, she decided enough was enough and had the car repainted chocolate brown, then gray, and finally black, its present color.

Her pink AMX was being built at the time publicity photos of her were being shot. Thus, the car in those shots was a stand-in model painted pink on the surface only.

The original car handed over to Dorian was painted pink all around, including the engine compartment, the trunk and the floors under the carpet. It was equipped with the 290 V-8 and automatic transmission. Options included air conditioning, power steering and power brakes, tilt steering column, AM/eight-track radio, tinted windows all around, rear bumper guards and chrome five-spoke wheels. In place of the normal AMX identification number glovebox plaque

The AMX-GT was another styling exercise. The front end was basically stock AMX, but the rear portion became the basis for the production 1970½ Gremlin.

The AMX for 1969 was basically unchanged. The optional five-spoke wheels were toned down and the car received detail refinements and improvements.

is a plaque reading AMX 36-24-35, Dorian's measurements.

Dorian still owns the car. Besides the new black paint job, she has replaced the rocker panel moldings and outside rearview mirror with flat-black pieces and replaced the factory wheels with five-slotted mags.

Incidentally, when Dorian was on tour as Playmate of the Year she had a new AMX waiting for her use at every major city.

Vice-President of Styling Dick Teague used his personal AMX as a rolling cosmetic test bed for styling changes that could and would appear on later two-seat AMXs and four-seat 1971-74 Javelin AMXs. This car is also now in the hands of an AMC club member and is under restoration.

One important show car that was an offshoot of the production 1968 AMX was the AMX GT (Grand Touring) Super Sports car, first shown at the International Auto Show in New York in April 1968. The rear end of the car gave a glimpse of what the production 1970 Gremlin would look like.

Standard items on the 1969 AMX included a 140 mph speedometer, 8000 rpm tachometer, Space Saver spare with inflatable bottle and the rugged Borg-Warner four-speed transmission.

Optional styled steel wheels and the 390 V-8 were still available on the little-changed 1969 AMX.

Built on the AMX's ninety-seven-inch wheelbase, the body was constructed of fiberglass. A deeply recessed wire mesh grille and wire mesh hood scoop opening were used. (The hood scoop would appear as a dual inlet opening on the production 1970 AMX.) The only modification to the front bumper was the addition of bull's-eye-type side-marker lights like those used on 1968 Mopar cars. Rally-style wire mesh headlight guards were also used. NASCAR-style hood pins and Formula-One-style racing outside mirrors were added, along with functional side exhausts. A quick-fill gas cap was used in the center section of the rear.

A small roof spoilerette was incorporated into the body design above the large rear window. The car had a bobtailed look with a minimum of overhang. The rear bumper containing side-marker lights was integrated into the sculptured body tail with the taillights cut in immediately below, flanking a centered and indented license plate boss. AMX-GT letters appeared on both quarter panels. Fifties-style moon disc wheel covers were used but were later replaced by five-spoke flat and aluminum-finish aftermarket American mag wheels with center caps.

The car was painted a beautiful deep shade of Candy Apple Red with a white racing stripe running from each fender tip to the length of the doors, sweeping up the quarter panels following the rear contour of the side windows, and joining in the middle of the roof section to make one complete running stripe. All windows were nicely tinted.

1969

For 1969, AMC could see no reason to alter such a winning combination, but a few important changes were made. The interior was spruced up with a woodgrain applique fitted to the center dash panels, the armrests, and the door panels. The carpeting was improved in both quality and fit, and genuine saddle or charcoal leather upholstery could be ordered for the bucket seats. A standard grab bar was added to the right side of the dash, and headrests were made standard. Also made standard were a 140 mph speedometer and an 8000 rpm tachometer, repositioned to make room for a new optional clock. Stainless steel trim adorned the pedals.

Guard rails, which were boxed steel members mounted inside each door to help protect passengers in side-impact accidents, became standard equipment in 1969 by federal mandate. This was an important safety feature incorporated into the AMX as well as the Javelin.

Aside from these few cosmetic trim changes, the new AMX was virtually identical to its 1968 counterpart. AMC proved that the overall car still had a lot of appeal by selling 8,293 units that year, with most again being 390 V-8 four-speed-equipped models. The base price of the car rose slightly to $3,297, a difference of $52 compared with the 1968 model.

Super Stock and Drag Illustrated magazine described the car as "currently the most far-out car on the American scene stylewise." *Industrial Design* magazine cited the AMX for "excellence of design." Again, why mess with a winning combination?

The Big Bad paint option was available on any base Javelin, Javelin SST or AMX.

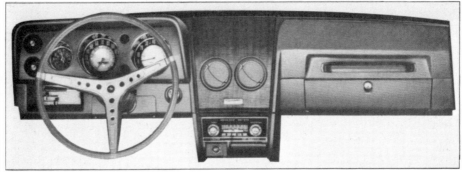

With the introduction of the Big Bad Javelins and AMXs came a Hurst four-speed shifter, chrome instrument tunnels and full eyebrow pad over the instrument panel.

The optional all-chrome five-spoke wheels were toned down a little for 1969. They were painted black with the spoke's flat surfaces painted silver, and had a stainless steel trim ring snapped on.

Other options available were a center cushion with folding armrest and a convenience tray between the bucket seats for the four-speed cars, and a new and improved console with a storage compartment for automatic transmission models. Ten new exterior colors were added along with three new optional over-the-top dual racing stripes (red, blue and silver) to go with the previously available black and white. A new platinum color was offered as an option for the vinyl upholstery.

Performance was emphasized even more in the factory literature: "It doesn't drive you; you drive it.... "You look through the wheel at a big speedometer and tach. Rev up and shift. With the 390, you leap from 0-60 in less than seven seconds.... The standard AMX is a sportscar you can buy and maintain at about the cost of a sedan. Or you can change to big carbs. Put in headers. Hop up axle ratio. From the special performance equipment listed in your Dealer's Performance Activities Book." Obviously AMC was pushing the full racing potential of its little baby even more than before.

A few dealers also realized the potential of the AMX and decided to offer dealer-installed high-performance bolt-on packages to further boost sales. One noted dealer was Westbury Rambler in Westbury, Long Island, New York, owned at the time by Leon Sporn, Gary Stowe and Alfredo Bergna. Their package was called AMX/S and was identified as such with emblems installed on the fenders just behind the side-marker lights and in the stock location on the roofline side. The package started with an unblueprinted 390 engine with an Edelbrock aluminum intake manifold and Holley carburetor, solid or hydraulic hi-po cam

and kit, full centrifugal advance distributor and Mallory coil, Doug Thorley headers with cherry bomb mufflers, Schiefer clutch and pressure plate assembly with scattershield, Hurst shifter with T-handle, special traction bars, functional ram-air hood scoop and 3.90, 4.44 or 5.00 rear end gears.

All this equipment produced an AMX that could do the quarter-mile in the high elevens to low twelves at 110 to 113 mph. This was achieved with open headers and a set of 9.7 inch wide 10.65x15 M&H slicks mounted on Cragar wheels. Even with closed headers and street tires, the car could rip off high twelves all day long.

All three four-barrel V-8s were carryovers and virtually unchanged. Thus the 290 was still the base engine, with the optional 343 and 390 being available with the Go Package. All other convenience and performance options remained the same except the ones previously mentioned.

New dealer-installed performance items could be ordered, such as forged connecting rods for the 290 and 343, high-rise aluminum manifold and carb, heat-blocker manifold gasket, new superflow 5:1 ratio ring and pinion gear set, and even body spoilers. Numerous other items were available through the *AMC Performance Activities Manual*.

Specials

The success of the 1968-69 models gave birth to yet another wave of specialty and idea show cars that were direct offshoots of the superb production AMX. One unique car was the street replica of the Craig Breedlove 1968 AMX record setter. Although it has been reported that between twenty-five and fifty units were built, and supposedly all were 1968 models, only one has surfaced and it came with documentation proving it to be a 1969 model.

The original record-setting Breedlove AMX was put on display at Detroit's Metropolitan Airport after the record-setting runs were made. Rumor has it that about fifty street replicas were made, but only one 1969 model has surfaced.

This car was special-ordered by a dealer in Oshawa, Ontario, Canada, as a giveaway for the winner of a race at Mosport Racetrack. It went through five hard owners and 125,000 cold Canadian miles before Canadian representatives contacted AMO president Darryl Salisbury, who is now in the process of restoring it.

The build-order sheet found with the car indicates that it is an authentic AMC factory replica, painted red-white-blue, in that order from back to front. Interestingly, the tri-tone paint scheme does not match the Breedlove record-setting AMX; instead, it matches the scheme on the 1970 Trans-Am Javelin street replica. Under the special instructions on the build sheet appears "Scheme 2" for the paint pattern. The paint code reads "00," indicating it is not a regular production code. According to the codes, the colors used on the car are 1968 Caravelle Blue, 1969 Frost White and 1969 Matador Red. The blue is metallic and the other two colors are nonmetallic.

The car also appears to have been painted all around, meaning under the fenders and body panels, whereas other tri-tone red-white-blue AMCs carried the paint scheme only on the outside surfaces.

All the replicas were supposedly made with the 290 V-8 only, which this car has coupled with the four-speed transmission. The car is also equipped with E70x14 redline tires and 1969 five-spoke AMX wheels. It has no convenience options such as power steering and brakes, air conditioning and the like.

The instrument panel gauge tunnels are chrome-plated. These were introduced midyear and installed on a limited number of AMXs until the federal government banned them saying there was too much reflection. Before and after that the tunnels were finished with silver paint.

Although Craig Breedlove was not involved directly in the building or sale of his record-setting AMX replicas, he and automotive designer Bill Moore did design and construct a $700 bolt-on Aerodynamx Kit. The kit used the stock front fenders with an integrated fiberglass extended nose and custom grille which also acted as a partial belly pan. The car also sported a fiberglass hood with flush hood locks and functional ram-air NASA- (National Aeronautics and Space Administration) type ducts similar to the 1969-70 Shelby Cobras. The grille and headlight openings were covered with riveted plexiglass pieces. The front end of the car resembled a modern Porsche 928 model.

A unique fiberglass rear window roof spoiler from the 1968 Speed Spectacular Javelins was also part of the package. A single wide solid over-the-top racing stripe ran from the hood to the deck lid and covered the roof spoiler. Different-type rocker panel moldings were used along with special ID badges put in place of the AMX circle emblems on the quarter panels.

The car was known as the Breedlove AMX 600. It is not known how many cars had the kit installed.

Customizer George Barris was not going to be left out of the picture. He worked out a deal with AMC to market through its dealerships, on a nationwide basis, his customized version of the AMX called El Toro. This car retained the AMX's basic stock appearance with a few changes that were not as severe as those on the Breedlove 600. The grille was changed into a plain square pattern with horizontal and vertical bars. The most striking change was the phony injecter clusters set on top of the stock hood blisters. Each was made up

A 1969 AMX was chosen to be the pace car for the 47th Annual Pike's Peak Hill Climb contest. The car was completely stock and was equipped with the 290 V-8.

of four individual units, with engine ID numbers placed on the sides just forward of them.

A rear trunk spoiler almost identical to the 1970 Mark Donohue design was molded into the deck lid and quarter panels. Custom Cragar mag-type wheels were mounted on redline tires.

One stripe was added, encircling the grille opening. Another stripe started out thin at the upper fendertips, tapering as it went back toward the door and running its length, sweeping up and following the rear side window contour, back toward the door window contour, ending just behind the windshield. (This stripe scheme became the optional racing stripe for the 1970 models.) Tapered stripes also outlined each hood blister, separated by the engine ID numbers, and special badges replaced the stock AMC circle ones on the quarter panels.

There was also a Frost White AMX used as a pace car for the 47th Annual Pike's Peak Hill Climb Contest, which took place on June 29, 1969. It was identified with appropriate markings and decals and was sponsored by the AMC Dealers Association of Denver, Colorado. Other than the pace car identification on the vehicle it was not specially built or modified for the occasion.

Another group of AMXs worth noting were the 100 that were used as giveaways in the 1969 Remming-ton Auto-Home Shaver Contest sponsored by Sperry Rand Corporation. The contest involved comparing the dial setting in a Remmington ad with the dial setting display at a Remmington or American Motors dealer. A match would produce an instant winner.

All 100 cars were equipped with the 390 V-8, four-speed transmission and Go Package, which included all the heavy-duty components and suspension handling pieces. All the cars were reportedly given away to contest winners.

These cars did not have any special serial numbers or sequence. Without the original invoice stating the car to be a Remmington Shaver Contest giveaway, there is no way to distinguish the car from any other production 1969 AMX. Since not one of these documented cars has surfaced, owners of any surviving units probably do not even know they have one.

One rare AMX was the Australian-built right-hand-drive version. Only twenty-four of these units were made, and one has recently been brought back to the United States and completely restored.

AMI (Australian Motors Industries), located in Melbourne, Australia, was interested in the AMX because of its exciting styling. The Australian-owned company purchased cars from various world manufacturers, had them shipped to Australia, and then converted many to right-hand drive for their own domestic

The AMX/2 was so designated because of its numerous twin features. It was the clear-cut winner over the Italian proposal.

Teague and his staff came up with an elegantly styled design that still looks contemporary today.

use. The cars arrived in Australia completely knocked down for assembly and conversion by AMI.

All twenty-four cars were ordered with the same equipment. They were equipped with the 343 ci 280 hp V-8, automatic transmission with console floorshift, 2.87:1 open rear, power steering, power front disc brakes, tilt steering column, Rally-Pak instrument package and five-spoke rally wheels mounted on Dunlop Aquajet ER70x14 redline radial tires. Only two cars were equipped with air conditioning, one a through-the-dash installation and the other an aftermarket hang-type unit. All the cars were equipped with clear, nontinted glass.

The cars were carefully hand-assembled. Close attention was paid to the fit of each component, especially the trim. The roll-up side windows fit tightly inside their channels with the windows closed, and were well sealed.

Trim colors differed from the US version, with only three being used: Pure White, Light Yellow and Fire Engine Red. The optional over-the-top racing stripe and rear bumper guards were not offered, and the quarter panel AMX circle emblems were covered in black vinyl to match the upholstery. Some cars had the 343 V-8 emblem on the right-hand side of the deck lid, and all had a Rambler nameplate on the hood or deck lid. An AMI logo containing the outline of the Australian continent was placed on each quarter panel where the engine emblems would normally be.

The interior of the Aussie AMXs differed quite a bit from the US-built versions. The dashboard was made out of fiberglass and used trim pieces from the US Post Office Rebels and Ambassadors, while other pieces were AMI handmade. Instruments used were the AMC Rally-Pak cluster consisting of the 140 mph speedometer, 8000 rpm tachometer, oil and amp gauge, and military-style electric clock. A European-style radio or stereo was installed with rear speakers. The console was a standard 1968 Javelin/AMX unit containing an ashtray and cigarette lighter.

Although the reclining bucket seats were standard AMX without headrests, they were overstuffed to produce a cushy ride, and the vinyls used were thicker, had a coarser grain and were much more durable, being sewn with a heavier thread. The matching door panels contained ashtrays and embossed AMI logos. To finish off the interior, AMI installed its own high-quality carpeting.

All the cars were converted to right-hand drive, and this required a few modifications under the hood. The oil filter had to be relocated to the top of the engine to clear the steering column by using a special mount taken from the 1967 Ambassador US Post Office right-hand-drive car. The battery was moved from the right to the left fenderwall, and the power-brake booster and heater motor changed sides on the firewall.

The complete conversion was professionally executed. Its price was $7,500, which was twice the amount of the US version. For roughly $1,000 more you could get an XJ6 Jaguar—but the AMX was more of a match for the 350 Chevy-engined Holden Monaro GTS 350 and the 351 Ford-engined Falcon GTH 351. Both cars could be had for half the price of the AMX.

Big Bad cars

Back in the United States, the big news for mid-1969 was the introduction of the Mod or Big Bad Javelins and AMXs, so-called because of their availability in three new body colors of Big Bad Orange, Big Bad Green and Big Bad Blue with matching painted bumpers. If the optional $12.65 rear bumper guards were ordered, they were painted to match the bumper and body color.

To retain the grille opening theme normally carried out by the chrome bumper, an aluminum molding was applied to the upper edge of the bumper grille opening on both Javelins and AMXs. The 343 and 390 Go Packages could be ordered with the Big Bad option, as could the black or white over-the-top racing stripes.

The Big Bad option was a mere $34. With it, three new standard features were introduced to all 1969 AMXs. A Hurst Competition Plus four-speed shifter finally replaced the sloppy AMC unit, and a padded hood or "eyebrow" was installed over the instrument cluster. The third feature, chrome plating on the deep tunnels of the instruments, was quickly banned by the federal government, and only a couple hundred or so AMXs were so equipped. Production numbers for the Big Bad AMXs were 195 blue, 283 green and 284 orange.

There could have been a fourth Big Bad color in a deep shade of banana yellow had Dick Teague had his way. He tried to convince management to offer the color because it was one of his favorite, but management turned it down, stating that yellow cars could not be sold. Teague liked it so much that he had his own AMX/3, the production version of the AMX/2 show car, repainted the yellow color.

There was also a limited number of Big Bad Green AMXs built and called the California 500 models. These cars were replicas of the car made to pace the 1969 California 500 race for Indy-type cars held at Ontario Motorspeedway in California. All of these limited edition cars had tan leather interiors and most were equipped with the 390 V-8 and four-speed transmission. Special California 500 emblems emblazoned the hood. These cars are quite rare and the exact number of units made is not known.

AMX/2

Probably one of the most nicely styled show cars coming from the AMX was the experimental studio-designed AMX/2. This project was initiated as a contest to determine who could produce the better styling proposal for a sleek mid-engined sports car. Dick Teague showed the group vice-president in charge of product, Jerry Meyers, a sketch proposal of the car, which Meyers liked very much. The two then decided to travel to the 1968 Geneva Auto Show and to Italy, where Meyers commissioned stylist Giorgetto Giugiaro to construct a prototype to compete with AMC's own proposal. An actual-size white Styrofoam carved model arrived in the United States from Italy, but it was no contest when compared to the AMC proposal. Teague and his styling staff had done a superb job.

AMC's iridescent red AMX/2 mockup was a work of art. It won the contest hands down. Two versions were actually built, differing only slightly in side window design.

The car was shown publicly for the first time at the February 1969 Chicago Auto Show, although it was unveiled at an American Motors stockholders meeting earlier that month. AMC designers described the car as a "significant exercise in styling ideas for the future," and the car was a prelude to the limited-production AMX/3 of 1970.

The car was a nonoperational fiberglass-bodied prototype having no engine, drivetrain or suspension, the same theme as the original AMX prototype. It was shown at major auto shows across the United States. It sat on a 105 inch wheelbase and was 171.5 inches long, 70.4 inches wide and forty-three inches high. The front track was set at fifty-nine inches and the rear track at sixty inches. It was estimated that the dry weight of the car was roughly 3,000 pounds with a forty percent front/sixty percent rear weight distribution.

The sleek sportster contained numerous twin features, hence its number two designation. Twin movable spoilers flared at their outboard ends into the quarter panels, twin flat-black functional hood scoops and rear recessed deck hatches, twin backlights, twin

outside racing mirrors, twin functional side scoops, twin vinyl rub strips and twin side racing stripes were some of its unique features. The car also sported hidden headlights.

The engine was to be mounted amidship using the standard AMX 390 V-8 coupled to a manually shifted transaxle. Suspension was to be independent all around.

The body was beautifully designed by Bob Nixon and Fred Hudson. It was aerodynamic in every way and was expected to be able to top 160 mph. The long low front blended nicely with the sleek upswept rear that slightly resembled the 1968 AMX-GT show car. The two movable spoilers on the rear could be operated from the cockpit together or separately thanks to the raised body spine that divided the rear deck providing the pivoting point. The interior was to feature separate consoles for both driver and passenger and to contain an array of engine instruments and a full complement of accessory and convenience controls.

Hot Rod magazine described the color of the car as follows: "The overall color effect of the AMX/2 is an iridescent candy apricot, although it actually blends from a gold tone on the top into a fiery red along the lower body sections."

The lettering, AMX/2, was painted in at the rear of each flat-black racing stripe just forward of the rear wheelwells. The taillight section was also finished in flat-black. A rear integrated bumper was blended in with the taillight area, which was outlined in chrome. A chrome protruding flat-type bumper adorned the front end, again nicely blended in with the fenders and the hood. Wheels were specially machined, featuring six thin spokes each with no center caps and mounted on wide-profile, raised-white-letter Goodyear tires.

In its last year, the AMX received new front- and rear-end styling. The over-the-top racing stripe was eliminated and a new optional rally side stripe was available.

In 1969, the greatest quantities of AMX production units were built. The decision to drop the two-seat configuration had been made in mid-1968.

1970

In its last year, a car or model will usually see few changes or alterations because of cost savings, low volume sales, buyer disinterest and so on. This was not the case for the 1970 AMX, making its last appearance as a two-seater. Its basic shape, size and overall dimensions were slightly altered, and numerous items were changed inside and outside of the body, engine, drivetrain and suspension. Most notable at first glance were the redesigned front and rear ends.

The front end now more closely resembled the original AMX show car that came out in 1966. The headlights and grille were not separated as on the original, but the signal lights were moved up from the bumper to inside the grille. The AMX shared the Javelin's front bumper, which contained the parking lights. On the AMX, these openings were covered with perforated plastic screens and were advertised as front brake cooling scoops.

The grille was made up of numerous thin horizontal ribs as on the prototype, but it had a nonglare finish and the four center bars were painted silver with silver letters AMX in the center, whereas the original prototype was all chrome.

A new Ram-Air Power Blister hood, made functional only with the optional Go Package, was standard and increased the car's overall length 1.82 inches to 179.04 inches. It was similar in design to the 1968 AMX-GT show car, except it had dual screen-covered openings.

The taillight treatment was still full-width but not of a wraparound design, necessitating new rubber-type end caps and quarter panel side-marker lights. The taillight was divided into five rectangles, with the center one being the back-up light and containing the letters AMX. New front side-marker lights were designed to match the rears, which now also contained reflectors.

The rocker panel moldings were simulated exhaust, introduced on the mid-1969 Big Bad Javelins, and the outside rearview mirrors were redesigned for a sleeker appearance. The five-spoke mag wheels were made standard, and a new optional five-slot mag wheel as used on the 1970 Rebel Machine was made available.

The engine ID emblems were moved from the quarter panels to the fenders just aft of the wheelwells. The AMX circle emblems on the buttresses were now red-white-blue instead of all chrome.

The over-the-top racing stripe was eliminated and a new stripe almost identical to that on the 1969 Barris El Toro AMX was used, with the exception of a slight difference in thickness. The stripes were available in black, white or red. Another optional paint scheme that originated from a past specialty model was the Shadow Mask or black scheme. The hood and fender tops as well as around the window area were painted glossy black. This scheme came from the 1968 Jeffords AMX-R custom-built unit. Whereas the AMX-R separated the colors with a gold pinstripe, the production

The dashboard on the 1970 AMX and Javelin was all new. This design was considered by many to be much cleaner and more appealing than the bulky 1968-69 model.

scheme separated them by a silver pinstripe. All three 1969 Big Bad colors were carried over, but without the matching painted bumpers.

One safety item made standard was the Chemcor safety windshield developed by Corning Glass Works. The glass was only two-thirds as thick as the old type and about thirty percent lighter. It was laminated with a flexible inner pane that made it shatterproof in low- to medium-speed collisions. In high-speed collisions, the glass would break into small, blunt-edged pieces that were not as hazardous to the passengers.

The interior was almost totally redesigned. Brand-new high-back turtle-shell bucket seats with integrated headrests were made standard in vinyl or Ventilair vinyl, or you could order the optional genuine leather or new corduroy. The instrument panel and dashboard were totally new and did not have the "pieced together" look of previous models. They were now flat straight across, with an integrated glovebox and grab handle underneath, both on the right side, and still retained recessed instruments. The production number plate was moved back to the right side of the dash, which had wood-grain applique all the way across. The door panels were also redesigned and had the wood-grain look. The steering wheel was of a new two-spoke design with a Rim-Blow-type horn.

The chassis and suspension system were integrated with the unibody, and the old front trunion setup was finally replaced with a new twin ball-joint front suspension system. This new setup provided smoother suspension travel and operation, and improved turning stability.

Also made standard in 1970 were seventy-eight-aspect-ratio fiberglass-belted tires and the Hurst four-speed shifter introduced mid-1969 on the Big Bad models.

Last, but certainly not least, was the introduction of a new engine line-up. The 290 and 343 V-8s were discontinued and replaced with versions displacing 304 and 360 cubic inches. The 304 was not available in the AMX. The standard engine became the 360 ci 290 hp four-barrel V-8.

The only optional engine was a new-design 390 V-8 producing 325 hp and also equipped with a four-barrel. The new 360 had a bore and stroke of 4.08x3.44 inches. Although the engine was basically a stroked version of the 343, head design, valve sizes, compression ratio and deck height were all changed. Exhaust valve sizes were increased from 1.625 to 1.680 inches in midyear. Deck height was increased from 9.175 inches to 9.208 inches, and compression ratio was decreased slightly from 10.2:1 to 10:1.

The important change in the heads was a new dogleg-design port, as opposed to the old rectangular port. The new port was reported to have fifty percent better exhaust flow characteristics. Although horsepower was still developed at 4800 rpm, the torque figure was rated at 3200 rpm as opposed to the 343's 3000 rpm figure. Torque rating was up to 395 pounds-feet compared with 365. Combustion chamber volume remained the same at 51 cc.

The new-design 390 V-8 retained its same bore and stroke but was also improved. It now developed 325 hp at 5000 rpm, although torque was down five pounds-feet to 420 at the same 3200 rpm. The 390 used the same heads, carburetor, and intake and exhaust manifolds as the 360. Provisions were now made in the block to accommodate four-bolt main bearing caps.

This rear end shot reveals the new divided full-width taillight treatment. Rubber end caps were used, and new large rectangular side-marker lights front and rear were incorporated.

Head bolts on both engines were new thicker-shank 1/2 inch size, replacing the 7/16 inch size on the older engines. This was to cure the chronic problem the older engines had of blowing their head gaskets. The Carter four-barrels used since mid-1966 on the 290 V-8 were replaced with the new-design Ford Autolite type.

All 1970 V-8 engines had their displacement figures cast into both sides of the block near the motor-mount bolt holes as did the previous 1966-69 V-8 engines. All V-8s from the 1966 290 on up were identified by a tag attached to the right-hand valve cover, which the new engines retained.

The new engines proved to be more responsive, with increased power throughout the entire rpm range. With all these new modifications and features, the base price of the car rose only $98 to $3,395, still pretty good for a solid, dependable, performance sports car.

Literature and advertisements for the 1970 AMX were somewhat subdued as far as straight-line performance was concerned. The emphasis was shifted to overall performance and luxury at a bargain price. As one ad stated, "But rather than elaborate any further, we'll rest our case on the standard AMX."

Some road tests praised the AMX for its brisk performance and improved handling, while others condemned the car for not being updated or keeping up with the times as far as brute power was concerned.

The 1970 model year became known as the peak of the supercar era. At that time there were factory muscle cars capable of turning mid- to high-thirteens in the quarter-mile right off the showroom floor. Such cars included the Buick GS-455 Stage I, Chevelle 454 LS6, Pontiac GTO 455 Ram-Air, Olds 442 W30, Hemi Cudas and Challengers, Mustang 428 Cobra Jets and the like. In stock form, the AMX was no match. With bolt-ons, it could equal or surpass the stock competition—but with bolt-ons the competition could dip into the elevens and twelves.

At any rate, the AMX did have adequate and respectable supercar performance for its size and intended purpose. *Road Test* magazine could not praise the sports car handling of the AMX enough: "For the doubters we can testify once again that the AMX feels like a sportscar, drives like a sportscar, handles like a sportscar and therefore in our book (and that of the Sports Car Club of America) it is a sportscar." The car tested was a 390 four-speed, Twin-Grip model.

Popular Hot Rodding staff members road-tested a 360 four-speed AMX and found the car to be quite a performer with the base engine: "Speaking of racing, this AMX with the 360 engine is a fulfillment of the racer's dream. It's quick, fast and economical too." They went on to say, "Without markings or a peek under the hood, anyone would have sworn our test car had the 390 engine. This 360 with factory optional

Ram-Air is a great package." They were able to record a 14.90 second time at 94.63 mph in the quarter-mile.

On the other side of the coin, *Super Stock and Drag Illustrated* testers had nothing good to say about the AMX. They criticized its styling, quality control, comfort, options, handling, performance and various other items. They very much disliked the inside of the car, saying, "the interior upholstery material, the seat fabrics, and the carpeting all look more like the product of an unimaginative home handyman than one of Detroit's styling teams. They're downright cheap looking and the color coordination is blah." They had this to say about the transmission: "The truckish four-speed is another item that will last forever, but doesn't perform up to snuff at the present." They also did not like the handling: "The car is very nose heavy, but power assists make it disappear or almost." They did admire the ruggedness of the engine: "The 390 engine will probably last a great deal longer than its peers, because it is built beefy."

The car was equipped with the 390 four-speed, Twin-Grip 3.91:1 rear, power steering and brakes, air conditioning and F70x14 tires. It was able to attain a best quarter-mile time of 14.46 seconds at 95.61 mph. This was considered to be adequate performance, but by no means earth shattering—how times have changed!

Final-year AMX production was the lowest of all three years, with only 4,116 units built, bringing the total to 19,134 for the little two-seater's life span. (Actual total AMX production for the three years did not match the dash ID number plaques.)

Dick Teague wanted the AMX to continue in its present configuration. To convince management to continue production for 1971, he modified his own AMX as a 1971 proposal and refinished it in silver-

Functional Ram-Air finally arrived for the AMX as an option in its last year of production. Cylinder head, intake manifold and carburetor designs were also improved. The 390 V-8 now pumped out 325 horsepower.

blue. From the cowl forward, the front end was totally redesigned with a bold look owing to the Group 7 racing car fender bulges.

With the exception of the hood scoop, locking hood pins, absence of wire mesh grille and Javelin script on hood, silver color and AMX letters on grille, slightly different grille signal and side-marker lights, and use of a flat-profile hood, the design went right onto the prototype and early-production 1971 four-seater Javelin/AMX. The base 1971 Javelin did not use the hood T-stripe or grille signal lights along with the previously mentioned items, but it did use the flat-profile hood and Javelin script. (The odd-looking hood scoop was made out of papier-mache.)

Teague was not successful in convincing AMC to continue production of the two-seater AMX, but the AMX name was used as an optional trim package on the 1971-74 Javelin, 1977 Hornet, 1978 Concord and 1979-80 Spirit.

The present and future collectibility of the AMX was secured by its 1986 induction into the Milestone Car Society's list of certified cars. Cars being certified for this list must meet criteria for excellence in at least two of the following areas: styling, engineering, performance, innovation and craftsmanship. The 1968-70 AMX had no trouble meeting the criteria.

Specials

There were not as many offshoot show or idea cars of the 1970 AMX as there were of the earlier models. According to its certificate of title, one was used in the NBC TV series "Banacek" starring George Peppard. The car was painted Commodore Blue with the white side stripes and had a black vinyl interior. It was equipped with the 390 V-8, four-speed, Twin-Grip rear, power steering, power front disc brakes, Go Package, and a clock and radio. This car has just recently surfaced.

Another AMX that was used on the same program was the customized 1970 Banacek TV mystery car built by West Coast customizer George Barris of California. The car played its starring role as a $100,000 safety car

Dick Teague wanted the two-seat AMX to stay alive. He modified his own AMX with the new front end shown to submit to management for approval. The proposal was turned down, but the front-end design was used on the 1971-74 Javelin.

hijacked for ransom that had to be found by insurance investigator Banacek.

It took George Barris roughly three months to complete the extensive modifications. The car featured an extended and very pointed front end that resembled Barris' 1965 Buick Wildcat Mystique customized show car. The car also had twin molded-in hood scoops, chrome fender side exhausts, custom mag wheels, tinted windows and a host of other special features. It was auctioned off in 1984 at the Chicago Historical Antique Automobile Museum in Highland Park, Illinois, by I.T.T. Kruse International.

AMX/3

One last-ditch effort by AMC to stay alive in the two-seater sports car market came in the form of the exotic mid-engined AMX/3. This "true" sports car took the two-seater configuration to its extreme.

The 1970 AMX/3 was a direct production version of the fiberglass prototype 1969 AMX/2 show car. The first unit was a nonoperational steel-bodied push-mobile, but an additional five units were fully operational and drivable.

The AMX/3 cars were built by the exotic Italian car maker Prototipi Bizzarrini in Livorno under the supervision of AMC. Owner Giotto Bizzarrini began as an engineer working on such famous cars as the renowned Ferrari 250 GTO and the less-well-known sports cars of Iso Rivolta. Bizzarrini began his own firm in 1965, racing an Iso Grifo at Le Mans and eventually building his own sports cars blending swooping Italian bodies with reliable American engines and drivetrain.

Prototipi Bizzarrini shut its doors in 1969, but reopened in 1970 to build the AMX/3s. Initially, 5,000 units were planned to be built per year, but that idea was scrapped almost immediately when problems started to develop. It was then announced that only two units per month would be built, or twenty-four per year. Chairman of the Board Roy D. Chapin, Jr., and AMC president William V. Luneburg said in an article appearing in *Hot Rod* magazine that the car would be manufactured to "test the market potential for the car's advanced engineering design."

Two problems destroyed any chance of AMX/3 quantity production. The new 5 mph federal bumper safety standards could not be incorporated economically into the present body design, and no coach-builder could produce the car for the targeted market price of $10,000 to $12,000. Had the market price of the car been around $20,000, there were houses ready and willing to build, but that price was way out of line for such a car in 1970. It cost American Motors $250,000 for each car actually produced including development and building costs.

Karmann of Germany almost became the builder of the AMX/3 bodies, and had that happened the car would have been designated the AMX/K. Almost everything had been agreed upon except price, which finally killed the deal.

All six AMX/3s that were eventually built were made basically the same, but each one had its own individual distinct characteristics. All rode on a 105.3 inch wheelbase and measured 175.6 inches long, 74.9 inches wide and 43.5 inches high. Front wheel track was set at 60.6 inches and rear track at 61.2 inches, with a 5.9 inch ground clearance. The sixth car had three additional inches of rear overhang to accommodate the mufflers and featured fully concealed windshield wipers.

The complete car had a curb weight of almost 3,100 pounds, roughly the same as a production 1968-70 AMX. Weight distribution was even at forty-three percent front/fifty-seven percent rear. Front and rear tire and wheel sizes differed. One of the cars had Campagnolo 15x6.5 custom wheels mounted on the front and huge 15x9s on the rear. The others had 205/70x15 Michelin X radials in front and 225/70x15s in the rear.

The AMX/3 used the 1970 Rebel Machine 390 V-8, which produced 340 hp at 5100 rpm and had a torque figure of 430 pounds-feet at 3600 rpm. The engine was mounted longitudinally behind the cockpit, thus giving the car its mid-engined designation.

No transaxle was available at the time that could handle the torque of the mighty AMC 390. The first car was built with a German ZF unit. Oto Melara of La Spezia, Italy, was then commissioned to build a new unit. Melara had extensive experience in building gears and gearboxes for both civil and military vehi-cles. The all-new gearbox featured Porsche-type ring synchronizers and hypoid ring and pinion gears.

A standard AMC clutch disc was used with Rhzeppa-type constant-velocity universal joints on the drive shafts. The wheels were chosen for their quietness and smoothness of operation. A 3.54:1 final drive ratio gave the sleek sports car an estimated 160 mph top speed.

The frame and suspension system were equally impressive. The frame was of a semimonocoque construction. Since all the cars were being built under Bizzarrini's direct supervision, numerous proven race car ideas went into the layout. BMW of Germany ultimately handled the testing of the car, even to the point of determining longevity of individual components. The independent suspension system used was of the parallel-wishbone type with pivots positioned to give a low and horizontal roll axis. Koni adjustable shocks were used all around, as were coil springs with unequal-length A-arms. The rear had two coils and two shocks on each side, a la XKE Jaguar.

Heavy-duty antiroll bars were used front and rear. Stock AMC spindles and ball joints were used up front, and special aluminum castings were made for the rear suspension uprights. All suspension pivots were either rubber bushed or lubed for life. A complete stock AMC steering column, and Saginaw steering box and steering linkage, made up a good, cost-effective steering system.

The car was equipped with vacuum-boosted internally vented disc brakes with German-made ATE brake calipers all around. The rear featured two cali-

The AMX/3 was an extension of the AMX/2 show car. Only six units were built, each a little different from the other. The first five are presently in the United States, and the sixth is in Italy.

pers per wheel, one being equipped with the mechanical handbrake. Each caliper had its own hydraulic circuit connected to its opposite wheel and to the dual master cylinder. In the event of a brake failure, one set of brakes should always work.

The body was of an integrated structure with boxed sills, central backbone and a permanently attached steel body. This permitted the car to be changed into a convertible or to have a facelift, if desired at a later date. Dick Teague states that the first nonoperational AMX/3 was built incorrectly and could not be converted to a running model.

The AMX/3 had ample luggage space under the front hood. It had six cubic feet of capacity just behind the air exit vents behind the radiator, with two electrically driven fans, and was handsomely finished and trimmed. The space-saver spare tire was placed in the rear above the gearbox.

The interior was quite spacious for a mid-engined car. It was wide and had plenty of leg- and headroom, although the bucket seats could not be fully reclined. A dead pedal was on the left for bracing yourself during hard cornering.

A small window behind the seats was double-glazed to act as a sound insulator between the driver and the engine compartment. Teague called this innovation a T-window. The engine hatch, which was hinged at the rear, was almost perfectly counterbalanced and used a production Pacer hood latch.

AMC used its excellent Weather Eye integrated heating and air conditioning system, which was blended into the dashboard quite nicely. A big 320 kph (200 mph) speedometer and a 7000 rpm tach with a 5200 rpm redline were placed under an overhanging shroud. Oil temperature, oil pressure and fuel level gauges were also present. The center console contained the shift lever and handbrake. A European three-spoke flat-type steering wheel was used.

A twenty-four-gallon fuel tank was positioned inside the left quarter panel, and the battery was placed in the opposite side.

From its first unveiling to the European press on March 23, 1970, people were awed by the car's sleek body. In its US debut at the International Auto Show in New York between April 4 and April 12, 1970, it drew the same reactions. All of its lines were meticulously blended to produce a sports car of unique and unequaled design. Many of the press writers could not believe the car came from American Motors.

The body design was basically that of the original AMX/2 show car but with new front- and rear-end styling. Front and rear painted steel bumpers blended neatly into the body sculpture. Pop-up headlights were on top of each fender. The windshield was sloped back

Mark Donohue poses with one of the AMX/3 sportsters. This shot gives an idea of the car's low stance (it was a mere 43.5 inches high).

42

at a sixty-six-degree angle. Standard Javelin/AMX flush door handles were used with racing-style outside rearview mirrors. A functional hood port placed at the leading edge between the headlights provided the interior occupants with fresh air. The hood also contained two large functional hood scoops to help break up the airflow over the cab for maximum antilift purposes at speeds over 100 mph. The hood was hinged at its forward point.

Air inlet ducts were placed forward of each rear wheel to provide cooling to the brakes and engine compartment. The rear deck hatch also contained functional air-venting louvers for additional cooling. AMX/3 emblems were placed on the hood and deck. AMX/3 or AMX/III appeared on each side forward of the rear wheelwells. Some cars had this emblem on or above the rocker panel, and other cars did not have it at all.

Although the AMX/3 was never wind-tunnel tested, its shape would appear to have a low coefficient of drag. One item that would have been beneficial was the rear flush body spoiler that was made to pop up at high speeds for stability, but the spoiler was never made operational. Consideration was even given to installing a front body spoiler for the same purpose, but that also was not finalized.

When Bizzarrini initially tested the car around the Nurburgring track in Germany, he was clocked doing 145 mph—but the car was becoming airborne, and had he not slowed down, disaster could have struck.

At first it was believed that only five AMX/3s were built, but a sixth was recently discovered in Italy which had been constructed from leftover parts by Giotto Bizzarrini's business partner in the project, Salvatore Diamonte, who now resides in Turin, Italy.

When the AMX/3 project was canceled by AMC, an order came from American Motors to Bizzarrini to chop up any and all remaining bodies. Diamonte reportedly destroyed four half-finished units which were then housed at his own new firm called Autoconstruzioni SD. But Diamonte could not bring himself to do away with a final AMX/3 which was nearly complete; he went on to finish the car, which he still owns today.

When Dick Teague heard of the discovery of the sixth AMX/3 several years later, he was intrigued, to say the least. The circumstances surrounding the destruction of the other four half-finished cars cannot help but raise doubts as to their actual demise. Could one or two more have been tucked away for a rainy day? Anything's possible in Italy.

Auction prices have been monumental for certain fifties and sixties GM, Ford and Chrysler dream cars which have surfaced intact in the past five years after reportedly being destroyed when their show-car duties were over. Odds on one or more AMX/3 making a future appearance are worth putting money on. As a matter of fact, Teague was quoted as saying in a recent article that "it wouldn't surprise me if someday a couple more surfaced."

The AMX/3 was ahead of its time. Only now, roughly fifteen years later, have successful production versions of the two-seater mid-engined sports car gained buyer popularity, in the form of the Pontiac Fiero and Toyota MR2. The AMX/3 was without a doubt the high point in American Motors design, styling, engineering and innovation. With the combined talents of AMC and Bizzarrini, the AMX/3 was probably the most successful of the company's joint projects with an Italian firm since the 1956 Rambler Palm Beach program.

Chapter 4

Javelin 1968-74

As was the case with General Motors and Chrysler, American Motors was caught off guard without a sporty model to compete with the runaway success of the Ford Mustang, introduced in April 1964. Every manufacturer scrambled to get a pony car of its own on the market to cash in on some of the sales Ford was reaping in.

The Plymouth Barracuda was introduced roughly two weeks before the Mustang, on April 1, 1964. It was a Valiant with a fastback added on, and was nowhere

The new Javelin sported the clean and well-contoured lines so typical of the times. The massive front bumper was nicely blended into the fenders.

near as successful as the Mustang. The Barracuda had to wait until the 1967 model year to receive a new original look.

It took Chevy three years to catch up, with the introduction of the 1967 Camaro in the fall of 1966. During its development the Camaro was called the Super Nova and almost received the name Panther, but Chevrolet kept up the tradition by having its name begin with a *C*. Until the Camaro came out, the Corvair and Chevy II had to take on the Mustang.

Pontiac was also late, coming out with the Firebird in mid-1967. It was essentially a sportier version of the Camaro.

Even Ford's relative, Mercury, could not come up with anything until model year 1967, when the luxury Cougar was introduced.

AMC was nearly the last to introduce its version of the pony car, the 1968 Javelin, in the fall of 1967. One more model came on board in the fall of 1969—Dodge finally came out with its 1970 Challenger. Until then, the Dodge Dart had to fight it out with the other pony cars.

The final Javelin prototype was completed in April 1966, after a period of about eighteen months, from drawing board through clay and several design changes. The production Javelin can trace its roots to a prototype called the Rebel II that used the basic 1964-65 Rambler American body style but with a landau-styled roof. AMC considered another prototype called the American Rogue, which introduced the 1968-70 two-seater AMX roof styling, but the AMX II from the Project IV Tour was ultimately the production Javelin's ancestor. The final design was so appealing and tasteful that Dick Teague stated, "It's the only car that we haven't wanted to change something on after seeing it outside our studios."

1968

When the production Javelin made its official debut on September 26, 1967, it was received very well by both the press and the public. AMC was quick to compare its new Javelin with the Mustang in an ad entitled "An Unfair Comparison between the Mustang and the Javelin."

The Javelin had a larger front bumper, ventless side windows, and bigger standard-displacement six-cylinder and V-8 engines. More important, its dimensions, based on those of a compact car, were much more generous. The Javelin could boast of more headroom and legroom and five inches more width for the backseat occupants, even more than the Cougar. The Javelin also had a larger trunk compartment, bigger gas tank and more powerful battery.

AMC also mentioned its superior flow-through ventilation system, wheel discs, reclining bucket seats and wood-grain steering wheel. The flow-through ventilation system was unique because it had air entering through a plenum chamber in the cowl and exhausting through the rear edge of the doors via manually controlled vents in the armrests.

AMC's new pony car was successful in its first year of production, selling 56,462 units. The year 1968 was the Javelin's best in terms of units sold, as the figures began to taper off in 1969 and continued to drop until the last year of production in 1974.

The Javelin's styling was clean and uncluttered. Its massive front bumper blended in nicely with the twin venturi grille openings and deeply recessed black crosshatch inner pattern. Standard headlights flanked the grille openings, with two large round parking lights directly below inside the body-contoured bumper. The hood contained twin indentations running its length, which were similar to the AMX II show car's and

The Javelin's profile carried out the familiar long-hood/short-deck theme well. It was available with an array of high-performance items and engines, including a 390 cubic inch *315 hp V-8, which came at midyear. The rally side stripe was optional, and the dual pinstripes were standard.*

Fully reclining bucket seats and the Shift-Command automatic transmission with console could be ordered.

almost identical to the 1967 Mustang's. Javelin scripts were placed on each fender behind the wheelwells and inside the left grille opening. Small side-marker lights were contained in the fenders.

The car had a semifastback roof style with a concave rear window that gently sloped to the rear of the fender tips. The same wraparound taillights with center red reflective lenses found on the AMX were shared with the Javelin, but with Javelin script in place of the AMX letters. The paddle-type flush outside door handles were featured along with the unique preset impulse locking system that eliminated the conventional front door push-button locks.

The Javelin could be had in fourteen different exterior colors, each with its own standard dual pin-

The Rally-Pak option consisted of an 8000 rpm tach with 270 degree sweep dial oil pressure and ammeter gauges and an electric clock. It could be ordered on column- (shown) or floor-mounted-transmission-controlled models.

stripes. Two models were available, the base Javelin and the SST, with the SST having its emblems placed under the fender Javelin scripts. The SST also included extra exterior chrome trim with an upgraded interior and reclining bucket seats. Like the AMX, the Javelin was available in one body style, the two-door hardtop sport coupe.

The dimensions of the car were right in pony car territory. Wheelbase was set at 109 inches, overall length was 189.2 inches and width was 71.9 inches, enabling the car to accommodate four passengers comfortably. Rear wheel track was 57.9 inches. Front wheel track varied between six-cylinder (57.9 inches) and V-8 models (58.4 inches). Curb weight was approximately 3,100 pounds, making it one of the lightest in its class.

The interior of the car had basically the same layout as the AMX. It was available in black, red or tan ventilated vinyl or fabric upholstery as a no-cost option on the SST, and had a rear seat. The base Javelin came standard with a black vinyl interior, with off-white being optional.

As with all 1968 AMC cars, the Javelin included a host of standard safety features to go along with its base price of $2,482.20. Even the sporty SST version was a bargain at just $2,587.20. Items such as illuminated side-of-car safety markers, safety shaped arm-rests, interior control knobs and handles, new mechanical brake light switch, seatback lock, padding for key interior areas and components, and nonglare finishes for certain interior items were built into the car. Two seatbelts were provided for the rear passengers and shoulder belts were reserved for the front occupants.

The Javelin could be tailored to fit any pocketbook whether it be for economy, luxury or performance.

The base engine was the 232 ci six-cylinder equipped with a one-barrel carburetor and producing 145 hp at 4300 rpm. Both the 232 ci and 290 V-8 two-barrel engines came standard with a column-shift three-speed manual transmission. The next level brought the first four-barrel-carburetor-equipped engine, the 10:1 high-compression 290 V-8 with 225 hp at 4700 rpm. This engine required premium fuel, but the

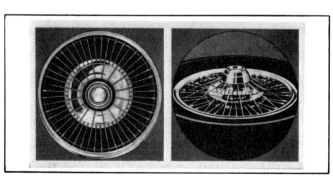

Optional wire wheel covers added a nice sports car flair.

two-barrel version with a compression ratio of 9:1 could get along on regular. The last and highest step until midyear was the 343 V-8 280 hp mill. This was the same engine as found in the AMX and could be ordered with optional dual exhaust and chrome tips, as could the 225 hp 290 V-8.

What turned the 343 Javelin into a performer was the combination of this engine and the optional Go Package. As on the AMX, the package included the 343 four-barrel V-8, dual exhaust system, power front disc brakes, handling package, E70x14 wide-profile redline tires and wide rally stripes on the side replacing the standard dual pinstripes.

A column-mounted three-speed automatic called Shift-Command, which could be held in each gear and shifted manually, was optional with the 343, as was the console shift with thumb-button control. The four-speed manual that featured a disc-type reverse lockout on the shifter handle, as on the AMX, was optional on all V-8s but was the standard and only gearbox available on the four-barrel 290. There was no standard transmission for the 343. Again, as on the AMX, standard axle ratios were 2.87, 3.15 an 3.54:1, with optional dealer-installed units available up to the deep 4.44:1.

AMC wanted the public to know that the Javelin was a performer as well as a good looker, so it came out with an advertisement entitled "Test Drag a Javelin." The ad stated, "It will move from a stand still to 60 in about 7.86 seconds and pin your back bone to the bucket in the process. . . . This SST in pure stock form will cover a standing quarter in 15.8." These times were for a 343 cube 280 hp V-8 with four-speed and 3.54 rear axle.

How good were these times compared with those of some of the other supercars that were around at the time? Surprisingly, they were very, very good. As a matter of fact, good enough to equal a Shelby GT500 dual-quad 428 and beat a Corvette 327 ci 350 hp model in the quarter-mile.

A quick glance back at *Road & Track*'s road test annual for 1968, summing up road tests conducted in 1967, was proof positive. A 343 ci 280 hp Javelin equipped with the four-speed and a 3.54 rear attained a 0-60 time of 7.9 seconds and covered the quarter-mile in 15.5 seconds at 90 mph. Curb weight of the car was 3,370 pounds.

A 1967 Shelby GT500 equipped with the dual-quad 428 producing 355 hp, with three-speed automatic transmission and 3.25 rear, did 0-60 in 7.2 seconds and covered the quarter-mile in 15.5 seconds at 95 mph. Curb weight was 3,520 pounds.

A 1968 Corvette equipped with a 327 ci 350 hp engine and a close-ratio four-speed with a 3.70 rear took 7.7 seconds to go from zero to sixty miles per hour. The quarter-mile was covered in 15.6 seconds at a speed of 92 mph. Curb weight was 3,260 pounds.

The Corvette was lighter and had more horsepower than the Javelin. The Shelby was slightly heav-

ier, but it had much more horsepower and its engine was known to be underrated. If the 343 Javelin was not considered a supercar by the competition then the Corvette and the Shelby were nothing but ma and pa grocery getters; AMC could truly boast of having a legitimate muscle car.

With a little work and a minimum of speed equipment, the 343 Javelin could be turned into a hot little street bomb. It could also hold its own on the strip, running in NHRA's G/Stock and Super/Stock classes and in the Trans-Am series.

Ranger Rambler in Florham Park, New York, was a very active AMC dealer promoting the new Javelin on the strip.

Numerous speed equipment suppliers realized the potential of the Javelin and thus offered high-performance parts almost immediately at the time of the car's introduction. Hi-po cams and kits could be ordered from Crower, Isky and others. Offenhauser and Edelbrock offered high-rise aluminum intake manifolds and high-cfm (cubic feet of air per minute) carburetors, while Jardine and Doug Thorley jumped in with their exhaust headers. Weber, Schiefer, Zoom and others produced clutches, pressure plates and gears. Hurst offered its excellent Competition Plus four-speed shifter.

Dealer Richmon Rambler Sales in Staten Island, New York, offered a specially equipped and prepared model called the Javelin RR-1 for a list price of $2,995. It started with a Javelin equipped with the 343 and the Go Package. Standard equipment on the car included the 280 hp engine, four-speed transmission, quick-ratio manual steering, Twin-Grip rear, dual exhaust, power front disc brakes, E70x14 redline tires, chrome valve covers, air cleaner, filler cap and master cylinder cover, racing fan belt, modified ignition, traction bars, heavy-duty valve springs with dampers, tuned carburetor with heat-blocker spacer, heavy-duty radiator, Power-Flex fan, fan shroud, heavy-duty sway bar, heavy-duty springs and shocks, and 5.5 inch rims. Optional equipment included a 3310 Holley carburetor, Cragar wheels, 8000 rpm Sun tachometer, Offenhauser intake manifold, AMC hi-po cam and kit, Hurst shifter, Schiefer clutch, AMC Rally-Pak gauge cluster, Autolite copper wire set and Thorley headers. It was quite a package for the price.

For those who preferred a well-balanced cruising and performance car, AMC offered an array of luxury and convenience options to suit individual buyer tastes. If the buyer wanted to stick with the base six-cylinder engine but demanded a little more beef, an optional handling package could be ordered that consisted of a front sway bar and heavy-duty springs and shock absorbers. Appearance items such as a black or off-white vinyl top really set off the Javelin's lines. An assortment of wheel discs or chrome mag wheels could be had with blackwall, whitewall or redline tires.

Still not enough? Wire wheels or turbo-cast wheel covers could be ordered for that extra sports car flavor. Visibility and light groups as on the AMX were available. Air conditioning, tinted glass and heavy-duty batteries and alternators were also on the list. As a matter of fact, just about every option that was available on the AMX could be had on the Javelin.

The car used the same advanced all-steel unitized body construction as found on all other AMC models. The complete suspension layout and components were basically compact Rambler American units (manufacturers commonly used as many existing and off-the-shelf parts as possible).

At the time of the Javelin's introduction, AMC came out with an assortment of TV commercials with the familiar "Hey Javelin" dialogue. One depicted a rich man driving an exotic European sports car. He came up beside the Javelin at a traffic light and asked its driver if he wanted to race. The Javelin driver declined, saying, "I have a bowl of goldfish on the seat." A group of young ladies and a young man on a motorcycle also challenged the driver of the Javelin. He declined in each case. The commercial ended with the safety-conscious driver pulling up to a multilevel parking garage and turning his car over to a young attendant who raced it up through the levels, screeching the tires. The message was that the Javelin could be docile or mean, depending on what the driver wanted it to be.

Road tests

The automotive magazines wasted no time in putting the car through its paces. *Motor Trend* magazine staged a six-car shoot-out between Mustang, Camaro, Barracuda, Cougar, Firebird and Javelin. The Javelin was equipped with the 343, four speed, 3.54:1 rear and dealer-installed traction bars. It surprised everyone by beating all the other competitors in the quarter-mile, running it in 15.1 seconds at 93 mph. The other pony cars turned in the following figures: Barracuda, 15.2 at 92; Camaro, 15.6 at 92; Cougar, 15.4 at 91; Firebird, 15.4 at 93; and Mustang, 15.2 at 94. Their engines were as follows: Barracuda, 340 ci 275 hp; Camaro, 396 ci 325 hp; Cougar, 390 ci 335 hp; Firebird, 400 ci 335 hp; and Mustang, 390 ci 335 hp. The Javelin was the lightest of them all, weighing 3,461 pounds; the heaviest was the Cougar at 3,882 pounds. With the exception of the 340 ci 275 hp engine in the Barracuda, which was underrated, the Javelin had the smallest-displacement and lowest-rated powerplant.

Motor Trend had this to say about the Javelin: "Really startling performance from smallest engine of all cars tested in category." It also praised the car's handling: "In SST form with the 343 V-8 which includes a stout handling package, the car turned and cornered as if it were nailed to the road." It went on to say, "If auto racing were relegated to strictly stock cars, we'd put our bet here." And finally, "Too few cars have brakes equal to the optional front disc/rear drum power units on the Javelin. We made many passes up and down mountain roads and 'through the eyes' on the drag strip, never once suffering deterioration of stopping power. The car pulled to a halt a scant 150 feet from 60 mph in a nearly perfect straight line, and repeated this test several times in the same distance."

The AMX/3 not only forecast the new Javelin's front-end styling, but also inspired the concept of the 1971 Hornet Sportabout station wagon.

Motor Trend was very impressed with the car's results in its first year out.

Car Life also tested a 343, four-speed 3.54 twin-grip rear model. It came up with a 0-60 time of 8.1 seconds and a quarter-mile time of 15.4 seconds at 93 mph. Those times supported the AMC ads' claims. *Car Life* was also impressed with the Javelin's overall styling, handling and performance.

Mid-1968 brought an addition to the Javelin's engine line-up that would enable it to better compete with the other pony cars. When the two-seater AMX was introduced in February of that year, it brought with it a new 390 V-8 that was named, appropriately, the AMX 390. This engine was made available in the Javelin SST only, as the top-of-the-line optional power-plant, and it produced 315 hp at 4600 rpm. This put the Javelin in the same league as the 396 Camaro, 400 Firebird, 383 Barracuda and 390 Mustang and Cougar.

The new AMX 390 V-8 was available with the four-speed manual or Shift-Command console automatic. With the automatic, the 2.87 axle ratio was standard and the 3.15 was optional. If you ordered the four-speed, the 3.15 was standard and the 3.54 was optional. The 3.15 ratio was standard with the optional Go Package, and 3.73, 3.91, 4.10 and 4.44 dealer kits could be substituted.

Car and Driver magazine decided to evaluate the six pony cars and see just how they stacked up against each other. All the cars were equipped with three-speed automatic transmissions, front vented disc brakes (with the exception of the Javelin's, which were solid), heavy-duty suspension, wide oval tires, tach-ometer, and power steering and brakes. The Barra-cuda was equipped with the 340 V-8 instead of the 383.

Since the results of the 343 Javelin test were so favorable, one might think the 390 version blew away the competition—but it did not. This time the Javelin SST came in last. The 0-60 run was covered in 6.9 seconds, but the quarter-mile took 15.2 seconds at 92 mph, which was slower than the 343 model.

The automatic transmission and 3.15:1 rear did not help. This Javelin was the first 390 version ever made, and AMC had promised the car to the *Car and Driver* staff; thus, it was built and rushed off to them for the test. Had the car been properly tuned and prepped and equipped with a four-speed and a 3.54 rear, it probably would have turned better times and perfor-mance than the previously tested 343. The production models that were later tested did much better.

Car and Driver praised the handling of the car, saying, "It felt very much like a British sports car—with the same advantages as well as the same disadvantages. The Javelin is nearly neutral when pushed through a hard corner and a controllable, power-induced over-steer can be obtained whenever desired. On the tight handling course the SST was everyone's favorite because of its versatility and predictability." They con-cluded with this: "The Javelin because of its handling turned out to be the most fun to drive of any of the sporty cars."

The styling of the Javelin received equal recogni-tion. *Car and Driver* summed it up this way: "It has a clean understated appearance that is not marred by phony vents, power bulges, mounds or bizzare sculp-turing of whatever variety. The Javelin is an honest-looking car with a dramatic flair." Once again, the magazine staff was pleased with the new Kenosha pony car by AMC.

The Javelin helped AMC operate in the black for the first time since 1965. It joined the AMX, American, Rebel and Ambassador to put the company back on its feet after a loss of $75.8 million in 1967.

Like the AMX, the 1969 Javelin was restricted mainly to detail refinements and improvements. The optional rally side stripe design was also changed, as shown.

Specials

The Javelin was also marketed in Great Britain and Australia, where it was known as the Rambler Javelin. The models available there were the SST versions equipped with the 343 ci 280 hp V-8 coupled to the Shift-Command floor-shifted automatic transmission. Some European models were equipped with a lower 9:1 compression ratio 343 V-8 producing only 250 hp at 4800 rpm. Rear axle was either the 2.87 or the 3.15:1 ratio non-Twin-Grip unit. The cars also had power steering and power front disc brakes with the Go Package (minus the rally side stripes) and Rally-Pak instrument cluster. Some Javelins did not have the Go Package, but most customers felt the standard suspension was adequate for their use. Some even had the optional vinyl top.

Rambler Motors (AMC) Limited of London was one British importer. Most models shipped to London were fully assembled left-hand-drive US versions, although later 1969 versions were right-hand-drive

The imitation mag-style wheel disc blended in nicely with the optional redline tires still available for 1969.

models. AMI of Melbourne, Australia, had the cars shipped over in completely knocked down form and then converted over to right-hand drive in more or less the same fashion as the AMXs. Only about 200 Javelins made it to Australian shores.

Both countries praised the car for its brisk performance and good handling in any weather. But both agreed that in wet weather the car fell short of expectations. Whereas the Yankee magazine road testers rated the braking power of the Javelin as very good to excellent, both the Britons and the Aussies rated it marginal to inadequate for their driving needs. That is just a small part of the different tastes between US and European or other foreign car buyers.

As was the case with the Aussie AMX, price was against the Javelin. In both Great Britain and Australia the car sold for over $7,000, with the Australian version being roughly $500 more than the British unit. Cars in both countries saw limited appeal, thus resulting in a low number of units being produced.

Javelins were also shipped in completely knocked down form to Karmann in Germany. These were hand-assembled like the Aussie Javelins, and they featured a nice hand-stitched interior. The car was known as the Karmann Javelin.

Javelins were also made in Mexico throughout their 1968-74 life span, and a limited number of 1974 Javelins were assembled and converted to right-hand drive in Australia by AMI.

Others were equally impressed with the Javelin's clean lines and styling. Customizer George Barris wasted no time in offering a custom package for the new car. The same arrangement was made with AMC regarding the Bonanza Javelin as had been made with the El Toro AMX—that of offering the car for sale through nationwide dealers.

The Bonanza Javelin had the same rear spoiler integrated into the trunk and quarter panels as had the El Toro AMX. The grille was a throwback to the fifties, consisting of five horizontal chrome bars. Small twin phony scoops were placed side by side inside the hood indentations just forward of the cowl area. Another set of nonfunctional scoops was placed on each quarter panel forward of the wheelwells. A flat-black stripe encircled the headlight fender tips and grille opening.

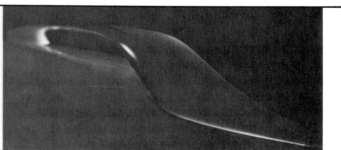

The simulated exhaust rocker panel molding and roof top spoiler were also available Big Bad options.

Flat-black stripes also ran on each side, starting behind the fender wheelwells and terminating into side scoops with special Bonanza logos. Standard five-spoke 1968 AMC chrome mag wheels were used with white sidewall tires. The deck lid, top surface of the spoiler and impressions around the rear window were also given the flat-black treatment, sort of a reverse scheme to what appeared on the hood and fenders of the Jeffords AMX and 1970 AMX Shadow Mask option.

Another custom package was marketed by Darel and Larry Droke, better known as the Droke brothers in the racing circle with their Ford funny car. Their package, the XP Javelin, did not have the add-on look of the Barris versions. Instead, it blended in nicely with the Javelin's existing lines and styling. It used the same type of trunk spoiler with integrated ends on the quarter panels as were used on the Barris models. One big difference was the use of a fiberglass hood with twin functional Ram-Air scoops running its entire length.

The design was almost identical to that of the 1970-72 Oldsmobile 442 with the functional Ram-Air hood. A stock 1968 AMX grille was used, with a Javelin script placed on the left side. A three-spoke slotted genuine-wood European-type steering wheel was installed, along with an interior-mounted padded roll bar secured to the floor using large flat steel plates. Cragar S/S chrome deep-dish offset wheels were mounted on redline tires. For $986, it was a clean and neat package that really enhanced the beauty of the stock Javelin.

One unique show car first exhibited at the Chicago Auto Show in February 1967, and then at the New York Auto Show in April, preceded the Javelin and gave a glimpse of the Javelin's front-end styling. It was the fastback sports station wagon model called the AMX III (not to be confused with the mid-engined AMX/3 sports car). This car inspired the Javelin's look and also served as the basis for the concept and styling of the 1971 Hornet Sportabout.

The car was finished in silver-gray. It sported two different side treatments toward the rear, which public viewers were asked to vote on. It was generally felt that the right side containing the post or pillar between the rear passengers and cargo area looked better than the left side, which was all glass. The rear roofline went right onto the production Sportabout.

The taillights were full-width nonwraparound type, and the car did not have front or rear side-marker lights. The dual exhausts had standard Javelin/AMX chrome tips, but the rear valance had bosses cut in to accommodate them—unlike the standard system that was hung underneath the valance.

The tailgate was a novel design that lifted up and, with scissor-action hinges, slid horizontally forward to rest on the roof. The idea was not new, it had been seen in similar form on the 1963 Studebaker Lark Wagonaire, designed by stylist Brooks Stevens before

he decided to form his own company called SS Automobiles Incorporated, makers of the unique Excalibur cars.

The Javelin was a successful model for American Motors in its first year out. It experienced its high point in production and sales for model year 1968.

1969

The Javelin received few changes for 1969, since the first-year 1968 model proved so successful. Both the base Javelin and SST models were carried over. The most notable difference when looking at the car head-on was the new bull's-eye motif on the left side of the recessed grille where the Javelin script used to be. That script was now located on the left-side leading edge of the hood. Bull's-eye motifs also adorned each sail panel, and the grille contained extra brightwork. The Javelin scripts that were formerly on the fenders were now placed on the sail panels, but the SST emblems remained in their original locations. A square American Motors emblem was placed just below the rear window.

Just about every small change that was made on the 1969 AMX was also made on the Javelin. Thus, the right-side dashboard grab handle and front bucket seat headrests were made standard, the spoked mag wheels were toned down with trim rings, and the new platinum vinyl option was made available. Subtle differences in options between the AMX and the Javelin included the blue and tan color interiors being restricted to the Javelin, and the AMX using a saddle rather than a tan-colored interior.

Other new stock and high-performance options available on the AMX also could be had on the Javelin. All engines and drivetrains were carryovers, with the exception of the new floor-shifted Shift-Command automatic transmission replacing the column unit.

Another appearance item change had to do with the optional Go Package. Whereas the 1968 rally stripe was single, running the body's length above the door handles, the 1969 version was a dual unit, running in line with the flush door handles. The bold nonfunctional twin hood scoops were painted flat-black and placed inside each stock hood indentation. Some thought they were a bit too severe; others thought they added that extra racing look.

One specialty model used by AMC to further promote the car's high-performance potential was the Blown 1969 Javelin 390 screamer. This car was inspired by Gene Amoroso of the American Motors Advertising and Sales Promotion Department. It was built by Hurst Performance in Detroit and became the personal transportation of Amoroso.

The engine was a fully blueprinted 390 AMX mill containing Crankshaft Company crank, rods and pistons topped by a GMC 6-71 blower with Cragar three-inch drive. A single four-barrel carburetor sat on top of the blower inside the triple venturi Bug Catcher scoop.

The car was also equipped with a four-speed and a 4.56:1 rear-end ratio. Goodyear Polyglas tires were mounted on American five-spoke deep-dish mags.

Large white-painted megaphone exhausts were later installed just forward of the rear wheels; these were similar in appearance to those found on the 1970 Dodge Challenger T/A and Plymouth Cuda AAR models. Originally the exhaust was made with four individual open header pipes on each side, terminating behind the front wheels. The car had a high stance, having been raised a few inches all around. A TV commercial's lines—"Butchered? It's a great car, dad. I only made it better"—were later painted in large white letters on both sides of the car. Incidently, the blower on the "butchered" Javelin used in the ads was a fake.

Performance was emphasized more in the factory literature. AMC put it this way: "It's great on the get-away, with any four-barrel V-8, you can order 4-on-the-floor with the same box the Javelins use in the Trans-Am races. Altogether, a car with dash." The literature also boasted of the spacious legroom and headroom in the Javelin's interior. The clean styling of the car with its built-in safety features was also touted.

Big Bad cars

AMC pushed the optional dealer-installed high-performance parts (cams and kits, intake manifolds and carburetors coupled with other Group 19 items) for "customizing your Javelin or AMX for fun and performance." Even the rear-deck adjustable spoiler from the Trans-Am racing Javelins was made available to the customer. An enthusiastic racer, equipping his or her new 390 Javelin with the right pieces, could do very well in NHRA's Super/Stock F class, for example.

The big news came in mid-1969 with the introduction of the Big Bad Javelins. The same Big Bad Orange, Big Bad Green and Big Bad Blue colors that were available on the AMX were introduced simultaneously on the Javelin, complete with matching bumpers. The padded eyebrow over the instrument cluster and Hurst four-speed shifter linkage became standard Javelin items. Again, a few models were equipped with the chrome-plated instrument tunnels.

There were a few items available on the Big Bad Javelin that were not available or were different on the Big Bad AMX model. The Javelin received the optional Craig Breedlove roof spoiler that was used on the 1968 Javelin Speed Spectacular models. Its design was changed to better blend in with the Javelin's roof, and it was no longer functional for its intended purpose. The optional simulated exhaust rocker panel molding available only on the Javelin became standard on the 1970 AMX and continued as an option for the 1970 Javelin.

The Big Bad option could be ordered on the base Javelin and on the SST version. If the optional Go Package was ordered, the twin hood scoops were still finished in flat-black. The same thin aluminum strip highlighting the grille-opening theme on the front bumper was shared by both the Javelin and the AMX.

One other cosmetic difference between the two-seater and four-seater was that the four-seater could be had with the optional black, white or red wide reverse-C flared rally stripe on the sides of the car, outlined with a matching color thin strip. The strip started at the quarter panel just ahead of the rear bumper and followed the beltline forward to the rear part of the front wheelwell, then turned down and back, finishing just forward of the door edge on the fender. Any regular Javelin option could be ordered, as well as a host of dealer-installed performance items. Only a few hundred Javelins were sold in each Big Bad color.

Unlike the AMX's sales, which increased for 1969, the Javelin's sales were down roughly twenty-eight percent to 40,675 units for the 1969 model year.

The Javelin received slightly new styling for the 1970 model year. The hood featured two raised sections with dummy chrome louvers on the leading edges.

The functional AMX Power Blister Ram-Air hood became optional for 1970, as did a new landau-style vinyl roof. The rally side stripe design was again changed, and the twin front ball-joint suspension was used on all 1970 AMCs.

Although 1970 did not bring an increase in sales for the Javelin, it did bring numerous body, interior and suspension changes to the last year for the original body style.

1970

Once again, most of what was changed on the AMX for 1970 was paralleled on the Javelin. The only body style available continued to be the two-door hardtop semifastback sports coupe, with models again being the base Javelin and luxury SST version.

The front and rear of the car were restyled. Although the grille and headlight treatment were now one piece instead of being divided, the deep recessed twin-venturi theme was retained. The hood was redesigned and extended almost two inches, bringing the overall length to 191 inches. Height was also down, from 51.81 inches to 51.60 inches. The standard hood now resembled more closely the optional hood that was available on the 1969 Javelin equipped with the Go Package. The hood scoops were also similar in design and layout to that package, but were nonfunctional and contained phony chrome louvers on their leading edges. The optional AMX Power Blister hood was now available with functional Ram-Air as part of the Go Package.

The Javelin scripts were in their same locations, and the bull's-eye motif was now also on the hood. The square AMC emblem just below the rear window was retained right up to the 1974 models. The SST and engine emblems swapped places, with the former now on the quarter panels and the latter on the fenders. New squared-off front and rear side-marker lights were used.

The full-width taillight treatment with end caps was identical to that on the 1970 AMX, except that no script was placed in the center back-up light. A landau-style vinyl half-roof available in black, white or blue was optional on the SST, and the full version could still be special-ordered. The vinyl half-roof was introduced in the spring of 1969 on the last '69 Javelins. The standard and optional rocker panels and outside rear-view mirrors were also redesigned for a smoother appearance.

A new rally stripe was a combination of the 1968 version and the 1969 reverse-C on the Big Bad models. The stripe started at the quarter panel, tapering out and following the body sculpture above the door handle all the way to the fender tip, turning downward and then back, following the beltline while tapering off to a point and ending in the middle of the door. The stripes could be had in black, white or red.

The interior was almost totally redesigned, with the SST version receiving a woodgrain finish. The instrument panel now had a full-width eyebrow crash pad around the top for added protection, which it shared with the AMX. As did the AMX of the same year, the Javelin had the high-back bucket seats with optional leather, new door and side panels, Pistol Grip automatic transmission floor shifter handle and optional Rim-Blow steering wheel.

The new twin ball-joint front suspension system was also shared, as was the new Chemcor safety windshield.

The rear shock setup was also changed. Manufacturers had found that one inexpensive way of controlling rear axle hop during acceleration on a limited basis was to stagger the shocks. AMC placed the right shock ahead of the axle and the left shock behind it. This little trick helped reduce the problem, but traction bars were still needed, especially on vehicles with modified engines and drivetrains.

All three Big Bad colors were carried over, minus the matching bumpers, and the roof spoiler still could be ordered. The Hurst four-speed shifter was still the way to go up and down through the gears.

The new engine line-up for the Javelin was similar, again, to the small AMX's, but with a few differences. The base engine was still the one-barrel 232 ci 145 hp six banger. The 290 and 343 V-8s were replaced with the 304 and 360 cubic inch versions. The 304 was available only with a two-barrel carburetor, and produced 210 hp at 4400 rpm. Torque was set at 305 pounds-feet at 2800 rpm, and was a good compromise between the old 290 ci 200 hp and 225 hp engines. Compression ratio was 9:1, permitting the use of regular fuel.

The next two optional engines were two- and four-barrel versions of the new 360 V-8. The low-performance version was rated at 245 hp at 4400 rpm. Compression ratio was the same as on the 304. The high-performance 360 pumped out 290 hp at 4800 rpm and had a 10:1 compression ratio, requiring premium fuel. Torque was healthy at 395 pounds-feet at 3200 rpm.

The final option was the improved version of the same 390 V-8 as found in the AMX, which put out 325 hp at 5200 rpm. Dual exhaust was standard on the 390 and optional on the four-barrel 360. This was the last year for the chrome-plated valve covers, air cleaner lid and oil filter cap on the big engine.

A new option on the Javelin as well as on the AMX was Goodyear E60x15 raised-white-letter Polyglas tires mounted on 15x7 racing-style steel wheels with center caps; this was later made standard equipment on the 1970 Rebel Machine. Another option was the fully functional Side-Winders side exhaust system available for both the Javelin and the AMX. This option had a

The 1970 Javelin grille design theme was carried out and extended to the new optional AMX Power Blister hood.

distinctive appearance and sound, and few cars were ordered with it.

Specials

In the full-line AMC catalog, the Javelin and the AMX were described as "the racy ones," emphasizing once again performance, although the luxury and convenience aspects of the cars were made more evident than before.

The hot news for the Javelin was the fall 1969 introduction of the 1970 street replica SST Trans-Am model. SCCA (Sports Car Club of America) rules at the time required that only 100 street versions be built for homologation purposes for the car to be eligible to race on the sanctioned tracks.

The street replica SST was patterned after the 1969 Trans-Am racing Javelin. Only 100 units were built and all were painted red-white-blue, in that order from front to back. All had the black vinyl interior and the same equipment, which included the 390 V-8, four-speed close-ratio transmission with Hurst shifter, 3.91:1 Twin-Grip rear, functional AMX Ram-Air hood, dual exhaust system, heavy-duty engine cooling, power steering, power front disc brakes, heavy-duty springs and shocks, 14x6 mag-styled wheels, F70x14 raised-white-letter Goodyear Polyglas tires, 140 mph speedometer, 8000 rpm tachometer, and front and rear body spoilers. Other options included were the visibility group, light group, AM push-button radio and space-saver tire with regular spare wheel. The Trans-Am model also included all the standard SST equipment minus the sill moldings and paint stripes. It was a complete package for the factory price of $3,995.

On January 1, 1970, SCCA rules were changed, requiring 2,500 units of a certain model be built to qualify it for the racing season. This led to the 1970 Mark Donohue Special, again based on the SST model. Mark Donohue and Roger Penske were not satisfied with the old adjustable rear deck spoiler found on the 1968 and 1969 Trans-Am racing Javelins. Donohue designed a more aerodynamic fixed unit that blended in nicely with the Javelin's existing lines. Ironically, the spoiler was almost identical to the Barris and Droke brothers designs of the previous year, although those were three-piece units, and the new Donohue model was a one-piece unit bolted onto the trunk lid.

Unlike the Trans-Am street replica, the Mark Donohue Special could be ordered in any exterior color including the Big Bad colors. It could be had with any of the SST options, although engines were restricted to the four-barrel 360 or 390 V-8s. Most, but not all, Mark Donohue Specials were equipped with a special thick-walled 360 ci V-8 that could be overbored 0.1075 inch to a maximum bore diameter of 4.1875 inches. The standard 360 could be bored only 0.045 inch to a maximum diameter of 4.125 inches. The thick-walled V-8 also had provisions for four-bolt main bearing caps.

The Mark Donohue Special started out with the SST model equipped with either the 360 or 390 V-8, Pistol Grip console-shift automatic or four-speed manual transmission with Hurst shifter, dual exhaust, functional AMX Ram-Air hood, power front disc brakes handling package, 14x6 mag-styled wheels, E70x14 raised-white-letter Goodyear Polyglas tires and the rear-deck-mounted spoiler with Mark Donohue signature on the right rear surface. From there buyers could tailor the car to their specific needs and tastes. Only 2,501 units were built, just to get AMC over the hump.

Road tests

How well did the Javelin perform with the new engine line-up? Again, pretty well when compared with other cars in its class.

Car Life magazine road-tested a 390 Javelin equipped with the three-speed Shift-Command console automatic transmission and 3.15:1 non-Twin-Grip rear. In the same issue it road-tested a 1970 Dodge Challenger convertible equipped with the 440 ci 390 hp Tri-Carb wedge V-8, coupled to a four-speed manual transmission and 3.54:1 limited-slip rear. The Challenger was faster than the Javelin, but not by much. The Javelin was praised for its nice compromise in performance, handling and comfort for the pony car. It recorded a 0-60 time of 7.6 seconds compared with the Challenger's 7.1. Best quarter-mile time for the Javelin was 15.11 seconds at 91.5 mph. The Challenger was quicker, doing it in 14.64 seconds at 97.82 mph.

One strike against the Challenger was its curb weight of 3,900 pounds, whereas the Javelin was a lightweight, coming in at 3,375 pounds. That was a difference of 525 pounds, and the performance times for the cars reflected it. *Car Life* had this to say about the Javelin's quarter-mile time: "A few more miles, maybe just more air in the tires, would drop it into the high 14s."

The car was once again cited by *Car Life* for its excellent cornering ability: "Powering out of a test curve, the new Javelin responds and goes where it is pointed. Front wheels hang on, the rear wheels track around."

Although the automatic transmission for 1970 was slightly improved by AMC standards, it really had not

The street replica red-white-blue Trans-Am Javelin saw only 100 units built for the 1970 model year. It was introduced with the rest of the 1970 AMC cars in the fall of 1969.

been improved when compared to the rest of the competition as *Car Life* commented, "The 1-2 shift was much faster than we expected. Move the lever and it happens at target 5000. In traffic or under part throttle, you'd never notice the shifts at all. We don't know of any domestic automatic transmission that isn't this good in daily driving."

And once again, the Javelin's brakes received a great applause. The *Car Life* staff put it this way: "If the Challenger brakes get good marks—and they do—then the discs on the Javelin win two gold stars. Stopping distance on the first stop was just about even. And short. The Challenger faded with use, which isn't that bad because the first one is the important one. But the Javelin didn't fade. On the eighth stop from 80 mph, the Javelin could still pull a high deceleration force, and stopped in ten feet less than it did on the first stop."

The completely redesigned interior also received excellent ratings by *Car Life*, as well as the AMC dealers, press and general public.

Earlier in the year, *Car Life* staged a shoot-out between four of the so-called showroom or pure stock versions of the Trans-Am racers. These were a Camaro Z/28 350, Firebird Trans Am 400, Mustang Boss 302 and Javelin SST 360. Horsepower ratings wre 360, 345, 290 and 290, respectively. All the cars were equipped with a four-speed manual transmission pulling 3.9:1 rear-end gears, except the Camaro which had 4.10:1 gears. All had front disc brakes, power steering and F60x15 Goodyear Polyglas raised-white-letter tires, with the exception of the Javelin which had smaller F70x14 skins, although E60x15 Polyglas tires could be optionally ordered. The Javelin had a horsepower disadvantage; it was also the lightest of the bunch at 3,100 pounds.

The following quarter-mile times and speeds were recorded: Camaro, 14.50 seconds at 100.22 mph; Firebird, 14.51 at 99.33; Mustang, 14.98 at 96.87; and Javelin, 15.46 at 91.09. Although the Javelin came in last in just about every category of the shoot-out, it was not too far behind the more-powerful-engined rivals. AMC also placed second, behind the Ford Mustangs, at the end of the 1970 Trans-Am manufacturers championship standings.

AMC even donated a 1970 Javelin, minus engine, to the University of California in San Diego for installation of a steam-driven two-cylinder Harley-Davidson motorcycle engine for the 1970 clean-air race at La Jolla. It was a six-day race that started from Cambridge, Massachusetts, to Pasadena, California.

Total 1970 Javelin production once again took a nose-dive, with 28,210 units being built for the model year. The annual production figures for the 1971-74 period hovered around that amount. AMC was quietly getting ready for the second-generation Javelin.

The Mark Donohue Special was introduced in mid-1970, and 2,501 units were built for homologation purposes for the 1970 Trans-Am racing season. Donohue's own-design rear spoiler was used, with his signature.

The Javelin was all new for 1971 and was available in base, SST and AMX versions. The AMX was developed in honor of the passing 1970 two-seater AMX model. This version is the SST with the optional rally side stripes.

1971

Although the 1971 model Javelin was totally redesigned, base price was kept reasonable, increasing only $159 to $2,879. All major body and chassis dimensions grew, as did the curb weight. Wheelbase was stretched one inch to 110 inches; overall length was now 191.8 inches, up slightly; width was increased to 75.2 inches; and height was again reduced slightly, to 50.9 inches. Front wheel track for the six-cylinder model was 59.3 inches, and the V-8 was slightly wider at 59.7 inches. Rear track for both was set at sixty inches. Curb weight was up to roughly 3,000 pounds.

The styling of the new Javelin was exciting, probably as much so as the first 1968 Javelin's and AMX's. The fenders now contained Group 7 bulges patterned after the Can Am race cars and the Corvette, and the windshield was set at a steeper rearward rake.

Although the only body style available was still the two-door hardtop sport coupe, there were now three models. The base Javelin, the SST version and the new top-of-the-line AMX version in honor of the passing 1970 two-seater.

The base and SST Javelins featured a new silver-lined recessed twin-venturi grille with integrated single headlamps. A thin front bumper carried out the bottom portion of the grille front-end theme, which now had a lower valance containing the parking lights. A flat-profile steel hood with a raised center section ran almost the entire length of the hood. The theme continued on the roof section, forming twin canopies to create a phony T-top appearance. Optional vinyl inserts could be ordered for the roof canopies; these also covered the A-pillars and small impressions behind the rear side windows. A small spoilerette was also sculptured into the trailing edge of the roof.

The quarter panels had matching Group 7 bulges sculptured in. Although the taillight treatment was still full-width, it was divided into only three sections rather than the previous five. The back-up light was still retained in the middle section. Front and rear side-marker lights were also rounded off for a cleaner appearance.

The entire car was completely redesigned and, aside from the bucket seats, it shared practically nothing with the older models. A new thermostatically controlled heater that kept an even temperature at all times was made standard. A curved, wraparound aircraft-cockpit-type instrument panel (first seen on the 1969 Pontiac Grand Prix) with three squarish pods, faced the driver. Four black-faced horizontal toggle switches running fore and aft controlled the inside dome light, headlights, and windshield wipers and washers, and were set on a shelf just below the instrument pods.

A stripe of backlight set immediately below the pods contained the signal light indicators, engine overheating light, seatbelt light and high-beam indicator. Heater controls were set just below the panel on the right, above the ashtray and cigarette lighter. The optional center console was an extension of the theme. The right side of the dash sported a grab handle and locking glovebox toward the middle. Door-locking buttons were now more antitheft, being placed horizontally just below the inside door handles inside the armrest bosses. A new flat-styled Hurst shifter handle replaced the older round unit, and a new inverted walnut stirrup-grip automatic transmission handle, available with the console option, replaced the previous year's Pistol Grip unit.

In 1971, the federal government mandated a compression ratio drop to permit engines to run on no-lead or low-lead fuels. While all other American producers were dropping high-performance engines from their line-ups or reducing the horsepower ratings of existing engines, AMC decided to introduce a new engine with the biggest cubic inch displacement it had ever produced.

New 401 power

The new engine was a stroked version of the discontinued 390 V-8, and it displaced 401 cubic inches. This was accomplished by increasing the stroke from 3.574 inches to 3.68 inches. The new engine featured a forged steel crankshaft and connecting rods, with provisions for four-bolt main caps. Valve sizes were the same as in the 1970 390 V-8, although combustion chamber volume was now 58 cc instead of 51 cc. Cam specs were also slightly hotter for the new mill. Improved free-breathing intake and exhaust manifolds were featured, along with a more performance oriented four-barrel carburetor that flowed over 600 cfm. With 1.56 inch primaries and 1.69 inch secondaries, this carburetor was the same type as used on the 1971 Ford Cleveland high-performance engines.

Early in the 1971 model year, the engine was released with a high 10.2:1 compression ratio, which was the same as on the old 390. It was rated at 330 hp at 5000 rpm. Torque was a healthy 430 pounds-feet at 3400 rpm. The engine was the strongest stump puller ever released by American Motors. Although the compression ratio was reduced to 9.5:1 later in the model year, it was still rated at the same 330 hp figure and still required premium fuel.

The complete engine line-up for 1971 was basically the same as for 1970, but there were a few changes. A new 258 ci six-cylinder engine, similar to the 252 ci engine that had been available in Mexico since the late sixties, was now made available as an option over the smaller 232 ci version. This new engine was rated at 150 hp at 3800 rpm, with 240 pounds-feet of torque at 1800 rpm. It had an 8:1 compression ratio and was equipped with a one-barrel carburetor. It was optional on the base and SST Javelin's.

The 304 V-8 had the same 210 hp, but compression ratio was down from 9.0:1 to 8.4:1. The two-barrel and four-barrel 360 V-8s also had compression ratios reduced, to 8.5:1. Although the two-barrel version had the same 245 hp rating as in 1970, the four-barrel verson was down 5 hp, from 290 to 285.

Trunk space was still the largest of any pony car at 10.2 cubic feet. An additional two cubic feet could be obtained with the optional space-saver spare tire. Chassis and suspension layout remained the same, as it did through 1974.

The SST version continued to be the spruced-up model of the base Javelin, costing only $120 more.

The top-of-the-line AMX used its own grille screen, fiberglass hood, wheels and optional front spoiler. Its dash panel also used a machine-turned pattern. Any 1971 401-powered Javelin was a superperformer.

Standard items included special trim and equipment in the form of simulated burled walnut on the door and instrument panel, pleated vinyl upholstery, Rim-Blow sports steering wheel and wheel covers.

The top-of-the-line AMX model of the Javelin was a nicely styled package influenced by lessons learned on the SCCA Trans-Am racing circuit. Driver Mark Donohue had an instrumental hand in the designing of various components on the car. The rear-deck-mounted spoiler was carried over from the 1970 Mark Donohue Special. It is reported that he designed the optional front spoiler, raised-profile fiberglass rear-facing cowl-induction hood and flush wire mesh grille, which was reminiscent of the 1969 Dodge Charger 500.

The AMX was further distinguished from the base and SST versions with its own running or signal lights inside the grille, front valance air scoops where the parking lights used to be, slot-styled mag wheels (as used on the 1970 Rebel Machine) and engine- or machine-turned dashboard and door side panels.

Standard engine-transmission combination was the 245 hp 360 V-8 coupled to a floor-shifted three-speed manual gearbox. The AMX had all the standard features of the base and SST Javelins, plus left and right outside rearview mirrors, center console with locking compartment without armrest, electric clock and E70x14 raised-white-letter Goodyear Polyglas tires. Base price started at $3,432.

As was the case with the first-generation Javelins, the new models could be ordered with just about any option imaginable. Options were more plentiful on the SST and AMX versions, but even a base Javelin could be tailored to any level of convenience, luxury or performance. Fourteen exterior colors could be ordered, of which eleven were new for the year. Embossed vinyl was standard on the base model, and SST and AMX had pleated vinyl. Power steering, power brakes, manual or power front disc brakes with new ventilated rotors, four-speed transmission with Hurst shifter, air conditioning, AM or AM/FM stereo radio, center console with or without armrest cushion, Adjust-O-Tilt steering wheel, rubber-faced steel bumper guards, light groups, visibility groups, leather or corduroy seats and insulation groups were just a few.

Heavy-duty batteries and alternators, handling packages and heavy-duty trailer towing packages were also available. The Rally-Pak gauges (with new Tic-Tac combination consisting of the clock and tachometer, oil, temperature, ammeter and fuel level gauges), dual exhaust for the 360 four-barrel V-8, Twin-Grip rear, quick-ratio manual steering and AMX 360 or 401 Go Packages were items still on the optional performance list.

The Go Package was available on the four-barrel AMX engines only. It retailed for $410.90 for the 360 and $498.95 for the 401. This was an excellent performance investment, consisting of the engine, dual exhaust system, cowl-induction hood, hood T-strip,

black rear panel, 15x7 slot-styled wheels, E60x15 raised-white-letter Goodyear Polyglas tires, Space Saver spare tire, handling package, Twin-Grip rear, power front disc brakes, Rally-Pak instruments with 140 mph speedometer and 8000 rpm tachometer, and heavy-duty engine cooling. Many of these items could be ordered separately on the base and SST models.

If the buyer was not satisfied with the optional factory performance items, there were still the hotter dealer-installed items available. For the engine, either the Trans-Am Cross Ram dual four-barrel aluminum or Edelbrock high-rise single four-barrel aluminum intake manifolds could still be ordered. The 780 cfm Holley carburetor could be had along with exhaust headers and heavy-duty valvetrain components to complement the hi-po cam. Side-Winders side exhausts could really brighten things up, and you could even get a Detroit Locker positive-locking rear with up to 5:1 ring and pinion gears. The AMX Torque Link kits was still a good, inexpensive traction aid invest-

The Javelin's interior featured a wraparound dash and stirrup-grip automatic transmission shifter handle. The base and SST versions used simulated wood-grain finishes on the instrument panel.

ment. If you wanted superwide tires, you could order 15x7 or 15x8 steel wheels.

The base model still had its own pinstripes, now running the length of the beltline under the door handles. The SST had twin thick rally stripes in the same location flanking the pinstripes above and below. The hood T-stripe available only on the AMX with the Go Package was applied on the center raised ridge of the hood, flaring out on the leading edge and running its width, spilling onto the fenders, squaring off and ending at the beltline. The complete stripe was highlighted with a pinstripe running inside its borders.

Early in the model year, the fender design of the hood T-stripe was changed. Instead of being squared off and ending at the beltline, the ends swept back into a point on the fender tops, terminating just forward of each Group 7 bulge. This design continued into 1974.

All V-8 engines were designated in large numbers behind the front side-marker lights. AMX emblems replaced the Javelin scripts on the quarter panels of the top-of-the-line model. AMX was also placed on the center of the wire mesh grille.

Factory literature described the new Javelin as follows: "The excitement of the new 1971 Javelin is truly international. For here is a luxury sports car that's at home cruising the autobahn or negotiating the Andes as it is in a North American traffic jam or an African bush road." A new ad campaign was launched, describing American Motors as perhaps being a little intimidated by the competition. Many of the ads were entitled, "If you had to compete against GM, Ford, and Chrysler, what would you do." One ad even described the Javelin as having a "1980 look." Still another stated,

"We made the Javelin the hairiest looking sports car in America, even at the risk of scaring some people off." This last ad offended some librarians, prompting an influx of nasty letters from that crowd, because it included the following statement: "We may lose a few librarians for customers, but we think we'll gain a few enthusiasts."

Road tests

The 1971 Javelin was probably the most improved model ever put out by American Motors. *Super Stock and Drag Illustrated* magazine road-tested a new 1971 Javelin/AMX 401 four-speed and said, "With its transformation from a two-seater crackerbox into a four-place styling bombshell, the Javelin AMX certainly qualifies for the title. . . . The most improved car of 1971." After its criticism of the 1970 two-seater version, the magazine had nothing but good things to say about the new model.

The model tested was a loaded-down AMX equipped with the four-speed transmission with Hurst shifter and 3.91:1 Twin-Grip rear. The car was gold with a black leather interior, black hood T-stripe and black twin-canopy vinyl roof treatment, Go Package with cowl-induction hood, E60x15 raised-white-letter Goodyear Polyglas tires mounted on 15x7 slot-styled wheels, Rally-Pak instruments, air conditioning, AM/FM stereo multiplex radio, power steering, power front disc brakes, front spoiler, front and rear bumper guards, and twin racing-style chromed outside rearview mirrors.

The car was loaded down with just about every available option, and even some that were not men-

The taillights were changed to a crosshatch design for 1972. The twin-canopy roof treatment continued as did most of the basic styling of the car overall.

tioned. Although these options made the car quite heavy, straight-line performance was not hampered.

The comfort and handling of the car were praised by the *Super Stock and Drag Illustrated* staff. The positive shifting action of the transmission was well liked: "Once mastered, the technique could be repeated over and over again without missing and the car went like gangbusters to almost 6000 rpm in every gear." On cruising, the magazine's staff had this comment: "With the high speed air flow through the grille and the back of the hood, there's always plenty of cold air on tap, and the car literally jumps when the pedal is floored in any gear at any speed."

The big surprise came when the car was taken to the drag strip for a few runs. As the staff put it, "On the drag strip, the AMX worked its way down from initial runs in the area of 14.8 and 94 mph to steady 14.30 elapsed times at a shade over 97 mph, smoothing it out of the gate and bringing in the quad 70 feet out. These performances were better than any previous AMX or Rebel Machine we've tested, and are indicative of really strong performances by a less loaded down car."

The Javelin AMX 401 was one of the fastest AMC models ever road-tested by any magazine before or after, even as a completely factory stock car right off the showroom floor with full smog emissions equipment and without the aid of traction devices, headers or anything else. If a heavy, loaded-down, 401, four-speed, 3.91 Twin-Grip-rear model could turn times like that, a bare-bones stripped model could have easily dropped into the high thirteens. And these times were achieved with the lower-compression 9.5 engine. The new 401 engine had to be producing more horsepower than the advertised 330, since the engine was able to push the 3,600 pound car to very respectable quarter-mile times.

Two other supercars were tested by *Super Stock and Drag Illustrated* in the same issue. One was a 1971 Ford Torino 429 CJ-R and the other a 1971 Mustang Boss 351. The Torino's best performance in the quarter-mile was a 14.49 elapsed time at 97.93 mph. The Mustang's best was a 13.93 elapsed time at 100.55 mph.

Performancewise, the Javelin reached its peak for 1971. As was the case with the first-year Javelin and AMX, numerous magazines couldn't wait to get their hands on the hot sporty model after previewing it and learning of its new powerful engine option. So road tests of the 1971 model were far more numerous than of any other year of the second-generation-design Javelin, which ended in 1974.

Supercar '71 magazine tested a 401, automatic Shift-Command, 3.54 Twin-Grip model and attained a 14.45 elapsed time at 96 mph in the quarter-mile. The 0-60 time came up in 7.6 seconds. This model was also loaded down with options such as air conditioning, AM/FM radio, power steering and power front disc brakes.

Speed and Super Car magazine achieved similar results testing a 401, four-speed, 3.91 Twin-Grip-rear model. Its times came in at 14.55 seconds and 97.82 mph. The magazine's staff felt the automatic transmission had better control against wheel hop as opposed to the four-speed. Even though the magazine's overall rating of the car was good, it did criticize the lack of quality control on the part of the United Automobile Workers on the assembly line. They also felt the engine should have had more top-end response and that the handling of the car could have been better. They summed it up this way: "We ended up liking the AMX more than we disliked it. If some of the faults could be corrected—and they can—we can really see ourselves becoming big Javelin AMX fans."

Hi-Performance Cars magazine had just about the same comments and complaints about its 401, four-speed, 3.91 Twin-Grip model. It felt that the quality control needed much improvement, axle hop was a problem and the automatic transmission model would have been the better choice. Its times were strong, registering 0-60 in 7.8 seconds and 14.60 seconds at 96 to 98 mph in the quarter-mile.

The optional side stripe for 1972 resembled the 1970 design turned upside down. Wheel covers were also new.

The top-of-the-line AMX model continued. Compression ratios were again cut, and net horsepower ratings were introduced. Even so, a 401 Javelin was still capable of quarter-mile times in the 14 to 15 second range.

During its test, *Hi-Performance Cars* discovered a weak point in the rear axle assembly. After thrashing around a racecourse and drag strip a few times at high speeds, and then coming out of a green light in town at about 8 mph, the right rear wheel parted company with the rest of the car. *Hi-Performance Cars* put it this way: "At approximately 5 mph, the wheel, tire and brake drum sheared off and the car went clunk! Had this happened at 90 mph on the thruway or at almost 100 mph through the traps, it would have been a bummer."

AMC learned of the fault and recommended a solution to the problem. Its 1972 publication entitled *Performance American Style* described how the wheel and flange assembly was retained on the axle shaft by a single 3/16-inch-wide key. It further explained that the

The plush-looking nylon corduroy interior was still offered on the 1972 Javelin. The leather seat option offered in 1971 was dropped for 1972.

key was adequate for regular passenger car use, but marginal for the mildest performance applications. It then went on to recommend installing two ¼-inch-wide keys 180 degrees apart on the axle shaft by precision machine. This seemed to cure the problem.

Hi-Performance Cars magazine summed up its road test as follows: "In spite of the quality control failings and rear end engineering, we learned to love the new Javelin." It also said the AMX's performance times were "boss."

In *Sports Car Graphic's* road test, the 401 Javelin again received high marks—but that nasty quality control problem was still evident in the finished product. The car had the Shift-Command automatic with a higher-ratio 3.15:1 non-Twin-Grip rear. The magazine commented how slowly the transmission shifted and how much it slipped. Still, the 0-60 time came in at 6.5 seconds and the quarter-mile took 14.3 seconds at 98.8 mph.

Again, with a properly tuned engine and positive-shifting transmission, the Javelin could easily rip off high-thirteens all day long. *Sports Car Graphic* was also able to achieve a calculated 0.70 g on the skid pad, which compared favorably with the 1970 two-seater AMX's 0.74 g.

Sports Car Graphic was impressed with the car's overall performance and handling. It concluded the test by saying, "If we could teach Americans how to drive, the quick reactions of a car like the AMX would make our roads a lot safer than padded dashboards, side marker lights and air bags could hope to."

Drag Racing U.S.A. magazine was known for its road test of stripped-down models with the biggest and baddest engine-transmission-axle combinations for maximum quarter-mile elapsed times. When it requested such a model from AMC, the only one available was a fully optioned luxury Javelin AMX 401 equipped with the Shift-Command and 3.15 rear.

Drag Racing U.S.A. had the following to say about the car: "It is, in fact, one of the most impressive and desirable cars we've driven this year. . . . It had every option in the book, including a few we didn't even know existed! . . . Yet, despite the weight of all this luxury equipment, plus the disadvantage of a relatively slippery automatic transmission and mild rear axle gearing, the car was good for quarter-mile times in the 14's at better than 95 mph! . . . We were left wondering about the potential of a stripped 401 Javelin with a four-speed and a strong rear axle. It ought to get into the 13's easily and, with some fiddling, we'd bet would nudge the 12's with strip preparation."

At the drag strip, the car came in at the top of NHRA's G/S and G/SA classes, which had a ten-pound breakout. A competitive machine indeed. The 3,600 pound car had a power-to-weight ratio of 1.9 pounds.

Supercar tests were almost always of cars equipped with the largest-displacement engines or highest horsepower ratings, since brute acceleration was the name of the game when it came to sales. Smaller-engined versions were road-tested and evaluated, also.

Road Test magazine, one of the most active at the time, decided to check out a 1971 Javelin SST equipped with the 360 four-barrel 285 hp V-8 coupled to the Shift-Command console automatic transmission. The car was also equipped with air conditioning, power steering, power front disc brakes, non-Twin-Grip rear, AM/FM stereo radio, vinyl canopy inserts, rally side stripes and a few other convenience items.

The car received a very good overall rating from the test staff, which said it had a high level of quality control, particulary in regard to the fit of the trim and carpeting. Apparently this Javelin SST did not have the chronic quality control problem of the previous AMX models tested by other magazines.

Performancewise, the car was no slouch. The 0-60 time was respectable at 9.5 seconds, and the quarter-mile time of 16.08 seconds at 83.5 mph was nothing to be ashamed of. This model was indicative of what the average buyer ordered at the time, as suggested by the road test headline: "The first non-muscle pony car we've tested for some time proves the breed can provide docile, comfortable transportation as well as look sporty."

Mark Donohue, who piloted the new Javelin AMX to its first SCCA Trans-Am manufacturers championship in 1971, liked his racer so much that he decided to modify his personal AMX into a better-handling street machine incorporating lessons learned from the track. Donohue, a brilliant Brown University engineering school graduate, described the modifications he made to his Javelin in an article in *Car and Driver* magazine.

The key to controlling the car's directional stability and attitude was in the steering assembly. Donohue used a small thirteen-inch-diameter padded-rim wheel that had been positioned away from the driver's seat; this permitted quick turns without crashing one's elbows against the door panels. The car's steering ratio was quickened by shortening the steering arms, but that modification did not prove to be satisfactory according to his expectations. The front suspension toe steer was reduced, and the pivot bushings on the lower control arms were stiffened laterally to reduce deflection steer. Stiffer springs and shocks were added, along with a rear antisway bar. To complete the package, larger tires and wider wheels were added all around. Front tires were E60x15 mounted on 15x7 wheels, and the rears were G60x15 tires mounted on larger 15x9 wheels.

As Donohue stated, "What we were trying to achieve is a car in which you can change lanes quickly and drive effortlessly at high lateral loads without worrying about going out of control. And a car in which you could drive down a country road and not be thrown around."

With these simple modifications, the car was able to pull 0.80 g on the skid pad, compared with the Javelin's standard 0.70 g ability. Donohue commented how well his car now performed, and the only other cars that could approach the Javelin's new handling were the 1971 Firebird Trans Am and Corvette. AMC and Donohue had certainly proved the performance and true potential of the new 1971 Javelin.

With such a winning, stunning new performance muscle car, one would think that tens of thousands would be sold, but it did not turn out that way. Only 28,866 units were produced, including 2,054 AMX models.

1972

After the major redesigning that took place on the 1971 model, the 1972 Javelin was restricted to cosmetic and detail changes and improvements.

For openers, the base model Javelin was discontinued, leaving only the SST and AMX models available. A bit of good news was that the base price of the SST went down $192 to $2,807 for the six-cylinder model. Even the 304 V-8-equipped Javelin was a bargain at $2,901.

The most notable change for 1972 was the new grille and taillight treatment. The grille was made up of numerous small rectangles formed by bright plastic horizontal and vertical thin bars. The taillights were still full-width but were now of a crosshatch design consisting of two rows, again resembling numerous small rectangles.

The bulky Rim-Blow steering wheel was replaced with a new three-spoke sport wheel having a smooth stainless-steel finish with a center horn button. The cigarette lighter was now above the ashtray instead of being combined with it as before, and the Tic-Tac speedometer-tachometer combination matched more closely the rest of the dashboard instruments. New international symbols were placed on all four dash toggle switches.

The optional SST rally side stripes were once again changed. The new design was a throwback to the reverse-C striping on the 1969 Big Bad Javelin. The stripe started at the lower portion of the quarter panel ahead of the bumper and ran the length of the car to the rear portion of the fender. When it continued at the front portion it flared out and up, engulfing the side-marker light completely, and then tapered back following the contour of the fender bulge and ending in a point just forward of the door handle. The complete stripe was paralleled by an inside running pinstripe.

Specials

The SST received a specialty version in the form of the Cardin Javelin, designed by French fashion designer Pierre Cardin. The car was available in a choice of five exterior colors—Trans-Am Red, Stardust Silver, Snowwhite, Diamond Blue, and Wild Plum—

and it has been reported that a few may have been painted Classic Black.

The interior finish of the car was very impressive, albeit unusual. The headliner, door panel inserts and cloth upholstery featured bold graphics in Chinese red, plum, white and silver arranged in a C shape. Chrome-plated Pierre Cardin emblems were placed on each inside door panel and on each fender forward of the door just below the beltline.

The Cardin special edition started out with the SST standard equipment and could be ordered with any available Javelin option. It was supposedly available only on the SST model, but later in the model year was quietly offered on the AMX version and fourteen 1972 AMXs were so-equipped.

The AMX, too, received a few noteworthy changes. As with the SST, its base price was reduced, down $323 to $3,109. A good portion of the price reduction came with the changing of the standard engine.

The 304 ci two-barrel carburetor V-8 was now standard, with the two 360s and the top-of-the-line 401 optional. The rest of the standard equipment on the car was more or less the same as in 1971. The 1970 Rebel Machine-type mag-styled wheels that had been standard for 1971 were replaced with a cleaner-design five-slot-styled type first introduced on certain 1971 Hornet and Gremlin models. The hood T-stripe that came with the optional Go Package had slightly different shading.

All engines for 1972 had SAE net ratings as opposed to the previous gross ratings. The lower net figures were arrived at by measuring the engines in nearly the same condition as when installed in a car, which meant having all accessory belts attached and coupled to a standard exhaust system. The gross figures were arrived at by measuring the engines without any accessories attached and with a free-breathing open exhaust system. Compression ratios remained the same on all engines except the 401 V-8, which was reduced to 8.5:1 permitting it to run on regular fuel.

The 232 inline six was now rated at 100 hp at 3600 rpm. The 258 six was rated slightly higher, producing 110 hp at 3500 rpm. Next up the line were the V-8s. The 304 had 150 hp at 4200 rpm. The two-barrel 360 was a low-performance engine, producing 175 hp at 4000 rpm. The four-barrel 360 engines promised a little more beef. The single-exhaust version was rated at 195 hp at 4400 rpm, and if optional duals were ordered the rating jumped up to 220 hp at the same rpm.

In an indirect way, AMC had shown how restrictive a single exhaust system could be (or how free-flowing a dual exhaust system could be). The 401, which came with standard dual exhaust, produced 255 hp at 4600 rpm. Torque was still strong at 345 pounds-feet at 3300 rpm. Carburetion on all engines was improved for responsiveness, for drivability and to reduce emissions.

One important feature on all engines was the use of new cylindrical bearings on the rocker arms. These eliminated adjustment and provided quieter valvetrain operation and longer service. The old AMC-type power steering pump with integral reservoir was replaced with a modern and compact GM Saginaw unit.

The old Borg-Warner Shift-Command automatic transmission, which dated back to a 1950s Studebaker design, was replaced by the Torque Command purchased from Chrysler. This was a modified version of Chrysler's famous Torque Flite which had backed up some of its wildest engines including the Elephant 426 Hemi. It is too bad the switch could not have been made in 1971 behind the high-compression 401—that would have produced an almost unbeatable combination.

Chassis and suspension components were virtual carryovers, although new front suspension zero-lash ball joints were featured for added durability.

Most of the 1971 options were continued. One expensive option dropped was the leather seats, but the corduroy upholstery could still be had in black, blue, green or tan for those who liked the plush look and feel.

It is generally accepted in the automotive circle that 1971 and 1972 were the last years for the true Detroit muscle car or supercar. Any model after that is considered to be a supercar in looks only when compared with its 1960s ancestors. But there were quite a few exceptions to this generalization.

Numerous supercars produced between 1972 and 1974 had more than adequate and respectable performance that could be traced right back to their 1960s origins. Once the catalytic converter syndrome hit and was joined by the single exhaust and low-octane unleaded fuel, however, the supercar was indeed dead.

The Pierre Cardin interior design used in 1972 and 1973 was considered a little too radical for some buyers' tastes. The option was available on the SST and AMX versions in 1972 and on the Javelin and AMX versions in 1973.

A small- or big-block Camaro properly optioned out could still turn the quarter-mile in the fourteen- to fifteen-second range. The Buick GS 455, Pontiac GTO 455 and Olds 442 could still burn up a set of tires in a day if pushed. Although Mopar dropped the big-block options in the sporty Challenger and Barracuda models, the 340 and 360 V-8 options could still be had with most of the optional performance and handling equipment. The compact Plymouth Duster and Dodge Sport (formerly Demon), with the same engine, were still great street sleepers. Ford's performance flagship was in the form of the Mustang with the 351 HO, an essentially detuned version of the potent 1971 Boss 351 which was equipped with solid lifters as opposed to the HO's hydraulics. And watch out for the potent 400 and 455 Firebirds, especially the 1973-74 455 SD (Super Duty) models. The SD cars equaled and sometimes surpassed many 1960s supercars in performance. In the end, the Javelin held its own with the desirable 360 and 401 four-barrel engines.

Just to show the performance potential of a 1972 Javelin AMX 401, *Super Stock and Drag Illustrated* tested another heavy, optioned-out four-speed Twin-Grip-rear model. Since it had road-tested a superheavy-weight Javelin AMX in 1971, the magazine decided to see what a similarly equipped but slightly lighter version of the same car could do. The 1971 engine had a bit more power than the 1972 engine.

In the previous test, *Super Stock and Drag Illustrated* had practically nothing but good things to say about the car. Its first comments were, "The Javelin AMX has changed little since its major restyling job last year, and remains one of the sleekest designs AMC or anyone else has come up with for a production four-seater."

The car started out as a blue Javelin AMX. For $3,109 it was equipped with the close-ratio four-speed transmission, 3.91 Twin-Grip rear, Go Package consisting of a white hood T-stripe, dual exhaust, blacked-out rear panel, rally instruments, cowl-induction hood, handling package, heavy-duty cooling system, power steering, power front disc brakes, five-slot-styled steel wheels, E60x15 Goodyear raised-white-letter Polyglas tires and Space Saver spare tire. Additional equipment ordered for the interior included a console, AM radio, soft gray corduroy-covered bucket seats and light group.

The *Super Stock and Drag Illustrated* staff were skeptical of the Javelin's performance, however. They estimated the car would be able to do the quarter-mile in the low to middle fifteens at 90 to 91 mph. So, they strapped themselves in and recorded a 15.15 elapsed time at 94.43 mph. The next pass netted a 15.05 elapsed time at 95.10 mph. The final pass of the day proved it all as the car registered a 14.68 elapsed time at 95.24 mph. The staff concluded the test having this to say: "If you have any doubt about the AMX's performance capability stacked up against some other so-called supercars, go back and read the tests in this and other magazines, and you'll be as surprised as we were."

The magazine went on to comment on how competitive the car could be made to run in NHRA's stock competition classes: "As a plain Javelin SST, the car breaks at 10.07 in the 10-pound B/S-B/SA class, but as an AMX it goes down deeper, breaking at 10.17. The current minimum record for the class is 12.80, and since our car ran easy 14.60s at over 95 mph, we wouldn't hesitate to recommend it for that racing application." The car could even be made to run quite competitively in the Super Stock I and IA classes. The 401 Javelin was a car that many competitors wanted to forget about.

One more feather in the Javelin's cap that year was the introduction of the buyer protection plan on all AMC models. The concept of the plan was good: For the first twelve months or 12,000 miles, AMC guaranteed that, except for tires, it would pay for the repair or replacement of any part on the car that was defective in material or manufacture. In the end this would result in a better car being built on the assembly line. *Super Stock and Drag Illustrated* echoed the AMC effort during its test by saying that "there's a special esprit de corps among AMC factory personnel that amounts to pride in product, and fortunately it shows up in the cars themselves."

Police Javelin

The 1972 Javelin AMX performed and handled so well that Alabama decided to purchase 100 models for its state police department as pursuit vehicles on Interstate 20 between Atlanta and Birmingham.

The police cars were used in 1971 and 1972, and were equipped with the fleet-style 401 V-8, three-speed Torque Command automatic transmission, 3.54:1 Twin-Grip rear, and numerous other performance and convenience options. The cars did not have back seats because they needed room to store flak jackets, riot gear, first aid kits, road flares and an assortment of Mace. There were also two riot shotguns mounted in the dash and some sophisticated radar equipment on board.

If you were ever lucky enough to have one of these cars pass you, you would see State Trooper written across the rear surface of the trunk-mounted spoiler in very large easy-to-read letters. These specially equipped Javelins could top 140 mph, and few cars could outrun them.

One of the cars is on display at the Alabama Department of Safety Building in Montgomery, Alabama. Another police Javelin has been fully restored and is now in storage under the protection of the Alabama troopers. The remaining ninety-eight cars were reported to have been sold off at public auction.

The emphasis on the new Javelins, however, was shifting to a compromise balancing performance, economy and handling as an overall package, instead of just brute straight-line acceleration. Road tests began to reflect this new trend.

Road tests

Road Test magazine decided to test a 1972 Javelin SST equipped with a 304 ci 150 hp V-8 and automatic transmission. Other options on the car included 3.15 Twin-Grip rear, handling package, E60x15 Goodyear raised-white-letter Polyglas tires mounted on 15x7 styled steel wheels, air conditioning, power steering, power front disc brakes, tinted glass, bumper guards, insulation, heavy-duty battery, remote outside rearview mirror, electric clock, three-speed wipers, light group, AM/FM radio and floor mats. Total price jumped up to $4,389.35 from the base price of $2,786.

As was the case for the Javelin right up to its last year of production, the car's handling and braking power were rated very good. The testing staff liked the comfortable and firm ride, although they found it a bit choppy on some roads owing to the heavy-duty suspension, and the power of the 304 V-8 was plenty for this type of car. The times were changing rapidly. The top speed of the car was estimated to be 100 mph, while the average city and country fuel economy came out to 14 and 15.5 miles per gallon, respectively. It took 9.8 seconds to go from 0-60, and the quarter-mile was covered in 17.5 seconds at 78.19 mph.

The *Super Stock and Drag Illustrated* staff liked the Javelin SST. They concluded their test by stating, "It's a rather tidy sum but well worth it if a sports oriented package is what you're after."

Although performance was no longer the number one selling factor, AMC did endorse the AMX as a performance vehicle in two of its ads as a result of Mark Donohue's Trans-Am victories. One ad showed his 1971 red-white-blue racer above with a stock Trans-Am Red Javelin AMX below. It was an excellent contrast. Another ad showed a black AMX with gold T-stripe coming at you on a two-lane blacktop road, with the picture itself banked to create a racing effect. It was entitled "The closest you can come to owning the Trans-Am Champion." Both ads spelled performance.

Production for 1972 remained pretty steady at 26,184 units, of which 2,729 were AMX models.

1973

Threats of an oil embargo were starting to surface even as early as 1972, although the full impact was not felt until late 1973 and early 1974. This did not seem to bother Detroit car makers for the new 1973 model year beginning in the fall of 1972. They were more concerned with meeting the ever-tightening federal government safety and clean-air emissions standards.

Two 1971 Javelin prototype police cars were built for the Alabama state police prior to their purchasing the 100 production 1972 versions. This particular prototype looks like an AMX from this angle, but is actually a Javelin with the AMX rear spoiler and AMX slotted mag wheels with Goodyear

E60x15 Polyglas tires. Some of the troopers who were fortunate enough to drive the Javelins stated that they were among the fastest and best-handling cars they had ever piloted.

Almost all the new cars had the huge 5 mph bumpers installed front and rear. Some makers could get by with merely adding long, thick rubber bumperettes on their existing bumpers, thus cutting down on tooling costs. Other makers were forced to redesign and retool for large, heavy, telescoping hydraulic units to meet the standards. This new requirement drove up the price on just about every car in the industry.

The emissions standards were also becoming more and more stringent each year. The EGR (exhaust gas recycle or recirculating) system now had to be incorporated into each engine, adding weight and hindering performance however slightly. The supercar's performance was being nickeled and dimed to death.

The 1973 Javelin was no exception to these new standards; it received the EGR system and small rubber bumperettes or biscuits on the front and rear. Some AMC models even qualified for collision insurance discounts from several national insurance companies because of their new safety bumpers.

The buyer protection plan was expanded to include free trip interruption protection. The new element provided reimbursement of up to $150 for food and lodging if an AMC dealer kept a car overnight for warranty repairs and the owner was more than 100 miles from home. In addition, for a minimum charge the plan could be expanded to twenty-four months or the first 24,000 miles over the standard twelve-month, 12,000 mile plan.

Induction-hardened exhaust valve seats were fitted to all six-cylinder engines for the coming of the nonlubricating low-octane no-lead fuels, and the four-barrel carburetors received new electric-assist automatic chokes for faster and easier warm-ups to reduce emissions. New captive engine mounts that maintained normal position under torque-rotating conditions were also introduced.

The model line-up was once again changed for the Javelin in its sixth production year. The SST was dropped and the base Javelin was resurrected, while the AMX version was continued. The imitation T-top twin-canopy roof was abandoned in favor of a new smooth-roof design, and the optional vinyl top inserts were changed to cover the complete roof and rear pillars as had been done on the 1968-69 Javelins.

The base Javelin received yet another grille change made up of a recessed plastic crisscross design, much like that of the AMX. The parking lights were also moved up into the grille and placed in the same locations as on the AMX. The openings left in the valance below the bumper (as a result of the move) were now covered with what AMC called air-scoop screens. The AMX had had these screens since 1971 whenever the optional front spoiler was not ordered, because of the location of its grille-mounted parking lights.

A new rally side stripe replaced the C design. It ran the full length of the car at the beltline and flared

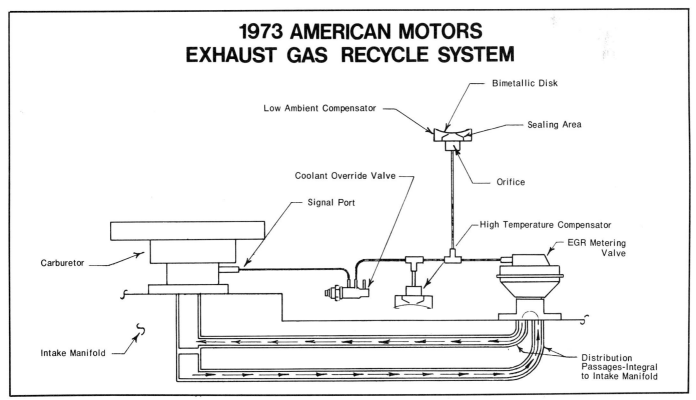

The exhaust gas recycle system was introduced on the 1973 models. This necessitated a new intake manifold design that hindered performance even more. Quarter-mile speeds and elapsed times were affected.

out over the front and rear wheelwells. The complete design was outlined by a thick pinstripe.

Both the Javelin and AMX received a new large twin-pod taillight arrangement with the inboard units being the back-up lights. A plastic AMC logo was placed on the left rear surface of the AMX trunk spoiler, and in the same location on the Javelin trunk lid. The interior of the car was virtually unchanged, with the exception of the bucket seats. A new slim-shell design replaced the heavy-looking turtle-back shells that had been used from 1970 to 1972. Rear seat legroom was also increased by the elimination of the older front buckets.

Although the Javelin had had protective side guard beams inside the doors since 1969, additional structural reinforcement was added to that area on all Javelins built after January 1, 1973.

Once again, virtually all standard features and optional equipment including dealer-installed high-performance items, were carried over, although the latter were not openly advertised in standard AMC literature. One noted change was the availability of a four-speaker system with the optional AM/FM multi-plex stereo radio.

The Pierre Cardin special edition was once again offered, but this time it could officially be ordered on the AMX as well as on the base model. Price on both models rose a modest $82 to $2,889 for the Javelin and $3,191 for the AMX.

Trans-Am Victory

There was one new special edition model that came out for the year, called the Trans-Am Victory Javelin. This model was in honor of the back-to-back SCCA victories recorded by the Javelins for the 1971 and 1972 Trans-Am racing seasons. The model was nothing more than a standard Javelin with a $167.45 option package added on at no extra cost to the buyer.

The special model retailed for $2,939 and included E70x14 Polyglas raised-white-letter tires

Both the Javelin and the AMX received a new twin-pod tail-light treatment for 1973, as shown on this AMX version. New front and rear rubber bumper guards were standard.

mounted on 14x6 slot-styled steel wheels, Space Saver spare and Trans-Am winner decals placed on both front fenders behind the wheelwell just below the beltline. The car could be ordered with any engine-transmission combination and anything else on the order sheet. Aside from the fender decals, there was absolutely no way of distinguishing the model from any other Javelin. Once the original invoice was lost or the car repainted, the car lost its identity.

Although performance was being downplayed by most manufacturers, AMC still outwardly advertised its 1973 Javelin AMX as a performance leader. In one ad, a blue model with white hood T-stripe was shown facing you, with a young couple leaning on the right side of the roof at the windshield. The ad was entitled "Its nice to know you're driving the winner." The Trans-Am victories of the car were discussed, and how well built it was inside and out, not to mention its racy looks. Even AMC factory literature described the 1973 Javelin and AMX as "a performance pair for the open road (or track)." Further endorsement of performance was put this way: "We've translated winning performance on the track into a superb street machine." The Javelin brochure described them as "a performance pair in the highest tradition of motor sports and touring."

Road tests

The performance of the 401 Javelin was still right up there with the best of them. *Road Test* was once again ready and willing to test one of Kenosha, Wisconsin's latest factory hot rods. It titled its test, appropriately, "Power to the people" and added the caption, "With the Javelin AMX, we can almost return to those days of yesteryear when the people had power, horsepower that is."

The smog and nonperformance days were really starting to close in, as evidenced by *Road Test's* opening statements: "Performance is supposed to be a dirty word in today's motoring world. Speed equates with air pollution and traffic deaths if you listen to government agencies and believe their frequently publicized reports."

The model chosen for the test was a Javelin AMX equipped with the 401 V-8, four-speed transmission and 3.91 Twin-Grip rear. The car also had the Go Package, power steering, power front disc brakes, E60x15 Polyglas raised-white-letter tires mounted on 15x7 slot-styled steel wheels, front spoiler, AM radio, light group, visibility group, tinted glass, interior map pockets, protection group, insulation group and the unique Pierre Cardin interior, making for another heavily optioned out car.

The Javelin continued to perform and handle well. It did 0-60 in 7.1 seconds and covered the quarter-mile in 15.4 seconds at 91 mph. The car was a bit slower than the 1972 version, and the testing staff felt it would have been better with the Torque Command automatic transmission and 3.54 rear.

Road Test had this to say about the performance aspect of the entire US auto industry: "It is also evident that the people are not getting what they want unless they shop in the showrooms of the poor boy of domestic auto makers, American Motors." As for the AMX's performance, the magazine put it this way: "So, from the outside and inside the Javelin AMX looks very much like a muscle car. But, does this appearance carry through to the drivetrain? The answer is yes, when you consider that a car's performance is relative to its competitors' capabilities."

When the AMX showed its superb handling by pulling a 0.724 g lateral acceleration figure, *Road Test* said, "To be labeled a performance car, an automobile should combine good straight-line acceleration with above average handling characteristics. The Javelin AMX does not fail this definition since it exhibits cornering capabilities that some sports cars would be proud to claim."

The road test was summed up this way: "In an era of blasé automobiles characterized by sluggish engine operation and bloated appearance, the AMX is a refreshing change. While living up to government regulations, it is not afraid to retain the looks and performance capabilities of a muscle car. The AMX is an exciting car, a fast car for its time, and these two things alone make it worth owning and driving."

This car was a winner, as verified by the road test staff. On the strip, the 401-powered Javelin was competitive in NHRA's B/Stock or Super Stock I classes.

Total production for 1973 amounted to 27,536 units, including 4,980 AMX models. A total of 4,152 Pierre Cardin Javelins and AMX models were built between 1972 and 1973. Sales were up 21.5 percent over 1971 and ten percent over 1972 (for comparison, Ford sales were up 12.2 percent over 1972, Chrysler 9.3 percent, and GM 3.6 percent). AMC was enjoying its best sales year in six years.

1974

The Javelin entered its seventh and final production year in 1974. Base price once again took a hike on

The twin-canopy roof design was eliminated and replaced with a new smooth-roof design as described by AMC. A full vinyl roof as used in 1968-69 was reintroduced. Parking lights for the Javelin moved up into the new grille.

both models. The standard Javelin went up $110 to $2,999 and the AMX increased $108 to $3,299. The cars were still well equipped for their prices.

Changes were kept to a bare minimum. The external appearance of the car did not change at all. Inside, a sharp eye was needed to detect the small changes that took place. In 1973, the plastic medallion in the center horn button had American Motors spelled out. For 1974, AMC script and the red-white-blue AMC logo replaced the former design.

The Slim Shell bucket seats had a slightly different pattern and the seatback latch was relocated from the upper center to the lower outer portion. The front and rear seatbelt designs were also changed. The rear belts were now encased in plastic shields. The shoulder belts were now combined with the front seatbelts in what was called a three-point lap-and-shoulder system. This was suspended from the upper rear portions of the roof with reels inside the lower side roof panels of the rear seats. An engine interlock starting system was incorporated into the shoulder belt mechanism. The window crank knobs also received a new smoother-looking design.

The fender engine ci numbers were eliminated completely (in 1971 all V-8s had been designated, and in 1972-73 only the 401 had been identified). A new optional heavy-duty bumper system was available that consisted of extra large and thick front and rear bumperettes. All engines were virtual carryovers from 1973, with the V-8s now having induction-hardened exhaust valve seats as were installed on 1973 six-cylinder engines.

At the beginning of the 1974 model year, the 401 V-8 was rated at the same specifications as the 1973 version. When the oil embargo hit in late 1973 and continued into the first quarter of 1974, the specifications were slightly changed but on paper only. Changes in insurance company policies and premium ratings based on advertised engine horsepower contributed to the need for this change. The horsepower rating in the AMX brochure was now 235 at the same 4600 rpm

The 1974 Javelin and AMX were virtually identical to their 1973 counterparts. Compression ratio on the 401 was cut down to 8.25:1, and its horsepower rating was cut from 255 to 235 net. Performance was still respectable.

figure, but torque was now 335 pounds-feet at a lower 3200 rpm. Some nonfactory repair manuals and specification charts rated the 401 at only 225 hp. Both the 360 and 401 compression ratios were dropped from 8.50:1 to 8.25:1.

There were quite a few options dropped from the regular Javelin options list. The cowl-induction hood (part of the Go Package) was deleted, although quite a few 1974 factory-installed systems exist. Another deleted option was the front underbody fiberglass spoiler, although it could still be dealer-ordered and installed.

The 1971 401 cowl induction system had dual non-thermostatic control air cleaner snorkels with no exhaust manifold heat riser tubes. The 1972-73 systems had a single thermostatic control snorkel with an exhaust manifold heat riser tube.

Performance axle ratios were also done away with. The 2.87 and 3.91 ratios could no longer be had on the 401 V-8, and the only ratio available on the four-speed 360 and 401 models was the 3.54 unit.

The former performance dealer-installed ratios could be ordered, but this option was not advertised. Even though it did not appear in any of the factory literature, the four-speed transmission could be special-ordered on the 304 V-8 from 1970 to 1974. This made for a nice economy supercar.

High-performance advertising was just about gone in the AMC and Javelin literature, although traces of it were still there. In the AMC brochure, the dashboard was described as "very performance conscious and very functional." If the optional 401 Go Package was ordered, AMC said, "Put it all together and you've got a truly tough performance car." The Javelin brochure endorsed the Javelin and AMX as "race circuit bred and competition proven the best in its class. Try one!" And that was it, performance advertising had really reached the bottom of the barrel.

Road tests

In an article in December 1973, *Road Test* magazine still endorsed the Javelin AMX as a first-class performance car. When equipped with the 401 V-8, Go Package and handling package, it said, "You've got the closest thing to an American-made Supercar available." In the midst of the lingering fuel crisis, the road test staff were forced to take a few steps back and regroup their strategies when it came time to road test the cars.

A sedate Javelin equipped with a 304 V-8 and automatic transmission was chosen as a typical economy pony car. The road test was conducted in June just months before the introduction of the new 1975 models. To fully understand how drastically the supercar scene and overall picture had changed, read *Road Test*'s opening paragraph: "With this issue *Road Test* is inaugurating a somewhat different mode of driver's report that we feel is suited to the problems facing all motorists today. We have a program designed to inform readers on the economy aspects of a car—everything from the initial cost, comfort and usability, and above all the fuel economy and driving range the car provides. In these driver impressions we will eliminate such data as acceleration values on the drag strip, g forces on the skid pad, and the like. Instead we will depict the convenience of the vehicle in today's world of queues for gasoline. Concern with distance availability on one tankful and the comfort for the entire family, along with general specifications." The supercar era was dead.

Throughout the test, the staff gave the car high merits on just about all aspects concerning luxury, convenience and performance as related to economy. The car was equipped with the 304 V-8, Torque Command automatic transmission, 3.08 Twin-Grip rear, power steering, power front disc brakes, Adjust-O-Tilt steering with sport steering wheel, air conditioning, handling package, Goodyear steel-belted radial whitewall tires mounted on five-spoke-styled steel wheels, white vinyl roof, white rally stripes, Rally-Pak instruments, visibility group, heavy-duty bumper system and AM/FM stereo multiplex radio.

The test was concluded with this statement: "So the Javelin 304 does have a definite niche in today's scheme of cars that are chosen for economy as well as appearance and outright performance." Luxury, convenience and economy now spearheaded the pony car's ratings in its last days, while performance took a back seat.

Javelin production for 1974 peaked at 27,696 units, with 4,980 being AMX models.

The Javelin was not the only pony car to bite the dust at the end of the 1974 model year. Because of the new federal government bumper and firewall safety standards, a whole new design would have been required to keep the Javelin and other pony cars like it alive. GM had the finances to retool, and so continued the Camaro and Firebird models, which survive today. The Ford Mustang was downsized and built on a modified Pinto platform. The Cougar went totally luxury and was kept as a separate model, being built with the existing Mercury Montego body and platform. The Dodge Challenger and Plymouth Barracuda succumbed to the same fate as the Javelin.

It is too bad that AMC did not have the finances to update the Javelin to the new federal safety standards. The road tests of the day proved the car's performance capabilities and potential. It would have been interesting to see modern, aerodynamically designed Javelins doing battle on US streets and drag strips against Camaros and Firebirds.

Unlike the Javelin's competitors, the big 401 V-8 was available right up to 1974. GM, Ford and Mopar had dropped their big-displacement V-8s in their respective pony cars roughly two years prior. The Firebird was the exception. Shown is a non-cowl-induction 1972 version.

Chapter 5

Rambler American 1966-69

The Rambler American served as the basis for the construction of the Javelin, AMX, Hornet and Gremlin platforms, not to mention most of their basic body structure and components. To better visualize the concepts of the aforementioned models, it is necessary to take a few steps back and trace the roots of these cars that turned American Motors' image around from economy to performance.

The styling of the second-generation Americans from 1961 to 1963 was dull—the cars were merely boxes on wheels, although they were economy champs when it came to gas mileage.

When Dick Teague came over from Chrysler Division to American Motors in 1959 (after spending two years with Chrysler as chief stylist), he took one look at the current Rambler American model and decided it was a car going nowhere fast. Almost immediately he set out to completely restyle the car into something much more appealing and salable.

The styling of the 1963 Chrysler turbine car was quite evident in the design of the all-new model for 1964, especially in the front fenders. The new model was a 100 percent improvement over the old workhorse. Almost every body dimension was increased to provide a true six-passenger automobile. Rear seat width was increased from forty-two to fifty-seven inches. Rear legroom was a little over thirty-four inches, which was only two inches less than in the larger Classic series, and only four inches less than in a 1964 Chevrolet Impala. The rest of the interior dimensions were just as roomy.

The car's styling was pleasing and well proportioned, and it looked elegant in two-door hardtop form. The car was available as a two-door sedan, hardtop and convertible, four-door sedan and station wagon. The car had respectable performance with the optional overhead valve 196 ci 138 hp inline six-cylinder engine, although there was plenty of room

The 1966 Rogue two-door hardtop was available with optional two-tone paint, as shown. This model is equipped with the optional 232 six, which was the largest engine offered at the time of its fall 1965 introduction.

inside the engine compartment for a V-8. The standard flathead six of the same displacement was the gas mileage miser of the line.

The new Rambler American had just about everything going for it except the most important item the public was demanding at the time—good old performance in the way of a V-8 engine. This is where the car fell short when compared with its direct competition.

Studebaker was way ahead of everyone, having made its 259 V-8 available in the first-year Lark in 1959. The 289 V-8 was offered in 1961, and in 1963-64 you could even get the hot 289 and 304 Avanti supercharged engines. Ford offered the new 260 V-8 in its 1963½ Falcon Sprints, and Mercury countered by offering the same engine in its 1963½ S-22 model. In 1964, both the Falcon and the Comet could be had with the larger 289 version, and Chevrolet finally offered the 283 V-8 in its Chevy II. The Dodge Dart and Plymouth Valiant received the 273 V-8 a few months after their fall 1963 introduction. Before that they had offered the floor-shifted four-speed manual transmission behind the optional 225 ci slant six-cylinder engine. Aside from the Corvair, which was doomed to carry the horizontally opposed aluminum flat six-cylinder engine during its entire life span from 1960 to 1969, the Rambler American was the only compact without a V-8 engine in 1964.

1965

The 1965 model received only a few cosmetic changes in the way of a slightly redesigned grille and taillight treatment, along with a new side molding spear. These few changes made the car look even sportier, but it was still lacking the power needed to match its looks. A modest increase in performance did

The 1964 Rambler American convertible with a 440 ci engine under the hood.

come about, as the new 232 cubic inch seven-main-bearing six-cylinder engine, first introduced on the 1964 Classic-based Typhoon two-door hardtop model, was now optional in the American. This engine had a two-barrel carburetor, and it produced 155 hp at 4400 rpm and 222 pounds-feet of torque at 1600 rpm.

It was still not enough for the buying public, who wanted to boast of having a V-8 under the hoods of their sporty-looking compacts. Remember, 1965 was the year of 289 Mustangs, Sprints and Calientes; 273 Darts, Valiants and Barracudas; and hot 327 Chevy IIs and Chevelles. People wanted horsepower, and if a manufacturer did not offer it, people went elsewhere to buy.

The stalwart 1965 Rambler American 220 with optional two-toned roof. Note the Rambler R symbol on the hubcap centers.

The Rogue hardtop came standard with fully reclining bucket seats and bright chrome trim.

1966

The 1966 Rambler American was redesigned on the 1964-65 body panels, and just enough was changed so that the car was a first-class eye catcher. It sat on the same 106 inch wheelbase as the older models did, but overall length was increased 3.75 inchest to 181 inches. Most of the length went into the hood for a better-proportioned look. Width was set at 69.5 inches, front tread at 56 inches and rear tread at 55 inches. Height varied according to body style, at 53.4 inches for the hardtop, 54.4 for the convertible and 54.5 for sedans and wagons. Curb weight was a light 2,800 to 3,000 pounds.

New front-end styling was in the form of an extruded aluminum horizontal grille outlined with

The 199 ci six-cylinder engine turned the American into the all-time gas mileage economy champ. It produced 128 horsepower with a one-barrel carburetor.

chrome moldings and having vertical splits and headlights set into squarish bezels. The rear end was also changed, and featured long, narrow rectangular taillights. The outside door handles were of the same protruding push-button type as on the 1964-65 models, and these would continue into the last year of production in 1969. Outside chrome trim depended on the model of the car, which also saw a change in the line-up.

The 330 and 440 H series were dropped. The 220 and 440 series were retained and a new top-of-the-line Rogue series was added. Body styles included a two-door sedan, four-door sedan and four-door station wagon in the 220 series. A two-door hardtop and convertible could be had on the 440 series. The Rogue was restricted to a two-door hardtop model only, with its own distinctive chrome ribbed panel between the taillights, roof and deck chrome trim, and interior package.

The dashboard layout was also new. All instruments were now contained in one long rectangular housing, replacing the old individual cluster type. Heater controls were also redesigned, along with the seats. Even the ashtray slid out on ball bearings. The carpeting and upholstery were also upgraded, and the convertible featured a standard power top, which was formerly an option.

A choice of thirteen Lustre-Gard acrylic enamels was offered, and the 440 convertible tops could be ordered in black, white, tan or aqua. The Double-Safety dual hydraulic brake system, Ceramic-Armored exhaust pipes and mufflers, and Weather Eye heating system were some of the American's long-time standard features. One item the American did not share with the rest of the AMC line was its Hotchkiss drive. All other AMC cars were in their last year of the torque-tube driveline.

The engine line-up for the little American was also new. The flathead and overhead valve 196 ci inline six-cylinder engines, which dated back to the early forties, were finally replaced with the new seven-main-bearing 199 and 232 cubic inch inline sixes. The 199 produced 128 hp at 4400 rpm and had 182 pounds-feet of torque at 1600 rpm. It used a one-barrel car-

The 199 and 232 sixes featured rugged crankshafts with seven main bearings. The pistons included moly-filled top rings to help stop cylinder wall scuffing.

buretor and had a bore and stroke of 3.75x3.00 inches. The 232 had the same bore but a longer 3.50 inch stroke. Horsepower and torque remained the same as on the 1965 engine. Both engines had an 8.5:1 compression ratio and used regular fuel.

The Rambler American could be built as one of the most frugal economy cars or optioned out to a full-fledged personal sporty-type car. An array of wheel covers could be ordered, from the plain small hubcaps to the top-of-the-line wire wheels with spinners or the unique turbo-cast design. Just about any color to suit any taste could be had, with matching vinyl-covered roof or two-tone paint on the Rogue model.

Fully reclining bucket seats, headrests, vinyl-covered roof, vinyl upholstery on wagons, retractable seatbelts, visibility group, light group and visor vanity mirror were just a few other popular items.

If you needed more, you could get power steering, power brakes, Twin-Grip rear and air conditioning. If you wanted better handling, heavy-duty shocks and a front sway bar could improve that aspect of the car. If you wanted a little more sportiness, a console with a floor-shifted automatic transmission along with the dash-mounted tachometer were a couple of nice touches. Other transmission choices were column-mounted three-speed manual, overdrive and automatic. Rear axle ratios were pretty mild, in the form of a 2.73, 3.08, 3.31 and 3.58.

The bare-bones 220 model had little exterior chrome. American was spelled out in script on the front of each fender. A large plastic A was placed on the leading edge of the hood on the center. The trunk (or tailgate on wagons) had a Rambler American plate on the right side, and the grille also had a Rambler plate on its left side. A rectangular 220 plate was placed under each fender script.

The 440 model had the taillight panel outlined with chrome moldings. Chrome side spear moldings ran the entire length of the car, following the fenderline and then turning down at the end of the quarter panel, terminating just above the bumper.

The Rogue had all the 440 trim plus the taillight chrome ribbed panel, broken up by the gas tank filler cap in its center. The side spear moldings were painted semigloss black inside their full-length indentations, and the American and 440 emblems on the fenders were replaced with Rogue emblems spelled out in script. Two small chrome ribbed spears were placed on each side of the car separating the roof and quarter panels. Other trim items unique to the top-of-the-line

A convertible was available in the 440 series. Optional headrests, center console with armrest and Shift-Command transmission made the American's interior sporty.

The 440 series offered a clean-looking convertible body style. This year a power-operated top was made standard instead of optional. This model is also equipped with the optional 232 six-cylinder engine.

Even the four-door sedan was a good-looking compact. The base 220 series offered the same body style along with a two-door sedan and four-door station wagon.

Rogue model were the chrome moldings separating the bodyside sculpture and quarter panel deck surfaces. When the two-tone paint scheme was ordered, the roof and rear deck, including the interior rear package shelf, were painted a different color than the body.

If the big six was ordered, a small rectangular 232 engine ID plate was placed at the rear section of the quarter panel. The 199 engine was not designated.

Once again, the compact sporty American for 1966 had just about everything going for it. The car could be optioned out to an acceptable degree of performance and handling combined with luxury and convenience.

An ad campaign proclaiming the 1966 AMC cars as the friendly Giant Killers was initiated. Even though AMC still advertised the American as America's lowest-priced car (at $2,017 for a 220 two-door sedan) and stated that it would still be right at home winning the Mobil Gas Economy Run, performance was starting to

be endorsed in AMC literature and magazine advertisements. The company boasted how much more powerful its car was than the Falcon, Chevy II, Corvair, Valiant and Mustang with the new standard engine. One of its magazine ads showing a 440 convertible had these opening statements: "Does this Rambler really come with Rally stripes? . . . No, but with the new engine it drives that way."

Other ads showing 220 two-door sedan and two-door hardtop Rogues had similar captions. They even capitalized on the American's wins in the Class IV acceleration test of the NASCAR-supervised 1966 Pure Oil Performance Trials. The American finished first and second in the 25-70 mph acceleration test, and AMC made sure the public knew it was with the same engine that logged 24.5 mpg in the economy test.

The Flash-O-Matic Shift-Command automatic transmission with center console could be ordered behind the 232 six or 200 hp V-8 engines.

A dash-mounted tachometer and Turbo-Cast wheel covers were options extended to the American.

The 290 V-8 and four-speed transmission were introduced at midyear to the top-of-the-line Rogue two-door hardtop. Shortly after, both options were extended to all Rambler American body styles. This 22,000 mile original is owned by the author. It has had the Rambler nameplate removed from the left side of the grille for a cleaner look. The V-8 Rogues also used black anodized grilles instead of bright ones.

With the optional four-speed transmission and dash-mounted tach, the American and AMC finally joined the modern supercar scene.

In the AMC and American brochures, the new Rogue was described in this manner: "It's a sassy new kind of Rambler American. The styling is new. Sleek. Racy. The new Rogue is a real mover." And the performance aspect was described like this: "To go with its new performance, some great sports options. A new electric tachometer. A 3-speed floor-shift, automatic transmission, with a new thumb-button release for quicker shifting."

The American, especially the Rogue, had everything a prospective buyer could want—styling, luxury, convenience, practicality, handling, price or what have you. And it finally got the one thing the buying public was crying for—performance in the form of a V-8 backed by a four-speed manual transmission. Since the sporty-looking Rogue was the top of the line, it received the new-design AMC V-8 engine.

Even a six-cylinder Rogue came standard with a host of features such as the new 199 cubic inch six, fully reclining contoured bucket seats with center cushion and armrest, full-width loop pile carpeting, wheel discs, light group, custom steering wheel, plus all the standard features found on the 440 model. The interior of the car was dressed out with quite a bit of chrome brightwork. Moldings outlined the fiber foam one-piece white waffle-patterned headliner. Moldings also adorned the door and rear seat side panels. The buckets had chrome trim on the seat cushions and backs.

The 290 V-8 engine was just icing on the cake. It came in a choice of two- and four-barrel-carburetor versions of 200 and 225 hp, respectively. The fully synchronized Borg-Warner four-speed manual transmission and column-shift three-speed automatic were offered as no-extra-cost options. If you wanted the thumb-button-control floor-shift automatic that was called the Shift-Command, you had to order the optional console. The new four-speed shifter handle

The new corporate 290 ci V-8 engine was a welcome addition and a much needed option to change the performance image of the new Rogue. Shown is a Carter four-barrel-equipped 225 horsepower version. A milder 200 horsepower Holley two-barrel version was also available.

The large ten-inch brakes from the Classic/Ambassador series were made standard on the V-8 Americans. Power front disc brakes also became an option.

featured a T-handle-controlled reverse lockout. The larger and stronger 8.75 inch ring and pinion rear axle assembly, taken from the Classic-Ambassador series, was modified to fit and was available with Twin-Grip.

Many other items were changed as a result of the V-8 installation to enable the car to safely handle the added horsepower and weight. Heavier front and rear springs and shocks were installed, as was a standard front sway bar. The front suspension components were beefed up and a boot was added to the front ball joints for added protection between lubrication periods (the boot was incorporated into all American-model front ball joints).

The five-inch rims continued to be used, but larger 6.95x14 tires were mounted in place of the smaller 6.45s for the sixes. Larger 7.35x14 tires were also available. The larger ten-inch-diameter brakes, also taken from the Classic-Ambassador series, replaced the nine-inch units. For the first time, power front disc brakes could be ordered for the V-8. The automatic transmission was water-cooled, as opposed to the lighter-duty air-cooled six-cylinder versions. All these changes and modifications increased the vehicle's overall curb weight 260 or 290 pounds, depending on transmission choice.

When the V-8 Rogue made its debut at the Chicago International Automobile Show in April 1966, initial production was to be 1,700 units specially painted in metallic Sun Gold with a Classic Black roof and deck, equipped with a special handling package consisting of heavier-duty springs and shocks and 5.5 inch wide wheels. Other special equipment was to include rocker panel moldings, spinner wheel discs and whitewall tires. Only 623 cars received the 290 V-8, however, and it is reported that some were Classic and Ambassador models. Approximately 500 1966 Rambler Americans got the new V-8, but not all of these were Rogues because the 290 was made available in any 1966 American. And many of the two-tone Rogues were painted similarly in Apollo Yellow with a black roof and rear deck.

Two other appearance features distinguishing V-8-equipped Rogues were a new flat-black anodized grille and three-bar spinners installed on the standard full wheel covers. To further confuse the issue, the black grille was installed on many 1966 Rogues, thereafter replacing the former chrome grille. The spinner wheel covers also could be ordered as an option. The one unmistakable distinguishing feature of the car was the installation of a 290 V-8 emblem on each quarter panel where the optional 232 emblem normally would be.

The 290 engine was AMC's first new-design V-8 in ten years. It was of a modern thin-wall block casting design with compact dimensions. The bore to stroke were oversquared, set at 3.75x3.28 inches, and featured stud-mounted stamped-steel rocker arms, pent-roofed-type valve covers, distributor up front and integral-design aluminum front timing case cover incorporating the oil filter, fuel and oil pumps, and distributor. It was a nice design that was close in appearance to the 289 Ford V-8.

The 9:1 compression ratio 200 hp version used a Holley two-barrel carburetor, and the higher 10:1 compression ratio 225 hp version used a Carter AFB four-barrel requiring premium fuel. This same basic engine was eventually produced in displacements of 304, 343, 360, 390 and 401 cubic inches, and powered all AMC cars during and after the supercar era.

Road tests

The V-8 Rogue was a long-awaited model, and the magazine testing staffs wasted no time putting it through its paces.

Motor Trend was one of the first to wring the car out. It tested two Rogue hardtops, both equipped with automatic transmissions. One had the 232 ci 155 hp two-barrel six, and the other had the 290 ci 200 hp V-8 also equipped with a two-barrel carburetor. The six-

The convertible body style moved to the Rogue series for 1967, and this was the last year the American offered the convertible. The 343 cubic inch 280 hp V-8 was available with a mandatory four-speed transmission.

cylinder version reached 60 mph in 12.5 seconds, and the V-8 took only 10.4 seconds. Quarter-mile performance for the six was 19.0 seconds at 72 mph, and for the V-8 was 17.6 seconds at 78 mph.

The 290 car was equipped with the optional handling package, and the testing staff was pleased with its handling abilities, commenting on the suspension's nice firm road feel without the harshness that was normally associated with such heavy-duty systems during most of the car's time on maintained roads. They summed up their evaluation of the car in one sentence: "Here at last is an enthusiast's car—and a pretty good one—from American Motors."

Car Life was so enthusiastic about the new Rogue V-8 that it titled its road test "Can an over/underdog survive the catcars?" meaning the so-called underdog was now ready, willing and able to compete head-on against the latest Detroit pony cars. Remember, the American would have to hold down the fort until the Javelin and AMX models came roughly a year to a year and a half down the road.

The car tested was equipped with the 200 hp 290 V-8, four-speed transmission and 3.15:1 non-Twin-Grip rear. Options included power front disc brakes, power steering, handling package consisting of heavy-duty springs and shocks plus front sway bar, radio, electric windshield wipers and undercoating. The car was one of the original gold-and-black models equipped with the rocker panel moldings, whitewall tires and spinner wheel covers. Its base price was $2,668 and it cost only $3,080 with the added options.

Although it was not known at the time, the 1966½ Rambler American Rogue 290 would serve as the basis for the mighty 1969 Hurst SC/Rambler Rogue 390 hardtop. Its immediate goal, however, would lead to the hot little 1967 Rambler American Rogue 343.

A total of 93,652 Rambler Americans were produced for 1966, which included 8,718 Rogues. Only three American 440 convertibles were built with the 290 ci V-8, four-speed combination.

1967

The 1967 Americans came on board with few changes, and most of these were cosmetic. Body dimensions and body style remained basically the same. Although the taillights were still rectangular, they were made shorter and higher, necessitating a new opening in the rear panel. The grille design was changed slightly with the elimination of the two vertical splits that divided the 1966 grille into three sections. The headlight bezels were made with a flatter profile on their bottom portions.

Most exterior emblems remained in their same locations as before, with the exception of the 220 and 440 plates, which were now relocated behind the front wheels on the fender. A full-length side strip of a wide ribbed design was now placed just above the rocker panels. The strip was the same for the 440 and Rogue

The 1967 Rogue hardtop featured new chrome side trim, as did the 440 American. A new two-tone paint scheme covered the hood and fender tops as well as the top and deck lid.

but was not available on the base 220 model. The 440 also shared the Rogue's rear panel trim between the taillights, which were of a new engine-turned design.

The large Rambler American emblem on the right side of the trunk lid or tailgate was eliminated. The same American emblem as found on the fender was put in its place, but on the left side. The same Rambler emblem found on the grille was placed next to the right taillight on the panel's lower portion on all models. All American emblems were replaced by Rogue emblems on that model line.

The Rogue still had three items of exterior trim unique to its line. The full-length side spear moldings were redesigned, now being half as thin as the old ones. They were still placed in their same locations, following the fenderlines, except that when they ended at the quarter panels they were turned down slightly to meet the new moldings that outlined the engine-turned rear panel completely. Two pieces of

The caption in large bold letters said it all in this AMC ad. The 343 ci 280 hp V-8 was now optional in any 1967 American body style except wagons. The announcement came in December of 1966.

trim that were unnecessary and lasted only one year were the grille theme extensions tacked onto the fender tips. They did nothing but ruin a clean-looking front-end design.

The optional two-tone paint scheme, available on the Rogue only, was carried out a little further. Not only were the roof and deck lid painted, but the quarter panel top sections and body sculptures, the section outlining the rear panel, and the hood and fender tops were all painted in the same color. An optional vinyl roof could also be combined with the two-tone paint scheme.

New optional mag-style wheel discs, which were also used on the 1968 AMX, added a nice touch to the overall appearance of the car.

The dashboard had the same padded eyebrow going all the way across the top, and the glovebox was unchanged. The instrument panel, however, was completely redesigned and contained five round gauges similar in layout to the 1964-65 models. A large speedometer was in the middle, flanked by two gauges on each side. The only real gauge was the water temperature gauge; the oil pressure and alternator were still idiot lights. Immediately below, on the Rogue, was an engine-turned panel of the same design as found on the 440 and Rogue taillight panels. The 220 and 440 had a silver rib-design panel that contained the headlight, wiper and ignition switches and cigarette lighter.

A new deep-dish three-spoke steering wheel replacing the two-spoke design topped off the standard energy-absorbing steering column with four-way hazard flashers and lane-changer signals built in. A

sportier wood-grain type was also available. Front and rear seatbelts were made standard this year.

Brightwork inside the interior was toned down a little bit. All the moldings outlining the ceiling headliner were finished in semigloss black, and the chrome trim on the bucket seats was now made out of light-weight plastic instead of metal.

The model line-up remained unchanged except the convertible body style was moved to the top-of-the-line Rogue series (this was the last year for any Rambler American convertible).

Engine availability was basically unchanged, with the exception of two new additions introduced at different times. At the beginning of the model year, AMC added a one-barrel-carburetor-equipped 145 hp 232 ci six that had been available in the 1966 Classic and Marlin series. The 145 hp was developed at 4300 rpm as opposed to the 4400 rpm figure for the 155 hp version. Torque ratings for the 145 and 155 hp engines were 215 and 222 pounds-feet, respectively, both at 1600 rpm. Both 290 V-8s were unchanged in their horsepower and torque ratings.

A few detail changes on the V-8 consisted of a new fuel pump without the bowl filter, compact-design air cleaner housing, upright coil mounting and gold-color engine paint for the 290 as opposed to the copper color of the 1966 engine. Some 1966 290s were also painted gold.

The big announcement came a few months after the beginning of the 1967 model year. In December 1966, the new 343 ci 280 hp Carter four-barrel-carburetor V-8 engine was made available in any Rambler American body style, except wagons. The 343

The base 220 series used little chrome side trim yet looked good. A few of these two-door sedans were turned into inno- cent street sleepers with the 343 V-8 four-speed transmission combination.

was painted copper to visually distinguish it from the 290. This engine had all the basic features of the 290 V-8, but with such important differences as a larger 4.08 inch bore, larger valves and ports, and a higher 10.2:1 compression ratio requiring premium fuel. This was the same engine that later powered the 1968 Javelin and AMX sportsters to supercarlike performance.

A 235 hp, two-barrel, 9:1 compression ratio version was also offered on the Classic, Marlin and Ambassador, but not on the American.

As a result of the new engine addition, the transmission selection was changed around quite a bit for all engines concerned. Standard transmission for both sixes was the column-shifted three-speed manual, which also became standard for both 290 V-8s. The 200 hp version could be had with the column- or floor-mounted automatic or the four-speed manual. The only optional transmission available for the 225 four-barrel engine was the four-speed manual, which was also the only one offered for the new 343. Options for the sixes were restricted to overdrive or column-mounted automatics. No more floor-shifted models.

AMC called its column-mounted automatics Flash-O-Matics regardless of the AMC cars they were installed in. Its floor-shift models were called Shift-Command because they enabled the driver to hold each gear as long as desired.

Axle ratio availability was slightly changed on the sixes. A 3.54 was the V-8's top option, although a new screening 4.44 dealer-installed gear set could be ordered, and the hi-po cam and kit also could be had.

The 343 American was touted as the hot setup that would have to do battle with the Ford, Chevy and Mopar pony cars for one more year. AMC described the hot compact in its literature with this opening line: "Now—Typhoon V-8 thunder comes to America's low-price economy champ." It also emphasized the new transmission availability, saying "And when you go for the Typhoon V-8 thunder, you can add four speed floor shift lightning."

A 290 V-8 200 hp Rambler American two-door sedan equipped with an automatic had a good power-to-weight ratio of 14.50—the ratio of a 1967 Mustang fastback equipped with the 200 hp 289 V-8 and automatic was almost identical at 14.49. On paper, this made for a very good combination as the basis for a competitive drag car on the strip.

Bud Gregson of Tacoma, Washington, who later campaigned a 1969 Hurst SS AMX, was one of the new personalities around proving the competitiveness of the 290 Rogue on the strip. Records in G, H and I stock classes were now being challenged by the V-8 Americans.

The 1967 American Motors cars were advertised as "the now cars," and the Rogue 343 ad was right at the head of the pack with its caption in giant bold letters reading, "343 Cubes." The car could be optioned out with, as AMC put it, "a fat pile of goodies,"

The 1968 American received a new black anodized grille with a bright accent bar running completely across. Although the *343 V-8 was no longer available, performance was still good with the two- or four-barrel 290.*

which would turn an innocent-looking Rambler into an instant street sleeper.

Road tests

Car and Driver decided to find out just how much of a sleeper the car was. It put in an order for a 343 Rogue and then put the car through the wringer.

The model tested was equipped with the 343 ci 280 hp engine backed up by the mandatory four-speed manual transmission. It was also loaded with quite a few options that included a 3.54:1 Twin-Grip rear, power steering, power front disc brakes, handling package consisting of heavy-duty springs and shocks plus front sway bar, heavy-duty battery, heavy-duty alternator, visibility group, light group, heavy-duty cooling system, sport steering wheel, seatbelt retractors, Solex glass all around and Firestone wide-oval tires.

Dealer-installed items included the high-performance camshaft and kit, traction bars, tachometer

The optional woodgrain steering wheel for 1968 was a nice touch.

and Cragar wheels. The car had a curb weight of 3,101 pounds.

With all this equipment and from all other indications, the car should have been a GTO beater. The best the Rogue could do was 88 mph with an elapsed time of 15.8 seconds in the quarter-mile. The car's 0-60 time should also have been better than the recorded 7.9 seconds. This performance was certainly not indicative of the car's true potential.

Stepping into the future for a moment, a 1968 Javelin equipped with the same engine, transmission and rear axle could turn the quarter-mile in 15.8 seconds at approximately 92 mph. Its 0-60 time was equally quick at 7.86 seconds. These times were turned with a bone stock engine and drivetrain, and the Javelin's weight was about equal.

So why was the 343 Rogue so slow? It's all in the engine's ability to blow out its spent exhaust gases; the Rogue was equipped with a superrestrictive single exhaust system. The Javelin, with its optional dual exhausts, showed the way to performance.

Getting back to the 1967 road test, the *Car and Driver* staff did not care for the car's overall interior and exterior styling, although they did praise its good handling characteristics and excellent brake stopping power and control. They concluded that the 343 Rogue was definitely a step in the right direction that could change the staid image of the company. They closed with this statement: "They've got the right idea, and now all they have to do is make it work."

With the new emphasis shifted over to performance, AMC still found time and space to advertise the American as the defending champion of gas mileage economy. And this year it managed to win Class VII of the Union/Pure Oil Performance Trials.

The 440 and Rogue side trim was moved up to the beltline for 1968. This year the only two-door hardtop available was in the Rogue series.

At the beginning of the model year the base price of a 220 two-door sedan was set at $2,073, which was only $56 above the 1966 model. On February 21, 1967, AMC dropped the base price to an incredibly low $1,839. The company stated, "The new pricing policy for Rambler American is the latest step in the repositioning of American Motors cars that began with the introduction of the luxurious 1967 Ambassador and the intermediate-size Rebel." The American was placed squarely in the middle, pricewise, of the imports and domestic compact cars, and it paid off big for AMC.

In the first forty days after AMC's announcement, American sales jumped 140 percent to more than double the sales of the preceding forty days.

Total Rambler American sales for the 1967 model year were a disappointing 62,692 units, down 30,960 units from the previous year.

The low-production models produced during the year included only 921 Rogue convertibles and of those, only seven were equipped with the 343 V-8. Fewer Rogue hardtops were produced for 1967 than for 1966 at 4,129 units, which closely rivaled the 440 hardtop's 4,135.

When AMC lowered the price of the American, it stated that it was able to do it "primarily by eliminating all future changes in our Rambler American line to essential changes that will further enhance the safety and reliability of these cars."

1968

The changes made to the 1968 model related directly to safety and reliability. Just when the 343 Rogue was starting to become one of the hottest little compacts around, the high-performance rug was pulled out from under it. This was done so as not to steal the show from AMC's new pony car, the 1968 Javelin. As a result, the 343 V-8 engine was dropped from the entire Rambler American line-up, leaving the 225 hp 290 as the top option.

A similar fate fell on the 1965 Ford Falcon Sprint V-8 for 1966 to make way for the Revolutionary Mustang. In 1967, the high-performance 1966 327 ci 350 hp Chevy II Nova also had to yield to Chevy's Mustang fighter, the Camaro, for at least a while (the car sprang back in 1968 because of buyer demand, with just as many high-performance engine options as its Camaro cousin). The 180 hp turbocharged Corvair Corsa of 1966 was also shelved for 1967 to prevent it from treading on Camaro territory.

The American line was trimmed from nine body styles to just five. The 220 designation was dropped and the low-line car was simply called the standard or base model. It was offered in two- and four-door sedans. The 440 model was retained and was available in a four-door sedan or four-door station wagon. The top-of-the-line Rogue was restricted to a two-door hardtop as it had been in 1966.

Once again, emblems and chrome trim were rearranged. The full-length side strip on the 440 and Rogue was relocated from the wheelwell area to the beltline running under the door handle. The federal government required safety side-marker lights for 1968, and these were placed at each end of the strips but were only reflectors (the other 1968 AMC models had lights with bulbs).

The American emblems on the front portions of the fenders were moved behind the wheelwells. The American script was eliminated from the left-side trunk lid, although the Rambler emblem was retained on the rear panel. The 440 model had 440 emblems on its C-pillars on both the sedan and the station wagon. Rogue scripts replaced the American scripts on the

The American station wagon from 1966 to 1969 was one of the most compact and best-looking wagons of all AMC models built during the 1960s. With V-8 power and excellent interior space utilization, it could serve any purpose desired by the owner. Shown is a 1968 model.

fenders, and Rogue was still found on the left side of the trunk lid.

Engine ID emblems were also relocated from the quarter panels to the fenders under the American scripts on base and 440 models. On the Rogue model, the emblem was placed behind and in line with the Rogue script. The American was the only car in the AMC line-up for 1968 to wear a Rambler name.

All of the American models sported a new grille that was now black anodized, with a full-width single bright accent bar set toward its upper portion and the same Rambler emblem placed on the left side. Taillights remained the same, as did the 440 and Rogue engine-turned rear panel. The only major body design change was in the roof C-pillar and rear window of the two- and four-door sedan models, which was made slightly lower and sleeker. The pillar was widened, which in turn reduced the length of the rear window. The American sedan was not similar in appearance to the Rogue hardtop model. Although all other AMC models received flush door handles for 1968, the American retained its old protruding push-button type until its last year of production in 1969.

Inside, the car received its share of safety-related changes. Legroom was increased one inch in the front and reduced one inch in the rear, by angling the front seatbacks slightly rearward. The engine-turned panel below the instruments was replaced with a thick padding which contained new recessed safety-shaped control knobs, and the safety theme was extended to new-design door handles and armrests. Brightwork was once again toned down or eliminated inside the car for the sake of safety.

Quite a few items were eliminated or changed on the American option list. Although two-tone paint was still available, it was restricted to different colors between the roof and the body only.

A small detail change was the reverse lockout T on the four-speed floor-shift handle. It was now of a disc design, and was used on all other AMC models until the coming of the Hurst shifters in mid-1969 on the Big Bad Javelins and AMXs.

Bucket seats were dropped in favor of individually reclining full-width seats butted up against each other, with no console, center cushion or floor Shift-Command automatic transmission available. (All 1968 automatic transmissions were now fully manual-controlled Shift-Command type, whether on the floor or on the console.)

The 155 hp 232 six was dropped, as was the 343 V-8. That left only four engines in the American line-up: the 199 and 232 sixes and the 200 and 225 hp 290 V-8s. Although all engines featured new engineering improvements, power ratings remained the same. The 232 ci 145 hp six was now the standard engine in the Rogue and remained the optional engine in the two lower lines. The 290 V-8 could be had in any body style, and the 225 hp four-barrel version was restricted to a

four-speed manual transmission with a choice of a 3.15:1 or 3.54:1 rear axle. Deeper ratios of 3.73, 3.91, 4.10 or 4.44 could be ordered as dealer-installed options.

Just about all the luxury, convenience and performance options available in 1967 could be had on the 1968 American. Items like power steering, power front disc brakes, Twin-Grip rear and handling package could still make the car into a respectable performer.

The year 1968 was one of the hottest performance years ever. The array of high-performance cars coming out of Detroit in the way of production, specialty or limited-production models was simply mindboggling. Cars like 400 Ram-Air GTOs, SS 396 Chevelles, small- and big-block Camaros, 427 and 428 Shelby Mustangs, 440 Wedge and 426 Hemi Chargers, Coronet RTs and Plymouth Road Runners, not to mention L88 427 Corvettes, could be seen just about every day battling it out at the streetlights.

With a few mild modifications, the high-performance 343 and 390 Javelin and AMX models could compete with these cars in almost every category. It was definitely a year of all-out brute strength and straight-line acceleration to reach the end of the quarter-mile in the fastest speed and lowest elapsed time possible.

Here was little American Motors introducing a supereconomy package on the American, just to remind the buying public that it could still order a car that combined comfort, practicality, performance, luxury and mileage at an affordable price quite ahead of its domestic and imported car competition. The package was restricted to the top-of-the-line Rogue two-door hardtop with the standard 232 cubic inch six. The engine featured a water-heated intake manifold, 205 degree thermostat, specially calibrated carburetor and ignition timing, and economy calibrated automatic transmission governor and valve body. The clincher of the complete package was the standard 2.37:1 rear axle ratio. A 2.73 or 3.08 was optional. It was an excellent buy for the $2,244 base price.

Since the spotlight was on the new Javelin and AMX for 1968, the American did not receive much in the way of performance advertising. Although a 225 hp American could be optioned out to be a respectable performer including the dealer-installed Group 19 hi-po parts, the issue was not pushed.

About the only piece of high-performance hype that the American received was in the 1968 brochure: "Other options; Eye-level tach, V-8 engines, Shift-Command, 4-On-the-floor, specially tuned springs-shocks-and-swaybar, power disc brakes. Roguish."

The hot little American that had received AMC's first modern-design V-8 and high-performance equipment was forced to take a back seat to its new offspring, the sporty Javelin and AMX.

Total production for the American was up at the end of the model year, peaking at 94,369 units, of which 4,549 were Rogue hardtops. Overall AMC had a good fiscal year for 1968, reporting a profit of $11.8 million.

1969

The American entered its last year of production minus a name that had been with it since its reintroduction in 1958 as the Rambler American. The car was called simply the Rambler for 1969. All models and body styles remained the same as for the previous year. All exterior trim and emblems remained nearly identical, with only a few minor detail changes.

The American scripts behind the fender wheelwells on the base and 440 models were replaced by square-letter Rambler emblems with red-white-blue rectangular symbols in line with them. Once again, Rogue emblems superseded the Rambler emblems on the top-of-the-line model. A small AM square emblem was placed on the lower portion of the rear panel next to the left taillight. The A hood emblem was now also made with the red-white-blue scheme. The grille design was identical to the 1968 model, except that the Rambler nameplate on the left side was eliminated.

Engine, transmission and rear axle choices were also changed quite a bit on the last-year model. The 199 six was still standard on the base and 440 models, with the 232 optional. The three-speed manual, overdrive and Shift-Command automatic column-mounted transmissions were offered on both sixes, except overdrive was not offered on the 232.

The Rogue still came with the big six and the economy 2.37 axle ratio as standard. The 290 cubic

inch 200 hp V-8 was available only in the 440 and Rogue, and could be teamed only with the Shift-Command automatic column-shift transmission with 2.87 standard or 3.15 optional rear. The 225 hp four-barrel 290 V-8 was now restricted exclusively to the top-of-the-line Rogue two-door hardtop and could be had only with the four-speed manual transmission and 3.54:1 rear axle ratio. The sixes had rear-end ratios of 2.73, 3.08 and 3.31 depending on transmission choice.

A new supereconomy 232 ci engine was introduced this year, but it was seldom ordered in any Rambler. Specifications were almost identical to the

The interior on the 1969 Rogue and all other Ramblers received numerous new safety features. The SC/Rambler used a Sun tach on the steering column and Hurst shifter with T-handle.

Although the American was renamed the Rambler in its final 1969 model year, the Rambler nameplate was removed from the left side of the grille. The car featured numerous new safety and mechanical improvements.

85

232 six that had been around since 1964, but the new engine featured an ultralow 7.7:1 compression ratio as opposed to the standard ratio of 8.5:1.

Nine new exterior colors were offered, and interior fabrics featured new trim styles and color selections. New standard headrests, door trim panels with deeper embossed pattern, deeply padded armrests and a padded hood over the dashboard were a few of the year's design changes.

For the sake of consistency with the rest of the AMC line, a new accelerator cable linkage with suspended gas pedal replaced the floor-mounted type that had been around since day one, and the parking lights now remained on with the headlights. As had been done in 1968, interior brightwork was toned down to lessen the hazard of glare.

The Rambler was still the economy champ when it came to gas mileage. It was once again advertised as the lowest-priced US-built car at $1,998, which was a very good buy when compared with the imports and other domestic compacts.

Road tests

Just how good it was against some of its direct competition was checked out by *Motor Trend* in a four-way compact car shoot-out. The contestants were a base Rambler two-door sedan, Chevy Nova two-door sedan, Ford Falcon custom four-door sedan and Dodge Dart custom four-door sedan. All four cars were ordered with the step-up six-cylinder engine option and three-speed automatic transmission. Rear axle ratios were 3.08:1 in both the Rambler and Nova 2.76:1

in the Dart and 2.83:1 in the Falcon. The Nova had the highest horsepower rating at 155 and the Falcon had the lowest at 115. The Rambler and Dart had 145. Curb weights were comparable, hovering around the 3,000 pound mark, with the Rambler the lightest at 2,667 pounds.

The *Motor Trend* testing staff found all the cars to be more or less equal in performance, economy, utility, comfort, convenience, handling, ride and braking. Where one car fell short in one aspect, it made it up in another. Considering its base price of $1,998, the Rambler did stand out from the rest as described by these *Motor Trend* experts: "Rambler comfort is good considering base price. Upholstery materials and quality aren't overly plush compared to the Dart, Nova or Falcon, but fill the basic needs and are satisfactory for a base price under $2,000.00 . . . Instrumentation is excellent for under $2,000.00 base price."

Unfortunately, the AMC factory literature did not advertise performance when it came to the Rambler. The Rogue was competitive when properly equipped; with the 290 cubic inch 225 hp V-8, four-speed, 3.54:1 Twin-Grip rear, handling package and variable-ratio power or quick-ratio manual steering, it was a well-balanced car overall. Surprisingly, AMC discontinued the power front disc brake option for the car, although power drum brakes could still be had.

The Rogue could also still be ordered with a host of dealer-installed high-performance equipment from the Group 19 option list. They were not extensively advertised for the Rambler, but Twin-Grip rears of up

The hot SC/Rambler was introduced at midyear and was an instant success with its numerous standard high-performance features. The 390 cubic inch 315 hp AMX V-8 was used with AMX rear Torque Links. The car was capable of low 14s at over 100 mph. This was the ultimate Rambler.

to 5:1 ratios could be ordered, along with a dual exhaust system that was little known and should have been standard equipment since the first mid-1966 models. *Super Stock and Drag Illustrated* summed up the Rogue in two sentences: "Even in stock shape, the Rogue is a doll to drive. Shifts are positive, acceleration adequate and comfort and roominess out of sight."

SC/Rambler

AMC was not about to let the Rambler just fade away. After all, it had brought the company much success in the late fifties and early sixties, not to mention being its first sporty car to receive the new-design 290 V-8.

The 1968 Plymouth Road Runner introduced in the fall of 1967 was practically a runaway success in creating the street sleeper image of a bare-bones two-door sedan having a big-block or high-performance engine lurking under its hood.

AMC had been collaborating with Hurst Performance to create a super sleeper for under $3,000 to drop on the unsuspecting supercar market for mid-1969. The car was based on the Rambler Rogue two-door hardtop without the wide-ribbed-design full-length side strips. Although the concept was the same as the Road Runner, the 1969 Hurst SC/Rambler, better known as the Scrambler, came off with an abrupt if not shocking appearance. The outrageous red-white-blue paint scheme on the Scrambler made the Road Runner look like a sedate grocery getter.

The car was jointly announced by AMC and Hurst on February 13, 1969, as a limited-production offering to incorporate the latest and most sophisticated in high-performance equipment. It made its public debut at the Chicago Auto Show held from March 8 through 16. It went on sale shortly after that at selected American Motors dealers throughout the United States. Drag racers Walt Czarnecki of AMC and Dave Landrith of Hurst were the two most responsible for the car's final configuration.

As put by AMC vice-president of marketing services R. W. McNealy in a bulletin release, "The SC/Rambler is the ideal vehicle for the motorist who wants better than average performance and also a car that is uniquely different from 70 million others on the streets today." In the same bulletin release AMC also stated that "the car is designed for the motorist who wants a customized car, but has neither the time nor inclination to build it himself." Those were the under-statements of the year; you couldn't miss the car if you tried.

Initial production was supposed to be only 500 units, but that supply was exceeded almost immediately by buyer demand. In all, 1,512 units were built at the AMC Kenosha plant, with on-site modifications directed by Hurst.

The first 500 and last 512 units built were painted in what has come to be known as the A scheme. The first 500 were finished in white with a 00 paint code,

while the last 512 were also finished in white but had an 88A paint code. The major portions of the body sides up to the middle of the wheelwells were painted red and outlined in black pinstriping. A wide blue racing stripe ran the length of the top and onto the deck lid. A large blue arrow painted on the leading edge of the hood pointed to the hood scoop, whose front opening was angled upward about ten degrees from the horizontal plane. The arrow itself was separated by large six-inch red letters saying "390 Cu. In." Both the blue arrow and racing stripe were also outlined in black pinstriping, as were all the red letters. The hood scoop contained large red four-inch letters on both sides saying "AIR." The center indentation of the hood scoop was painted blue and outlined in black pinstriping. There were three different but very similar hood scoops produced for the three groups of SC/Ramblers built.

The middle 500 units were also finished in white, but with a Spec (special) or regular Rambler paint code, and were called the B scheme. The overall appearance was subtle, having the lower portions of the body sides painted blue with a blue racing stripe just above running the car's full length.

The grille was completely blacked out, without the chrome accent bar as on the stock Rogue. Letters on the right side of the rear panel formed the word Scrambler, and SC/H emblems were placed in front of the Rambler emblems on both fenders: SC stood for Supercar and H stood for Hurst (the SC designation was also used by Don Yenko for his 1969 SC/Yenko 427 Camaros). Standard AMC 390 V-8 emblems were placed on each fender behind the side-marker reflectors.

The interior of the car was stock Rambler, finished in charcoal vinyl upholstery with the exception of the color-keyed red-white-blue front seat headrests, large-shank Hurst T-handle shifter and 8000 rpm Sun tachometer mounted on the steering column with an ordinary stainless steel hose clamp.

The mechanicals of the SC/Rambler were just as impressive as its appearance. AMC sent out a "car ordering and price list" sheet which described the SC/Rambler to its dealers. It became effective April 1, 1969, and it described what equipment was included in the price. One footnote read, "NO OTHER OPTIONAL EQUIPMENT ITEMS WILL BE INCLUDED OR PERMITTED TO BE ORDERED ON THESE CUSTOM-BUILT CARS."

For $2,998 including federal tax (about two-thirds the price of a Hemi Road Runner), the car came with the following standard equipment: 390 cubic inch 315 hp AMX V-8 engine; Borg-Warner close-ratio all-synchromesh four-speed manual transmission; 3.54:1 Twin-Grip rear with AMX Torque Links and staggered shocks; heavy-duty U-joints; heavy-duty 10.5 inch clutch disc; handling package consisting of heavy-duty springs, shocks and large-diameter sway bar; heavy-

Vice-President of Marketing Services R. W. McNealy and George Hurst look over their latest creation for the crowded 1969 supercar scene. The SC/Rambler project was a joint venture between AMC and Hurst Performance (also makers of the 1969 S/S AMXs).

duty cooling system consisting of heavy-duty radiator, Power-Flex fan and fan shroud; AMX 11.2 diameter power front disc brakes; AMX-type 20:1 quick-ratio manual steering; special Hurst four-speed shift linkage with T-handle; Sun tachometer on steering column; dual exhaust system with special-tone Thrush Glasspac mufflers and chrome tailpipe extensions; vacuum-controlled mailbox-type functional cold-air-induction hood scoop; five E70x14 Goodyear Polyglas redline tires mounted on 14x6 specially painted blue five-spoke Magnum 500 mag-styled steel wheels with trim rings; two chrome hood tie-downs with locking safety pins and cables; right and left outside custom teardrop rearview mirrors; custom blacked-out grille; flat-black-finished taillight bezels and rear deck treatment; wood-grain-look sports steering wheel; individually adjustable reclining seats; all-vinyl charcoal seat upholstery with full carpeting; front seat headrests in matching red-white-blue vinyl upholstery; special SC/Rambler Hurst emblems on fenders and rear panels; and special application of red, white and blue exterior colors. All the regular Rogue safety and comfort equipment including the Weather Eye heating and ventilation system plus electric windshield wipers were also part of the package. Wow!

The complete package making up the SC/Rambler was nothing short of spectacular. This was probably the only production street car of its type built and promoted for a specific drag racing class, which was the NHRA F/Stock class where cars like the Mopar 340

and Olds W-31 ran. The equivalent AHRA (American Hot Rod Association) class was designated E/O. The car also qualified for Super Stock J class, for those who were thinking about an all-out assault on the strip. The car weighed only 3,160 pounds, and with the advertised 315 hp it came out with a power-to-weight ratio of 10.03.

In an AMC bulletin, the SC/Rambler was described as follows: "Well imagine the looks on the faces when you lay down an et in the low 14's at say, 98 mph . . . right off the showroom floor! And set up for the strip with a little sharp tuning, who knows? You might be turning 12's." And in big bold red letters on the bottom of the bulletin, AMC said it all in one short sentence: "It only hurts them for 14 seconds!" The ad for the SC/Rambler that was run in some of the major auto magazines was entitled "A Rambler that does the quarter mile in 14.3."

AMC would not have made such a strong statement if its factory preliminary tests had shown otherwise, but just to keep everyone honest, the testing staffs of the various auto magazines decided to take AMC up on its latest boast. The SC/Rambler defended its maker's claims that "with this car you could make life miserable for any GTO, Roadrunner, Cobra Jet or Mach 1."

Road tests

Car Life was one of the first to road test the SC/Rambler. It recorded a 0-60 time of 6.3 seconds, and the quarter-mile was covered in a quick 14.20

seconds at 100.8 mph. *Car Life* had this to say about the times recorded: "And, by George (sorry), it is a fast little car. We could turn quarter-miles in the mid-14s all day, with a full gas tank and two people." And it confirmed AMC's ad by stating, "Even the ads only claim a 14.3 E.T."

For comparison, a 1969 Chevrolet Camaro SS 396 was tested in the same issue. The car had the high-performance 375 hp solid-lifter engine, coupled to a 2.20 close-ratio M21 Muncie four-speed transmission leading to a 3.73 limited-slip rear. The car was able to do 0-60 in 6.8 seconds, and it took 14.77 seconds to cover the quarter-mile at a terminal speed of 98.72 mph.

There was no doubt about the Scrambler's performance. *Car Life* also praised the superior braking power of the little Rambler, rating it excellent because it recorded one full g. Although the car's handling around the test track was nothing special, the magazine's staff felt that with a little suspension work and the addition of a rear antiroll bar, the car could be made to handle quite well.

Car and Driver recorded the same 6.3 second 0-60 time but its quarter-mile elapsed time and track speed were a bit slower owing to thirty-degree temperatures and a damp track after snow removal. Even with these handicaps testers were able to obtain a 14.7 elapsed time at 96.3 mph, and they felt the car was indeed capable of turning its advertised elapsed time under normal conditions. They too complimented the car's excellent braking power and also had this to say: "American Motors, you've created a car which makes it in almost all the categories by which they judge the Hall of Famers in the Great American pasttime—it can run and it can stop." Their overall impression of the car was that "for lack of a better classification, the SC/R is a street rod."

Road Test was equally enthusiastic about testing the car. Its recorded times were even better than those previously mentioned. Quarter-mile elapsed time was just 14.14 seconds at a speed of 100.44 mph. The *Road Test* staff liked just about everything on the car with the exception of the striking paint job and color-keyed front seat headrests. Performance, braking, ride and handling received high points. They concluded their test with this statement: "The SC/Rambler might just be the ultimate Q-ship. Think it over—it now only takes three grand to get into the quick league."

Car Craft was able to test one of the first Scrambler prototypes. Its car lacked the rubber seal that went around the cold-air-induction air cleaner assembly (which was similar to the production version of the optional setup available on the 1970 Javelin and AMX models). This small handicap did not affect performance in the least, as *Car Craft* recorded a 14.34 second elapsed time at a shade over 98 mph.

Some of the positive things *Car Craft* had to say about the car were as follows: "Handles surprisingly well due to beefed suspension and quick steering . . . steering could be a little quicker. . . . Performance is very good for a pure stocker. When you put your foot in it, it's hard to believe it's a Rambler. . . . Leaves line well . . . no wheel hop. . . . Shifter position excellent. Can bang off shifts like greased lightning."

Super Stock and Drag Illustrated was invited by Hurst Performance to take a slightly different approach to testing the car. Hurst decided that if one was good, two were better—so it staged a shoot-out between a stock and a modified version of its latest pocket rocket.

The test took place at Miami Speedway Park in Hollywood, Florida. The title of the test made sure you read it meticulously from start to finish: "SC/Rambler gets it on! The 390, a 4-speed, HD suspension, and the wildest stock paint in captivity make a Rambler go 12.6!"

A Rambler running in the twelves? Impossible, you say? That was 1969 Camaro ZL-1 territory—but with the few modifications made to one of the cars, its performance was changed from outstanding to mind-boggling.

Ed Beyer and Dale Young handled the strip-testing of the cars. The stock version was no disappointment, recording a best quarter-mile elapsed time of 14.31 seconds at 98.86 with Ed Beyer at the controls. "See the ads don't lie," was what *Super Stock and Drag Illustrated* had to say after that run.

The modified Scrambler was something else. The only modifications performed were the installation of the AMC hi-po 302-degree-duration 0.477-inch-lift cam without the kit, Edelbrock aluminum high-rise intake manifold with matching 780 cfm Holley carburetor, modified distributor deleting the vacuum advance, Champion N-12Y spark plugs, a set of Doug Thorley 290 V-8 headers modified to fit and a pair of 8.00/8.50x14 Goodyear slicks. With these few simple, practically bolt-on modifications, the car was turned into a neck-snapping beast.

Dale Young strapped himself in and pulled three hard smoky burnouts. He made five passes altogether. The first pass netted a 12.92 elapsed time at 107.86 mph. The last two passes were astonishing: a 12.69 at 110.50, and finally a 12.67 at 109.99

One of *Super Stock and Drag Illustrated*'s closing statements went like this: "Either way you look at it, stock or Super Stock, the SC really has potential." And the staff concluded their overall impression of the car in this manner: "The Hurst SC/Rambler is not just another supercar. It was conceived and built for that purpose but it goes just a little further and a little differently in that direction than the rest."

Wayne Greer and Sam Taylor, operating out of Bond Rambler in Huntington, Indiana, were just one of the many successful teams campaigning an SC/Rambler in the F/Stock class. They managed to win twenty trophies in one year running their car at the

Muncie, Avilla and Bunker Hill drag strips in the Indiana area.

Modifications to the car included Doug Thorley headers, air bags added to the rear, homemade traction bars, carburetor rejetting and altered ignition timing. The engine had never been blueprinted or balanced, and with the exception of a degreed cam, it had never been opened.

With just these few simple modifications, the car was running in the 12.4 to 12.5 second range. Its best elapsed time for the 1969 season was recorded at Bunker Hill Drag Way, where it clipped off a blistering 12.10. The car managed to win stock eliminator among its twenty trophies, and also captured the F/Stock laurels at the Muncie dragway in the same season.

Ken Rose and Rick Leonard ran another SC/Rambler, called *American Image*, in F/Stock on the East Coast. The car was owned by Paul Franzetti and Lakeview Rambler in Woodcliff Lake, New Jersey. Rose did most of the work on the car himself, and the machining was handled by Bob O'Brien at his competition engines shop in Fairfield, New Jersey.

O'Brien started out by boring the 390 V-8 to 3.187 inches to produce a 401 cubic inch displacement. (AMC arrived at the same number two years later by stroking the 390 crank to 3.68 inches over the stock 3.574 inch dimension.) The crankshaft and pistons came from Forgedtrue and were of the thermorev type. Connecting rods and Dykes rings were supplied by Crankshaft Company. Although the valvetrain was left stock, a Crower hi-po cam was used.

The stock Carter AFB carburetor and cast-iron intake manifold proved satisfactory. Stock primaries and 104 secondaries were fed by dual Stewart-Warner fuel pumps. The stock distributor was curbed to thirty-six degrees total with an initial setting of twelve

degrees. A reinforced deepened oil pan holding three extra quarts of oil was installed to protect the engine internals and the pan itself when the car came down hard on the track after a first-gear tire burner.

The 2.23:1 first gear was replaced with a 2.36:1 unit, and the Hurst shifter was modified for quicker shifting action. A Schiefer 10.5 inch long type clutch and pressure plate assembly were protected by a Lakewood scattershield. A 4.44 rear end gear set replaced the stock 3.54 unit. Front coil springs were American six-cylinder versions (the same as those used on the Hurst S/S AMXs). Cure-Ride 90/10 shocks were used up front with Delco airlift units on the rear, set at 10 psi. The bottom four leaves on the left side of the rear spring were reversed, and homemade traction bars rounded out that area of the chassis.

To complement the overall package, Cragar SS chrome wheels were installed all around, Atlas 8.15x15 tires were mounted on the front and a pair of Goodyear D5 9.50x15 wide slicks filled up the rear wheelwells. For added safety, the slicks were pinned to the rim to keep the valve stems from pulling during hard smoky burnouts.

The track division test director made Rose reroute the front brake lines because their stock locations made them prone to damage in the event of a clutch explosion. Rose rerouted them up front by the radiator.

Rose was successful with the car as a result of his trial and error experiences with different parts and combinations. The car's best performance in the quarter-mile was a 12.49 second elapsed time at 112.89 mph.

Another East Coast team of drag racers operating out of Charlie's Fair Deal Carburetor Emporium of Ozone Park, Long Island, New York, were the Demaria brothers, Phil and Tommy. They had purchased their

The SC/Rambler also saw duty as the official pace car at the Golden Spur Raceway in Abington, Massachusetts.

Two SC/Ramblers at the Orange County International Raceway.

car new in 1969 and after the engine blew a few years later (still under warranty), they decided to rebuild the car after the dealer refused to honor the fifty-thousand-mile drivetrain warranty, citing that the car had been abused—this was even after the dealer tear-down had proven that the wrong piston rings were installed at the factory. The Demarias modified the car for the 1972 season to run in NHRA's B/Modified Production class, where times were in the low twelves. The complete project cost only $1,500!

As with the Greer and Taylor car, the engine was not blueprinted but did receive quite a few modifications. It was assembled by Bob Labarara of S&K Speed of Lyndhurst, New York. A Crane hydraulic cam with 302 degree duration and 0.483 inch lift was installed with matching anti-pump-up lifters and stiffer valve springs. Although the stock pushrods, rocker arms and valves were used, the heads were cc'd and milled 0.022 inch and given a competition valve job.

The Trans-Am dual-quad AMC aluminum cross-ram STR-11 intake manifold, manufactured by Edelbrock, was installed with two Holley 660 cfm double pumper four-barrels. The carburetors were also rejetted and calibrated by Fair Deal Carburetor. A Carter Superpumper electric fuel pump with homemade cool can and Jardine exhaust headers coupled to Thrush mufflers rounded out the engine modifications.

A Zoom clutch disc and Hays 10.5 inch pressure plate were mounted on the stock flywheel. All were protected by a Lakewood scattershield, and the Hurst shifter was modified for quicker shifts. As with the Rose car, Cure-Ride 90/10 uplock front shocks were used, while the rear end of the car was jacked up with Delco air shocks set at 16 psi. Finally, a set of M&H 8.25x14 eight-inch slicks put the power to the ground, and for safety a roll bar was installed.

So how good did the car run? It could turn 12.30s at 112 mph all day long. For $1,500, the project was a complete success.

Other SC/Ramblers were breaking records and capturing new titles at drag strips across the United States. It is too bad the car lasted only one year, for it could have easily dominated its intended and other strip classes.

Total Ramber production for its final year of 1969, including the Scrambler models, was a healthy 97,541 units, with Rogue production of 3,543 models being at its lowest since its introduction in 1966. Only 102 Rogues equipped with the 290 V-8 four-barrel four-speed combination were built.

The Rambler, better known as the American, was truly a competitive car in the luxury compact market. Although it had received most of the modern improvements extended to the rest of the AMC line, its body style, suspension and certain mechanicals were outdated; thus, it was scheduled to be replaced by AMC's compact car for the seventies, the Hornet. The Scrambler had permitted the little Rambler American to bow out in a blaze of high-performance glory.

The SC/Rambler large mailbox-type hood scoop was angled up into the airstream. The functional Ram-Air setup used a vacuum-operated solenoid and rubber seal around the air cleaner housing.

Chapter 6

Rebel, Ambassador and Matador 1968-74

Because of the major restyling job in 1967, practically from the ground up, the 1968 Rebel and Ambassador were little changed for the new model year. Most of the few changes made were related to the new federal government safety requirements mandated for all domestic production vehicles for 1968.

Body styles and model availability were slightly changed for both lines. The intermediate Rebel, formerly offered in eight models, now had nine models in four body types and three series, with the addition being a new low-priced two-door convertible in the 550 series (body styles for 1967 and 1968 did not parallel each other exactly).

The same held true for the luxury intermediate Ambassador, which was reduced from eight models to seven models offered in three body types and three series by deleting the convertible body style altogether. This was the last year for any AMC built as a convertible.

All the popular body styles in the industry were offered in both series in the form of four-door sedans, two-door hardtops and station wagons. Two-door convertibles were restricted to the Rebel. The two-door sedan body styles were discontinued.

Series designations for the Rebel were 550, 770 and SST. The Ambassador also had three series, identified as standard, DPL and SST. The standard model was formerly called the 880, which still appeared as the last three symbols in the series designation. The car was simply referred to as the Ambassador.

Before the Rebel could hope to compete with the hot intermediates of the day, it needed an image. AMC

The 1968 Rebel SST two-door hardtop was little changed appearancewise from the 1967 model. It was still considered to be one of the cleanest looking intermediates in the American auto industry.

realized that this would have to be more than just a performance image, for if the overall package was not pleasing to the eye, it would not matter how much horsepower was under the hood. It would be necessary to engineer performance, handling and luxury into a sporty-looking design to attract the youth market to the showrooms.

AMC knew it had to cover all bases in an attempt to swing the young buyers away from the more popular GM, Ford and Mopar performers. It had done a pretty good job with its first attempt in the form of the totally new 1967 Rambler Rebel line.

1968

For 1968, the car was basically the same but was called simply the Rebel, since the Rambler designation was dropped on all AMC models except the American line. Before 1967, the Rebel had been known as the

Classic and could not begin to compete against such cars as the SS 396, 389 GTO, Olds 442, GS 400, Fairlane GT and the Plymouth GTX when it came to straight-line performance.

AMC started out with a 114 inch wheelbase for the Rebel and a slightly longer 118 inch wheelbase for the Ambassador (the old Classic had a shorter wheelbase of 112 inches). Both cars shared basically the same body panels with modified grilles, fenders, quarter panels and taillight treatments.

Both the Rebel and the Ambassador were classified as intermediates by AMC, although the Ambassador was termed a luxury intermediate and was almost always compared to the full-size models of the Big

The interior of the 1968 Rebel was available with an array of performance and convenience options. Note the fully reclining individual seats with headrests, woodgrain steering wheel, air-conditioning outlets, eight-track tape player, four-speed transmission and dash-mounted tachometer.

This custom steering wheel was optional on the Rebel 550 with its own series designation in the center. Shown is one with the Ambassador crest.

The 1968 SST convertible was AMC's last convertible. There is no getting around the elegance of this body style.

93

The Ambassador shared many of the Rebel's body panels with its own sculptured front- and rear-end designs. Once again the two-door hardtop model showed how good a job the AMC stylists had done.

Three, which had only a one-inch-longer wheelbase. The other full-size cars were also at least 500 pounds heavier and ten inches longer, and had two to four inches more wheel track than the Ambassador.

Just to get an idea how good a value the car was when classified as a full-size model, *Motor Trend* road-tested four of the latest full-size offerings. The cars chosen were all two-door hardtops with notchback or fastback styling. The candidates were a Chevrolet Impala SS, Ford XL, Plymouth Sport Fury and Ambassador DPL. All four were equipped with three-speed column- or floor-mounted automatic transmissions and four-barrel carburetor V-8 engines. Engine ratings were as follows: Chevy, 427 ci and 385 hp; Ford, 428 ci and 340 hp; Plymouth, 383 ci and 330 hp; and Ambassador, 343 ci and 280 hp. Axle ratios were 2.73, 2.80, 3.23 and 2.87, and curb weights were 3,800, 4,200, 4,000 and 3,500 pounds, respectively.

The Ambassador was a lightweight, but it provided just as much interior and trunk space as the rest of the cars, if not more. Even though it had the smallest engine, its power-to-weight ratio made it perform quite well when compared with the other big-block monsters.

The following 0-60 and quarter-mile elapsed times and terminal speeds were given: Impala, 7.0 seconds, 15.4 seconds at 90 mph; Ford, 8.0 seconds, 16.4 seconds at 86 mph; Plymouth, 7.9 seconds, 16.2 seconds at 87 mph; and Ambassador, 9.2 seconds, 17.0 seconds at 84 mph.

Motor Trend had this to say about the Ambassador's performance: "The Ambassador, with the smallest engine of all—343 cubic inches—nevertheless gave all occupants sufficient confidence. Nearly all of this can be attributed to its tight, heavy-duty suspension, though much credit goes to its lighter weight, better proportions, excellent space utilization and lower

height. By far, it was the most agile of all four cars, and where sheer power enabled the Impala SS and Ford XL to overwhelm our adversary, the Ambassador's clever broken-field running did a perfectly adequate job."

In the handling department, the Ambassador won hands down. The testing staff could not praise it enough, saying, "The Ambassador was outstanding, and yet it was handicapped by an engine that had suffered a combination of maladies and was running at about 50% efficiency. Its handling was so far superior to the other three that it required only four miles to build up a margin of a half-mile between itself and the second fastest car—the Impala SS—and this was done without either tire squeal or dirt-tracking. The car tracked beautifully, its taut dimensions and suspension being detectable at all moments.

The Ambassador also had the shortest stopping distance from 60 mph of all four cars, and this was done with the standard drum brakes. Its suggested retail price was also one of the lowest, second only to the Ford XL's.

The Rebel had been one of the AMC performance leaders for 1967. For 1968, its narrow oval grille with several thin horizontal bars (and blacked-out theme on some models) was nearly identical, as was the horizontally placed four-headlight system. The taillights were changed from a single large horizontally split unit to three narrow individually stacked rectangles. The two center bars on the SST grille were highlighted in silver.

The hood design was also slightly altered. Whereas the 1967 hood had two raised profiles on each side, the 1968 version had a single one running down the middle, with two indentations placed where the twin raised sections had been in 1967. The theme blended into the fresh air intakes for the interior occupants at the cowl area.

Although not required by federal law, the 1967 Rebel had rear side-marker lights. In 1968, all domestic production vehicles were required to have front and rear side-marker lights defining the length of the car at night. On the Rebel, rectangular side markers graced the fenders and a new arrow type, formerly rectangular pointing to the rear, were placed on the quarter panels. The luxury Ambassador used the arrow type on the front and rear. Flush door handles replaced the push-button type on both cars.

The Ambassador shared the Rebel's basic body panels, modified for its own individual distinction. Its headlights were stacked vertically and made squarer than in the 1967 design, with a horizontal grille bar combining a grid-style insert with blacked-out finish.

On the SST model, two running lights were set at each end and were the signal lights. This same theme was used on the 1967 Ambassador and Rambler Marlin. The standard and DPL models had their signal lights set into the bumper, as did all Rebel models. A thicker horizontal center divider split the grille in half over its 1967 counterpart.

The Ambassador's front end was lengthened about six inches over the Rebel's. Taillights were also slightly changed from vertically to horizontally split individual units. The taillight treatments on all 1967-68 Rebel and Ambassador wagons were nearly identical.

Rear panel decorative trim on both cars was slightly changed from 1967. Full-length moldings following the Rebel's bodyside sculpture were added for 1968, except on the 550. The dummy air scoops located on each quarter panel ahead of the wheelwells on SST models were retained. Side trim on all Ambassadors was only slightly changed, although the standup 1967

hood ornament was eliminated. Emblems on both cars were little changed.

Rambler was eliminated from the Rebel hood, as was the SST emblem on the left side of the grille on that model. Rebel was placed on the left-side leading edge of the hood in block letters. Rebel scripts were still on both fenders behind the wheelwells, with their series designations directly below. Rebel was still on the center of the trunk trailing edge, but the Rambler plate placed on the right side of the 550 and 770 was eliminated. The SST designation on the right side remained unchanged.

The V-8 engine emblems on both the Rebel and Ambassador were relocated from the front portions of the fenders to the rear portions of the quarter panels. All Ambassador emblems remained unchanged, except that the 880 designation numbers were deleted from

The Ambassador interior for 1968 was literally a living room on wheels. Just about any popular fabric or color could be ordered for AMC's luxury leader.

The Ambassador SST four-door sedan was AMC's luxury flagship. This car could be optioned out to rival a Cadillac.

under the Ambassador scripts and placed on the fenders behind the wheelwells. Ambassador scripts also adorned the left-side leading edge of the hood and right-side trailing edge of the trunk.

About the only major body change on the Ambassador, if it can be called a major change, was the addition of twin recessed fresh air scoops set into the cowl area that blended in with the sculpturing of the hood similar to the Rebel design. These were for the fresh air ventilation going to the interior occupants.

For the Ambassador interior, one more inch of legroom was added up front, with the sacrifice of one inch of rear legroom. The same was true for the Rebel. The new preset impulse door locks were featured on both cars. All the standard safety features that went into the Javelin, AMX and American were extended to both the Rebel and Ambassador.

Exterior body dimensions on both cars were also quite close to each other. Width for both was 77.2 inches, and front and rear wheel tracks were nearly identical at approximately fifty-eight inches. Even trunk luggage and wagon cargo spaces were the same at 18.2 and ninety-one cubic feet, respectively. Height for both cars was approximately 53.5 inches.

At the beginning of the 1968 model year, engine and transmission choices for the Rebel and Ambassador were virtual carry-overs of the same units available in 1967. Nevertheless, the 290 and 343 V-8s featured improved intake-manifold and cylinder-head breathing, along with thermostatically controlled air cleaner assemblies and full engine-modification emissions equipment on all engines.

The 232 ci 145 hp six was the standard powerplant in the Rebel 550 and 770 and the base Ambassador and DPL, and the higher 155 hp 232 six was optional. Standard engine for the SST versions of both cars was the 290 cubic inch 200 hp two-barrel V-8 engine. The four-speed manual transmission was standard with the

Rebel SST 290. The rest of the engine line-up was optional at extra cost on all models.

The next step was the 343 ci 235 hp two-barrel V-8. The four-barrel version at 280 hp had a high 10.2:1 compression ratio and required premium fuel.

The two-seater AMX was introduced at midyear, in February 1968. That model's top-of-the-line 390 ci 315 hp V-8, called the AMX 390, was made available in both the Rebel and Ambassador starting the middle of May 1968. This engine had the same compression ratio as the 280 hp 343, and provided the car with brisk acceleration. Because of its late introduction, Rebels and Ambassadors equipped with this engine are quite rare.

Transmission choices were extended to both models across the board. The three-speed column shift was standard on both sixes and the 290 V-8. Overdrive was available on the 145 and 200 hp engines. The column-mounted Shift-Command automatic transmission could be teamed with any engine, and the floor-shifted version could be had with all except the sixes.

The automatic transmissions also incorporated a new self-adjusting action for the front band, thus eliminating periodic adjustments. The four-speed manual was restricted to the 200, 280 and 315 hp V-8s.

Factory-available axle ratios were 2.87, 3.15 and 3.54, depending on transmission choice. High-performance dealer-installed ratios of 3.73, 3.91, 4.10 and 4.44 also could be ordered. The four-link trailing arm rear suspension, introduced in 1967, was carried over.

Luxury, convenience and heavy-duty options were plentiful for both cars at the buyer's request. A handling package consisting of heavy-duty springs and shocks plus front sway bar could be ordered for V-8s as well as six-cylinder models. On the Rebel six-cylinder wagon, all V-8s and all Ambassador models, the front sway bar was standard.

In 1967, the special edition Rebel Briarcliff, Mariner and Westerner station wagons were introduced to different parts of the country. Each model had its own distinguished side treatment. These models were not carried over into 1968. Shown is the Westerner version.

Just about every option available on the Ambassador was available on the Rebel. As stated in the 1968 brochure, the Ambassador was "the first car under $10,598 with air conditioning standard." A wide choice of rich-looking fabrics could be matched to just about any popular body color the buyer could think of. Two-tone paint and black, off-white or blue vinyl-covered tops could be had. Individually adjustable reclining bucket seats could be ordered if the customer wanted to combine sportiness with extended trip comfort.

Air conditioning was a popular option. When it was teamed with the Cruise-Command automatic speed control and Adjust-O-Tilt steering wheel, one could glide down the highway. The Power-Lift electric side window option was restricted to the Ambassador DPL and SST versions of both cars. A Power-Lift electric tailgate window was a very convenient and sensible option to air out a stuffy interior on long trips.

An array of wheel discs could be mounted on the standard 7.35x14 black- or whitewall tires. If you needed more you could step up to a 7.75, 8.25 or, for that sporty finishing touch, F70x14 wide-profile red-line tires on V-8-equipped models, except wagons.

AMC also offered visibility groups, light groups, AM/FM stereo radios with two speakers, 8-track tape players, insulation groups, electric windshield wipers and washers, appearance groups, heavy-duty batteries, alternators and clutches, and just about anything else the buyer could think of. Both the Rebel and Ambassador could be optioned out to rival a Cadillac.

The Javelin and AMX were heavily promoted for 1968, especially in the performance department, and AMC did cover this aspect with the Rebel and the Ambassador. AMC did not push the Rebel and Ambassador, however, because it wanted to sell as many of the new Javelins and AMXs as possible, as the AMC performance leaders. Thus, the hot Rebel SST that had been promoted so much in 1967 along with the Rogue was forced to take a back seat in 1968.

Both the Rebel and Ambassador could be optioned out as intermediate supercars, although the percentage of those ordered in performance trim was probably low.

At the beginning of the 1968 model year, one could order the 343 ci 280 hp V-8 and optional dual exhausts. This could be teamed with the four-speed manual transmission and a 3.54 Twin-Grip rear. Throw in the handling package and wide-profile F70x14 tires with a few convenience or luxury items, and wrap the complete package in the Rebel or Ambassador hardtop or Rebel convertible, and you had one tough-looking car with respectable performance.

With a shipping weight of approximately 3,000 to 3,500 pounds depending on body style, the cars could be made into formidable street sleepers with the right doses of dealer-installed Group 19 high-performance parts. With the midyear introduction of the AMX 390 V-8, these models were probably the most overlooked supercars of the era. Add to this a lack of advertising, and the scarcity of 1968 Rebel or Ambassador 343 or 390 road tests is understandable.

AMC did conduct its own road test of a 1968 Rebel equipped with the 390 V-8, four-speed transmission and 3.54:1 rear. (This car was used as the basis to create the limited edition 1970 Rebel Machine, which became the apex of Rebel performance.) AMC recorded a 0-60 time of 8.25 seconds, and the quarter-mile was covered in 15.78 seconds at a speed of 85 mph. These times were by no means earth shattering, but they were indicative of what the car could do. With just a few simple modifications and hot rodding tricks, the car could be made to perform. High thirteens and low fourteens were easily within the reach of a properly prepared 390 Rebel or Ambassador.

Production of both cars was substantial at the end of the 1968 model year. The final tally for the Rebel was a healthy 79,325 units. Only 377 units were built in

The 1969 Rebel's lines were rounded off for the new model year. The 390 V-8 and four-speed manual transmission were also absent from the option list.

the 550 convertible series and 823 units in the 770 convertible series. Fully optioned out examples of these models are quite rare.

A few Rebel specialty cars worth mentioning, that were built as 1967 models introduced in February of that year and not carried over into 1968, were the limited edition Briarcliff, Mariner and Westerner Stationwagons. The Briarcliff was sold in the eastern portion of the United States and only 400 units were built. The Mariner was sold in the coastal areas to just 600 customers, and the Westerner was sold in the Midwest and found 500 new homes. Each model had its own distinctive full-length side panel treatment with the model ID placed on the quarter panels.

Total Ambassador production for 1968 trailed Rebel production with 60,872 units built. Again, fully optioned out 390 V-8 four-speed models were scarce.

1969

AMC entered the 1969 model year with yet another approach as to how it would market the Rebel

and Ambassador, since the Javelin and AMX had proven to be runaway successes in spearheading the new corporate performance image.

What happened to the 1967 Rambler American 343 happened to the 1968 Rebel 390. Just when those cars were beginning to become performance leaders, AMC yanked their high-performance plugs to ensure that they could not cut into the performance territories of the Javelin and AMX. Consequently, the 390 V-8 and four-speed manual transmission options were shaved from the Rebel's option list. Although the Ambassador was still available with the 390, it too lost its four-speed transmission. The four-speed never returned to the Ambassador's option list, but the Rebel regained it for 1970.

The Rebel's exterior dimensions remained basically the same except that its front and rear track measurements were increased to an even sixty inches.

Although the big-displacement 390 was no longer available, an adventurous enthusiast could still order up a Rebel to be a competitive street contender. The 343 two- and four-barrel V-8s could be ordered with optional dual exhaust and any high-performance equipment offered under the dealer-installed Group 19 program. If the buyer did not mind the lack of a four-speed, the Rebel could still be made into quite a street screamer, but few buyers bothered.

The year 1969 was a big performance year for compacts, pony cars and intermediates. The streets were crawling with such stompers as the Plymouth GTX, Dodge RT, Torino Cobra Jet, Chevelle SS 396, GTO 400, Olds 442 and the like, most with 400 cubic inch engines or larger, not to mention the 455 ci Hurst Olds. If you showed up at the local drive-in or supercar

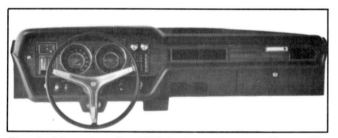

The dashboard on the 1969 Ambassador was all new. The Matador design was similar, the main difference being in the instrument panel.

The Ambassador received a new grille for 1969. This remained basically the same up to 1973. The taillights were also of a new design.

hangout with an automatic transmission AMC Rebel 343, you were probably laughed out of the neighborhood.

Fortunately, AMC realized this and attempted to change the Rebel's image for 1970, but it was too late for 1969. On the cover of the *1969 Rebel Product Sales Information* pamphlet, the car was described as "the machine that likes its work." A similar phrase was used in the standard AMC brochures. Could this have been a prelude to the 1970 Rebel Machine?

For 1969, the grille design was slightly changed. It featured a horizontal bar theme made of injection-molded plastic and incorporated the inner high-beam headlights. The outer low-beam headlights were contained in their own square housings. Both the grille and the headlight housings were outlined in bright chrome moldings.

Taillights were also redesigned into large wrap-around units doubling as the rear side-marker lights. The deck lid and lower panel were slightly resculptured for a cleaner look. The overall profile of the car was basically unchanged, however.

Models and body styles were trimmed extensively. There were only two series in the line-up, the Rebel and the Rebel SST, and both were available in four-door sedan, two-door hardtop and two- or three-seat four-door station wagons—and that was it.

Model series and engine ID emblems remained in their same locations, with a few changes. The 550 and 770 emblems were dropped, and the SST badge moved back into the left side of the grille, where it had been in 1967. Also on the SST the phony rear wheel-well air scoops were replaced with four chrome side strips on each side. The Rebel was void of any side trim, but the SST had a chrome strip running the entire length of the car at the beltline just above the door handle.

A neat item made standard on all Rebel and Ambassador station wagons was the Dual-Swing tailgate. It could swing out like a door or down like a conventional tailgate.

On the inside, a completely new dashboard was designed for both cars. It resembled a guitar case laid on its side, with the wide base portion serving as the instrument panel. The Rebel instrument panel was a rectangular design housing the speedometer, temperature gauge and fuel gauge flanked by the heater and air conditioning controls on one side, clock and radio on the other. Immediately below were the windshield wiper and headlight controls and cigarette lighter on their own upward-slanting panel.

The Ambassador had a similar arrangement except the speedometer, temperature and fuel gauges were housed in two large round central pods. A large

The Dual-Swing tailgate was made standard on all 1969 Rebel and Ambassador station wagons. Here the luxury Ambassador demonstrates how convenient it was.

99

padded eyebrow covered both dashboards completely across. New pure nylon cut-pile carpeting was also introduced on the Ambassador.

The Ambassador had its wheelbase lengthened four inches to 122 inches. As a result, overall length also took a four-inch jump to 206.5 inches, with most of the length added in the hood. Width and height were unchanged, but the wheel track was increased to an even sixty inches, as was done on the Rebel. Both cars also received a redesigned steering linkage and front and rear suspensions for improved handling, more stabilized ride and reduced vibrations.

The Ambassador's front end was redesigned with a bold squared-off grille made of injection-molded plastic in a deep-section honeycomb design, which featured a bright horizontal accent bar running through the middle, completely across, connecting the horizontally placed four-headlamp system. It resembled the Chrysler 300s of the late fifties and early sixties.

The new sculptured hood was described by AMC as a Power-Dome design. This front-end design remained little changed right up to 1973, which was the next-to-the-last year for Ambassador production.

The new taillight treatment was a little odd and fortunately, it lasted only one year. AMC installed blunt quarter panel end caps where the taillights had been for the 1967-68 models. It then set the new taillights into the rear panels directly below the deck lid. They were of a horizontal-bar design with integral back-up lights. The same design was extended to the outside surfaces of the quarter panel end caps that served as the side-marker lights, which were also redesigned. On the SST version, the theme was continued in a full-length rear panel design set between the taillights themselves.

The Ambassador line still consisted of the base DPL and SST series. The new line-up consisted of seven models in the three series. The DPL cross-country wagon was dropped. The two-door hardtop was dropped from the base series and a four-door station wagon was added to the SST series. This new SST wagon had such standard features as a 290 cubic inch V-8, rooftop travel rack, individually adjustable reclining front seats, the Dual-Swing tailgate, and nylon cut-pile carpeting covering the front, rear and cargo areas. The rooftop travel rack was standard on all Rebel and Ambassador wagons.

As on the Rebel, emblem placement on the Ambassador was once again rearranged. Ambassador appeared in script on both rear portions of the quarter panels and on the left upper side of the grille. Ambassador in block letters adorned the center of the rear panel. The DPL and SST versions were identified on the C-pillars, and all V-8 engine emblems were moved from the quarter panels to the fenders behind the side-marker lights. Ambassador crests finished off the rear surfaces of the quarter panel end caps.

Side trim for the base series consisted of a single chrome strip running the length of the car, intersecting the middle of the wheelwells. The SST and DPL had double parallel running strips, and the SST four-door sedan could be had with a stainless steel insert. The SST wagon in both the Rebel and Ambassador lines featured simulated woodgrain exterior paneling on the side and rear of the body.

The Ambassador for 1969 could be optioned out quite heavily—a little more so than the Rebel—because it was AMC's luxury flagship. You could choose any one of fourteen solid exterior colors or thirty-three optional two-tones. Vinyl tops could be ordered in black, white or blue.

Another exclusive Ambassador option was the deeply channeled velour upholstery in place of the standard brocade or optional vinyl. Power steering, power front disc brakes on V-8s, power windows, handling package, electric clock standard on some models, Twin-Grip rear, fiberglass-belted tires, Cruise-Command speed control, rich interior fabrics and sports steering wheel were just a few of the numerous luxury, convenience, appearance and performance options for both cars.

Engine and transmission choices for the intermediates were significantly changed. All Rebels came standard with the 232 ci 145 hp one-barrel carburetor six-cylinder engine. The two-barrel carburetor version producing 155 hp was optional on the Rebel and standard on the base and DPL Ambassadors. The 290 ci 200 hp V-8 was standard on the Ambassador SST and optional on all other Ambassadors and Rebels, as were the two- and four-barrel 343 V-8s. The AMX 390 ci 315 hp V-8 was restricted to the Ambassador SST model only.

Transmission choices were cut-and-dried. The Rebel 145 hp six could be teamed with a column-mounted three-speed manual, overdrive or Shift-Command automatic. The Ambassador 155 hp six

The grille on the 1970 Rebel was a modified version of the 1968 Rebel SST's, with a vertical split added.

came standard with the three-speed manual, and the column-shift automatic was optional. The 290 V-8 in both cars was restricted to automatics on the column or console, and the console shift was standard on the Ambassador SST. The 235 hp 343 had only one transmission choice, the column-mounted automatic, but the four-barrel 343 and 390 could be ordered with the column- or console-shift automatic.

Standard rear axle ratio for all V-8s was the 2.87, with the 3.15 optional. All sixes came standard with the 3.15 ratio, except the overdrive-equipped Rebel six which had a 3.54 rear. There were no optional ratios for any six cylinder.

When compared with the rest of the AMC performance cars for 1969, the Rebel and Ambassador models were clear-cut budget performance or sedate luxury cruisers.

For 1969, the Rebel took a back seat to not only its bigger brother, the Ambassador, but the entire AMC line in terms of options. In its literature, AMC promoted the Rebel as "the car for people." A touch of Volkswagen cliche, to say the least; the Rebel was clearly experiencing an identity crisis.

Despite AMC's decision to de-emphasize performance for its two senior car lines, both cars were quite improved for 1969. The numerous new standard and safety features introduced on the Javelin, AMX and Rambler were also extended to the Rebel and Ambassador.

Some of those features included head restraints, a cable-controlled accelerator system with a suspended pedal, a lighter and more compact battery with a translucent polypropylene case, parking lights that remained on with the headlights, Guard-Glo safety headlights featuring a standby filament as a back-up in case of failure, and a Command Air ventilation system con-

sisting of easy-operation controls and a high-capacity three-speed blower which forced air through the normal air conditioning outlets.

Aside from the Command Air system, the Rebel and Ambassador featured an increased-capacity air conditioning system exclusive to their series only. This unit was capable of dropping inside temperatures considerably faster than had units previously used. The control marked "for desert only" could really chill the occupants.

Additional AMC standard safety features beneficial to all occupants were excellent double safety brakes, seatbelts for all passenger positions, shoulder belts for driver and right front seat passenger, energy-absorbing steering column, padded dash and visors, and left outside rearview mirror. Numerous options were available to fit just about any and every taste. The Rebel and Ambassador models were among some of the finest and safest cars in the industry.

A new Pistol Grip Shift-Command automatic transmission floor-mounted control lever was introduced on both the Rebel and Ambassador for 1970.

The quarter panels and rear bumper appeared quite massive on the 1970 Rebel. Lines were still clean.

The mighty Rebel Machine from 1970 used a modified version of the standard 390 V-8. With modified intake and exhaust manifolds it produced 340 hp. The optional red-white-blue paint scheme looked neat.

Road tests

Super Stock and Drag Illustrated had this to say about the Rebel's styling: "For 1969, the AM Rebel and Rebel SST are even cleaner-looking than last year, if that's possible." But the magazine's staff were disappointed with AMC's decision to drop the Rebel as a performance model, saying, "The Rebel could be a spirited road car if AMC would allow use of hot rodded 390 V-8, but as it is, the 343 4-BBL. is tops for this clean-cut hardtop."

Super Stock and Drag Illustrated also confirmed the luxury aspect of the Ambassador, commenting that "Ambassador seating is very luxurious, considering the price range, with Brocades in the middle DPL series, and real velour in SST sedans." Its ride was also praised: "The Big Ambassador has a lot going for it as a

road car." Finally, its handling and overall package were summed up in one sentence: "Shifts were positive, wheel feel very good, and the disc/drum brakes were so effective that they were hard to get used to."

The Ambassador was such a good car that Robert F. Estes of Trans-World Leasing in Chicago, Illinois, built several Ambassador custom limousines based on the four-door sedan model. These were stretch-type limousines featuring facing seats, and they saw a lot of airport service.

As in 1968, road tests for both cars were scarce in 1969 because the Javelin and AMX models were in the spotlight as the performance leaders. *Road Test* magazine did, however, perform a complete evaluation of a 1969 Ambassador SST 390 four-door sedan's roadability and handling, comfort and convenience, power and performance, and braking.

The model tested had the console-shift automatic transmission and 3.15:1 rear axle ratio. It also had the optional power front disc brakes, 7.75x14 whitewall tires and an overall curb weight of 3,660 pounds.

Road Test opened with its initial reaction to the car: "Luxury in a small package is a ploy successfully peddled for years by European carmakers, notably Mercedes-Benz and BMW, but not too many Americans realize that equal or better standards are offered for far less money right out of Wisconsin's cheese belt. They are found in the Ambassador." And about the car's interior: "In no domestic car at any price will you find a plusher interior." *Road Test* went on to comment about the car's excellent interior dimensions when compared with the Chevrolet Caprice, Ford LTD and Plymouth VIP.

Although the car's handling and roadability were nothing special, its comfort and convenience aspects were rated tops. Once again, AMC's integrated Weather Eye heating and air conditioning system was unequaled in the industry.

For 1969, the Ambassador also became the first domestic car to place five air conditioning outlets on the dashboard, further ensuring that no one inside could ever complain of being uncomfortably warm on a blistering hot summer day. AMC was also praised for retaining its front vent side windows, an item most manufacturers sacrificed in the name of styling.

The power and performance of the AMX 390-powered Ambassador was just another good trait of the car. Gas mileage was only 14.2 mpg, but its 0-60 time of 8.9 seconds and passing range of 50 to 70 mph in 5.7 seconds were good enough to make you forget about that rather average figure. Quarter-mile performance was not too bad for a luxury car with a highway-cruising axle ratio, registering an elapsed time of 16.01 seconds at 88.58 mph. The power disc-drum brake

The lighted 8000 rpm hood-mounted tachometer was right in the line of the driver's vision. The model was identified by the decals on the fenders, and the side and deck stripes glowed in the dark.

combination enabled the car to stop straight and true in a short 142 feet from 60 mph.

Road Test was impressed with the Ambassador: "We strongly suggest that a habitual buyer of a Ford, Chevrolet or Plymouth at least take the time to visit his nearest AMC showroom, kick the tires and go for a demonstration drive."

As it had in 1968, *Motor Trend* again staged a four-car luxury shoot-out between an Ambassador SST, Chevrolet Impala, Ford LTD and Plymouth Fury III. Again, all models were two-door hardtops equipped with bench seats and column-mounted automatic transmissions, with the exception of the Impala which had a Muncie four-speed manual box.

Engine and rear axle combinations were as follows: Chevrolet, 427 ci 390 hp, 3.31; Ford, 429 ci 360 hp, 2.80; Plymouth, 383 ci 330 hp, 3.23; and Ambassador, 343 ci 280 hp, 2.87. All cars had four-barrel carburetors and at least 10:1 compression ratios requiring premium fuel. The Ambassador was the lightest at 3,805 pounds, and the Impala was the heaviest at 4,475 pounds. All but the Ambassador had G70 or H70 series tires mounted on fifteen-inch wheels. The Ambassador had small 7.75x14 skins.

The Ambassador was again at a power disadvantage, and consequently its 0-60 and quarter-mile performance figures could not match those of its more powerful rivals. Zero-to-sixty and quarter-mile times and speeds were as follows: Chevrolet, 7.7, 15.7 at 93 mph; Ford, 8.7, 16.3 at 86 mph; Plymouth, 7.5, 15.7 at 93 mph; and Ambassador, 12.0, 18.2 at 78 mph.

Despite this disadvantage, *Motor Trend* said this about the Ambassador's performance: "With AMC's 343-c.i.d. mill under the hood, our Ambassador SST had the lowest hp rating of the four cars tested, with 280 hp at 4800 rpm. Even so, performance was still brisk for a family car, with a 4-bbl. Carter carburetor and 10.2:1 compression."

In the handling, steering and stopping departments, the Ambassador was well rated when compared with its competition: "Anything other than a soft, boulevard ride, would be a surprise in the Ambassador, and we weren't surprised." Although the handling of the car could have been better, it still received a favorable rating.

The braking power of the newly styled Ambassador was one of its many strong points, even though the car tended to be a little touchy and swerved a bit. It was summed up this way: "Stopping distances were excellent though, and there was never any fade problem. Tires also made a difference in braking. Without the advantage of the wide treads, the SST performance was very good compared to the other cars."

Production of both the Rebel and Ambassador for the 1969 model year was quite good, despite the Javelin and AMX being the center of attraction. The 1969 Rebel ended with 60,106 units built, which was roughly 20,000 units shy of its 1968 counterpart. Ambassador production shot up to 76,194, which was about 15,000 more than in 1968.

1970

The year 1970 was the height of the Detroit supercar, especially for the GM intermediate A-bodied cars

The Rebel Machine also came with its own design five-slot steel wheels and Goodyear Polyglas E60x15 raised-white-letter tires.

The interior of the Rebel Machine was pretty much standard Rebel with a few nice touches such as the custom Rim-Blow steering wheel and optional center console with floorshift and armrest.

To promote the Rebel Machine a set of four of these decals could be had by sending a whopping $.25 to AMC.

which were by far the most popular. The corporate 400 cubic inch engine limit for those cars was lifted, and the streets began to crawl with high-compression, premium-fuel-gulping cars like the 454 LS6 Chevelle SS, 455 W30 Olds 442, 455 Ram-Air IV GTO and 455 Buick GS Stage I. The Mopar 426 Hemi and 440 Wedge GTXs, Road Runners, RTs and SuperBees that had reigned supreme since 1967 now faced some stiff competition. And, with a minimum of tweaking, the mighty Torino and Cyclone 428 and 429 Cobra and Super Cobra Jet sleepers were superterrors.

AMC had no choice but to immediately build up and promote the Rebel as its performance intermediate. There was just no way a 343 Rebel could be classified as a competitive intermediate muscle car, so the inevitable happened. The 390 V-8 was reintroduced to the Rebel SST line for 1970, minus the four-speed manual transmission. Not to worry; the four-speed was soon available again, but only for the Rebel Machine.

Most exterior dimensions remained the same, but the overall length on hardtops and sedans was increased two inches to 199 inches, and the Rebel Machine was almost an inch taller than the standard hardtop, at 54.4 inches. Models and body styles in both the Rebel and Rebel SST series were carry-overs, except for the addition of the Rebel Machine two-door hardtop.

Again, AMC used as many existing and off-the-shelve parts as possible. The overall body design was once again used, with the new sculptured quarter panels, rear deck lid and panel, and rear bumper and taillights. The rear bumper was quite massive and contained horizontal rectangular taillights with Rebel spelled out in block letters between them. This same bumper and taillight treatment was shared with the

Ambassador in slightly modified form, the only difference being that the larger car had full-width taillights with center-mounted back-up lights.

The new grille and headlight treatment was almost identical to that of the 1968 Rebel SST unit, with the addition of a vertical center bar splitting the grille in two. It now had the appearance of a four-rectangle design with the horizontal center bar inside.

New longer rectangular-style side-marker lights were used front and rear on both the Rebel and Ambassador and on all AMC models for 1970. (American Motors seemed to like rectangular designs in everything.)

Model and engine identifications were only slightly rearranged. The SST emblems on that model were now placed at the bottom of the roof C-pillars. Engine emblems for V-8s moved from the quarter panels to the rear portions of the front wheelwells under the Rebel letters. Rebel and SST emblems were removed from the deck lid and rear panel. The SST had a new bright chrome ribbed molding connecting the front side-marker light to the front door handle.

The Ambassador still rode on the larger 122 inch wheelbase. The grille design was now of a crosshatch pattern made up of, again, numerous small rectangles. The center bar was now blacked out, and the headlight bezels were smaller, less ornate and slightly separated over the 1969 design. Ambassador written out in script adorned the rear portions of the front wheelwells and the right side of the deck lid. SST or DPL was identified on the roof C-pillars, and V-8 engine numerals were placed under the Ambassador fender scripts.

The Ambassador continued to be the company's luxury cruiser, with options available to turn the car into a floating living room. A new wood-grain vinyl called Bavarian Oak was introduced for the dash-

The Ambassador's rear-end styling was similar to the Rebel's. Its major difference was the full-width taillight treatment, which blended in well.

106

board. Instrument panels, dashboards and interior layouts for both cars were basically unchanged. The integral headrest turtle-back-type bucket seats replaced the old design. All AMC cars for 1970 received the all-new twin ball-joint front suspension system.

The big news for 1970 was the complete change in engine line-up. Both cars now shared basically the same standard and optional engine, transmission and rear axle combinations.

Starting with the Rebel, the 232 ci 145 hp six was standard in both models. The 155 hp six was optional for the Rebel and Rebel SST and standard for the base Ambassador. The 304 ci 210 hp V-8 engine was standard in the Ambassador DPL and SST and optional on all other Rebel and Ambassador models. The 360 ci 245 and 290 hp V-8s were also optional in all Rebels and Ambassadors, but the 390 ci 325 hp V-8 was restricted to the Rebel SST and Ambassador SST and DPL models only.

Transmission selection was quite similar to that in 1969. The three-speed column-shift manual was standard on the Rebel 145 hp and Ambassador 155 hp sixes, with the column Shift-Command automatic optional. The 155 hp Rebel six came only with the Shift-Command.

The 304 V-8, both 360 V-8s and the 390 V-8 all came with Shift-Command automatic transmissions mounted on the column or floor console. No three- or four-speed manual transmissions were offered for the Rebel or Ambassador V-8 engines.

Axle ratio availability was again quite conservative, with a 2.87, 3.15 or 3.54 offered depending on transmission choice, and the hot 3.73, 3.91, 4.10, 4.44 and 5.00 dealer-installed ratios still to be had.

The Rebel could now be made into a high-performance intermediate, a capability it had needed since 1957. With a curb weight of approximately 3,500 pounds, it was easily one of the lightest in its class. A typical young buyer might have ordered the 390 V-8 backed up with the Shift-Command console automatic (because there was no four-speed) and the 3.54:1 Twin-Grip rear. From there, heavy-duty cooling might have been added, along with the handling package consisting of heavy-duty springs, shock absorbers and rear sway bar. The extra-wide-profile E60x15 Goodyear Polyglas tires mounted on 15x7 slot-styled steel wheels would nicely complement the buyer's choice of exterior and matching interior colors.

The Machine

With the variety of options available, a Rebel could be tailored to fit just about any taste imaginable, except one. The Rebel had been given a performance image, but it still needed a visual image, something you would never forget. The dealers needed something striking to pull in potential buyers just passing by the AMC showroom; something was needed to follow in the footsteps of the successful 1969 Hurst SC/Rambler.

Enter the 1970 Rebel Machine, which was introduced just eight months after the SC/Rambler and shortly after the fall introduction of all the 1970 AMC cars. It made its debut at the National Hot Rod Association World Championship Drag Race in Dallas, Texas, on October 25, 1969. Both the SC/Rambler and the Rebel Machine were joint projects between AMC and Hurst Peformance.

Whereas Hurst had received top billing in the Scrambler's advertising campaign, it received practically none when it came to the Rebel Machine. With the exception of one short sentence in the main 1970 AMC brochure—"We really did a job on it (in collaboration with Hurst Performance Research)"—AMC took all the credit for the car. In fact, the Hurst nameplate was nowhere to be found on the car, other than the four-speed shifter handle inscription, and even that was absent when the Shift-Command automatic transmission was ordered with Pistol Grip shifter handle.

AMC's ad campaign for the car was endorsed with the slogan "Up with the Rebel Machine." Decals could be ordered with the catchy slogan; one decal showed a long-haired hippy with dark glasses riding on a gear-shaped unicycle going off in a cloud of dust and carrying a protest sign with the slogan—a typical attempt to catch the young people's attention. AMC vice-president of marketing services R. W. McNealy stated, "We expect the machine to accelerate American Motors' developing image as a producer of cars that will meet the demands of the performance car market, as well as cars that fit the more conventional needs of the buying public."

Unlike the Scrambler, which was available only as a complete package for $2,998 and could not be ordered with any additional equipment or options, the Rebel Machine was offered in a choice of colors and with just about any regular Rebel SST option available. It was based on the Rebel SST two-door hardtop model and started out at a price of $3,475, which included most of the SST's standard equipment plus a host of high-performance items similar to the Scrambler's: a choice of any of the sixteen Rebel exterior factory colors; Shadow Black paint on major portion of hood, hood scoop and fresh air cowl panel; silver paint accent on front opening of hood scoop and silver pinstripe over center rib on hood and hood scoop; The Machine decals on rear portions of fenders and on right-side bottom corner of deck lid; venturi grille with blacked-out rear panel and headlight bezels; Rebel and 390 V-8 emblems on fenders, with fender and door ribbed side moldings and SST emblems on quarter panels deleted; high-back bucket seats upholstered in Ventilair vinyl with matching rear seats, minus center cushion and fold-down armrests, available in black, blue or brown; rear armrests and ashtrays deleted; full carpeting including baseline of door and rear side interior panels; Javelin-AMX two-spoke

Rim-Blow steering wheel; The Machine emblem on glovebox; dual horns; special 390 cubic inch 340 hp V-8 with modified intake and exhaust manifolds; 680 cfm four-barrel carburetor; removal of heat-riser control valve; 2.23 close-ratio four-speed manual transmission with Hurst linkage; 3.54 non-Twin-Grip rear; dual exhaust system with special-tone low-restriction mufflers and larger 2.5 inch exhaust pipes; handling package consisting of heavy-duty springs, shock absorbers and rear sway bar; heavy-duty cooling system consisting of high-capacity radiator, shroud and Power-Flex

The Machine continued as an option package only on the 1971 Matador two-door hardtop. Although the same type of mag wheels and Goodyear E60x15 Polyglas tires were used as in 1970, there were no decals, emblems or graphics identifying the car as a Matador Machine. This rare model is owned by AMC club member Patrick Wnek of Wisconsin.

fan; power front disc brakes; functional Ram-Air fiberglass hood scoop with vacuum-operated flapper valve and integrated 8000 rpm lighted tachometer; Space Saver spare mounted on regular fourteen-inch orange-painted wheel, and E60x15 Goodyear Polyglas raised-white-letter tires mounted on 15x7 Kelsey-Hayes-styled steel wheels with trim rings.

To finish off the complete package, AMC jacked up the rear two inches with the installation of heavy-duty Rebel station wagon coil springs to give the car a special raked look. It was another superbuy that followed right in the footsteps of the Scrambler!

If that wasn't enough, more hot items could be ordered to really turn the car into a performer. A 3.91 Twin-Grip rear was optional on the four-speed-equipped model. If you ordered the automatic transmission, the 3.15 rear was standard and the 3.54 was optional. Twin-Grip was available for any rear-end ratio and was required on the 3.91. The dealer-installed 3.73, 4.10, 4.44 and 5.00 ratios were also extended to the Rebel Machine option list, and for the serious racer, a no-slip Detroit locker could also be dealer installed.

Still needed more? How about power steering, an AM or AM/FM radio with or without rear speakers, a fold-down center armrest with automatic transmission or the same armrest upholstered in red-white-blue, or a black, white or blue vinyl-covered roof.

The Rebel name was dropped for 1971 and the series was renamed the Matador. The car featured a new hood, grille and bumper design. This was the last year for the four-speed manual transmission with the Go Package.

If the buyer wanted something a little more striking, for just $75 option code 768 could be checked off giving the Rebel Machine a Frost White paint job with red-white-blue stripes, which were decals that glowed in the dark. Electric Blue replaced the Shadow Black on the hood, hood scoop and cowl panel. The same blue also finished off the lower bodyside panels from front to rear, including the rear bumper lower valance. A red-white-blue decal was placed on the lower flat surface of the grille with the colors in that order from right to left.

A red stripe started at the fender just above the bumper and went up and back, following the side of the body at the beltline, traveling above the door handle to the middle of the deck lid, going across it and connecting to the opposite side. There were also white and blue stripes, in that order, behind the red stripe going over the deck lid. All three stripes were outlined and separated with black pinstriping. The red-white-blue body and grille decals were optional on any of the sixteen body colors for the Machines. If the buyer ordered the Frost White body color, no two-tone scheme or vinyl roof was available.

The Rebel had managed to flag down the attention of the buying public, but the supreme test would be its quarter-mile performance. On paper and in person, the car looked to be a real winner.

Its 390 V-8 was not new, but with an advertised rating of 340 hp at 5100 rpm and 430 pounds-feet of torque at 3600 rpm, it was the most powerful engine ever produced by AMC. With a shipping weight of 3,650 pounds, the car had a power-to-weight ratio of 10.735 as advertised in *The Rebel Machine* brochure, which was enough to qualify the car for NHRA's F/Stock class.

In the same publication, AMC stated that the car could cover the quarter-mile in 14.4 seconds at 98 mph with a top speed of 125 mph, while delivering 13 mpg. The car was also capable of turning a 0-60 time of 6.6 seconds, according to AMC engineering tests. These statements were just as bold as the ones made in the SC/Rambler ad.

In one of its ads, AMC pointed out that the car was not as fast as certain big-block performers: "For instance, it is not as fast on the getaway as a 427 Corvette, or a Hemi, but it is faster on the getaway than a Volkswagon, a slow freight train, and your old man's Cadillac." This was true, but still the Rebel had finally started to become competitive with the rest of the cars in its class.

Road tests

How competitive? *Car Craft* magazine was able to test what appeared to be a preproduction prototype of a 1970 Rebel Machine. The car pictured was a standard Rebel SST two-door hardtop with all the appropriate trimmings and equipped with a vinyl roof. The underhood shot clearly identified the engine as a 390 V-8, which was reintroduced in the Rebel line for 1970.

But note this quote from the test: "Our test Machine was equipped with a four speed, 3.54:1 Twin-Grip rear differential and E70-14 tires. As with all Rebel four speeds, a Hurst shifter was standard." The only four-speed offered in the Rebel line was on the Rebel Machine!

Another statement provides further evidence that *Car Craft* was testing a Rebel Machine prototype: "This particular car did not have a cold air package, but this option is supposed to be available very shortly." The magazine's closing statements said it all: "We hope this doesn't hurt first quarter sales, but we've seen some artists' projections of the midyear version of the Rebel, and it is really sharp. The use of paint treatment and stripes (on the renderings we saw) is extremely creative and attractive. If approved for production, you'll probably see more Rebels than showed up for the battle of Bull Run." As we know, the Rebel Machine was approved for production.

The model *Car Craft* tested was a standard 390 cubic inch 325 hp engined Rebel SST that recorded a 14.50 second elapsed time at 98.37 mph in the quarter-mile. In the same issue, a Chevelle 454 ci, Challenger 440 ci, Torino 429 ci, Cougar 429 ci, Olds 442 445 ci, Cuda 426 ci and GTO 400 ci were tested. All were between ½ and 1½ seconds quicker in the quarter-mile.

Although the Rebel was catching up, it still had a long way to go and it had started too late. The next year, 1971, would be the year of the compression ratio drop, 1972 the year of the net horsepower ratings, 1973 and 1974 the years that the EGR and additional related smog emissions systems strangled the supercars to death, and 1975 the year of the final blow with the introduction of the catalytic converter.

Road Test had a chance to put a Rebel Machine through its paces. Its car was equipped with the four-speed, 3.91 Twin-Grip rear and variable-ratio power steering.

From the start of the test to the finish, the testing staff had just about nothing but good things to say about the Rebel Machine. They commented about the red-white-blue paint scheme, citing how much more subtle and pleasing it was when compared with the SC/Rambler's.

The road test took place in California, and the car's delivery to *Road Test* from Wisconsin took a slight detour to the Tulare shop of H. L. Shahan. Once there, the heads were shaved 0.030 inch, carburetors rejetted, distributor checked for balance and transmission linkage checked for clearance. These few modifications probably had little effect on the car's performance.

Despite a test weight of over 3,800 pounds, the car was able to record a 14.57 elapsed time of 92.77 mph in the quarter-mile. Although the elapsed time and speed were off from what the factory advertised, the testing staff encountered quite a bit of rear-end bounce and wheel spin caused by the car's high-pronounced rake. They all agreed the car could have easily turned low fourteens at almost 100 mph if it were not for this handicap.

Roadability and handling of the car were superb. *Road Test* put it this way: "Even though down just a bit on power compared to some of the muscle cars, the Machine scores high points in the handling department." Although the magazine's staff felt the suspension was too stiff, they praised the cornering ability of the car: "While you can feel anything thicker than a cigarette paper under your wheels, you also get around corners with sports car aplomb or the kind of handling that brings home the bacon in Trans-Am racing." Apparently, the lessons AMC was learning on the track were being incorporated into its street cars.

The braking power of the car was tops in its class, and *Road Test* stated, "The brakes on the Machine are among the best yet tested on a muscle car." It went on to say, "Under very hard braking the Machine exhibits almost no nose dive. Braking is among the best found in an intermediate domestic sedan."

Hot Rod also had a chance to road-test a red-white-blue Rebel Machine equipped with the four-speed and 3.91 Twin-Grip rear. The testing staff commented that the potential was there, but the car did not perform as well on the track as it did on paper. Although its braking power was rated excellent, its handling could have been better and only suffered because of its high stance.

The dashboard and instrument layout did not receive good marks, and neither did the hood-mounted tachometer. *Hot Rod* had this to say: "Dash is too blank. In the words of one viewer: 'Looks like a taxi.' Tach is hard to read in this location, and rather optimistic with 8-grand scale."

Despite these comments, when the Rebel ripped off an easy 14.49 second elapsed time at 93.0 mph flat in the quarter-mile, the testing staff immediately realized the car's potential, saying, "Can't say this is all bad for such a boxlike front-ended car, but dropping the car closer to the ground, richening the carburetor, bumping the ignition lead a couple of notches, and adding stiffer rear shocks ought to bring this near-4000-pound car close to 14 seconds even."

With a little tinkering, the car would come alive— *Super Stock and Drag Illustrated* discovered when it decided to investigate the untapped performance potential that lurked within the clean-looking Rebel Machine, just as had been done with the Scrambler. The testing staff started out with a four-speed-transmission-equipped 3.91:1 Detroit locker rear model. The heads were cc'd to 49.1 cc, deburred and given a competition valve job. The stock cam was replaced with the AMC hydraulic hi-po unit, which featured a 302 degree duration and 0.477 inch lift. The matching kit consisting of lifters, studs, springs, retainers, keepers, pushrods and locknuts was installed. The intake system received an AMC-Edelbrock aluminum hi-rise manifold with 850 cfm Holley four-barrel carburetor. Doug Thorley headers with 1⅝ inch primaries and 3¼ inch collectors, along with a 2½ inch exhaust

The Ambassador was mildly restyled for 1971. It was available with a new 401 cubic inch 330 hp V-8, which was also offered on the new Matador.

system with Thrush mufflers, were installed. The stock distributor was curved for twelve degrees initial advance and thirty-six degrees total advance.

The stock clutch disc was replaced with a 10.5 inch Chevrolet L88 disc to solve prior problems, and the stock pressure plate and throw-out bearing were used. With everything apart, a couple of two-inch-diameter holes were drilled in the bottom of the bell housing for ventilation. Shifting was much improved at 5800 rpm, but the stock E60x15 tires were not up to the task, so a set of Goodyear seven-inch 8.00x14 slicks was installed. This led to the axle shaft hub flanges being snapped off at the keys but, a set of S/S AMX heavy-duty axle shafts cured that problem. The high rear stance of the car again produced severe wheel hop. Installation of the standard Rebel rear springs or heating of the coils recommended by Hurst would cure the problem.

With everything buttoned up and ready to go, the car made its first pass down the quarter-mile recording a 13.53 second elapsed time. This was accomplished with open headers and with the slicks set at 22 psi. With closed headers the car was still impressive, recording a 13.68 elapsed time. By simply bending the carburetor accelerator pump rods for a larger shot of fuel, the elapsed time dropped to 13.34.

With the timing set back to thirty-six degrees total and open headers, quarter-mile times reached the thirteens. Dropping the tire pressure to sixteen pounds and readjusting driving techniques by shifting at 5500 rpm allowed the mighty Rebel Machine to record a best elapsed time of 12.81 seconds at 107.35 mph.

As was the SC/Rambler, the Rebel Machine was another super street sleeper. Both cars were among the top five fastest street AMCs ever produced (the other three were the 1968-70 390 AMXs, 1971 401 Javelin and junior 1971 Hornet SC/360).

The Rebel Machine had just about everything going for it, but it lacked a performance instrument panel in the form of gauges instead of idiot lights, and the hood-mounted tachometer needed improvement.

Pricewise, the Rebel had the edge on the competition. In full street-racing trim it cost about $200 less than its nearest-priced competitor.

Production figures for the Rebel Machine are conflicting. *The Hurst Heritage* by Robert C. Lichty and Terry V. Boyce states that 2,326 were built, with the first 1,000 units being finished in the red-white-blue paint scheme.

A more detailed breakdown is given by the Rebel Machine Division of the National American Motors Drivers and Racers Association (NAMDRA) AMC enthusiasts club: a total of 1,936 units were built with 1,340 finished in the red-white-blue paint scheme and the remaining 596 finished in the sixteen available factory solid colors. This group also states that the first 300 off the assembly line were red-white-blue models, and the balance of 1,040 were optional ordered. For transmissions, 1,210 were equipped with the four-

speed and 726 with the Shift-Command console automatic transmission. Total Rebel production for 1970 was 49,725 units, including Rebel Machines.

Total Ambassador production for 1970 exceeded Rebel production by roughly 10,000 units, at a final count of 59,941 cars produced.

1971

For 1971, AMC's intermediate received yet another name change, after keeping its Rebel name for only five model years. The car was now known as the Matador, a name used by Dodge for one year in 1960.

Another change was in the car's wheelbase. It inherited the Ambassador's larger 118 inch platform, last used by that model in 1969. Width remained the same at 77.2 inches, but length was increased seven inches to 206 inches overall for sedans and hardtops, and the wagons were one inch shorter at 205 inches.

There were only three models offered in the one series called the Matador, the SST series having been dropped. The only body styles offered were a four-door sedan, two-door hardtop and four-door station wagon.

The front end of the car was finally redesigned. It now featured an integrated bumper-grille theme, with the grille arranged in twin horizontal venturi sections divided by a band of body color. The hood was also resculptured and had a slightly raised center section. The rear bumper was of the same basic design as on the 1970 Rebel, except the taillights were now three individual rectangular units on each side, with the center ones being the back-up lights.

High-back turtle-shell bucket seats could be ordered on the 1971 Ambassador. This would also be the last year any floor-mounted transmission control would be offered on both the Ambassador and the Matador, with the exception of the upcoming 1974 Matador coupe.

The center panel between the taillights was made up of four rectangular sections containing thin vertical and horizontal bars. Front and rear side-marker lights had rounded-off corners as did the rear units on the Ambassador.

Matador in block letters appeared directly above on the deck lid and on the left leading edge of the hood. Matador in script was placed on the roof C-pillars of all models including wagons. All V-8 engines were designated in block letters on the fenders behind the wheelwells.

The exterior appearance of the car was upgraded with bright trim moldings as standard equipment, since there was now only one series in the line-up. These moldings were placed around the front and back window openings, along the drip rails, on the lower rear portion of the deck lid and quarter panel end extensions, and on the outline of the four wheel-well openings. For added protection and to emphasize the Matador's side profile, channeled metal moldings ran the entire length of the car.

Other standard equipment included color-co-ordinated full carpeting in red, blue, green or black, full-back bench seat cushion on sedans and wagons (split back on hardtop), front and rear armrests, rear ashtrays, embossed interior door panels with Matador nameplate and front seat head restraints. The Dual-Swing tailgate was still standard on wagons.

Although the mighty Rebel Machine of 1970 with its unique appearance package was gone, AMC offered a carry-over Machine Go package for the Matador hardtop. The Rebel Machine's red-white-blue paint scheme was not offered, but a good portion of its performance equipment was.

If you checked off option code 3 you had a choice of the 360 four-barrel or 401 four-barrel V-8. The dual exhaust system, 15x7 slot-styled wheels, E60x15 Poly-glas raised-white-letter tires, front ventilated-rotor power disc brakes, handling package consisting of heavy-duty springs, and shock absorbers and rear sway bar, and Space Saver spare tire were all standard items.

As of this writing, only one Matador Machine has surfaced. This model was quite rare indeed.

The Ambassador continued to be upgraded with luxury items. It came standard with air conditioning, an automatic transmission and a transmission oil cooler. The oil cooler was also standard on the Matador big six and V-8s. Model and series availability was basically unchanged, although a new series name added to the others made it appear as though the complete line had been revamped.

As in 1970, there were seven Ambassador models. The standard Ambassador was dropped and the DPL was offered as the base model, available in a four-door sedan only. The SST and new Brougham were both available in a two-door hardtop, four-door sedan and four-door station wagon.

The Ambassador's exterior dimensions were carried over with the exception of the length, which was increased 2.8 inches to 210.8 inches by the addition of standard rubber-padded front bumper guards. Rear bumper guards were still optional. As with the Matador wagons, the Ambassador wagons were one inch shorter.

A new diecast rectangular grille highlighted the front end, complemented by new fender caps incorporating large side-marker lights. Ambassador in script still adorned the left side of the grille and the fenders behind the wheelwells with the V-8 engine numerals designated directly below. The taillight treatment was still full-width, but the center back-up light was replaced with twin units set inboard of each lens. Ambassador in block letters was set into the center red reflective taillight panel. Exterior trim moldings were upgraded in a fashion similar to those on the Matador.

Overall interior and dashboard layouts for both the Ambassador and Matador were virtually unchanged. Brougham wagons featured a new translucent wood-grain side that picked up the tone of the body color for a subtle, attractive color-keyed effect, and had reflective rear paneling as standard equipment. The same paneling was optional on Matador wagons. Other standard equipment on the new Brougham wagons included special interior and exterior trim, individually adjustable reclining seats, six-foot roof rack and integral rear window air deflector. Rocker panel moldings were standard on both SST and Brougham wagons.

Engine line-up for both models was similar to what it had been down through the years. The standard 232 cubic inch inline six-cylinder engine in the Matador was down 10 hp from the previous year, now being rated at 135. A new larger 258 cubic inch six rated at 150 hp was optional. The 304 V-8, both 360 V-8s and 401 V-8 were all optional in any Matador body style. The base-line Ambassador DPL received the new 258 six (which was exclusive to that series) as standard. The standard engine in the SST and Brougham was the 304 V-8, with the two 360s and the 401 as options. The DPL could be had with any V-8 except the 401.

Both the Matador and Ambassador continued to be refined and updated in terms of luxury. With the exception of the optional Machine Go package, which was only a footnote in the brochure, AMC's emphasis had shifted to convenience and comfort coupled with luxury appointments and adequate moving power.

Although optional dealer-installed low axle ratios were still offered, the standard ratios and transmission choices were geared to economy and cruising. The only three-speed manual transmission available on the Matador was offered on the standard 232 six. The column-mounted Shift-Command automatic was optional and was the only transmission offered on the 258 six in both cars. The Ambassador lost its three-speed manual transmission forever. The four-speed manual with Hurst shifter could be ordered only on the 360 four-barrel and 401 V-8s in the Matador hardtops, and only in conjunction with the Machine Go package. The V-8s in both cars were offered with either the column- or console-shifted automatic. The column shift was standard on the Ambassador 258 six and 304 V-8.

Rear axle ratios were again straightforward. Both sixes had 3.15 ratios as standard, with 3.54s optional. With the exception of the four-speed Matadors and console automatic 401s, all V-8s in both cars had the 2.87 axle as standard, with the 3.15 as the only option. The 401 had just one additional ratio, that being the 3.54.

The mighty Matador Machine four-speeds were a little different. Their standard rear-end ratio was 3.54, with 3.15 and 3.91 as optional. This was also the last year any Matador was offered with the four-speed manual transmission.

Pressure from the insurance companies combined with federal government safety and emissions standards were starting to halt the muscle cars. A four-speed coupled to just about any size V-8 engine meant just one thing to the insurance companies: the vehicle was classified as a muscle car and a premium surcharge was immediately tacked on.

Despite the performance wind-down, AMC continued to upgrade both the Matador and the Ambassador with more safety and convenience items as standard equipment. Some of those items included high-intensity headlights for better roadway lighting, seat and shoulder belts, more easily applied brakes, larger rear brakes on station wagons, suspension refinements for a more comfortable ride and better handling, impact-absorbing front sections that exceeded federal standards, improved exhaust emissions controls, improved automatic transmissions, a more reliable electrical system and fiberglass-belted tires. There were also eleven new exterior color choices offered, along with rich-looking vinyl and fabrics, including a new fabric called Serape on the Matador.

Some of the new options that joined the list were an adjustable air shock rear suspension, 258 six and 401 V-8 engines, improved variable-ratio power steering, air deflectors to help keep rear windows clear and infinitely variable reclining seats. Handling packages still could be had, along with heavy-duty electrical items and trailer towing packages. An array of optional

If the dashboard of the 1972 Matador looked familiar it was because it was borrowed from the 1971 Ambassador.

A new grille was about the only major exterior styling change made on the 1972 Matador. All floor-shift transmissions were deleted, but the big 401 V-8 could still propel the car to high 15s in the quarter-mile.

appearance, convenience and luxury items could turn both cars into unique cruisers.

The 401 Javelin-AMX and Hornet SC/360 spearheaded AMC's performance image for 1971. The Matador had no choice but to take a back seat to these faster and sportier-looking models. Even so, at the end of the model year, production figures for both cars were still good for AMC. The Matador edged out ahead at 45,789 units built. The Ambassador wasn't too far behind with 41,674 units built.

1972

The supercar scene continued its downward spiral for 1972. All manufacturers cut compression ratios down even further, and net horsepower ratings were introduced across the board (some car makers, including Plymouth, had introduced net ratings beginning with the 1971 model year).

Both the Matador and Ambassador came on board for the 1972 model year with few changes. All

Likewise, the dashboard for the 1972 Ambassador was taken from the 1971 Matador. A very odd switch indeed.

exterior dimensions and wheelbases were left unchanged for the two cars. The buyer protection plan was introduced and this improved overall quality control on the assembly line.

Model line-up for the Matador remained the same, with a four-door sedan, four-door station wagon and two-door hardtop available.

The Matador's grille was slightly redesigned. It now consisted of nine thin horizontal bars divided into four sections by three vertical color-keyed bars. The taillights also received their share of redesigning. Eight vertical bars divided each taillight into small rectangles, with the center lens being the back-up light. The center taillight panel was again only slightly altered.

A dual parallel pinstripe was added running the length of the car just below the door handle, turning down at the quarter panel and ending in line with the side-marker light.

The 1972 Ambassador, too, was little changed from its 1971 counterpart, although power drum brakes and 304 V-8 engine were made standard. Power front disc brakes were still optional. With three bright horizontal bars added to the 1971 design, a grid of large square openings was formed on the grille. The Ambassador taillights and center panel also received slight alterations.

Series and model line-ups were cut to just the SST and Brougham, both offered in four-door sedan, four-door station wagon and two-door hardtop. The DPL series, or base Ambassador, was discontinued.

The Ambassador received another slight grille change for 1972. Several features that were formerly optional were made standard.

114

For some reason, the Ambassador switched to the 1971 Matador instrument panel design, and the Matador switched to the 1971 Ambassador design. All exterior emblems for both cars remained in their same locations.

Engine, transmission and axle ratio choices were becoming more straightforward with each passing year. The 232 cubic inch 100 hp six-cylinder engine was standard on the Matador four-door sedan and hardtop, and the 258 ci 110 hp six was optional, standard on the station wagon. The six was discontinued in the entire Ambassador series. The 304 cubic inch 150 hp V-8 was made standard in the Ambassador SST and Brougham, and optional in both cars. The two-barrel 360 produced 175 hp, and the four-barrel version produced 195 when equipped with single exhaust. When dual exhaust was ordered on the four-barrel 360, the horsepower jumped up to 220. The 401 V-8 had one horsepower rating of 255 net. Only the 401 V-8 engine was designated on the fenders of the cars.

For the Matador, the full-synchromesh column-mounted three-speed manual transmission was standard on the 232 six in the sedan and hardtop only. The column-mounted Torque Command was optional. The three-speed manual was available on the 258 six but only for wagons, and the column automatic was optional. The one and only transmission offered on all the V-8s was the column-mounted Torque Command automatic.

Axle ratio availability for the Matador was just as simple. The 3.15 was standard with the 232 six, and the 3.54 was optional. If the car was destined for California, the 3.54 was standard with no option available. If the three-speed manual transmission was behind the 258 six you received a 3.54, with no optional ratio offered. If the automatic was behind the 258 six, the 3.15 was standard with the 3.54 optional. For all the V-8s, a 2.87 was standard and a 3.15 was optional.

The Ambassador's choices were even simpler. AMC listed the column-mounted Torque Command as standard equipment on the 304 V-8 in the SST and Brougham, and it was the only transmission offered on both 360 V-8s and the 401 V-8. For axle ratio availability, the 2.87 was standard and the 3.15 was optional for all V-8s.

When you come right down to it, there was nothing to get excited about for the 1972 model year. This was not happening just at AMC, but throughout the entire domestic auto industry. Manufacturers had to spend a good portion of their time and money on meeting the stringent federal government safety and pollution standards that were getting tougher each year.

Despite all that, both the Matador and Ambassador continued to receive changes and refinements for the sake of comfort, convenience and luxury. The plush Ambassador seats were still made with coil springs. Although both cars lost their luxurious optional consoles with sporty Pistol Grip shifts, new interior vinyls and fabrics were introduced and upgraded for even more of a living-room feel and look. A new Chrysler automatic transmission replaced the old Borg-Warner unit, and all engines received new and revised detail improvements for more efficient operation.

Numerous other small changes were made; AMC boasted of a total of 102 engineering changes made across the board on all its models. It had this to say: "We cut the number of models from 21 to 15. We eliminated 'stripped' models and concentrated on the

1972 AMBASSADOR

Although not as popular as the Matador version, the 1972 Ambassador was available as a police model as well.

models people really want. Starting from scratch with each model, we looked at 17 areas of function, from design to final assembly. Then we put in more quality control steps, more tests and more people to be sure the cars are right when they leave the factory. Overall, we put more time, men and money into this program than anything else we're doing this year." AMC was serious about its quality and overall product building program.

Police Matador

The 1972 Matador was so good that the Los Angeles Police Department (LAPD) chose it for a 500 car fleet on the basis of quality, performance and price. AMC was quick to capitalize on that honor in its advertising.

Road Test had a chance to put one of these torrid LAPD cars through its paces around the training facilities, with the assistance of the terminal island instructors. The car that was used came from American Motors but was built for testing purposes by the LAPD. It was not equipped with the police lights, siren or radio, and looked rather ordinary—just like a plain Matador four-door sedan. It did, however, have the dual A-pillar spotlights, Goodyear Police Special G78x15 blackwall tires, gray vinyl interior with extra-firm bench seats featuring additional springs and padding, and rubber floor mats.

Included was what AMC called the law enforcement package, which was installed on every vehicle sold to police forces. It consisted of heavy-duty engine, transmission, suspension, calibrated speedometer and special seats. The 401 cubic inch 255 net hp four-barrel V-8 engine was used, coupled to a heavy-duty Chrysler-built column-mounted three-speed automatic transmission with a manual low-gear lockout mechanism.

Regular 10-weight engine oil was used in the transmission, and its heavier viscosity helped prolong gearbox life. The car was also delivered with a 3.15:1 rear axle ratio, although many officers preferred the lower 3.54:1 ratio.

The internals of the engine were beefed up considerably to withstand the rigorous punishment dealt to the car. Extra strength was incorporated into the silichrome valves, springs, keepers, oil seals and rocker arms. The Ford Autolite carburetor featured larger throttle bores plus modified jetting and accelerator linkage. Floats were of a different construction, and float level settings were also changed to permit the car to run smoothly and without hesitation during high-speed cornering and hard acceleration. A specially baffled oil pan prevented foaming and loss of oil pressure during a Hollywood-style high-speed chase, if the occasion called for it.

All LAPD cars had air conditioning combined with the heavy-duty cooling system, which included a seven-blade fan, radiator shroud, Dayco DS-7 nonslip fan belt and larger hoses. To keep the extra police lights working at peak efficiency, an 80 amp battery was needed along with a 62 amp alternator.

The chassis and suspension were equally reinforced to handle the added stress and loads imposed on them. Heavier-rate springs and shocks were installed with a rear antisway bar. Both front and rear sway bars were adjustable by the use of mounted spacers. The front strut rods and control arms plus the four rear torque links were made of heavier-gauge steel, and all bushings were encased in separate housings and then pressed into place as a guard against unwanted wear.

Front brakes were power-assisted 10.9 inch discs incorporating a semimetallic bonded lining, and rear

1972 MATADOR

The 1972 Matador Police Model was popular with law enforcement agencies across the country.

brakes were heavy-duty 10x2.5 inch drums giving a total swept area of more than 375 square inches. The discs were made by Kelsey-Hayes and featured full-floating calipers, and the drums had integral wear tabs on the brakeshoes. The discs were vented and the drums were cross-ribbed for adequate cooling.

All critical components on the Matador Police Car were made of a special heat-resistant material for protection against severe usage. Depending on police department destination, either manual or power-assisted steering was used. The LAPD preferred the power-assisted unit in conjunction with Cooper instead of Goodyear tires mounted on stronger steel wheels.

On the interior, the extra-firm bench seats were featured with a thick-rimmed steering wheel which offered good leverage and arm position. A police calibrated speedometer and fuel and temperature gauges were also present.

How did the mighty Matador Police Car perform? Stopping distance from 60 mph was in 140.9 feet at a deceleration g load of 0.838. Interior sound level at 70 mph was seventy-eight decibels. The car also generated a 0.763 g load on the skid pad and could do 0-60 in eight seconds flat. Quarter-mile elapsed time was sixteen seconds flat at 85 mph, with an estimated top speed of 120 mph (not too fast, but remember, you can't outrun the officer's radio). The car was capable of cruising at a constant 120 mph for more than 100 miles with no resulting engine damage. Gas mileage averaged out to about 11.3 mpg for the 3,920 pound Matador.

Overall, the Matador Police Car was quite popular with numerous law enforcement agencies. Here are just a few of the comments made by the driving instructors: "In order to perform safely and satisfactorily, a vehicle's chassis has to combine strength with good handling characteristics. The Matador Police Special does this and, according to the instructors at the LAPD training facility is one of the best handling machines they have driven. . . . The net result of these suspension modifications is a car with almost neutral steering habits. Although the ride is very stiff and choppy, the handling is among the best we've experienced in a sedan as the Matador. . . . In all, it was a confidence-inspiring vehicle to toss around a road course, even a tight one like that used by the Los Angeles Police Department. . . . Policemen claim the Matador's interior comfort is superior to other patrol cars. As examples, they cite excellent legroom and headroom along with superb visibility in all directions."

AMC still offered performance for both cars. Optional equipment was little changed from 1971, and all of the hot Group 19 dealer-installed performance parts were still offered. One performance model available in the Matador line was not well-known. It followed in the footsteps of the optional 1971 Matador Machine Go package and was called the NASCAR equipment package. This package was available only on the two-door hardtop. It was offered to honor Mark Donohue and the Roger Penske racing team in their efforts on the high-speed banked oval NASCAR racing tracks.

The NASCAR equipment included the following: slot-style wheels, E60x15 Polyglas tires, sports steering wheel, bucket seats, handling package and NASCAR decals. Few Matadors ever received this package. AMC promoted this model quite a bit in literature, decals, pins, ticket premiums in race areas, fan club activities, membership cards and NASCAR showroom displays, and even offered buyers a membership in the NASCAR International Club. It was a good program, but unfortunately few people were listening.

After the passing of the 1970 Rebel Machine little was heard about AMC's intermediate in the way of performance, but a 401-powered Matador hardtop was still a formidable foe on the street or on the strip.

Gary Farthing of Odin, Illinois, an AMC enthusiast, wrote to *Hot Rod* magazine telling about his adventures with his 1972 Matador 401 hardtop. The car was equipped with the Torque Command on the column, optional 3.15:1 rear and full power, and had a shipping weight of 3,810 pounds. Right off the showroom floor, the car covered the quarter-mile in 15.09 seconds at 95.4 mph. It ran in NHRA's H/SA class and took home the showroom stock trophy.

After that a few changes were made, including Walker Continental mufflers, a Mr Gasket distributor curve kit, a set of Accel points and N1-Y Champion spark plugs, carburetor accelerator pump moved to its maximum setting and ignition timing set to fourteen degrees initial. With just those simple modifications, the car ran in the mid-fourteens at 100 to 102 mph. *Hot Rod* was so impressed that it titled the brief article "She's Real Fun, My 401." AMC most definitely was not out of the performance game.

Total Matador production for 1972 was almost 10,000 units higher than for 1971, peaking out at 54,813 units. Although the Ambassador's total production for the year was lower at only 44,364 units, it was still roughly 3,000 units more than in 1971.

1973

With the exception of additional federally mandated safety and pollution standards, AMC introduced the 1973 Matador and Ambassador series with few changes. Once again the Matador received a new grille in the form of four groups of narrow rectangles stacked three high with a thin horizontal bar inside each one. The taillight and center panel designs were left basically the same. The same four-door sedan, four-door station wagon and two-door hardtop models were carried over in one series.

The Ambassador SST series was discontinued, and the lone series that remained was the Ambassador Brougham, available in a four-door sedan, four-door station wagon and two-door hardtop. The Ambassador, too, was only slightly redesigned. Although the grille was of the same design it featured thicker vertical and horizontal bars. The front bumper also received a thick rubber impact strip on the upper center edge as wide as the grille itself. As on the Matador, the Ambassador's taillight and center panel designs were virtually unchanged, with new deck trim stripping.

Both cars continued to be refined. The Ambassador now featured a 304 V-8, automatic transmission, power steering, power front disc brakes, AM radio, tinted glass in all windows, whitewall tires, undercoating, hood insulation, remote control outside rearview mirror, visor vanity mirror, deluxe intermittent electric wipers and electric clock. It was without a doubt one of the best buys in its class.

The Matador was also upgraded with new interior colors and fabrics. Just about all dimensions and wheelbases for both cars remained the same. The overall length of the Matador sedan and hardtops increased two inches, and the length of the wagon increased 2.5 inches, all because of the new rubber bumper guards replacing the rubber-faced metal units used previously. The Ambassador wagon also increased two inches in length, and the sedan and hardtop went up one inch.

All exterior emblems and chrome moldings remained the same for both cars. The new plastic red-white-blue corporate logo with AMC spelled out in chrome letters was placed on the left lower rear panel of all models. It appears as though some 1973 Ambassadors had Ambassador scripts placed in the left side of the grille and some did not. The 401 V-8 engine designation on the fenders of both cars continued for 1973.

AMC, like all other manufacturers, incorporated a host of new convenience and safety features into all of its cars. The buyer protection plan was increased to twenty-four months or 24,000 miles for a modest fee, including another option of free trip interruption protection. There were also more than a dozen new manufacturing and testing procedures added to the extensive quality control system already in effect, to further emphasize the company's commitment to quality-built automobiles for customer satisfaction.

Both cars featured a new front and rear telescoping impact-absorbing 5 mph bumper system, which could pass 1974 standards and incorporated body-colored filler panels for a smoother appearance. These bumper systems qualified the cars for collision insurance discounts from several national insurance companies. There were also improvements in engine emissions controls, thus reducing the amount of hydrocarbons emitted into the air. Captive engine mounts were introduced to maintain normal position under torque-rotating conditions, and for greater side-impact protection all cars built after January 1, 1973, incorporated guardrail steel beams inside the doors.

Heating and air conditioning systems were improved, headliners were molded out of fiberglass for better sound absorption resulting in a quieter ride and window crank mechanism gear ratios were changed to reduce crank handle turns from 5.5 to 3.75. There were even more detail improvements such as seat adjusting mechanisms for less operating effort and more positive adjustment. Both cars had reduced-diameter steering wheels and quieter ignition key, seatbelt and headlight warning buzzers, and the use of steel-belted radial tires was extended to all models.

Another slightly redesigned grille was tacked onto the 1973 Matador front end.

The Ambassador hardtop received new slim-shell high-back bucket seats to increase rear seat legroom. Headrests on the Matador were slightly smaller, with a new shape, and were mounted on the top of the seatbacks. Color-keyed wood-grain inside and rear panels were standard on the Ambassador Brougham station wagon and optional on the Matador wagon.

As had generally been the case with AMC models each year, new-style steering wheels, dashboard knobs, wheel covers, interior upholstery vinyls and fabrics, and vinyl tops were introduced for 1973. Exterior colors changed with the wind.

The Matador four-door sedan was once again the choice of the LAPD and numerous other law enforcement agencies across the United States.

AMC's Matador Fare-Master-Taxi, also based on the four-door sedan, became popular with cab companies in many major cities. The car was equipped with numerous standard items such as a 258 six or 360 two-barrel V-8, heavy-duty automatic transmission, heavy-duty front and rear springs and shock absorbers plus rear sway bar, transmission oil cooler, front and rear armrests, dual horns and a host of others. All cars came with the AMC Safe-Command standard features plus the added bonus of being covered under the buyer protection plan. Just about any regular Matador option could be ordered. Another excellent buy.

Engine and transmission choices for all the Matador and Ambassador models were identical in every aspect to the 1972 offerings. Rear axle ratios were slightly different. The only changes made to the Matador were the availability of the 3.15 ratio as optional with the 258 cubic inch six-cylinder engine and three-speed manual column-shift transmission in the station wagon. The only other change was that all V-8s in both cars were now available with the 2.87 as standard and the 3.15 as optional. Starting with 1973, the high-performance dealer-installed rear axle ratios and

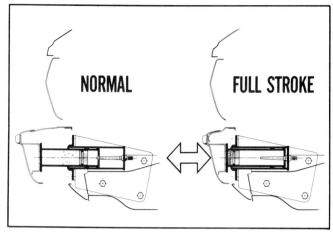

AMC introduced its hydraulic recoverable bumpers on the Matador and Ambassador models.

Group 19 parts were no longer advertised in the brochures.

All in all, 1973 was practically a carbon copy of 1972, except when it came to the production figures. Matador production fell off over 6,000 units for a total of 48,533 units built. Ambassador production was only slightly down, less than 1,000 units, for a total of 43,676 units built for the model year.

1974

The styling of the new 1974 Matador coupe, which replaced the old two-door hardtop, was said to be a direct result of the experiences learned on the NASCAR superspeedways. The old boxy two-door hardtop design had not proven to be aerodynamic enough to compete with the Big Three on the track, so AMC responded with a sleek-looking and aerodynamically efficient body design taken almost directly from one of its former production cars. Which car? The limited-production 1970 AMX/3 mid-engined sports car.

It was the same story for the 1973 Ambassador. Little was done to the car's exterior styling, but ten new features that were formerly optional were made standard.

AMC and Dick Teague could not let the styling of that beautiful sports car just fade away with six units produced. So they incorporated some of its features into a complete new line; from the beltline up, the new Matador coupe replicated the AMX/3. American Motors president William V. Luneburg said, "The introduction of the Matador Coupe means that now we have freshly styled cars for all the market segments in which we compete—cars with appeal for the widest range of buyer preferences."

One feature that looked undesirable to many was the large frog-eyed pods in the hood and grille incorporating the headlights. This feature may have been the only distracting element in an otherwise clean-looking design.

The new Matador was available as a two-door only in three levels—coupe, coupe X and coupe Brougham. It sat on a shorter 114 inch wheelbase compared with the Matador four-door sedan and four-door station wagon, which retained the longer 118 inch wheelbase. The styling on those two models was also completely changed.

The integrated bumper-grille assembly was dropped in favor of conventional separate units. The grille was now of a vertical louver pattern divided in two sections with a vertical bar. It had square headlight bezels with an Argent Silver finish and round parking lights mounted inside the grille inboard of the single headlights. The vertical grille fins, headlight bezels and grille perimeter molding were chromed to accent the new front-end treatment. The front and rear

bumper were of a heavy shelflike design with thick rubber bumper guards on each side.

Side trim for the sedan and wagon ran from behind the front wheelwell at the midsection of the car to the end of the quarter panel just above the side-marker light. This same side molding design was used on the Ambassador Brougham. Taillight design for the sedan was also new in the form of long, wide rectangular units set on each side. For the station wagon, a wide vertical design divided into three sections was featured, with the lower units being the back-up lights.

Matador in block letters was located on the left-side leading edge of the hood, the rear section of the fender wheelwells and the right side of the deck lid. The AMC plastic logo once again adorned all AMC models on the left side of the deck lid or rear panel. All fender V-8 engine designations were dropped. Overall length for the sedan and wagon took a jump to 216 inches. Width and wheel treads remained the same as on the 1973 models.

The Matador coupe was a sleek design, approximately three inches lower than the old Matador hardtop. The overall length of the new coupe was only about one inch longer, and all other exterior dimensions were retained.

The car was built with the traditional long hood-short deck design. The headlight tunnels were sculptured into the hood and the lower theme was continued inside the grille. The grille itself was a crosshatch design made up of horizontal and vertical rectangles, with the parking lights mounted inside

The Matador was completely restyled for 1974. This design remained basically the same right up to the last year of production in 1978.

inboard of the headlights. Front and rear bumpers were of the same design as on the sedan and wagon, with the thick rubber bumper guards. The front and rear bumper vinyl nerfing strips were optional on all Matadors.

Taillight treatment for the new couple was an age-old design that fit the integrated quarter and rear panel assembly perfectly. Twin round taillights were located on each side, both acting as the stop and signal lights. The license plate housing was sculpted into the rear panel and flanked by two back-up lights, one on each side. The rear quarter window and fastback styling were almost identical to those on the AMX/3.

Specials

A very stylish trim package priced at $299 was made available on the Matador coupe Brougham. It was called Oleg Cassini and was designed by the Paris fashion designer himself. The package was marketed in 1974 and 1975, and included custom wheel covers with copper-colored inserts, copper-colored protective side moldings, copper-colored vinyl roof, copper grille and headlight bezels, copper hood and body pinstriping, black-carpeted trunk compartment and tire cover, special black seat and door trim with copper buttons, black headliner and instrument panel with copper dials and overlays, black steering wheel with copper inserts in horn rim and copper-colored floor carpeting. Upholstery was plush, and the individually reclining seats were covered in black nylon knit fabric having a tufted look, which was popular in the late fifties and early sixties. The Oleg Cassini crest was embroidered on each front headrest and medallions were placed on the rear portions of the fender wheelwells just below the beltline.

The base Matador coupe was the stripped model only when compared with the X and Brougham models.

The X coupe included all of the base features plus the 304 V-8, column-mounted automatic transmission, 14x6 slot-styled wheels with trim rings, three-spoke sports steering wheel, blacked-out grille, bodyside and deck lid stripes, and Matador X fender nameplate. The stripes started at the fender tips and tapered out, running the entire length of the car at the beltline and the complete width of the deck lid, forming a wraparound design. A second thinner stripe paralleled the full primary stripe.

The Ambassador in its last year featured standard Abbington fabric upholstery.

The Ambassador too was totally restyled for 1974, which was its last year. Almost every past optional luxury feature was now made standard.

The top-of-the-line Brougham also included all the base model equipment plus the bumper vinyl nerfing strips and full wheel covers.

All coupes had Matador in block letters placed on the rear portions of the fender wheelwells, the left-side leading edge of the hood and the right side of the deck lid. Matador X nameplates replaced all Matador nameplates on that model, and the deck lid stripe Matador X name was die-cut into the decal itself. The Brougham was identified in script on each side of the roof C-pillars. Dashboard and instrument panel layouts were rather sedate looking, with three large square pods facing the driver, similar to the Javelin's, and a pronounced eyebrow containing the instruments, radio, heater and dash switches, and air conditioning outlets. A locking glovebox was to the far right on the passenger's side.

It is unusual for a model to enter its last year totally redesigned, but that's just what happened to the 1974 Ambassador. The two-door hardtop was discontinued and what remained was the four-door sedan and four-door station wagon Brougham models. Wheelbase was retained at 122 inches but overall length was increased seven inches on the sedan to 219.4 and six inches on the wagon to 218.8. Width and wheel treads remained unchanged as did trunk and cargo space. Fuel tank capacities were increased from 19.5 to 21.0 gallons on the sedan and from 20.3 to 24.9 gallons on the wagon.

The grille was of a completely new design and was similar in theme to the Matador sedan's. A fine-grid pattern insert was used, and this was divided horizontally by two thicker bright moldings. The parking lights were set into the grille just inboard of the four-headlight system, and the headlights were set into

The new Matador coupe for 1974 arrived at the end of the supercar era. From the beltline up its styling was borrowed from the limited-production AMX/3 two-seater sports car.

The one-year 401-powered coupe could turn mid-15s to low 16s in the quarter-mile.

square bezels. A chrome molding outlined the entire grille and headlight design. As had been done with the Matador grille, the Ambassador's grille stuck out ahead of the headlights approximately four inches. The Matador sedan had chrome headlight bezels that were blended into the fender design and were visible from the side. The Ambassador's fender was flush with the headlights, which were quite recessed.

Front and rear bumpers were basically Matador design, with rubber bumper guards. The middle section lacked the stripe. The cosmetic body-colored panels between the bumpers and body on both the Matador and Ambassador were removed because of the new and improved energy-absorbing bumper systems. Taillights again were similar to the Matador's.

Ambassador appeared in block letters on the left leading edge of the hood, the right trailing edge of the deck lid and the rear portions of the fenders just behind the wheelwells. Brougham in script adorned the sedan and wagon roof C-pillars, and a standup hood ornament was used. Even a color-contrasting hood pinstripe was featured.

The Ambassador continued to offer one of the most complete standard equipment packages in its class—and even out of its class. In all there were seventy-two various comfort, convenience and road-ability items included as standard items on the Ambassador.

Engine and drivetrain availability on the Ambassador was about as straightforward as you could get. The standard engine and transmission combination was the 304 V-8 and column-mounted Torque Command automatic transmission. The two- and four-barrel 360 V-8s and four-barrel 401 V-8 were the only other engines offered. The only transmission offered for all engines was the column Torque Command, and the rear axle choice was the 3.15 ratio standard, with the 3.54 optional.

With the introduction of the Matador coupe, the line-up for the Matador was quite different. The 232 cubic inch 100 hp six was standard on the four-door sedan, base coupe and Brougham coupe. The larger 258 cubic inch 110 hp six was standard on the wagon and optional on the three previously mentioned models. The 304 V-8 was standard on the Matador X and optional on all others. Both 360 V-8s and the 401 V-8 were optional on all.

Transmission choice was not extensive. The column three-speed manual was standard on the 232 and 258 sixes, with the column Torque Command optional. The three-speed manual was not available on the coupe. The 304 V-8, both 360 V-8s and the 401 V-8 were available with either the column- or floor-mounted Torque Command automatic transmission, but there was a catch: the floor-mounted automatic could be ordered only on the coupe, and the column automatic was standard with the Matador X model.

Rear axle ratios were constant with only one exception. All six and V-8 engines had the 3.15 ratio as standard with the only option being the 3.54 ratio. The only exception was that when the 258 six was coupled to the three-speed manual transmission in the sedan and wagon, only a 3.54 ratio was offered.

There were quite a few new standard features for 1974. The energy-absorbing front and rear bumper systems supposedly reduced low-speed collision cost, but they added quite a bit of weight to the cars, thus hurting gas mileage. The three-point lap belts and shoulder harnesses incorporating the ignition interlock system prevented starting of the car if pressure was sensed on the front seats and the belts were not buckled. It was a nice safety item, but could become very annoying by preventing the car from starting if you put a bag of groceries on the front seat beside you and did not buckle the belt around it.

The induction-hardened exhaust valve seats were installed in the V-8 as well as in the six-cylinder engines for use of low-lead or no-lead gasoline.

The sleek-looking Matador X was introduced at the end of the supercar era. With its low stance and relatively light weight, a 401-powered Matador was capable of supercar performance. Just how capable was something *Road Test* wanted to find out.

The candidates chosen for the shoot-out were a 401 ci 235 hp Matador coupe, 460 ci 215 hp Torino Brougham, 400 ci 150 hp Chevelle Malibu Classic, 350 ci 200 hp Oldsmobile Cutlass Salon and 455 ci 230 hp Buick Regal. All cars except the Chevelle were equipped with four-barrel carburetors and all had

The interior of the 1974 Oleg Cassini Matador coupe featured diamond-tufted-design seats with copper buttons. The same theme was extended throughout the rest of the interior.

three-speed automatic transmissions, power front disc brakes and, with the exception of the Torino, variable-ratio power steering. The Matador was the lightest at 4,055 pounds, and the Torino was the heaviest at 4,615 pounds.

As with the 1968 Javelin SST 343, the Matador 401 shut them all down in the quarter-mile. The Matador scored 15.96 elapsed time at 87.37 mph, with the Regal on the bottom at 16.66 elapsed time at 83.17 mph. In the 0-60 mph test, the Matador again was victorious overall. The Matador and Regal both did 0-60 in 8.5 seconds, edged out only by the Torino which did it in 8.3 seconds. In the 40-60 and 50-70 mph passing speed tests, the mighty Matador once again showed everybody up, although the Torino was able to equal its 50-70 mph time of 5.4 seconds.

The Matador's braking power was equally impressive. Only the Torino and Cutlass were able to beat it, and by only nine and two feet, respectively.

Road tests

Super Stock and Drag Illustrated also road tested a Matador coupe equipped with the 401 V-8. Its version was a loaded-down X coupe with the 401 four-barrel V-8, Torque Command automatic on the floor, 3.54 Twin-Grip rear, air conditioning, power steering, power front disc brakes, handling package and so on.

The testing staff liked the overall layout of the interior, citing its convenient controls. The car's new exterior styling received mixed reviews from both the staff and onlookers. One passerby asked, "What . . . is that, a Ferrari or something?"

The transmission performed up to expectations, and the handling of the X coupe was described in this manner: "Over the road, the Matador X test car was a sweetheart." The variable-ratio power steering and power front disc brakes also received high marks. The overall road package was much liked by the staff, which said, "Driving the 401 4-Barrel Matador X is pure, unadulterated fun, a commodity that hasn't been associated with new cars for a couple of years, and especially with the AMC Matador."

Even though the 401 V-8 was bogged down with every type of emissions control required at the time, its performance surprised everyone. With absolutely no modifications, the Matador was run half a dozen times down the quarter-mile into a prevailing head wind and was able to record a best elapsed time of 15.38 seconds at 94.26 mph. The staff reacted this way: "We came away with a slight case of blown mind, because we honestly didn't think the car would do that well under the prevailing weather conditions, and we're convinced that there is a great deal of potential in the Matador 401 package for the tinkerer who is willing to spend the time."

The *Road Test* staff were so impressed with the 401 coupe against the other intermediates that they decided to conduct another test on the car a few months later, this time by itself. The Matador was once again praised for its handling, smooth ride and power. They found the power of the 401 Matador to be just about on par with the sixties supercar and very good for a typical emissions-equipped car: "When you drive away the engine not only pulls well but does so willingly and anxiously, which is quite a switch from the flaccid, even grudging, performance typical of today's emissions controlled engines, which you have to practically beat with a stick to make them hurry."

The car tested was again a heavily optioned out model consisting of the 401 V-8, floor-shift automatic transmission. With a curb weight of 4,070 pounds, the car was able to cover the quarter-mile in 16.17 seconds at 87.60 mph. Zero-to-sixty time was quite good at 8.5 seconds.

Although it was a little difficult for a tall person to get into the back of the car, its comfort was summed up this way: "As a people hauler, the Matador is on the whole a highly pleasant car."

The Matador proved to be a very efficient car, as *Road Test* concluded with these statements: "As for its direct competitors, the intermediates offered by the Big 3, the Matador can do a pretty good job of holding its own on a feature for feature basis. Against its sisters from Detroit, this belle of Kenosha has the charm of a fresh, clean, pretty face and the solid virtue of AMC's Buyer Protection Plan to woo would be buyers."

The 401 Matador coupe was only a one-year combination, for after 1974 the 401 V-8 was dropped from passenger car use. It is reported, however, that eighty-nine 1975 Matadors, probably four-door police sedans, were produced and sold, and recent information indicates that four of those cars were Matador coupes.

Matador production jumped in 1974. There were 99,922 units built, including 6,165 Oleg Cassini coupes. Only 1,817 units of the same designer series were built for the 1975 model year.

Total Ambassador production for 1974 was a dismal 24,971 units, down almost half from the previous year. The Ambassador was quietly put to rest, but the Matador continued until model year 1978, when it too bit the dust to make way for the increasingly popular compact and subcompact domestic and foreign models.

Chapter 7

Hornet and Gremlin 1970-74

In 1969, Roy D. Chapin, Jr., chief executive officer of AMC, announced that the company would launch an entirely new car every six months until 1972. The Hornet would be that car, and it also would be AMC's new compact car for the seventies, replacing the aging Rambler American series of 1964-69. The Hornet name was resurrected from the racing Hudson Hornets that terrorized the NASCAR tracks in the early to mid-fifties.

1970

It was no accident that the Hornet's interior and exterior dimensions were close to those of the model it was replacing. Wheelbase was only two inches larger at 108 inches, overall length rivaled the Ramber American's at 179.3 inches, height was set at 52.4 inches and width was set at 71.1 inches. Front and rear treads for six-cylinder cars were 57.5 and 57 inches, respectively. Front tread on V-8 models was only slightly narrower. The trunk compartment was quite spacious for a car of its size at 11.2 cubic feet.

Hornet

As Chevrolet was with its SS designation, AMC was liberal with its SST badging, extending it to the new compact. The Hornet was available in two series, called the base Hornet and the Hornet SST, both offered in two- and four-door sedans only. Shades of the Vixen and Cavalier from the Project IV Tour could

The new Hornet for 1970 replaced the 1969 Rambler. Shades of the Vixen from the Project IV show cars were evident in the model's front end and overall styling. This is the base two-door sedan model.

be readily seen in the front- and rear-end styling of the Hornet.

The grille was of a horizontal thin-rib wrap-around design. It was blacked-out and contained two headlights with the parking lights just inboard of them. The side-marker lights were recessed into the wrap-around end caps. Taillight treatment was just as simple, with large horizontally divided rectangular wrap-around units that were as wide as the back panel itself.

The SST version had an aluminum machined rear panel pattern. Front and rear bumpers were of a simple design and, as on the Rambler American, were interchangeable.

Hornet in block letters appeared on the front portions of the fenders and right rear panel, preceded by a flying Hornet medallion. The square AMC logo was placed on the left side of the rear panel, and SST letters adorned the roof C-pillars on that model. The 304 V-8 was designated on the rear sections of the quarter panels.

The base Hornet was just about as plain as you could get, with practically no chrome moldings or trim. The SST was handsomely done with wheelwell and rocker panel moldings, drip rail moldings, and chrome trim around the two-door sedan's window frame and B-pillar.

The car also had unique large-diameter front and rear protruding wheelwell arches, which blended in nicely with the overall body design, but were vulnerable to those nasty parking lot dings.

Engine line-up for the newest AMC car was conservative. The 199 cubic inch 128 hp six-cylinder engine was standard in the base Hornet. The 232 ci 145 hp one-barrel six was optional in the base Hornet and standard in the SST. The two-barrel version of the same engine producing ten more horsepower was optional in both the base and SST models. The lone optional V-8 was the 304 ci two-barrel 210 hp engine, and that was supposed to be available only in the SST, although a few base Hornets were equipped with it.

Transmission and rear axle choices were again plain. The column-shift three-speed manual and column Shift-Command automatic transmissions were offered on the 199 and 232 ci 145 hp six-cylinder engines. The 155 hp six and 304 V-8 were offered only with the column Shift-Command automatic.

The 3.08 rear axle ratio was standard and a 3.31 was optional on all engine and transmission combinations except the 232 ci 145 hp six Shift-Command automatic and 304 V-8. On the 232 ci 145 hp six, the 2.37 ratio was standard with a 2.73 optional. This was a carry-over from the economy package offered on the 1968-69 Rambler American. The 304 V-8's standard ratio was 2.87, with the 3.15 optional.

A hot Hornet equipped with the 360 cubic inch V-8 was almost launched in the winter of 1970 as a limited edition model to follow in the footsteps of the 1969 Hurst SC/Rambler. Management decided, however, to extend it to the Rebel series, thus creating the 1970 Rebel Machine. Although the Hornet came on board in its first year as a sedate model, it too would get a chance at an appearance in the supercar market the following year.

A Hornet equipped with the 304 V-8 was also a strong performer. AMC stated in its main brochure, "If you get the big engine, you can go from 0 to 60 in 10 seconds flat." That same time had been used to advertise the 1966 Rambler Marlin equipped with the 327 cubic inch 270 hp four-barrel V-8. As with the Marlin in 1966, no transmission or rear axle ratio was specified. It would be safe to assume that AMC was referring to the Hornet equipped with the optional 3.15 ratio.

AMC offered an extensive choice of convenience, appearance and luxury items on its new compact. Exterior Lustre-Gard choices were abundant, with color-coordinated pinstriping and vinyl roofs offered in three colors. Interior fabrics and vinyls were plush, and individually reclining front seats could be ordered. Power steering, power brakes or power front disc brakes for the V-8 could make vehicle maneuverability and stopping easier and safer. Optional tire sizes up to a D70x14 redline could be had with an array of different-style wheel covers. Air conditioning, tinted glass, and convenience light and visibility group options could make life on the road more pleasant, and the insulation group and antiscuff side molding could further protect your pride and joy from rusting or getting parking lot dings.

Although there was no performance engine available for the Hornet, the customer could order the Twin-Grip rear, handling package, heavy-duty cooling system and cold-start package. With a few basic hot rod modifications to a 304 V-8 Hornet plus the heavy-duty factory items discussed earlier, the car was definitely a competitive junior supercar.

Road tests

As with any new compact car or intermediate introduced at the time, the popular magazines wasted no time in evaluating the AMC Hornet. *Car and Driver* was one of the first to check out a two-door SST equipped with the 304 V-8, column Shift-Command automatic transmission and 2.87:1 Twin-Grip rear. The car was only mildly optioned out with power steering, power brakes, vinyl roof, air conditioning and AM push-button radio.

This car was a preproduction prototype model assembled on a makeshift assembly line from early production parts, mainly to see if all the parts fit together properly as engineered. As a result, a full-fledged road test was not conducted.

Car and Driver's first impression of the car's styling was good. Its staff had this to say: "It's very smooth and clean and its attractiveness lies in the basic body shape rather than in clever use of add-on trim. It's big on tumblehome, as is the current trend, but the greenhouse flows smoothly into the body sides rather than having shoulders like most American cars."

They also liked the general interior layout, but felt the car was slightly overweight at 3,198 pounds. They said that "because of the Hornet's mass and because AM engines are invariably modest in their output, acceleration is pleasant but not exciting."

The road test was conducted in the fall of 1969, and even then a prototype Hornet 360 must have existed as evidenced by this statement: "Thrill seekers are advised to be patient until January when AM will turn loose a super Hornet packing a 360 cubic inch V-8." But the thrill seekers would have to wait until the fall of 1970.

Car and Driver's staff felt the handling of the car was adequate but could have used quite a bit of improvement: "Handling is secure in normal maneuvers, but the variable-ratio steering quickens alarmingly as you turn and will require some getting used to." Braking power was also not up to par.

When compared with the Maverick, Valiant and Nova, the Hornet was just about in the middle, with the Maverick being on the bottom and the Valiant and Nova toward the top. The Hornet's interior dimensions were more than generous when compared with the competition's.

Road and Track's impression of the new Hornet was both good and bad. The model tested was an SST four-door sedan equipped with the optional 232 cubic inch 145 hp six coupled to the column Shift-Command automatic transmission and superhigh 2.37:1 rear axle ratio. A supercar it was not.

Road & Track praised the car's exterior styling: "It has the lean, efficient look we like so much in the best continental sedans. To our eyes, it's a better looking automobile than its direct competitor, the Ford Maverick." It went on comparing the Hornet with the Maverick, giving it high marks for its comfortable front seats and its tasteful layout of the dashboard and full-width parcel tray underneath.

The instrument panel contained three medium-size round gauges; centrally located radio, ashtray and heater-air conditioning controls; and a lockable glovebox on the right side. Rear seat legroom was rated excellent and the car was said to have a "satisfactory ride," again better than the Maverick's.

After mentioning so many positive aspects about the car, *Road & Track* made an about-face and agreed with *Car and Driver* that the handling of the car was only adequate. Apparently the car had excessive understeer, and the power steering unit was so slow that even parking became a tedious chore. *Road & Track* also agreed with *Car and Driver* that the small nine-inch brakes were not adequate, saying, "We rated the Hornet's brakes as poor, the only car we've tested in 1969 to get that overall rating."

Acceleration and performance also received a poor rating: "As it was we got nothing more neck-snapping than a 20.0-sec standing quarter-mile—which is just barely adequate for getting out of your own way in typical rush-hour traffic." The car covered the quarter-mile with a terminal speed of 68 mph and did 0-60 in 15.7 seconds.

The car averaged about 20 mpg, which *Road & Track* did not think was too good for a car of its size. With the right factory options, the magazine's staff agreed that the car could be made to perform and handle quite well.

This Hornet was not a muscle car by any means, but *Road & Track* concluded its test with this statement: "The Hornet is a perfectly satisfactory transportation package and will undoubtedly give thousands and thousands of miles of faithful service."

There are, however, two sides to this story. *Motor Trend* conducted a three-way-comparison road test of the Hornet, Ford Maverick and Plymouth Duster. The Hornet was the clear-cut winner in almost every category tested. All three cars were economy models. The Maverick and Duster were available in two-door models only, and *Motor Trend* compared them both with the Hornet four-door sedan.

The Hornet had the optional 232 cubic inch 145 hp six coupled to the column automatic and 2.37 final-drive-ratio rear. The Duster had the optional 225 cubic inch 145 hp slant six, also with a column automatic, and a 2.76 rear. The Maverick had the smallest engine at 200 cubic inches and 120 hp. It too had the column automatic but was equipped with deeper 2.83 rear end gears.

The 1970 SST version had more trim than the base model. The car sported extra-large wheelwells and was elegant looking from any angle. This model is equipped with the 304 V-8, which was the largest option for that year.

All three cars had power steering and none had power drum brakes. The Maverick was the lightest at 2,497 pounds and the Duster was the heaviest at 3,260 pounds. The Hornet fell right in the middle at 2,870 pounds. The Hornet and Duster had 108 inch wheelbases and the Maverick had only a 103 inch wheelbase. All other exterior dimensions were about the same on all three cars.

Another road test of a four-door Hornet, conducted by *Car Life*, gave the car mixed but favorable reviews. The model tested was an SST version equipped with the 304 V-8, automatic transmission, 2.87 non-Twin-Grip rear, variable-ratio power steering, Solex glass, vinyl roof and Decor group. With these options the car was brought up to a price of $3,026 from a base price of $2,221.

The one big disadvantage the V-8 Hornet had was weight distribution—fifty-nine percent front and forty-one percent rear would explain its somewhat unpredictable handling. Its new twin ball-joint front suspension for 1970 contributed to the car's ability to control its nose-heavy attitude.

Car Life rated the car's ride as fair and judged its overall handling as acceptable despite its weakness. The brakes did not perform the way they should have, and it was felt that the small D-78 tires were not adequate for this size car when equipped with the V-8 engine.

The Gremlin came on board as a 1970½ model in April 1970, roughly six months ahead of the competition. The chopped-off back was taken from the 1967 AMX-GT show car, which also used a modified 1968 AMX front end. The car was restricted to six-cylinder power and was available in a two- or four-seat version.

The testing staff did praise the rich look and quality of the interior and the versatility of the individually reclining front seatbacks. Dashboard layout, including the instrument panel and switch accessibility, was well received and rated.

Although the car's performance was not spectacular, it was rated as equal to that of a Pontiac Tempest or Buick Skylark equipped with the 350 V-8. With a curb weight of 3,120 pounds, its 0-60 time of 10.1 seconds was close enough to its advertised time, and it was able to cover the quarter-mile in 17.5 seconds at 80 mph flat. With the 304's 16.3 mpg figure (compared with the six-cylinder's 19 mpg figure), the V-8 was a good choice.

Production output at the end of the 1970 model year was a healthy 73,548 units built, of which only 100 base Hornets were equipped with the 304 V-8. Some of those could well have been modified by their owners into innocent-looking super sleeper sedans, since the optional dealer-installed and Group 19 high-power parts could be ordered on any Hornet V-8.

Gremlin

Now that AMC had its new compact for the seventies, it, as well as GM, Ford and Chrysler, began to eye yet another profitable segment of the automobile market. This segment was called the people's car, and it was best exemplified by Volkswagen's Beetle. The Volkswagen was introduced to the United States in 1949. It dominated the subcompact, or minicar, market for over a decade before any serious competition challenged it.

As early as the mid- to late sixties, the Big Three plus American Motors were all working on their own versions of the minicar for introduction in the early seventies, or sooner if possible. Chevrolet was working on the Vega, which resembled a scaled-down version of the 1970-73 Camaro. Ford was busy with its new Pinto, which slightly resembled the Maverick, introduced a year earlier. Chrysler used existing mini models manufactured in Japan and introduced them under the badges of Dodge Colt and Plymouth Cricket.

American Motors also took advantage of existing models to cut down on tooling costs and shorten the length of design and introduction time, as it had with the 1968 Javelin and AMX. The final design was introduced on April 1, 1970, roughly eighteen months after Dick Teague made his first sketch on a Northwest Orient motion sickness bag in June 1968. It made its debut as a midyear model, about six months ahead of the competition, and was labeled the 1970½ Gremlin. The car was the second in a series of new models promised every six months.

From the trailing edge of the door, forward, the car's styling was almost all Hornet with its own hood and grille design, and even those were interchangeable. The rear-end styling could be traced back to the 1967 AMX/GT show car, which used a modified 1968-70 production AMX front end.

Two other styling concepts had been tried for the Gremlin design. The first, called the Wasp, had more or less the same dimensions but was conventionally styled and had nothing really new to offer. The second, the Stinger, also conventionally styled, sat on a six-inch-longer wheelbase. Both were finally rejected in favor of the AMX/GT styling.

The rear-end styling of the car was controversial, and was the target of industrywide humor. The slanted kammback theme angled about a foot or so behind the bottom portion of the rear wheelwell opening to a point on the roof about even with the rear wheel centerline.

Only two models were offered, a two-passenger commuter with storage area in the rear, and a four-passenger version with fold-down rear seat which did not have much rear legroom. The car also featured a flip-up rear window on the four-passenger model only, and a fixed rear body panel instead of a more desirable swing-down tailgate.

The Gremlin sat on a ninety-six-inch wheelbase, which was only one inch shorter than the two-seater AMX's. The VW had a shorter 94.5 inch wheelbase, and it was a little over seven inches taller than the Gremlin, which was set at a low 51.8 inches. Width for the Gremlin was 70.6 inches compared with the VW's 61.0 inch width, and the Gremlin edged out the VW in length by only 2.6 inches, with an overall dimension of 161.2 inches. Front/rear tread dimensions of the Beetle were 51.6/53.1 to the Gremlin's wider 57.2/56.6 stance.

The Gremlin really shined with its turning radius, which was a scant thirty-two feet, eight inches compared with the VW's thirty-six-foot radius. Another aspect of the Gremlin that readily stood out was its cruising range. With a twenty-one-gallon gas tank coupled to an approximately 23 mpg, the car could go almost 500 miles on one tank of gas.

The VW had 7.3 cubic feet of usable luggage space to the Gremlin's smaller six-cubic-foot capacity. The Gremlin was also about 762 pounds heavier than the Beetle, a comparison AMC did not like to emphasize.

The car's grille design was wraparound, like the Hornet's, and contained a blacked-out-center rectangular oval pattern with a silver finish on the outside. Parking lights were inside the oval just inboard of the headlights, and the side-marker lights were set into the wraparound fairing ends. Front and rear bumpers were shared with the Hornet, as were the large wheel-well openings.

The rectangular rear depression panel contained recessed rectangular taillights and center-placed gas cap with a defined arch at the top. Immediately above the arch was a T-handle controlling the flip-up window.

The Gremlin's hood was slightly different than the Hornet's but was also interchangeable. A raised sculpture ran almost the complete length of the hood's center section. The same flush-type door handles used on all other AMC cars were used on the Gremlin and Hornet, minus the integrated locking key cylinders, which were placed immediately below.

Gremlin in script was placed on the left leading edge of the hood and also on the sail panels between the two angular body depressions. A chrome Gremlin cartoon character adorned the front sections of the fender and the gas cap. The square AM log was just above the flip-up window's handle.

The dashboard was the same as on the Hornet, except that the instrument panel used only two round gauges instead of three, set into its own oval design.

Because of the Gremlin's extra-short wheelbase, the rear semi-elliptic leaf springs were of a new design modified from the conventional units. They were quite short, and the spring hanger at the rear portion of the leaves was set so far back it almost attached to the bumper.

The Gremlin was restricted to six-cylinder power for its first half model year. The V-8 version had to wait roughly eighteen months for the fall introduction of the 1972 models. The 199 ci 128 hp six was standard, with the only option being the larger 232 ci 145 hp one-barrel carburetor version.

The three-speed column shift was standard on the base engine, with the column Shift-Command automatic optional. The 232 had a three-speed manual on the floor as standard, with the column automatic and the column automatic with air conditioning as options.

The 2.73 rear axle was standard on the 199 and automatic transmission, air-conditioning-equipped 232, with a 3.08 optional for both. The 232 three-speed came standard with a 3.08, and a 3.31 was optional. If you checked off the column Shift-Command automatic for the 232, the high 2.37 was standard and the 2.73 was optional.

Although the Gremlin was relegated to six-cylinder power only, it performed well because of its

The new Gremlin interior was patterned after the Hornet. It used two, as opposed to three, round dials for the instrument panel. The rear seatback folded down for additional cargo space. The Gremlin cartoon character was a unique feature.

light curb weight of approximately 2,635 pounds. In the Gremlin brochure, AMC claimed a 0-60 time of 15.3 seconds with manual transmission for the 199 cubic inch six. It described this as "the kind of pickup you need for expressway driving." AMC also claimed 15.8 seconds for the automatic. Even quarter-mile elapsed times and speeds were cited. The 199 three-speed could do it in 19.7 seconds at 67 mph, and the automatic took twenty seconds flat at 66 mph. Top speed was said to be 95 mph. The 232 version was even faster.

The Gremlin had a long standard features list that was similar to the Hornet's, including the dual pinstripes running from the fender tips to the rear portions of the doors above the door handles, sweeping up and following the fixed rear window contours and ending at the roof drip rails. The pinstripes could be matched with any one of thirteen Lustre-Gard exterior colors offered. An optional thick tapered rally stripe that ran inside the pinstripes' boundaries could be ordered in red, white or black.

Options for the car were plentiful. The customer could order power steering, power brakes, Twin-Grip rear, handling package and heavy-duty cooling. An interior appointment group, visibility group, air conditioning group, light group, radio, tinted glass, roof travel rack, engine block heater and insulation group were just a few more options. Optional appearance and trim items included bucket seats in pleated vinyl, custom steering wheel, custom interior and exterior trim packages, wheel discs and vinyl insert antiscuff side molding. The standard 6.00x13 inch polyester cord tires could be replaced with 6.45x14 inch tires or with larger B78x14 fiberglass-belted tires, which were standard on air-conditioned models.

At the time of the Gremlin's introduction, it was the smallest, lowest-priced model at $1,879 for the two-seater and $1,959 for the four-seater, and it had the best gas mileage of any production car made in America.

Road tests

As is usual with first-year models of any car, numerous road tests were performed by the various magazines for a complete evaluation of the car's characteristics and capabilities. *Rod and Custom* was able to test one equipped with the 232 six, three-speed on the floor and standard 3.08 rear axle ratio. It also mounted on a set of Cragar SS wheels with fat (for the Gremlin) F70x14 Goodyear Polyglas raised-white-letter tires. Although it was felt these two items could have improved the handling of the car, they actually hurt it because they added unsprung weight to the standard suspension. But they did made the car look great.

The Gremlin's handling was touchy and the car had built-in understeer. In the words of *Rod and Custom*, "As it comes off the showroom floor, even with its top of the line, three-on-the-floor shift and 232-inch optional six the Gremlin is no sports car. Sporty, yes;

nimble, definitely but a sports car, no." The magazine summed up the car's handling as follows: "The larger tires felt good on gravel and dirt roads but on any washboard the extra weight, coupled with stock shock absorbers created an uncomfortable skittering and jounce at the rear end. Disconcerting!" The Gremlin needed help in the handling department.

Rod and Custom staff also felt that the two-seater version would have limited appeal in the market unless someone was looking for an absolute bare-bones, no-frills means of transportation. Their version of the ideal Gremlin that would probably appeal to most buyers was one equipped with the 232 six, Shift-Command automatic with air conditioning and 3.08 rear end gearing. To make the car handle better, the buyer should order the handling package consisting of heavy-duty springs and shocks plus front sway bar and the larger B78x14 fiberglass-belted tires. Aftermarket adjustable shocks were also recommended. The variable-ratio power steering was another worthwhile option, as the standard steering box was too slow even in a car of this size. Bucket seats along with the interior appointment group could make living inside much easier. Finally, *Rod and Custom* recommended hopping up the six-cylinder with aftermarket items such as carburetors, headers and whatever else was popular at the time.

Rod and Custom was impressed with the Gremlin, saying, "The Gremlin is a nice car, a lot of car for the 'under $2,000' price tag and an intriguing platform on which to build a wild sleeper of a street machine. Especially if you're an apple-pie-and-mom, True Blue patriot and wouldn't buy foreign even if. . . ."

Motorcade borrowed the same Gremlin from *Rod and Custom*, complete with the Cragar SS wheels and F70x14 tires, and apparently was just as impressed with the little sportster. *Motorcade* concluded its test by saying, "We suspect that Gremlin and the other forthcoming Bugbombs will fail to stop the Beetles and the public still will be all the better for it. We'd like to see Detroit automakers, just once, produce a car that could stand on its own." Although it was not known at the time, *Motorcade* was absolutely right: the Gremlin was never able to put a dent in VW sales.

Car Life's full-fledged road test of the Gremlin came a few months later, and the staff decided to load it up with options. The magazine's first impressions of the car were not favorable, especially when driving the car from the dealer to the *Car Life* offices, as its handling and braking created some dangerous situations. In the staff's opinion, the rather large sail panels created obscure vision, right and left, although the use of the rearview mirror more than compensated for this. *Car Life* agreed that a tailgate should have been designed into the rear because it required more than a three-foot lift off the ground to clear the tailgate wall.

Because the car was so heavily optioned out, its test weight jumped up to 3,200 pounds. With a sixty percent front and forty percent rear weight distribution, corners could not be taken too fast or disaster could easily strike. Handled with moderation, the Gremlin was a pleasure to drive. You got into trouble only if you started pushing the car, and that was also the case with the VW.

As did the three early cars tested, this Gremlin still had "gremlins" inside of it. During the brake testing the car swerved and stalled, and the rear drums locked up. Worse yet, the oil warning light still came on, indicating a definite engineering problem that should have been remedied as a result of the earlier tests. Another problem was the throttle linkage sticking as you depressed the pedal, causing the car to jerk. The car's automatic transmission was rated good, but its gas mileage was a poor and disappointing 16.8 mpg. Although the car was equipped with the 2.73:1 axle ratio its numerous options added too much weight, which pulled the car out of the economy class.

Acceleration, however, was brisk. The car was able to jump from zero to sixty in 12.5 seconds and covered the quarter-mile in 18.6 seconds at a speed of 73.8 mph. At least it had the VW beat in that area.

In the name of economy and practicality, AMC built an experimental Gremlin equipped to run on both natural gas and conventional gasoline. Five 100 cubic foot capacity gas storage cylinders hooked up in parallel with a switch, were squeezed into the car, allowing it an additional driving range of 100 miles.

Total production for the first midyear Gremlin was 26,209 units, which included both two- and four-passenger versions.

1971

Since the Hornet and Gremlin had been totally new for 1970, few changes were made to both cars appearancewise for the 1971 model year. The 1971 Hornet was available in a six-model line-up consisting of two- and four-door sedans in the basic and SST series, a high-performance SC/360 two-door sedan and the new four-door Sportabout station wagon. The Sportabout was the third and last new model in the series, despite AMC's earlier promise to release a new model every six months until 1972. The Sportabout name was not new, having been used by Dodge in the early fifties to designate its Wayfarer roadster series, which was the convertible.

The Hornet's exterior dimensions and wheelbase for the sedans were carry-overs. The Sportabout had the sedan's exterior dimensions plus a 58.3 cubic foot storage capacity with an additional 3.8 cubic feet of underfloor storage as a bonus feature.

The grille was of the same basic design except the horizontal ribs were now highlighted in silver, and the clear parking light lenses were replaced with amber-colored units containing a chrome three-bar-encircled design on the surface. A similar facelift was also given to the Gremlin front end. Out back, the plain body-colored gas cap was replaced with a large diecast plated

The Hornet's styling for 1971 was little changed. The SST four-door sedan was the series' luxury compact.

131

cap bearing the flying Hornet emblem. Nameplates and exterior chrome trim were virtually unchanged.

Inside, high-back vinyl-trimmed front seats were standard on the Hornet two- and four-door sedans as well as on the two-door SST. Interior door panels for both the Gremlin and Hornet had a new deep embossed pattern, and the armrests were redesigned and repositioned for added comfort and convenience. Also shared was a small brake pedal on automatic transmission models which gave more footroom, and a redesigned steering wheel which gave the driver more thighroom.

The Sportabout was all new. It was a direct descendant of the 1967 AMX III show car, and it retained a good portion of the show car's side window treatment. It came standard with such features as a carpeted cargo area, rear liftgate, cargo compartment lock and space-saver spare. Sportabout in script appeared on both quarter panels.

There was also a Sportabout D/L (deluxe) package, which included individual reclining seats with Serape fabric upholstery or vinyl trim, Serape fabric on door panels, sports steering wheel with Rim-Blow, custom wheel covers, roof rack with integral rear air deflector, wood-grain instrument cluster trim, translucent wood-grain side and rear panels, and D/L decals.

Specials

A one-of-a-kind Sportabout was designed by internationally known Italian designer Dr. Aldo Gucci. Six months were spent customizing the car's interior and exterior to provide a pullout writing desk, a picnic table, a fitted vanity case and a pair of folding center armrests that housed a variety of games. The model used was powered by a 304 V-8 with automatic transmission and had a modified machine-turned rear panel design. Gucci in block letters preceded the quarter panel Sportabout scripts.

The limited-production SC/360 picked up where the Rebel Machine left off, just as the Machine had picked up where the Scrambler had left off. The car

listed for only $2,663. Like its ancestors, it included a host of high-performance features as standard equipment, such as 360 ci 245 hp two-barrel V-8, full-synchromesh three-on-the-floor manual transmission, heavy-duty clutch, 14x6 eight-slot mag-styled wheels without trim rings, D70x14 Goodyear Polyglas tires, Space Saver spare, individually reclining seats, lower rear deck red plastic reflective panel and unique SC/360 rally side and deck stripes.

The side stripes, available in black, white or red, started at the fender tips, tapered out and ran the length of the car above the door handles, and then swept up behind the roof C-pillars and joined in the middle of the deck just forward of the deck lid to form one complete stripe. As on the Gremlin, a pinstripe paralleled the rally stripe, and SC/360 was die-cut into the rally stripe at the rear portions of the fenders.

The SC/360 was potent enough in standard form, and could be optioned out to be even more powerful. Items that could be ordered included the 360 cubic inch 285 hp four-barrel V-8, four-speed manual transmission with Hurst shifter, Ram-Air induction with flat-black-finish hood scoop, dual exhausts, tachometer, handling package and D70x14 Goodyear Polyglas raised-white-letter tires. The same items made up the Go Package when the automatic Shift-Command on the column was ordered instead of the four-speed.

As the supercar scene began to wind down for 1971, AMC advertised the SC/360 with this title: "Introducing a sensible alternative to the money-squeezing, insurance-strangling muscle cars of America. The Hornet SC/360." The concluding statement said it all: "As a leading car magazine has said 'the day of the heavy 400-cube, 400-horsepower supercar may be just about over." AMC was so right.

The little Gremlin also came in to 1971 with a sporty-type model, called the Gremlin X. It was a $300 or $334.35 package, depending on tire sidewall choice. The Gremlim X could be ordered on the four-passenger model only and consisted of body-colored grille, 14x6 eight-slot mag-style wheels without trim rings, D70x14 black or raised-white-letter Polyglas tires, custom interior appointments, front bucket seats

The hot 1971 SC/360 Hornet two-door sport sedan was AMC's first junior supercar since the 1969 Hurst SC/Rambler. With the optional 285 hp 360 four-barrel V-8 engine, the car was capable of turning low 14s at almost 100 mph in the quarter-mile.

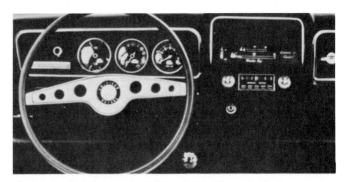

The dashboard layout of the SC/360 was just about stock Hornet with its own Rim-Blow sports steering wheel and optional four-speed transmission with Hurst shifter.

in pleated vinyl, engine-turned instrument cluster, Space Saver spare, three-on-the-floor manual transmission and special Gremlin X rally side stripes.

The standard two- and four-door sedan Gremlins were still offered, but base prices rose to $1,899 and $1,999, respectively. The dual struts that supported the liftgate on the four-passenger model were replaced with a single spring cylinder.

The standard thick rally side stripe was of the same design as in 1970, but the Gremlin X side stripe was new. It ran slightly lower, out of the body sculpture, but still above the door handles. The quarter panel design was different. It went wider just after the door line and remained rectangular going back, but ended in a knife-edge. A pinstripe again paralleled the rally stripe, and Gremlin X in script was die-cut into the stripe itself. The two angular body depressions on each sail panel were outlined with dual pinstripes as part of the X package.

There were also rear panel stripes used on the Gremlin X, and for the first time AMC used engine liter decals. These were placed to the left of the right taillight on the rear panel. The 232 six used a 3.8 liter, and the new 258 six used 4.2 liter.

Both the Gremlin and Hornet sported a new engine line-up for their new model years. The 199 ci six was retired and the larger 232 ci 135 hp six was standard in the Gremlin, base Hornet, SST and Sportabout, with the new 258 ci 150 hp six optional. The 304 V-8 was optional only on the Hornet SST and Sportabout, and the two- and four-barrel 360 V-8s were restricted to the Hornet SC/360.

When under the hood of the Gremlin, the 232 six was offered with the column and floor three-speed manual or column automatic. The floor-shift three-speed manual was the only one not offered on the 232 Hornet. It was, however, offered on both the Gremlin and Hornet, along with the column automatic, for the 258 six. The 304 V-8 could be had only with the column automatic, and both 360 V-8s came standard with the floor-shift manual three-speed or optional column-mounted automatic. The four-speed manual box with Hurst shifter was optional on the four-barrel 360 V-8.

Vehicle weight and wheelbase can have a big effect on a car's performance. Thus the final drive ratio must be tailored to the car for maximum and efficient operation. With the Gremlin, the manual 232 offered the 2.73 ratio as standard, with the 3.08 and

The new 1971 Hornet Sportabout combined the best of the sedan and station wagon body styles. The new model featured a large 58.3 cubic foot storage capacity with an added 3.8 cubic foot underfloor storage.

3.31 as options. In the Hornet, the manual was offered with a 3.08 standard and a 3.31 optional. In both cars, if the automatic was ordered without air conditioning you got a 2.37 standard ratio, with optional ratios of 2.73 or 3.08. In both cars, if you ordered air conditioning with the automatic you got the same choices as with the Gremlin manual transmission 232. In both cars, the 258 six came with the same ratios as did the Gremlin manual transmission 232 six regardless of transmission choice, with one exception: the 3.08 ratio was standard, with a 3.31 ratio optional on the floor-mounted manual transmission Hornet. The 2.87 was standard and the 3.15 was optional on the column automatic 304 and 245 hp 360s. The 3.15 was standard and the 3.54 was optional on the column automatic and three-speed manual 360s. Last but certainly not least, the four-speed manual, four-barrel 285 hp 360 V-8 had the 3.15 as standard, with the 3.54 and 3.91 optional, and the 3.91 was mandatory with Twin-Grip.

New colors and fabrics were introduced for both cars. There was still a long option list to choose from. The customer could tailor the car to just about any level of convenience and performance.

In the spring of 1971, AMC offered "the first spring special that has something to do with spring. Free sunroofs from American Motors." If the customer purchased one of AMC's specially equipped Gremlins, two-door Hornets or Sportabout station wagons offered, AMC would include a free sunroof with canvas pullover. The specially equipped models included white-sidewall tires, custom wheel covers, rally stripes or pinstripes depending on model chosen, light group and special visibility group.

One special Hornet model was the Williams Turbine Hornet four-door sedan built by Williams Research of Walled Lake, Michigan. Built at an estimated cost of $240,000, including research, two cars were supposedly completed, with one being delivered to the Environmental Protection Agency of New York for testing and evaluation.

The turbine used was a small unit producing only 80 bhp at 4450 rpm and having a torque output of 190 pounds-feet. The turbine speed ranged from 30,000 rpm at idle to 51,000 rpm at maximum power. The small unit weighed only 315 pounds stripped and 400 pounds with accessories, and was coupled to the standard Hornet Borg-Warner three-speed automatic transmission by way of a circuitous drive. The car was sluggish because of its overall 3,150 pound weight. The model was identified by a buffed chrome plaque mounted on the right side of the dash that said "turbine-powered by Williams Research."

The Gremlin still lacked a V-8 engine option, but a 258-equipped model was a lively performer—although not lively enough for the magazines to take serious notice as they had done the year before. Consequently, when it came time to select a performance candidate

The 1971 Gremlin received detail improvements and refinements for the new model year. A 258 cubic inch six was optional.

The one-off 1971 Gucci Sportabout prototype was designed by Aldo Gucci of Italy. The car incorporated numerous inside and outside styling touches and innovations.

from the new wave of compact and subcompact cars, the Hornet SC/360 fit the bill perfectly.

Road tests

Car Craft selected an SC/360 and a Dodge Demon 340 for a comparison road test, since they represented the ultimate in junior supercars of the time. The SC/360 was one of the most potent combinations around, and *Car Craft* opened with this statement: "We don't want to blow the ending to this story, but the new Hornet SC 360, a Gremlinish compact with a 360 cubic inch ram-air engine nestled snugly under the hood, could easily qualify as sleeper of the year in the small-block/small body ponycar category."

The styling of the Hornet was well accepted, and the shifting actions of the linkage and transmission were rated better than most. The one big headache was the driving position. The seat would not go back

The rear seat occupants were treated to a fold-down picnic table and pullout writing desk. The center armrest housed a variety of games. Seats and upholstery were plush.

far enough and the steering wheel was too large. The reclining back helped some, but it was felt a tilt wheel or one of a smaller diameter would have remedied the situation. (AMC did cure the problem on the 1973 models.)

The car's performance was tested at Orange County International Raceway. In stock form, coming off the line at between 3000 and 3500 rpm and shifting

The interior shot of the Gucci model shows the unique upholstery pattern and modified dashboard and console.

A matching color luggage set was also included with the unique model. Note the matching rear body panel.

at 5000 rpm, the car netted a 14.54 second elapsed time at 98.90 mph with a back-up run of 14.50 seconds at 99.11 mph. With the vehicle weight at 3,230 pounds and the floor jack and toolbox removed from the trunk, the car was staged and covered the quarter-mile in 14.18 seconds at 99.55 mph. A back-up run produced a better 14.08 elapsed time at 99.88 mph.

Opening up the headers resulted in excessive off-the-line wheel spin and tire smoke and a disappointing 14.23 elapsed time at 101.01 mph. The ignition timing was advanced to ten degrees before top dead center, and the car responded with a very good 13.90 elapsed time at 100.67 mph. After an hour cooldown period, the last two runs of the day were 13.86 seconds at 101.35 mph and the best at 13.78 seconds at 101.92 mph. The best run of the day was 0.04 second quicker than a 454 Chevelle *Car Craft* had tested previously!

Car Craft concluded the SC/360 Hornet's performance as follows: "Anyway you look at it, American Motors has at last released a car competitive in price, performance and economy to anything on the market today."

Final Hornet production for 1971 remained steady with only a slight increase over 1970's. Total units built came to 74,685, of which only 784 were SC/360 two-door sedans. As in 1970, approximately 100 base Hornet 304 V-8s were built, again possibly indicating that there were a few modified super sleepers terrorizing the streets.

Total Gremlin production was up because it had a complete model year to build, but when compared with 1970's half model year, production remained steady. Total units built for 1971 peaked at 53,480, including two- and four-passenger models.

1972

Model year 1972 brought few changes to the Gremlin and Hornet. The base Hornet series was dropped and only the SST series remained available, in a two-door sedan, four-door sedan and four-door Sportabout station wagon. Wheelbases and exterior dimensions remained the same for both the Gremlin and the Hornet.

The Sportabout was now available in three levels of trim: the base, D/L and X models. The base model could be ordered in any number of ways to suit the customer's individual tastes and needs.

The D/L version could be had in two ways, with either vinyl upholstery at $236.25 or Scorpio fabric upholstery at $283.55. The rest of the equipment included color-keyed wood-grain side and rear panels, roof rack with integral air deflector, custom wheel covers, D/L decal and individually reclining seats.

The X package for both the Sportabout and the two-door sedan models retailed for $118.55 and consisted of a sports steering wheel, lower side body rally stripes, X emblems, 14x6 slot-styled wheels with C78x14 Polyglas black sidewall tires and rocker panel moldings. The rally stripes could be deleted on the Sportabout, which also had wider rocker panel moldings than the ones found on the two-door sedan X package.

A third, more luxurious trim level was available on the Sportabout. This was called the Designer Series

The Hornet for 1972 was again little changed. Although the SC/360 was gone, the two-door sedan was still available with the 360 two-barrel V-8 producing 175 net hp.

Gucci package, and was designed by Aldo Gucci. The package was available in four exterior colors—Snow White, Hunter Green, Grasshopper Green and Yuca Tan—and included seats, door panels, sun visors and headliner finished in beige with red and green stripes. If the optional sunroof was ordered the headliner was of the plain design. The wider rocker panel moldings were used, and the Gucci crest was placed on the inside door panels, front fenders and headliner.

Exterior emblems were only slightly altered. The flying Hornet was eliminated from the fender sides, and the Sportabout D/L and X models were designated under the quarter panel emblems. The two-door sedan X model was identified by an X placed under the Hornet emblems on the fender tips.

If the Rallye package was ordered (it was available on the two-door sedan only), the car became the Hornet Rallye X, with Rallye X die-cut into the side stripes at the quarter panels. With this package the X was eliminated from the fender tips. The 304 numbers were also deleted from the quarter panels on models equipped with the 304 engine, and the 360 was not designated.

The potent SC/360 junior supercar of 1971 was dropped, but it was still possible to option out a Hornet two-door sedan to almost the same specifications. The buyer could simply order the X package or the Rallye package.

The Rallye package consisted of vinyl bucket seats, manual front disc brakes, handling package, 20:1 quick-ratio manual steering, full-synchromesh three-speed floor-shift transmission, sports steering wheel and Rallye emblem.

With the manual three-speed transmission, the only engines offered were the 232 and 258 sixes and the 304 V-8. If the buyer wanted the 360 ci 175 hp two-barrel V-8, the transmission choice was restricted to a Torque Command automatic on the column, with a 2.87 rear standard and a 3.15 optional. The four-barrel 360 V-8 and the four-speed manual transmission were no longer offered.

Although dual exhaust was not available on the 360 Hornet, it was possible to order the 1971 system along with any of the Group 19 high-performance axle ratios and other parts, and have them dealer installed. A hard-core enthusiast could even opt for the four-speed manual transmission and have the dealer install it, if price was no object.

Road tests

Even in stock factory form, a 304 V-8 three-speed or 360 V-8 automatic Hornet X or Rallye X were good performers with the right factory options. *Motor Trend* decided to pit a 304-powered Hornet Rallye X against a Valiant Scamp 318, Maverick Sprint 302 and Rally Nova 350. All the cars were two-door sedans with the exception of the Scamp which was a hardtop, and all weighed within the same range. The Hornet was the lightest at 2,950 pounds, and the Nova was the heaviest at 3,250 pounds. All exterior dimensions and wheelbases were comparable.

The Hornet had small C78x14 tires, and the Valiant, Maverick and Nova had D78, D70 and E78 sizes,

Even with air conditioning and power steering, the 360 ci 175 hp engine could propel the lightweight 1972 Hornet to rival 1960's performance.

The Hornet's dashboard for 1972 was literally unchanged from 1971. The bulky Rim-Blow steering wheel was replaced with the newer three-spoke machined design.

respectively. The Valiant and Nova had power disc/drum brake combinations, the Maverick had power drum/drum and the Hornet had manual disc/drum. All cars except the Hornet had power steering. The Hornet was the only one that had a three-speed manual floor-shift transmission; the others all had column-mounted automatics.

Rear axle ratios were worlds apart. The Hornet had the deepest at 3.54:1 and the Valiant had the tallest at 2.76:1.

All engines were two-barrel carburetor versions with low 8.4:1 to 9:1 compression ratios that required regular fuel. The Nova had a slight power advantage with its 245 hp 350 engine. The Maverick's 302 V-8 was rated at 143 hp, and the Hornet's 304 and Valiant's 318 were both rated at 150 hp. All the cars were equipped with the optional heavy-duty suspension except the Valiant, whose handling suffered.

The Maverick and Nova were rated good in handling, but the little Hornet had them beat according to *Motor Trend*: "Hornet was the surprise of the field with the best handling of all. The little beast held it all together even with all four tires smoking in the turns." *Motor Trend* felt that power steering was a must and that the manual discs were good, but the power assist would have been easier on the right leg.

The Gucci trim package was now optional on the 1972 Sportabout. The car did not include any of the unique features found on the original 1971 prototype. It did, however, have its own distinctively designed interior color pattern and the Gucci crest on the fenders.

Although all four cars had good performance, the Hornet again came out on top. *Motor Trend* said, "Hornet came off quickest by virtue of a shorter rear end gear." The following 0-60 and quarter-mile elapsed times and speeds were recorded: Valiant, 9.7, 17.3 at 81 mph; Maverick, 9.4, 16.9 at 81 mph; Nova, 9.5, 16.8 at 82 mph; and Hornet, 9.0, 16.8 at 83 mph.

Although the Nova equaled the Hornet in elapsed time, the Hornet edged the Nova out in speed, even though the Nova was equipped with a larger and more powerful 350 V-8 engine (this shows the effects of a proper axle ratio). The Nova was able to beat the Hornet in only one other speed category, the 40-60 mph passing speed range. The Nova did it in 4.2 seconds, and the Hornet was close behind at 4.5 seconds.

Super Stock and Drag Illustrated tested the ultimate Hornet for 1972, a Hornet X equipped with the 360 cubic inch 175 hp two-barrel V-8. The car also had the column-shift Torque Command automatic transmission, special-order 3.31:1 Twin-Grip rear, handling package, X package, D78x14 black sidewall tires, power steering, power front disc brakes and so on. The car jumped from a base price of $2,285 to $3,955.40! With all the options, the car's weight also went up to approximately 3,300 pounds.

The *Super Stock and Drag Illustrated* staff had much praise for the luxury compact Hornet. The car was tested with a 401 Javelin AMX and 304 Gremlin X. Here is one of the magazine's opening statements: "Of the three cars tested, we'd have to say that the Hornet caught our fancy the most. The paint scheme, upholstery design and quality, quiet operation and drag strip performance all added up to a very pleasing car."

More than a dozen quarter-mile runs were put on the Hornet 360 by at least a half dozen different drivers. The first run netted a 16.64 elapsed time at 82.19 mph. With absolutely no modifications performed to the car, Gordy Foust of the Wally Booth crew recorded the best run of the day—a 16.17 elapsed time at 84.19 mph. These performance figures were not too far off from those recorded by the 1971 Hornet SC/360. This was good performance for a loaded-down luxury cruiser, according to the testing crew, which said, "Here we were with a bone-stock Hornet 8000 miles old, almost getting into the 15's in twelve tries with an automatic, 3.31 axle and no tricks to the engine, not to mention the extra weight we were hauling."

They also commented that with a few basic and simple bolt-ons such as headers, four-barrel carburetor, deeper rear-end gears and the usual hot rod tricks, the car would be able to dip into the low fifteens. They even agreed that the Hornet 360 could be quite competitive on the strip: "When it comes to class racing, there is only one Hornet model that's anywhere near competitive on paper, and that would be a 4-door 360 2-BBL., which breaks at 12.09 in the 12-pound D/S-D/SA class in NHRA's stock eliminator."

For the enthusiast who stuck to the streets and was not interested in the drag strip, *Super Stock and Drag Illustrated* concluded its test of the Hornet 360 with this last positive note: "Hornet 360 could well be a real street bomb if our test clockings are any indication of potential."

The Gremlin also came on board with few cosmetic and trim changes in 1972. The two-seater version was dropped because it had never sold well, and that left only the four-passenger version available in three levels of trim, standard, custom trim package and X package. All exterior emblems were left intact except

The Gremlin received the 304 V-8 as optional for 1972, and the two-seater version was dropped. To handle the added power, larger wheels and tires were used along with the AMX rear Torque Links from the 1968-70 AMX two-seater models.

that the chrome Gremlin cartoon character was deleted from the front portions of the fenders.

The Gremlin X rally side stripe design was unchanged, but the optional regular rally stripe was now split in half, forming two thinner parallel stripes. The parallel running pinstripe remained unchanged.

The custom trim package consisted of custom door panel and seat trim in pleated vinyl, carpeting, cargo area insulation, custom steering wheel, wheel opening moldings and drip moldings.

The X package was even plusher. It included spear side decal (rally stripes), painted grille (except with certain special paint options), 14x6 slot-style wheels with D70x14 Polyglas black sidewall tires, Space Saver spare, custom interior with bucket seats and cargo area insulation, fifteen-inch sports steering wheel, interior appointment package and special X decals.

Because of the introduction of the new Hornet, Sportabout and Gremlin sporty models, engine and drivetrain line-ups were considerably changed from 1971. In addition, horsepower ratings were lower because they were expressed in net rather than gross figures. The 232 cubic inch six with one-barrel carburetor and 100 hp was standard in both the Gremlin and Hornet. The 258 cubic inch one-barrel carburetor 110 hp six was optional, as was the 304 cubic inch 150 hp V-8. The 360 two-barrel engine was optional only in the Hornet.

In the Gremlin, the 232 was available with the three-speed column- or floor-shift manual with synchromesh on second and third only, the full-synchromesh three-speed on the floor and the column Torque Command automatic. The 232 Hornet was available with the same transmission except the three-speed manual on the floor with the 2-3 synchromesh was not offered. The optional 258 and 304 engines in both cars could be coupled to the full-synchromesh three-speed on the floor or the Torque Command automatic. The 360 V-8 could be ordered only with the column Torque Command.

Rear axle ratio availability was again a mixed bag, depending on which car the engine was in. The 2.73 ratio was standard in all Gremlin 232s with the manual transmission, and a 3.08 and 3.31 were optional. If the manual transmission was hooked up to a Hornet 232, the 3.08 ratio was standard and the 3.31 was optional. Automatics for both 232 cars had the high 2.37 ratio standard, with the 2.73 and 3.08 ratios as options.

To further complicate the issue, if the 232 automatic was in a sedan with air conditioning or in a Sportabout, the 232 Gremlin manual transmission ratios applied. Moving to the 258 six, again, the 232 Gremlin manual transmission ratios were used with one exception: the three-speed manual Hornet had the 3.08 standard with the 3.31 optional.

The 304 and 360 V-8s were straightforward: the manual 304 got the 3.54 ratio as standard with the 3.15

optional; the automatic 304 and 360 engines got the 2.87 as standard with the 3.15 optional.

V-8 Gremlin

During the 1970-71 period, AMC had been testing a V-8 Gremlin for possible future production. The big problem was that it experienced severe wheel hop and torque steer. The V-8 engine was just too much for the small ninety-six-inch-wheelbase car to handle. The problem was reduced to acceptable levels by the use of 1968-70 AMX Torque Links rear traction bars, staggered shocks and wider wheels with larger 6.95x14 tires.

There was even a prototype 1970 390 V-8 Gremlin built. It became the personal transportation of Dick Teague. The car had power steering, power brakes, air conditioning, aluminum hi-rise intake manifold with Holley carburetor, open air filter assembly, aluminum five-slot wheels with extra-wide-profile raised-white-letter tires, Side-Winders exhausts, roof rack, rear air deflector, SC/360 type flat-black hood scoop and the 1970 AMX Shadow Black paint scheme. A host of other personal touches and items were added.

The production 1972 304 V-8 Gremlin included quite a few heavy-duty items and components to help harness its newfound horsepower. Some of the equipment included a larger 8⅞ size rear axle assembly with AMX Torque Links, ten-inch brakes, wider wheels, 6.95x14 tires, front sway bar, heavier springs and shocks, and for comfort, contoured bucket seats and sports steering wheel. The 304 Gremlin was identified by a "5 litre V/8" decal placed beside the right taillight on the rear panel, only when the optional X package was ordered. The 3.8 and 4.2 decals identified the six-cylinder Gremlins.

A few other new items were introduced on the 1972 Gremlins, such as a full-synchromesh three-speed manual transmission, front door pockets, tilt steering, pop-out windows, sunroof, redesigned front seats, suspension improvements and reengineered rear brake cylinders to reduce rear wheel lockup during hard braking. New exterior colors and interior fabrics were also added. The new buyer protection plan was also extended to both the Gremlin and the Hornet.

Road tests

The testing staff at *Hot Rod* magazine wasted no time in thrashing around a 304 V-8 Gremlin. They were impressed with the acceleration and handling results turned in by the little subcompact with its new supercarlike performance. In fact, they voted the car as the best buy from AMC for 1972 because of its new engine option, modest initial price, low insurance rate and overall utility.

While attending the American Motors press review at the Michigan International Speedway, the *Hot Rod* staff had a chance to briefly test an early model. They found the car to have a well-engineered suspension and good handling. Off-line acceleration was brisk and the car had plenty of power to break the rear wheels loose if the driver wanted to bring the rear end of the car around a corner. They concluded that the V-8 Gremlin handled quite well overall on the road course, and was predictable and amazingly maneuverable in tight traffic—in short, fun to drive.

The full-blown road test of a production model took place a few months later, and was a comparison test between the Gremlin and its ancestor, the original two-seater 1968-70 AMX. The Gremlin tested was loaded with options, including the floor-shifted all-synchromesh three-speed transmission, handling package, D70x14 Goodyear Polyglas raised-white-letter tires mounted on aftermarket American Racing Equipment 200S five-spoke wheels, 3.54 rear with Twin-Grip, power steering, power front disc brakes and Weather-Shield sliding sunroof.

The Gremlin's wheelbase was one inch shorter than the AMX's ninety-seven inches. The Gremlin's overall length was almost sixteen inches shorter, but tread widths for both cars were within an inch of each other. The Gremlin had the added bonus of being a four-passenger car.

The *Hot Rod* staff's impression was that "the Gremlin X is an economy AMX." Base price of a 1968 AMX was $3,245, which was quite close to the test Gremlin's $3,400 price tag.

The Gremlin's V-8 engine was larger than the original AMX's engine in displacement, but the AMX had a four-barrel carburetor and dual exhausts producing 225 gross hp. The Gremlin had a single exhaust, two-barrel carburetor and 150 net hp rating. The equivalent gross horsepower rating for the 304 Gremlin was 210.

The handling of the V-8 Gremlin was a big improvement over that of the older six-cylinder. As *Hot Rod* put it, "We were quite surprised by this car's handling ability, mostly because of earlier samplings of Gremlin's that were a handful—to speak kindly of them—when negotiating turns more severe than entering a driveway." A slight bit of understeer was evidenced as the car entered a corner flat, but the car could be powered out of the curve in a safe line of travel by applying a judicious amount of throttle.

Although the car was found to ride a little harsh because of its heavy-duty suspension, its standard staggered rear shocks and AMX Torque Links produced absolutely no trace of wheel hop during acceleration and deceleration.

The three-speed manual transmission with floor-shift linkage was rated as one of the best, and the car's braking power was tops with the optional power front disc brakes. It took only 120 feet to come to a full stop from 60 mph, which translated into an average deceleration rate of 1 g—and the car remained in a straight line. Seating comfort was good, interior noise level was low and mileage was average at 14 mpg.

Despite the car's 3,090 pound weight and restrictive single exhaust system, quarter-mile performance was respectable. Its best recorded time at the Orange County International Raceway was a 16.33 second elapsed time at 83.87 mph. This was accomplished by setting the rear tire pressure to thirty-four pounds and the front tire pressure to forty-five pounds, advancing the ignition timing to ten degrees before top dead center, removing the air cleaner element and shifting at 5200 rpm.

Super Stock and Drag Illustrated also hopped on the bandwagon, and ordered a 304 Gremlin with just about every option available. The car was equipped with the column Shift-Command automatic, air conditioning package, power steering, power front disc brakes, 3.15 Twin-Grip rear, manual sunroof, AM/FM radio, luggage rack, rear roof air deflector, tilt steering wheel, D70x14 Polyglas raised-white-letter tires mounted on five-spoke-style wheels, bumper guards, visibility group, light group, locking gas cap, bucket seats, clear vinyl floor mats and X package.

The X package consisted of the side stripes, painted grille, sports steering wheel, Space Saver spare, outside decals, inside insulation package and interior trim. With the air conditioning package you got tinted glass, power steering, extra insulation and the D70 tires. The car's base price jumped from $1,999 to $3,909, and its weight from 2,500 pounds to 3,150 pounds, putting it at a disadvantage performancewise.

The car was a first-class boulevard and highway cruiser, and its ride became harsh only on the most severe roads. The car's interior and dashboard layout were liked by the *Super Stock and Drag Illustrated* staff, and its quality was topnotch. The little Gremlin handled any and all traffic situations with ease and comfort. It was also surprisingly quiet inside, according to the staff: "It did have some extra insulation built in,

The 304 V-8 was a natural fit inside the Gremlin engine compartment since it had shared the Hornet's front end from the start. There was still plenty of room for routine maintenance and modifications if desired.

but this class of car isn't supposed to be that quiet. A nice surprise."

As was done with the 360 Hornet, over a dozen runs were put on the 304 Gremlin by various drivers. In stripped stock form and letting the transmission shift for itself, the car recorded a 17.33 second elapsed time at 78.60 mph. After another run with worse results, the car was handed over to Gordy Foust and Wally Booth. After a few familiarization runs, both drivers recorded identical elapsed times of 16.86 seconds at a little over 79 mph, for the best performance figures of the day. The only trick employed was pumping up the rear tires to forty-five pounds, which helped traction. Removing the air cleaner produced worse performance.

Wally Booth and crew, and Bob Swain, AMC's manager of performance activities, all agreed that the car had hidden potential. It was summed up this way: "At Milan dragway, the car gave every evidence that it could be made into a pretty trick street bomb with the right selection of options and aftermarket pieces." This was further evidenced by the 14.30 second elapsed time that was turned by Wally Booth's pure-race E/SA Gremlin driven at the Pomona race.

Specials

Randall Rambler of Mesa, Arizona, was extensively involved in racing. One of its specialties was transplanting the high-performance four-barrel AMC

The rear hatch glass on the 1972 Gremlin was supported by a single cylinder. The 4.2 liter decal on the right-side rear panel indicated this model was equipped with the optional 258 ci six.

343, 360, 390 and 401 ci engines into small AMC cars, such as the American, Gremlin, Hornet and Pacer. To make things even better, the customer could order the engine and car in virtually any desired level of performance, including modified production. Just about any piece of equipment could be installed on the car, even if it was not on Randall's option list. You couldn't ask for anything more, right? Wrong. Randall Rambler also paid the airfare one way if a customer wanted to go to Mesa to pick up the car and drive it home!

To get an idea what one of these cars was like, *Super Stock and Drag Illustrated* road-tested a 1972 Randall Rambler 401 XR Gremlin. The car started out as a 304-equipped Gremlin X with larger ten-inch rear brakes, heavy-duty front sway bar, heavy-duty shocks and springs, and the larger 8⅞ inch rear axle assembly. Other equipment included power front disc brakes, air conditioning, flip-open rear side windows, Torque Command automatic transmission, Adjust-O-Tilt steering column and variable-ratio power steering. A three-speed or Borg-Warner four-speed transmission could be substituted for buyers not wanting the automatic.

The standard Gremlin X package also included 14x6 slotted steel wheels, D70x14 Polyglas tires, appropriate striping, sports steering wheel, engine-turned instrument panel, standard bucket seats and Space Saver spare tire.

Randall equipped this XR Gremlin with a Stewart-Warner speedometer, tachometer and oil pressure gauges. The 1972 401 engine was left basically stock with the exception of a 650 cfm double-pumper Holley carburetor, unsilenced full-open chrome air cleaner, Jardine headers and Thrush dual outside exhausts. Koni shocks, F60x14 tires mounted on custom 14x6 XR mag wheels and a custom Hornet dashboard rounded out the package. The car also had the standard AMX-type factory Torque Links to control wheel hop and a 3.55:1 axle ratio.

The complete XR package started out at $2,995. From there it could be taken to just about whatever the customer could afford.

Once strapped into the 401 Gremlin, one could feel the power on the freeway. Accelerating up to speed and passing was no problem at all, although handling on tight turns took getting used to.

On the drag strip the car was impressive. Using no special driving techniques and shifting at 5300 rpm, drivers put the car through several passes, netting a high elapsed time of 13.79 to a low of 13.59, all at about 103 mph. Uncorking the headers, installing a fresh set of plugs and shifting at 5500 rpm produced times starting at 13.37 and finishing with a best of 13.22 at 105.76 mph.

At the track the same day, another 401 Gremlin was being raced. This car was owned by Jim and Ledora Happ, and featured the optional hi-po dealer 0.477 inch lift cam, 750 cfm Holley carburetor, headers, 4.10:1 Twin-Grip rear and H60x14 rear tires.

A warm-up pass with this racing Gremlin, shifting at 5500 rpm, produced a 13.21 elapsed time at 106.62 mph. Several later passes, combined with all-out tire-warming burnouts, netted times of 12.81 at 109.40, 12.78 at 109.35, 12.76 at 109.55 and a best of 12.75 at 109.60. The 401 Gremlin was a potent piece of machinery.

A special 1972 Gremlin was built by Hurst Research and used in numerous highway accident and emergency situations. This Gremlin was called the Rescue System 1, and it was stuffed with emergency equipment for highway use. The car was a 304 V-8 automatic transmission model fitted with fiberglass-belted wide tires, wider wheels and Hurst's own air-adjustable shocks. These items were supposed to make the car handle better in adverse weather conditions, but they did not.

The car was painted white with Hurst safety oriented orange stripes and panels that were highly visible even at extended distances. It also had a twin flasher bar on its top, complete with an electronic siren and built-in speaker system.

The Rescue System 1 was equipped with the Hurst Rescue Tool, which was like a giant jaw capable of exerting a force of five tons to quickly open jammed doors, raise crushed roofs and even upright over-turned cars. It carried twenty-five gallons of water, a ten-pound purple-K extinguisher, a resuscitator, a stretcher, two first aid kits, an aluminized blanket, a set of jumper cables and an electric winch. Also standard for the $11,900 asking price were front and rear push bars, an external 12-volt electric outlet and power steering.

Another special Gremlin was the one-of-a-kind Gremlin Voyageur first shown at the Montreal International Automobile Salon in January 1972. This car had a distinctive side and rear paneling treatment and featured the Grem-Bin, which was a large slide-out tray that occupied the car's cargo area.

Total 1972 Gremlin production was up over 8,000 from 1971. Total units built were 61,717, of which approximately 8,500 were V-8 models.

Although Hornet production was good, total units produced for 1972 were slightly down from 1971, ending at 71,056.

1973

Popularity of the subcompact and compact cars was increasing. As a result, in 1973 AMC introduced numerous refinements to the Gremlin series and offered a new model in the Hornet series called the hatchback. This brought the total Hornet model series to four body styles available: two-door sedan, four-door sedan, four-door Sportabout station wagon and two-door hatchback. The SST designation was dropped, and the cars were now simply called Hornets.

The new hatchback combined the functions of a window and a trunk lid. To facilitate opening and closing, it was fully counterbalanced with two gas-filled assist cylinders and hinged at the top. With the rear seat in place there were 9.5 cubic feet of luggage space, and with the rear seat folded down there were twenty-three cubic feet.

The wheelbase of all Hornets was still 108 inches, but overall length was increased 6.5 inches to 185.8 inches. This increase was due to the federally mandated front and rear telescoping energy-absorbing bumpers. The telescoping front bumpers were standard on both the Hornet and Gremlin, but the rears were optional. With both systems, the Hornet and Gremlin qualified for as much as a twenty percent discount for collision insurance from several national insurance companies.

The Hornet received a new grille in the form of a full-width V-profile. The headlights and inboard parking lights were contained in a cavity outlined in silver, which continued into a full-width dual-center horizontal motif. Front fenders were redesigned, along with a recessed hood containing a raised center creaseline. The large front bumper was wider and heavier, and had full-width vinyl nerf strips.

The same rear bumper design was used on the hatchback, but the Sportabout and sedan rear bumpers were of the 1972 design, whether they were telescoping or not. The rear aluminum overlay panel now had a vertical theme. The taillights were only slightly changed, still being of a wraparound design and doubling as the side-marker lights. A new side molding on the Sportabout and Hornet sedans ran the entire length of the car at the middle section and over the wheel arches.

Because of the new front fenders, new side-marker lights were designed. A flying Hornet medallion was placed in the center leading edge of the hood, and Hornet in block letters was placed on the left leading edge of the hood and right rear panel beside the taillight.

The Sportabout was still identified on the rear sections of the quarter panels and could still be ordered in D/L, X and Gucci trim levels. The optional X package was also extended to the hatchback.

The hatchback X model was identified with a lone X under the Hornet emblem on the rear panel and included sports steering wheel, slot-styled wheels, X emblems and rally stripes. The rally stripes were of a dual thick design with a central pinstripe, running above the door handle at the beltline and following the contour of the body sculpture. The Hornet hatchback X model had the horizontal grille center motif color-keyed to the rally side stripes.

The D/L package on the Sportabout consisted of wood-grain panels, roof rack with air deflector, individual reclining seats with Scorpio fabric, D/L emblem and a few other distinguishing items.

The luxurious Gucci model again featured vinyl-upholstered individually reclining beige front seats with red and green stripes and door panel inserts. The door trim, sun visors and other trim throughout the car were finished in deep green, and the headliner was in light gray incorporating the Gucci crest in a double C pattern.

The Gremlin also received its share of changes for 1973, although its basic body design and exterior dimensions remained just about the same as in 1972. Front- and rear-end styling remained virtually untouched, but as with the Hornet, overall length increased five inches to 166.2 inches owing to the telescoping bumpers.

The rear seat in the Gremlin was redesigned to allow more rear seat room. It also provided greater torso support, using a contoured two-piece cushion back design. To make entry and exit from the rear seat easier, the front seatback locking mechanism was reworked.

In 1973, the Gremlin had the widest selection of optional packages of any AMC model. There were no less than eight packages, which were as follows: X package, custom trim package, interior appointment and Decor group, air conditioning package, handling

The Hornet hatchback was introduced for 1973. It was considered to be one of the best designs to come out of the American automotive industry. The model was truly a work of art.

package, Levi's custom trim and Levi's with the X package.

All of the packages were more or less carry-overs from 1972 except the new and distinctive Levi's custom trim package. This special treatment was developed in collaboration with Levi Strauss and was also offered on the Hornet starting in the spring of 1973. It consisted of a spun nylon version of the traditional blue denim Levi's trim, with Levi's buttons and door panels; storage-litter container in blue denim; blue headlining and sun visors; front fender Levi's decals; and color-keyed carpeting, cargo area insulation and custom steering wheel.

The buttons were in the form of copper rivets and the stitching was in orange thread to complete the western-style motif. The material was said to wear far better than the traditional denim, and even met federal flammability requirements. The Levi's decals were placed on the rear sections of the front fender. The Levi's crest also appeared on the outer welt of the front seats.

Body changes were minimal in 1973, relegated to small trim and appearance items. The vinyl nerfing strips were bonded onto the bumpers, but the bumper design itself was the same as in 1972. The standard rally side stripe was slightly altered, now being three thin and one thick parallel running stripes.

The Gremlin X rally side stripe was changed, but only at the quarter panels. It hopped up over the rear wheelwell openings and ran through the door and fender portions in line with the door handles, instead of above them.

One other small change made was removing the square AM logo above the rear window handle and replacing it with the new AMC logo and letters mounted next to the left taillight. The Hornet also received the new logo mounted in the same location.

Standard and optional equipment for both the Hornet and Gremlin were little changed from 1972 with the exception of the added government safety and pollution devices. The new high-back Slim Shell bucket seats introduced on the 1973 Javelin were also shared by the Hornet and Gremlin.

Engine line-up for both the Hornet and the Gremlin was unchanged from 1972. However, for the sake of emissions, economy and improved drivability, transmission choices and rear axle ratios were rearranged a little.

In both cars, the 232 was available with the three-speed full-synchromesh manual on the floor and with the column and floor Torque Command automatics. The Hornet also could be had with a full-synchromesh manual on the column.

All 232 sixes had the 2.73 rear standard, with the 3.08 and 3.31 optional. With the exception of the column-mounted manual three-speed, the 258 six was available with the same transmission and rear axle choices—with one small catch: in the Hornet series, the floor-mounted manual and automatic were offered only on the hatchback model.

The 304 V-8 again offered the same transmission choices as the 258 six, but rear axle ratios were different. The automatic transmission versions had the 2.87 standard, with the 3.15 optional; the manual versions had the 3.54 standard, with the 3.91 optional.

The 360 V-8 restricted to the Hornet was offered with the column- or floor-mounted automatic (the latter only on the hatchback). The 2.87 rear was standard and the 3.15 was optional.

Road tests

Since the new Hornet hatchback was such a clean and smooth design, it managed to attract the most attention as a potentially hot compact. *Hot Rod* magazine awarded the title of best buy for 1973 to the car. It said, "Without a doubt, the fastback coupe is one of the best-looking designs to come out of any door in Detroit."

Car Craft was equally impressed with the new Hornet hatchback's styling, and so put in an order for a heavily optioned out boulevard cruiser. The car was equipped with the largest engine option available, the 360 cubic inch 175 hp two-barrel V-8, Torque Command automatic on the floor and 3.54 non-Twin-Grip rear. Other options on the car were power steering, power front disc brakes, air conditioning, handling package, D70x14 Polyglas tires mounted on slot-styled wheels and a few other convenience items. The car was a lightweight at 3,360 pounds with a half tank of gas.

The test conducted on the Hornet was purely to see how the car performed in the quarter-mile. A few passes in showroom stock form netted a best elapsed time of 16.44 seconds at 82.0 mph. Traction was not good, however, and it was decided that more rubber was needed on the ground.

A set of Mickey Thompson F70x14 tires mounted on 5.5 inch wide GT wheels was installed on the front. In back, huge Mickey Thompson E60x15 skins were mounted on wider eight-inch GT wheels that really gave the Hornet a tough look. This tire combination did nothing for quarter-mile performance, as the speed fell off 0.5 mph.

A pair of Hooker equal-length headers with 1.75-inch-inside-diameter tubes terminating into three-inch collectors was installed, along with a pair of Hooker mufflers. With closed exhaust the car ran a 15.90 elapsed time at 86 mph, but with the headers opened it recorded a 15.50 elapsed time at 90 mph.

Installing M&H L60x15 rear tires resulted in a loss of both speed and elapsed time. Next came the installation of the Offenhauser dual port intake manifold and Holley 700 cfm double-pumper four-barrel carburetor. With the E60x15 tires back on, the car responded well with a 14.45 elapsed time at 99 mph. With the M&H L60x15 tires remounted, the time dropped to 14.28 seconds but lost 1 mph.

Things started to get interesting, so the headers were uncorked. The left rear tire was set at 20 psi and the right one was set at 15 psi. The car now ran 14.10 at 100.11 mph. The final change was to advance the ignition timing from five degrees before top dead center to ten degrees before top dead center. This produced an elapsed time of 13.97 seconds at 100.78 mph.

The modifications made were typical of those needed to make the new smog engines perform. *Car Craft* concluded its drag test of the Hornet hatchback with this: "It handles like a sports car, yet is as economical as many subcompacts. Dollar for dollar it's one of the best new car buys on the market." And that was probably the best compliment that could have ever been given to a car, especially at that time.

Canadians were also impressed with the hatchback. The *Driving* pamphlet, which is the Canadian equivalent of the US *Americana*, conducted a road test of a 304 V-8-powered hatchback with floor-mounted Torque Command automatic transmission. The car

also had a 2.87 non-Twin-Grip rear, power steering and power drum brakes.

The Canadians described their first impression of the car: "In all the Hornet must rank as one of the most effective designs to come out of North America in the last few years." They liked the way AMC avoided filling in the gap between the bumpers and body with rubber, electing to use a sheet of color-keyed ABS plastic instead. They also praised the way AMC redesigned the driver's seating position by allowing the seat to move farther backwards for a more comfortable driving position away from the steering wheel.

Although the seatbelt positions could have allowed the driver better access to the controls and rear seat legroom could have been better, the overall quality control of the car, especially that of the interior, was rated first class.

The Canadians also felt the car had excellent visibility and good control and riding characteristics, although the power steering was a little ticklish and the car's overall balance control would have benefited from the optional handling package. The drum brakes were not adequate in their opinion, and they strongly recommended the disc brake option.

The car's performance was respectable, with a 0-60 time in the nine- to ten-second range and the quarter-mile covered in 17.4 seconds at 80.5 mph.

Driving concluded that the new Hornet hatchback was a first-class car in just about every respect and could be tailored to any level of comfort, convenience, performance or economy.

Road Test again answered the call with a three-way comparison test of the Hornet hatchback, Nova hatchback, and Dart Sport Convertriple. The Hornet had the 360 ci 175 hp V-8, the Nova the 350 ci 145 hp and the Dart the 318 ci 150 hp. All three cars had two-barrel carburetors, three-speed automatic transmissions, power front disc brakes, power steering and 3.42 rear axle ratios. The Hornet weighed 3,290

Slim Shell bucket seats and a stick-shift-type automatic transmission floor control lever were just some of the new features on the new 1973 Hornet hatchback.

This custom wheel cover was one of the most popular options ordered for the 1973 Hornet by its buyers.

pounds, the Nova 3,470 pounds and the Dart 3,330 pounds.

As had been the case so many times in the past with various AMC models, the Hornet came out victorious in the speed contests. The following 0-60 and quarter-mile elapsed times and speeds are given: Hornet, 8.6, 16.52 at 84.66 mph; Nova, 9.7, 17.4 at 79 mph; and Dart, 8.8, 16.70 at 81.59 mph.

Road Test's choice of the three cars was clearly the Hornet.

Road Test liked the new Hornet hatchback so much that the following month it evaluated a 304 V-8 model. This car also had the floor-mounted automatic transmission and the air conditioning package, which included power steering, power front disc brakes, handling package, 3.15 Twin-Grip rear, DR70x14 radial whitewall tires, bucket seats and rear hydraulic bumper.

The staff's first impression of the car was described as follows: "In its own right, the Hornet is one of the better compact automobiles made. Then when you add the hatchback option it becomes something special: a fun little car which is also useful. How can you beat that?" And their opinion about the car's design? "The overall impression is one of a functionality of design which makes the Hornet probably the most stylish hatchback on the market."

Performance was respectable, with the hatchback attaining a 0-60 time of 9.5 seconds. The quarter-mile was covered in 17.3 seconds at 81 mph. Braking power was very good, with a minimum of fade and no fishtailing or instability of any kind even after repeated stops were made.

Road Test's concluding statements said it all: "The Hornet X, then, is an excellent example of that modern American phenomenon, the hatchback automobile. It combines style, comfort, quality, performance, and load-carrying ability in one inexpensive car." The Hornet hatchback was one of the best bargains in its class.

C. J. Baker, *Hot Rod* performance editor, privately entered a white 1973 Randall Rambler 401 Hornet

The Levi's trim package was introduced on the Gremlin for 1973. The front hydraulic recoverable bumpers were also added to both the Gremlin and Hornet. The rear hydraulic units were optional.

hatchback in the third running of the Cannonball Baker cross-country auto rally from New York to Los Angeles.

The original rally was simply known as Cannonball and was a thinly disguised cross-country trip conceived of by Brock Yates, former senior editor of *Car and Driver* magazine. In Yates' own way, he was protesting what he thought to be unrealistic highway speed limits in the United States and other motorsports with too many restrictions. Yates' rally had one rule and one rule only: "The winners were those people who drove from New York to Los Angeles in the shortest elapsed time." Any number of drivers could be used, any type of vehicle, any route and any speed.

The original Cannonball Run was a solo event with Yates and friends driving a Dodge van named *Moon Trash II*. They completed the run in a little over forty-one hours. Cannonball II was run in late 1971, and was won by Yates and race driver Dan Gurney in a Ferrari 365 GTB/4 Daytona with an incredible time of thirty-five hours and fifty-six minutes. The event drew eight vehicles and twenty-three eager drivers.

The 401 Hornet hatchback used by C. J. Baker was equipped with a cruising 2.87:1 rear axle ratio, Goodyear radials and Hooker headers. For the long trip coast to coast, three auxiliary twenty-two-gallon fuel cells were installed complete with an onboard aircraft five-way control valve system, giving a capacity of seventy-three usable gallons of fuel. Delco air shocks were installed to handle the extra weight, along with a pair of 100,000 candlepower aircraft landing lights and a digital read-out speedometer to keep on the lookout for Smokey.

During the cross-country run, a test was conducted on two radar detectors. One was the $40 Radatron and the other was the $80 Snooper, which proved to be very good.

For safety, a roll bar, competition seatbelts, shoulder harness and Velvetouch semimetallic brakes were installed. The 401 engine was just about stock, but the car did sport a floor-shifted heavy-duty automatic, Twin-Grip rear, handling package, deluxe interior and power steering, resulting in a sticker price of over $4,600. Base price of the 401 Hornet was $3,995.

A stock 360 two-barrel V-8-equipped Hornet accompanied the hi-po Hornet on the cross-country trip. Both Hornets completed the trip in a little over forty-one hours and finished thirteenth in a field of twenty-eight finishers, with no major mechanical mishaps.

During the run, out in the Nevada desert highway, the hi-po Hornet had a top speed of 128 mph with the 2.87 gears and the stock ERx70 street radial tires.

At the end of the test, it was decided to see what the 401 Hornet could do on the strip. The 2.87 gears were replaced with 4.10s, and G60x15 Super Stock Formula One street tires mounted on Fenton 15x8 Super Shark wheels were installed. With the exhaust closed, the car netted a low-fifteen-second elapsed time at 97 mph.

Too much wheel spin was encountered, and it was felt a set of slicks was needed. Those coupled to an open exhaust would have produced a fourteen-second car with ease.

A one-of-a-kind show car that was a blend of Hornet and Gremlin styling was the 1973 Hornet GT, first shown at the AMC stockholders meeting in February 1973. The car was essentially a Gremlin with modified tail and side treatments and with Hornet fenders, hood, grille and bumper. As did the 1967 AMX III show car, the Hornet GT featured two different side treatments to illustrate contrasting design proposals. The center section of the hood was finished in black, and the rally side stripe was a reversed downward version of the Gremlin X's.

The car was finished in bright orange, and had wide Polyglas tires mounted on custom ET-type crosshatch mag wheels.

Model-year production for both cars was up almost 100 percent from 1972. The Hornet totaled 133,468 units, and the Gremlin trailed slightly at 122,844 units built.

1974

The Hornet received a few detailed refinements and trim changes for 1974. Most noticeable was the elimination of the bumper vinyl nerf strips, which were replaced with large rubber bumper guards located between the headlights and parking lights. The center horizontal grille motif was now finished in black instead of silver, and the Hornet emblem was removed from the hood leading edge and placed behind each fender side-marker light. The parking lights were offered with or without the chrome three-bar-encircled design.

The Hornet hatchback X still had the horizontal grille center motif color-keyed to the rally stripe. A new

For 1974, the Hornet again received minor trim changes. Most notable were the large rubber bumper guards and relocation of the Hornet letters from the hood to the fenders. This was the last year for the Hornet with the 360 V-8.

pinstripe was set lower on the sides of the car, with a small turndown at the fender tip contour. New lower back panel moldings were also featured, and a new finer-grained material was used for the optional vinyl roofs.

The rest of the car was virtually unchanged in design and exterior dimensions. The same four body styles offered in 1973 continued for 1974. There were six new rally stripe colors (black, white, gold, blue, orange and brown) to complement the fourteen different body colors. The X and D/L trim packages were still around, but the unique Gucci package on the Sportabout was dropped.

The extra-quiet insulation package that was standard on the Matador and Ambassador was optional on the Hornet and Gremlin. It was also included as part of the optional Levi's and X packages for the Hornet hatchback and Gremlin, and in the Hornet Sportabout D/L package. The cargo-floor deadening material was unique to the hatchback, Sportabout and Gremlin.

A few more items were included in the hatchback X package. It now consisted of vinyl bucket seats or optional Levi's trim, hidden compartment with Space Saver spare, sports steering wheel, rally stripe, extra-quiet insulation package, X emblem and D70x14 tires mounted on 14x6 slot-styled wheels. The X package on the Sportabout included the same equipment except the first two items.

The Rallye X package, available on the Hornet hatchback and Gremlin only, returned after being offered in 1972 on the Hornet two-door sedan only. It included tachometer, oil pressure gauge, ammeter gauge, floor-mounted shift for manual transmission, manual front disc brakes, front sway bar for six-cylinder models, power steering, leather-wrapped sports steering wheel, and black steering column and instrument cluster.

All of the standard safety features introduced on the other 1974 AMC models were also extended to the Hornet and Gremlin, such as the new three-point lap and shoulder belt system with ignition interlock feature.

Road tests

The Hornet hatchback equipped with the 360 V-8 was still the main focus of the compact supercar scene. Consequently, it attracted a lot of attention, and *Motor Trend* was eager, once again, to evaluate the model.

Motor Trend conducted a five-car shoot-out between Detroit's latest offerings, electing to call them the Sports Compacts. Since the United States was right in the middle of the fuel crunch, the miles per gallon figures for each car were placed at the beginning of the test.

The shoot-out was between hatchback models of the Hornet, Pontiac Ventura GTO, Chevy Nova, Ford Maverick and Buick Apollo. The Maverick had the best gas mileage at 19.0 mpg, and the GTO had the worst at 14.6 mpg. The Hornet was right in the middle at 17.8 mpg. The Dodge Dart and Plymouth Duster models were not ready in time for the comparison test.

The cars were equipped with the following engines: Hornet, 360 ci 175 hp; GTO, 350 ci 200 hp;

The 1974 hatchback model was also virtually unchanged from the 1973 model. Shown is a car equipped with the *optional Levi's trim package, which was made available on the Hornet in the spring of 1973.*

Nova, 350 ci 185 hp; Maverick, 302 ci 140 hp; and Apollo 350 ci 150 hp. All five cars had three-speed automatic transmissions. The Nova and GTO had four-barrel carburetors, and the others had two-barrels. The Nova, Apollo and GTO had a 3.08 final drive ratio, the Hornet had a 3.15 and the Maverick had a 3.00. All cars had power steering and all were variable-ratio except the Maverick. The Nova, Apollo and GTO had power front disc brakes; the Hornet and Maverick had manually operated front disc brakes. The Maverick was the lightest at 3,180 pounds, and the GTO was the heaviest at 3,880 pounds; the Hornet was the second lightest at 3,340 pounds.

As with the 1973 shoot-out conducted by *Road Test*, the Hornet was the overall choice of the testing staff. AMC continued to offer what was probably the best bargain in its class, according to *Motor Trend*: "The Hornet is the class of the line. More thought and care has gone into the Hornet than has been lavished on the others of the compact genre." And the magazine said this about the car's ride and handling: "Hornet's combination of ride and handling leaves very little to be desired."

Even though the Hornet's engine was not the strongest of the bunch. *Motor Trend* liked it, saying, "Response from the 360 - 2V engine is strong below 50 mph, which is where you need it, right?" The comfort of the new bucket seats was also rated as good, and the floor-mounted shiftgate was described as "the best offered on a domestic." How about overall quality

control? "Fit and finish of the general car are very good. Our machine had a red and black color scheme which pleased this eye."

In the 0-60 times, the Hornet was victorious. The Nova and GTO with their four-barrel carburetors were able to edge it out in the quarter-mile, but only by about a half second and roughly 3 mph. The following 0-60 and quarter-mile performance figures were obtained by *Motor Trend*: Hornet, 8.5, 17.04 at 80.93 mph; GTO, 9.4, 16.50 at 84.03 mph; Nova, 10.0, 16.77 at 83.48 mph; Maverick, 10.5, 17.35 at 79.78 mph; and Apollo, 9.5, 18.00 at 74.00 mph. A 360 four-barrel Hornet could have shut the others down, but that engine was no longer offered.

Even in the 40-60 and 50-70 mph passing speeds, the Hornet was beaten only by a slight margin owing to the Nova and GTO four-barrel secondaries opening up.

Motor Trend concluded its comparison test with this: "They are (all) a pleasure to drive, but the Hornet is the most pleasurable of all."

Road Test had been so impressed with the 1973 Hornet hatchback that it immediately tested the improved 1974 version. The model chosen was the hatchback with the 360 V-8, floor-mounted automatic transmission, 3.54 Twin-Grip rear, manual front disc brakes, X package, air conditioning package (which included power steering), AM/FM stereo radio, DR78x14 radial whitewall tires mounted on 14x6 five-

The Gremlin finally received a new front- and rear-end styling treatment for 1974. The grille looked massive, and the X model here was clearly identified. The rear end was not changed as much.

spoke-styled steel wheels, and various trim and convenience options.

The overall power, ride, handling and appearance of the elegant hatchback were praised by *Road Test*. Here are its opening statements: "The response to the accelerator pedal pressure that you get from the Hornet with the optional 360 cubic-inch, 175 horsepower engine comes as a definite surprise in this age of debilitating emissions controls, and the feeling is gratifying." And, once again, the automatic transmission was described as "smooth and unobtrusive and a perfect mate for the big engine." Its handling and maneuverability were described as "one of the Hornet's strong suits when equipped as ours was."

Road Test was equally impressed with the car's steering: "The Hornet's rather short wheelbase makes the quick steering even quicker, giving the car an agility that is often referred to as 'European' in this country." The firmness of the handling package helped the car on the skid pad, and the staff found no sacrifice in ride quality.

The optional manual disc brakes needed no introduction: "Braking performance of our test Hornet was outstanding." *Road Test* concluded that "AMC rates two ears and the tail for these brakes."

The car's overall interior layout in terms of ease of control, convenience and quality finish received very good marks. The package was summed up as follows: "Not only is the aforementioned hatch quiet, the whole car is quiet for a compact, which allows full enjoyment of the good sounding AM-FM radio." The extra-quiet insulation package with the X option was certainly doing its job. The buyer protection plan was rated as "by far the best in the business for domestic cars."

The car was able to do 0-60 in 9.3 seconds and the quarter-mile in 16.80 seconds at 81.2 mph. It recorded a 0.679 g lateral acceleration force on the skid pad.

Gremlin

For 1974, the Gremlin finally received its first new look since 1970½ introduction. The grille was completely done over and was made up of twelve thin horizontal bars containing the rectangular parking lights. The grille itself was set into a cavity for a floating effect. The theme was continued on the headlight door-fender extension panels, which contained horizontal grooves from the middle of the headlights down. Front side-marker lights were also new.

New wider front and rear bumpers were almost identical to those used on the Hornet. Both the Gremlin and Hornet used free-standing recoverable front bumpers with new standard reinforced static rear bumpers. The Hornet used color-keyed filler panels.

For added durability and stability, two struts were added to the lift-up rear window. The angular body depressions on the sail panels were eliminated and were replaced with four vertical slanted depressions. On some Gremlin models, Gremlin in block letters appeared alongside the new depressions at the bottom, and it still appeared on the left leading edge of the hood bulge.

Both the standard and X package rally side stripes were redesigned. The standard one was almost identical to the 1971-72 X design. Instead of a pinstripe outlining the main thick stripe, a half-inch stripe ran parallel under it. The four side depressions were color-keyed to the stripes. The X rally stripe was of a hockey-stick design (as described in the main AMC brochure). It started at the fender tip and ran back, flaring out and continuing in line with the door handle. At the sail

The prototype Gremlin G/11 used a Hornet front end and gave a glimpse of what the 1979 Spirit liftback rear window and side styling was to look like. The car also had color- *keyed bumpers that would appear on the 1977 Hornet AMX hatchback.*

panel it went back a little and swept up, completely engulfing the four depressions, which were left body color. A pinstripe outlined the main stripe, and Gremlin X was die-cut into the stripe just forward of the door on the fender.

As on the Hornet, the optional X package contained more equipment than in the previous year. It now consisted of hockey-stick side stripes, painted back panel, engine liter decal, 14x6 slot-style wheels, D70x14 blackwall tires, Space Saver spare with regular wheel, custom interior with bucket seats, extra-quiet insulation package, cargo area insulation and carpeting, sport steering wheel, interior appointment package and special X identification. The X was rather large and placed on the upper center portion of the grille.

The Levi's custom trim package was still offered. Most of the heavy-duty equipment offered on the Gremlin and Hornet since 1970 was still available, plus the high-performance Group 19 items.

Engine and transmission choices for both cars were carried over from 1973, but the rear axle ratios were changed to conform to California state requirements. In the forty-nine states, the optional 3.31 ratio was deleted for all six-cylinder Gremlins and Hornets. In California, the 3.08 ratio was the only one offered.

The 3.54 ratio was the only one available on all 304 manual transmission Gremlins and Hornets, regardless of destination. The 304 column Torque Command in the Gremlin offered the 3.15 ratio, and in the Hornet it offered the 3.15 ratio as optional with the 2.87 ratio standard. The floor-mounted Torque Command in both the hatchback and the Gremlin came only with the 3.15 axle, again, regardless of the state it went to. The 3.15 ratio behind the Hornet 360 V-8 was standard, and the 3.54 was optional. If the 360 V-8 was in a Hornet two-door sedan, the 2.87 ratio was standard and the 3.15 was optional.

Both the Gremlin and the Hornet recorded good sales at the end of the model year. The Gremlin's total was 171,128, and the Hornet's was even higher at 176,275.

There was one last show car based on the Gremlin-Hornet design. It was called the Gremlin G/11 and it was first shown at the Detroit Auto Show in November 1973.

This car was basically a Hornet from the cowl forward, but the roof and side window design later appeared on the 1979 Spirit. The car was finished in bright red with color-keyed bumpers, twin black accents on hood, black grille and custom five-slot mag wheels with whitewall tires. The rear panel and taillight treatments were pure 1973-74 production Javelin.

Both cars carried AMC into the eighties. The Gremlin lasted until 1978 and became the Spirit in 1979; the Hornet turned into the Concord for 1978. The Gremlin's 304 V-8 was offered until mid-1976, and 1974 was the last year the 360 V-8 was offered in the sharp-looking Hornet.

The rear end of the G/11 used the production 1973-74 Javelin taillight panel. The rear-end opening also bore a slight resemblance to the one-off AMX/2 two-seater prototype sports car.

Chapter 8

Economy experts 1975-83

With the introduction of the catalytic converter and additional smog equipment, plus tighter emissions controls and mandatory low-octane unleaded gasoline for 1975, the new AMC cars' performance was nothing to write home about. The supercar's demise was imminent, but a few outstanding AMC cars remained.

Unfortunately, a performance car of the 1975-83 period was generally restricted to being an imitation, using scoops, spoilers, air dams, fender flares, ground effects packages and bold graphics (such as stripes and decals), coupled to resurrected supercar names or designations from the original supercar era.

Engines were generally big sixes or small V-8s, under 305 cubic inches, although there were some larger V-8s such as the GM 350 and the Pontiac and Chrysler 400s. There were even some four-cylinder-equipped cars called performance models, but true high-performance four-cylinder technology would not come into being until the mid-eighties.

Ford brought back the Cobra name and tacked it onto a specially painted 302 V-8 Mustang II in 1976. Chrysler created the Road Runner again, with a trim package that could be ordered on the Volare with such anemic power as the 225 cubic inch slant six-cylinder

The 1977 Hornet AMX hatchback was AMC's first use of a past muscle car's designation for what was really a muscle car in name only. Here it stands next to its ancestor, the two-seater AMX.

The midyear 1978 GT package brought back some styling flare to the Gremlin body design that had been little changed since its introduction in mid-1970. The 258 six with four-speed manual transmission was standard.

engine, which was a far cry from the original 1968 concept. GM was probably the most successful, having continued the Camaro and Firebird V-8 models.

1975

AMC was not to be left out. With the absence of the sporty Javelin for the 1975 model year, it was up to the Matador coupe, Hornet and Gremlin to carry on what was left of the high-performance image. The highest engine option available for the Hornet and Gremlin was the 304 V-8, which could be teamed to the floor-mounted three-speed manual or Torque Command automatic transmission. The optional X packages could still be ordered, along with most of the heavy-duty engine and suspension components previously available. The 360 cubic inch two- and four-barrel V-8s were restricted to the Matador and coupes.

The most powerful 1975 AMC car was the Matador coupe equipped with the four-barrel 360. Optional dual exhausts and the 3.54 Twin-Grip rear plus the previously mentioned heavy-duty items made for a respectable performer, and the X package made it look sporty.

The 401 V-8 was still around but was restricted to police use, although it is reported that a few Matador coupes were quietly equipped with the big stump-puller. The Pacer, which was the first wide small car, was introduced in mid-1975. It was not intended to be a performance model and was restricted to six-cylinder power only.

Randall Rambler in Mesa, Arizona, still specialized in transplanting 360 and 401 V-8 engines into Hornets and Gremlins, and decided to extend the option to the Pacer. A customer could order a V-8 Pacer (or Fishbowl, as it was quickly dubbed) from Randall in just about any stage of tune. The D/L and X packages could be ordered, and the dashboard design was reminiscent of the 1971-74 Javelins.

AMC did not promote high performance in its 1975 brochures. Its new slogan, in large bold letters, read, "The Economy Experts."

1976

The year 1976 was almost a carbon copy of 1975, except the Gremlin lost its 304 V-8 option at midyear and AMC began to produce imitation high-performance models.

The first was a 1976 customized Pacer called the Stinger, a name last used by Yenko for its limited edition high-performance Corvairs. The car was developed as a special project by American Motors' styling department. It was to be in the International Showcar Association, which consisted of a twenty-city tour throughout the United States and Canada.

The exterior was finished in yellow pearl that faded into pale yellow on the top and featured matte black bumblebee stripes on the rear section of the car from the rear door openings back. Also on the exterior were side-mounted exhausts, fender-mounted air scoops, flared wheelwell arches, Cibie road lights, front spoiler and oversized radial tires mounted on five-spoke Jackman Star wheels.

The interior of the Stinger featured black and yellow striped vinyl bucket seats, black headliner and sun visors, black leather shift boot, black twenty-four-ounce carpeting, black leather-wrapped sports steering wheel, yellow vinyl door pull straps, center console and rally instrumentation package.

1977

In 1977 came the first resurrection of a past AMC high-performance name. The legendary AMX designation that started it all was used for an optional trim package on the Hornet hatchback.

Called the Hornet AMX, it consisted of color-coordinated bumpers with black nerfing strips and bumper guards (from the 1974 Gremlin G/11 show car), color-coordinated front air dam, front and rear fender flares and backlight rear window louvers, five-spoke mag wheels, European-style brushed aluminum targa band a la Porsche with special insignia, floor console, rally instrumentation and tachometer, brushed aluminum instrument panel overlays, Soft-Feel sports steering wheel, custom interior door trim panels with assist straps, lower back panel molding, door and quarter window belt moldings and unique thick bodyside scuff moldings.

AMX in large letters with four hash marks preceding it was placed on the quarter panels just forward of the wheelwells and below the bodyside scuff moldings.

Other standard equipment included in the package were D78x14 black sidewall steel-belted radial tires and blacked-out trim consisting of grille, headlight bezels, dual mirrors (left-hand remote), door and quarter window frames, and lower back panel and license plate depression.

Exterior colors available were red, yellow, green or white, which reminded one of the 1969 Big Bad Javelins and AMXs.

Engine and drivetrain combinations were restricted to the 258 cubic inch six and the four-speed manual transmission, or the 304 V-8 with the floor-mounted automatic. Standard axle ratio for the six was a 2.73, with a 2.53 optional. For the V-8 it was a 2.87 standard, with a 3.15 optional. With a curb weight of a little over 3,300 pounds, performance was adequate.

Other downgrading performance aspects that took place in 1977 were the deletion of the three-speed manual transmission behind the 304 V-8 in all Hornets, and the discontinuation of the 360 four-barrel V-8 and dual exhausts in all Matadors including the coupe. This left the 360 two-barrel V-8 as the strongest AMC powerplant. Handling packages and heavy-duty

items could still be ordered. Although not advertised, a sympathic dealer could still order most of the Group 19 high-performance parts and install them.

Just to get an idea of how performance was defined in the late seventies, *Hi-Performance Cars* road tested a 1977 Hornet AMX. It gave the car a very good overall rating, despite its anemic acceleration and quarter-mile elapsed time and speed when one compared them to the brutes of the 1968-74 period.

The model tested was equipped with the 304 V-8 rated at 120 hp coupled to the floor-mounted Torque Command automatic with 3.15 rear-end gears. Steve Collisons' opening statements praised the new car's handling: "To a closet case Jackie Stewart like myself, AMC's newly restyled Hornet AMX comes closest to conquering the Curve." And he had this to say about the car's appearance: "Make no mistake, this one's a real head turner." Collisons described the car as "a perky little devil." He also had a chance to sample a 258 six four-speed version, and found it to be "surprisingly agile."

The six was given an added bonus because of its 20 mpg average versus the V-8's 14 mpg average. The 304 V-8 Hornet AMX recorded a 17.53 second elapsed time in the quarter-mile with a terminal speed of 76.46 mph. That was considered perky for the times.

The importance of a car's handling rather than its acceleration was beginning to become apparent, as evidenced by Collisons' closing statements: "Its properly engineered suspension components all worked as one to keep the tires glued to the ground and the body flat in the turns. In short the Hornet AMX has enough lateral chutzpah to keep it rocketing through the curve at nearly 50 mph, faster than anything we've driven since the Trans Am. And a recommendation like that certainly can't hurt your performance image." Between 330 and 376 Hornet AMXs were built for 1977.

AMC continued to offer special optional trim packages on its models, as did other manufacturers.

The Cassini Matador coupe was carried over into 1975 and was then replaced with the Barcelona coupe in 1976. For 1977, the package was continued and an even more plush Barcelona II coupe package was also available.

At mid-year, the 1977 Gremlin received a 2.0 liter version of the Porsche-Audi-style overhead valve four-cylinder engine coupled to a new four-speed manual transmission, and a station wagon was added to the Pacer line.

1978

For 1978, the Hornet became the Concord, AMC's first luxury compact car. The hatchback model was continued, and it looked even sportier than the old Hornet version, but the X package had been discontinued. The Hornet AMX now became the Concord AMX, also with an improvement appearancewise.

The design concept of the Concord AMX was nearly identical to 1977's Hornet version. A few of the most noticeable differences included flat-black fender flares, rear window louvers, front air dam, special grille, window moldings and rocker panels. Exterior color choices were Fire Cracker Red, Sunshine Yellow, Quick Silver Metallic, Alpine White or a special Classic Black with gold accents.

Engine line-up and transmission choice were unchanged. Conflicting reports indicate between 1,931 and 2,540 Concord AMXs built for 1978.

The 1977 Gremlin, now in its last year and powered with only four- and six-cylinder engines as in 1976, was right back where it started from. The X package was still available, and a mid-year GT package

Sporty-looking aluminum star wheels were a popular option on the new 1978 Concord AMX.

The AMX trim package was available on the new Concord for 1978, creating the AMX hatchback. It was basically the same as 1977's Hornet version.

was offered. Graphics and equipment differed slightly from the 1976 model's.

The GT package started with the Gremlin custom model and included as standard equipment such items as the 258 cubic inch six-cylinder engine; four-speed manual transmission; front and rear fender flares and front air dam in body color with special accent pinstriping; rally instrumentation with tachometer; GT spoke-styled wheels with trim rings; DR70x14 steel-belted radial tires; front sway bar; blacked-out back panel with pinstriping; GT bodyside stripe; blacked-out wiper arms, windshield molding, door and window frames, B-pillars and grille insert (with bright accents); Soft-Feel vinyl bucket seats and custom door panels; sport steering wheel; brushed aluminum instrument panel overlay; body color bumpers with bumper guards and nerfing strips; dual black mirrors (left-hand remote); color-keyed hood decal stripe; extra-quiet insulation; day/night mirror; and more. It was a neat-looking package, and only a limited number were built.

There was also a limited edition Gremlin Sundowner package made for the California market. The Barcelona package continued on the Matador coupe and was also offered for the first time on the four-door sedan. The coupe version retained its unique body-colored front and rear bumpers. This was the last year for the Matador models. The Pacer also received the 304 V-8 for the first time.

1979

In 1979, Renault of France purchased controlling interest in AMC stock. This merger ultimately led to the discontinuation of AMC performance models, and the last true AMC muscle car was the Spirit AMX.

Essentially a redesigned Gremlin, the Spirit was the company's new subcompact for the eighties. The fastback and rear side window treatments on the lift-back models were taken right from the 1974 Gremlin G/11 show car, which was an operational prototype of the design-study Javelin XT prototype. The old chopped-back model was still available as the Spirit sedan.

The 1979 304 V-8 AMX was probably the closest and best concept of all the 1971-80 AMXs to rival the original 1968-70 two-seaters. Even the wheelbases were only one inch apart. The new Spirit styling lent itself to the final version of the AMX trim package.

Standard features included front and rear black bumpers with bumper guards and nerfing strips; front air dam and rear deck spoiler with accent stripes; front and rear fender flares; blacked-out grille; turbo-cast II aluminum wheels; ER60x14 belted radial tires; dual remote mirrors; AMX letters and graphics; sport vinyl or Caberfae corduroy bucket seats; brushed aluminum instrument panel overlays; leather-wrapped sport steering wheel; center console with armrest; gauge package consisting of clock, electric tachometer, ammeter, oil pressure gauge, water temperature gauge and manifold vacuum gauge; rally tuned suspension package with front and rear sway bars; and performance tuned exhaust sound with the optional 304 V-8 and four-speed manual transmission. The latter was the big news for 1979.

The V-8 and manual transmission combination also could be ordered on the new Spirit liftback GT. An automatic on the floor was offered with a 2.56 rear standard and a 2.87 Twin-Grip rear optional. The 2.87 ratio was the only rear offered with the four-speed. The 258 cubic inch six was the standard engine available, with the same choices and with axle ratios of 2.53 and 3.08.

The AMC brochure described the AMX's performance as nothing short of inspiring. Its appearance, inside and out, was described as bold and command-

ing. The final word was, "AMX—a very moving experience. The only thing more exciting than its looks is the way it acts."

Car Craft decided to take AMC up on its claims and road-tested a 304 V-8 four-speed version. The testing staff was impressed with the visual impact. They liked the added-on spoilers, flares and air dams, but felt those could have been fastened in a more secure manner.

Also disliked was the absence of a key slot on the liftback, which was covered by the spoiler. A remote

The 1980 Spirit offered a new sports-car-type three-spoke steering wheel with leather-like grip.

The new 1979 Spirit received the AMX trim option, which blended in well with the body style. The car was available with the 304 V-8 and four-speed manual transmission. The last-year 1980 version was almost identical with the exception of the deletion of the V-8 option.

The 1979 Spirit liftback GT was available with the 304 V-8 four-speed combination with a sporty look. Spirit styling

remained little changed right up to the model's last year of production in 1983.

157

cable release was mounted inside the glove compartment to permit opening of the liftback itself.

Inside, the rally gauge package was placed underneath the radio and heater controls, which in their opinion was not good at all. Although they liked the throaty sound of the exhaust note, the engine was nothing but a "pinging" low performer. They even said a 305 Monza and 302 Capri had no trouble dusting off the 304 AMX.

The best the car could manage in the quarter-mile in stock form was a 17.50 second elapsed time at 79 mph. For comparison, the 258 six-cylinder AMX did it in 17.70 seconds at 77 mph. Not too much difference there, but as *Car Craft* stated, "Happily, the car's handling far surpassed its other abilities." And they went on to say, "The car is genuinely fun to drive. It feels peppy and responsive, and you really aren't aware of its limitations until you actually time it."

Car Craft stated that what the car really needed was a dealer-installed 401 cubic inch V-8. Many of the AMXs probably did receive 360 or 401 backyard conversions.

It was then decided to tap into the car's hidden potential. A set of Casler headers complete with smog fittings was hooked up to the stock catalytic converter and single exhaust, and an Edelbrock SP2-P aluminum intake manifold with a Carter 625 cfm four-barrel carburetor were also installed.

As a result, the overall drivability of the car and its usable rpm range were much improved. The car ran a 16.70 second elapsed time at an even 80 mph. Although that was good, the car would have benefited with a tuned free-flowing exhaust system and deeper gears.

Car Craft concluded: "With some real effort you can turn the AMX into a decent little street machine, and with some extraordinary effort you may come close to the type of performance available in the original AMX."

Car and Driver came up with more or less the same impressions and results when it road-tested a similarly equipped Spirit GT liftback. But *Car and Driver* was also impressed with the AMX as a complete package. The staff liked its performance, saying, "The early prototype AMX we drove had no trouble laying down two smooth black streaks on acceleration." They further stated, "Under all the wolf's clothing, there's a real wolf. The AMX is AMC's TransAm." And their driving impressions said it all: "We haven't had much more than a quick drive in a very rough facsimile of this aggressive little coupe so far, but the right parts are here to make the AMX a serious contender for modern muscle-car medals."

The Concord was still available in a sporty hatchback model with a 258 four-speed six or a 304 column automatic V-8. The Pacer could be ordered with the same power teams. But sadly, 1979 was the last year for any AMC V-8 passenger car, as the 304 was yanked from the option list on all future models. It was a farewell to the AMC performance car, forever.

It is a shame that AMC discontinued the V-8 Spirit and AMX (possibly under pressure from the Renault merger), because they could very well have paralleled and rivaled the development and performance of the Mustang GT five-liter 302 V-8 model.

Perhaps AMC could not be faulted completely. Just when it looked as though performance was coming back and things were returning to normal, when

The elegant-looking Concord hatchback body style was last produced for the 1979 model year. The Concord too received few styling changes up to its last production year in 1983.

the second oil embargo hit in 1979, and it looked as though we would all be riding bicycles for the rest of our lives. The car industry panicked; for the 1980 model year even Pontiac discontinued its large 400 V-8 engine, and Ford temporarily dropped the 302 V-8 in the Mustang and replaced it with a smaller and more fuel efficient 255 cubic inch version.

The 1980s

The AMX was continued for 1980 with more or less the same standard and optional equipment carried over from 1979, minus the 304 two-barrel V-8. There were slight differences in appearance, the most notable being that less subtle racing side stripes were used and the large AMX decal on the rear spoiler was replaced with a small AMX nameplate.

There were only 865 AMXs built in 1980, making them extremely rare today. The 1979 version saw better sales at 2,902 units built.

There were three new additional models introduced for 1980, called Eagles. These were America's first four-wheel-drive passenger cars. They were basically Concords with the four-wheel-drive systems. As was the Concord, the new Eagle was offered in two-door sedan, four-door sedan and station wagon models. The Concord hatchback model was dropped.

The Spirit sedan, liftback and liftback GT were continued, as were the Pacer hatchback and station wagon models. Luxury came to the Spirit series in the form of the Limited package, which had been introduced on the Pacer in 1979. In 1980, Spirit sales were up eighty-eight percent over 1979 sales. In December 1979, the Pacer was discontinued after seeing just a few months as a 1980 model.

After being used for only three years, the Porsche-Audi-style four-cylinder engine was replaced with the Pontiac 2.5 liter 151 cubic inch 90 hp Iron Duke four.

In the late seventies, turbocharging started to catch on as an inexpensive way of adding power to small-displacement four- and six-cylinder engines with few other modifications necessary. Turbocharging technology came into full swing in the eighties, and became instrumental in the quest for more fuel-efficient high-performance engines powering the newest and most sophisticated sleek sports cars.

There were two new models added to the 1981 line-up: the new four-wheel-drive Eagle Kammback

Two crew members of the Breedlove team place a section of the stressed Harvey Aluminum skin over the cockpit section of the monocoque frame.

A new five-speed transmission was introduced for 1982. The gauge package or rally instrumentation consisting of electric clock, vacuum, amps and oil pressure gauges was available from 1977-83.

The highly modified 340 ci version of the AMC 360 block featured an Edelbrock tunnel-ram intake manifold, a pair of Holley 4500 carburetors and a General Kinetics cam and kit. The engine was redlined at 9000 rpm and used Kendall GT-1 racing oil.

The 1983 Spirit GT bowed out with one of the most sporty-looking and functional cockpits in the industry. Too bad V-8 power was no longer available to go with this hot setup.

and SX/4. The Kammback was based on the Spirit sedan and the SX/4 on the Spirit liftback. Aside from these two new four-wheel-drives, 1981 was practically a repetition of 1980.

It was more or less the same story for 1982, but with a few surprises in the early months of the model year. Both the Spirit sedan and its four-wheel-drive cousin, the Eagle Kammback, were discontinued. One important item introduced in 1982 was a five-speed manual transmission on all models and engines across the board.

For 1983, the AMC model line-up was limited when compared with the previous year's. The Spirit and Concord entered their last production year with a total of three body styles available between the two. There was the Spirit liftback, the Concord four-door sedan and the Concord station wagon. There were also only three Eagles left: the SX/4, the four-door sedan and the four-door station wagon. The four-cylinder engine was pulled from the Spirit and Concord, leaving the 258 six as the only engine available. The four-cylinder was still offered in the Eagles. The hottest-looking car for 1983 was the Spirit liftback GT.

And how was the car's performance endorsed in the AMC brochure? "For still more sports flavor, there's an affordable new Spirit G.T. that really does a number on the competition." "Sports flavor" was right, "affordable" was right, but about the only kind of "number" it could do on the competition was the number of miles per gallon because that's about all the performance the car had left in it. But AMC was not the only one with mundane acceleration at the time; its performance was typical throughout the industry.

Chapter 9

Investment potential

AMC closed its high-performance chapter in much the same way as it had opened it: by producing pretty bodies with sporty looks but with a lack of power. With performance coming back to the automotive industry in the mid-eighties, AMC enthusiasts wondered if a true American Motors muscle car, or any car for that matter, might come down the assembly line again as an American-built car.

In January 1987, American Motors Owners Association board member Grover Cleveland launched a campaign to show how much interest there was among potential buyers. He petitioned owners of AMC cars to call or write American Motors urging it to return to American-built products rather than the French-Renault-designed cars being built at the Kenosha plant. AMO stated specifically that it wanted to buy an American car built by AMC and was not satisfied with the current offerings from the Big Three. Retired AMC vice-president of styling Dick Teague offered to come out of retirement to design the car should the campaign prove successful enough to justify the action.

The result of this campaign will probably never be known. On March 9, 1987, Chrysler Corporation announced that it was planning to purchase Renault's 41.6 percent share of American Motors stock.

Industry analysts generally agree that a transaction such as this usually spells doom for the company being purchased. It has happened too many times in the past not to be a strong possibility—remember what happened to Graham, Hudson, Packard and Nash, to name a few. In some cases even the buying company was dissolved, as with Kaiser, Frazer, Studebaker and Willys, but that is highly unlikely to happen to Chrysler.

On the favorable side, values for AMC cars will probably start to increase, although not immediately. On the minus side, parts will become scarce within a few years, and some vendor and junkyard hoarders, scalpers and pirates will inflate prices almost beyond reach. It will then be up to the various AMC enthusiast clubs to maintain a certain control.

What AMC vehicles look good as future collectibles and investments that should appreciate in value in the next five to ten years? Since AMC cars have almost always had fewer body styles and engines to choose from when compared to the Big Three, I would put my money on the limited edition and heavily optioned out big-engined high-performance hardtop and convertible models. Clean low-mileage and one-owner examples of six-cylinder or small V-8 models should not be overlooked, however.

The 1968-70 AMXs will certainly continue to increase in value, including all the limited edition models, especially since their recent induction into the Milestone Car Society's list of certified milestone cars.

The 1968-70 Javelins should not be too far behind, as well as the sleek 1971-74 Group 7 fendered beauties. Unique models in those years to especially keep in mind would be the 1969 and imitation 1970 Big Bad models, 1970 Trans-Am and Mark Donohue editions, 1971-74 AMX and 1972-73 Pierre Cardin versions, and finally, the limited edition 1973 Trans-Am Victory Javelin.

Although Rebels, Matadors and Ambassadors haven't caught on yet, with the exception of the 1967-68 Rebel convertibles and 1970 Rebel Machine, a 1971 Ambassador two-door hardtop in number two condition recently sold at an auction for $5,000. The 1967-70 Rebel and Ambassador 343 and 390 high-performance two-door hardtops should begin to catch on mainly because of their low production figures. A 1967-68 four-speed model would be even rarer.

About the only ones that look good in the 1971-74 period would be the 1971 Matador Machine or the 1972 Matador with the NASCAR package. The 1971-73 401 hardtops are also desirable.

With the exception of the 1971 Hornet SC/360 two-door sedan, interest in the Hornets and Gremlins

161

does not seem to be overwhelming. Still, a good bet would be a 1972 Hornet X or Rallye X model with the 360 V-8, and the 1973-74 hatchbacks with the same engine should hold their values. As far as the Gremlin goes, the 1972-74 304 X models will bring the highest prices in that series.

Getting back to the sixties, the 1969 Hurst SC/Rambler has made its mark and will continue to go up in value. A sleeper that is just now beginning to gain popularity is the 1966-69 Rambler American Rogue or 440 two-door hardtops. When equipped with the 290 or one-year 343 V-8 and four-speed, they make for a fun-to-drive and fine-looking compact combined with space and nice handling.

The limited-production competition and race cars such as the four-wheel-drive SC/Rambler and Hurst S/S AMX will be worth their weight in gold, as will any of the one-off show or prototype cars. The value of the six AMX/3 two-seater sports cars go without saying.

Going back even further, the 1957 Rambler Rebel 327, 1964 Classic-based Typhoon two-door hardtop, 1965-67 Marlins and, as the trend seems to indicate, just about any convertible in decent shape, are worth hanging on to. Again, don't pass up those one-owner, superclean, low-mileage, driven-only-on-Sunday grannymobiles, no matter what body style they may be or what engine-transmission combination they may have.

Happy hunting!

Chapter 10

AMC goes racing

By the early seventies, American Motors was involved in numerous racing events including NHRA, IMSA (International Motor Sports Association), Trans-Am, off-road, NASCAR, thrill shows and others. AMC often came from behind to score significant victories in those events, and as it gained experience, the company realized it could run with the best the competition had to offer.

For a company that had a policy against racing up to the late sixties, this involvement was spectacular.

Before 1967, American Motors had no racing program and only a few racing cars.

In 1960, a compact car rally took place at the Continental Divide Raceways near Denver, Colorado. A Rambler American co-driven by Jonny Mauro and Tommy Rice won the event against Corvairs and Falcons.

In 1963, *Hot Rod* magazine set up a couple of 327-powered Rambler Ambassadors for the drags, just to prove that AMC had at least a little punch to offer in

Motor Trend's 1967 Rogue project car was one of the first true AMC muscle cars to use the new-design V-8 engine. The model used was a two-door hardtop equipped with the 290 cubic inch 225 hp V-8 coupled to the four-speed manual transmission. The car was called the Rogue Runner and had a Road Runner cartoon character logo on both doors. Plymouth would use a similar logo for its sleeper 1968 Road Runner two-door sedan big-block model.

its models. The car had limited success owing to its outdated engine design, driveline and suspension, however. Right up to 1966, AMC still used the torque-tube drive, long abandoned by the Big Three.

A 327-powered 1966 Ambassador number 44 driven by Larry Hess, was even tried on a few short NASCAR tracks with little success.

Indy car builder Barney Navarro of Glendale, California, pulled the ultimate with a 199 ci 1965 Rambler six-cylinder-engined Indy car called the Navarro Injection. Navarro chose the Rambler six because it had seven main bearings, eight counterweights and half-inch head bolts. No Ford, Chevy or Chrysler six offered all three features in one package. These features were considered essential for the 203 ci rule limit for blown engines.

Initially, the highly modified engine was carbureted and turbo-supercharged to produce close to 560 bhp at 6000 rpm on alcohol. Later, in 1968, the engine had a Navarro-designed injection system that measured the airflow and matched fuel flow to airflow to produce 640 bhp at 7000 rpm. It still used a turbo-supercharger. The engine was installed in an A. J. Watson Indy chassis that was used by Roger Ward in the 1964 Indy 500.

During preliminary tests, Les Scott easily qualified for the Memorial Day brickyard race, clocking lap speeds of better than 150 mph, the fastest six ever at Indy at the time. Unfortunately, the car was unable to run on race day because of engine development problems.

When AMC came out with its new models for 1967, new engines, drivelines and suspensions had finally arrived. These offered a ray of hope.

One of the first active Rambler dealers to become involved in racing was Randall Rambler. Randall's was one of the first to realize the potential of the new V-8 Rambler American, and chose to campaign a 1967 Rambler American 440 two-door sedan equipped with the 343 four-barrel V-8 and four-speed transmission.

This was AMC's largest engine at the time, stuffed into one of its lightest body styles. The car was owned and raced by Skip Randall and Bob Wamsley of Mesa. It raced in AHRA's (American Hot Rod Association) 6D/SO class, turning elapsed times of 12.47 at 116.3 mph, proving its competitiveness.

The engine was bored out to 350 cubic inches and had Forgedtrue pistons with a 12.5:1 compression ratio. A 0.525-inch-lift Crower cam was used, with 310 degrees intake duration and 330 degrees exhaust duration. A single 780 cfm Holley four-barrel sat on the stock cast-iron intake manifold.

A heavy-duty Schiefer clutch, a 4.89:1 rear-end ratio and a pair of M&H slicks launched the car quite well. The car was all steel and weighed a mere 2,785 pounds.

Another Rambler dealer that was active in racing was K&K Rambler of New York City. Service rep-

resentative and drag enthusiast Jesse Schneider decided to campaign another 343 American, called *Beep-Beep*, and chose the top-of-the-line Rogue two-door hardtop model.

Hi-Performance Cars spent a day with Schneider at New York National Raceway Dragstrip. Right off the showroom floor, the car ran a best of 17.54 seconds at 83.0 mph in the quarter-mile.

The car was equipped with the stock single exhaust system and 3.54 Twin-Grip rear. Schneider then installed the factory high-performance cam and kit and a Sparkomatic transistorized tachometer and traction bars. Other modifications included using colder Champion N-9Y spark plugs, removing the air cleaner, uncorking the exhaust and removing the power steering system. The car then clocked a 15.7 elapsed time at 95 mph. That was more like it. With a set of 8.00x14 Casler slicks, the car ran 15.15 at 92 mph. Later the distributor was reworked by Dayton Ignition with hi-po wires, and valve cover breathers were installed along with a set of Dougs headers.

The car did not seem to be running right, so a check was made, uncovering a set of burnt and bent valves. A complete rebuild was done and a Chevy declutching fan was installed. Gabriel shocks, a Sparkomatic shifter linkage kit and the factory 4.44:1 rear axle gears were also installed. A supercharged Studebaker carburetor airbox was tried, but was discarded because instead of boosting airflow, it restricted it.

With all these modifications the car ran a 13.91 elapsed time at 100 mph. Different jets were tried with the stock Carter four-barrel, and 0.95s worked the best. The car then ripped a 13.98 elapsed time at 107 mph.

During the 1967 season, the little *Beep-Beep* took home a dozen class trophies from New York National Speedway and Dove Dragway in New Jersey. Its best time of the season was 13.4 seconds at 108 mph.

For the 1968 season, AMC and Sparkomatic sponsored the *Beep-Beep*. It ran in Super Stock E or C/Hotrod class at New York's National Speedway NHRA track. It held both records, running a best elapsed time of 11.88. Schneider was so successful that he was appointed performance manager of Richmond Rambler in Staten Island, New York, which also eventually sponsored the car.

Randall Rambler produced many other sleeper performance AMC models. In fact, AMC bought the V-8 conversion from Randall for its own 1978 factory V-8 Pacer model. Randall Rambler was instrumental in creating the first Rambler race cars. What follows are some of the most famous and notable racing cars, drivers and crews that carried AMC's red, white and blue colors.

1967 *Motor Trend* Rogue Runner project car

During its initial tests of the 1966½ Rogue 290 V-8 hardtop, *Motor Trend* magazine was impressed with the car, its handling traits and the overall package. It decided to show the performance aspect of AMC's new entry in the small car-big engine field. The project was run in the June 1967 through February 1968 issues.

The car used was a 1967 Rambler American Rogue two-door hardtop equipped with the 290 four-barrel V-8 rated at 225 hp, four-speed manual transmission, heavy-duty suspension and cooling, and electrical systems. A 343 V-8 car would have been preferred, but *Motor Trend*'s order went in before AMC announced that that engine was offered in the American.

The first items to be installed on the car once it was delivered were the factory hi-po cam and kit consisting of a high-lift 0.295 inch high-duration camshaft, anti-pump-up hydraulic lifters, heavier valve springs, valve stem oil deflectors, valve spring upper retainers and dampeners, adjustable rocker studs, modified pushrods, valve spring retainer locks and rocker arm stud nuts. The metal intake manifold with the blocked heat riser was also installed, along with the 4.44:1 rear axle gear set. These items really made the little Rambler sound tough at idle or cruising.

The car also had a factory stock single exhaust system, so a pair of dump tubes (or sneaker plugs, as they were originally called) was installed just below the bend of the exhaust Y-pipe coming off the exhaust manifolds. A set of Traction Master traction bars was installed along with an extra pair of rear shocks to prevent wheel hop.

At its initial pass at Irwindale Raceway with two people aboard and 100 pounds of test equipment, the car went down the strip and chirped the rear tires going into second and third, netting a 16.9 second elapsed time and a speed of 83.0 mph. The car also registered 3.4 seconds to 30 mph, 5.7 to 40 mph and 9.1 to 60 mph.

With the simple removal of air cleaner and uncorking of the bypass caps, the car clocked 15.3 seconds at 93.0 mph, clearly indicating that the exhaust system was superrestrictive. The other times improved significantly, with 0-30 coming in 2.9 seconds, 0-45 in 4.6 and 0-60 in 7.8. With removal of all the test equipment and the passenger, the car went 14.8 seconds at 94.0 mph. *Motor Trend* was quoted as saying, "This has got to be the sleeper of the year."

Motor Trend's associate *Hot Rod* borrowed the car for about a week to do its own testing. It too praised the handling of the car, and attributed part of it to the excellent D70x14 Goodyear blue-streak tires and 5.5 inch wide wheels.

The first thing the *Hot Rod* crew did was to tear down the Carter AFB, cleaning out all passages and properly setting the float levels. Tension was removed from the centrifugal advance weight springs, and a fresh set of Champion N-12Y plugs was installed. The first run at San Fernando Raceway netted a 16.71 elapsed time at 81.11 mph.

The smog pump belt was then removed, alternator belt loosened, air cleaner top removed, front tires set to 55 psi, rears set at 35 psi and gas tank filled with premium. With the exhaust still closed the car pulled a 16.32 elapsed time at 89.37 mph, qualifying the car in AHRA's H/Stock class.

The car was later taken to Irwindale again and run with a few more modifications. The float level was raised, the acceleration pump stroke lengthened, a Hurst shifter installed and the dump tubes opened up. The car now ran 15.15 at 93.0 mph. This was just about equivalent to a stock 1967 390 Mustang.

With a 1968 Olds 442 cold air package installed, the car went 14.89 at 95.0 mph. *Hot Rod* was quoted as saying, "Astonishing for a 3220 pound car with an unblueprinted engine."

When *Motor Trend* got the car back, modifications were once again performed. A new-design clutch and pressure plate system called the Rev-loc by Schiefer was installed. The quad-shock and Traction Master setup in the rear did not work well, so a set of lift bars was installed. The bars came from a Randall Rambler 343 American demo. These bars cured the wheel hop problem the Rogue was encountering with the old setup. Later, *Motor Trend* made up its own system. The lift bars netted a 0.1 second improvement. By installing a set of Casler 26x7 inch wide recap cheater slicks, *Motor Trend* realized a 0.25 second improvement.

Although they were not legal for NHRA meets, a set of Ansen E.T. tubeless magnesium wheels was installed just to set off the car's appearance. These were made of an aluminum and titanium alloy to resist oxidation.

When a set of Cyclone individual 1⅜ inch four-tube exhaust headers was installed the Rogue took off. A 3 mph speed gain was achieved, and a 0.3 second improvement came with unmuffled stock exhaust manifolds. With all modifications up to this point, the car was running between 95 and 97 mph at about 14.50 seconds elapsed time.

The next item to be tried was an Offenhauser aluminum hi-rise single four-barrel intake manifold while still using the stock AFB carburetor. An Offenhauser chrome low-height and low-restriction air cleaner was used. These two modifications improved the elapsed time by 0.2 seconds. A nice pair of same-brand aluminum valve covers was installed to enhance the engine's appearance.

Bill Hanyon of Scientific Automotive in Pasadena, California, and Grant MacCoon of Grant Industries helped tremendously throughout the project to make the Rogue as competitive as possible. A Grant dual-coil Flamethrower distributor was fitted to the engine to net a 0.1 to 0.2 second improvement. The distributor along with the dual-coil setup started to act up. It was found that the distributor had defective and inferior parts inside and that both coils were defective. Replacement of the parts cured the problem. Grant

The 1967 Grant Rambler Rebel SST was AMC's first attempt at the funny car class. The car was instrumental in changing the company's staid image. Various track records were set with this fuel-burning supercharged terror.

moly piston rings were installed along with another cosmetic touch, a Grant all-wood-type steering wheel.

The engine started to sound as if it had a burned valve. When the heads were pulled, sixteen bent valves were found, having contacted the piston tops. A quick phone call to AMC brought new valves and springs and a recommendation to notch all piston tops. Early cam kit springs were found to experience coil bind, but AMC guaranteed replacement with a new improved design to buyers of all initial models.

While the engine was apart, it was time for some machine work. The crankshaft was balanced with a new set of bearings, piston rings were replaced and the heads were cc'd, surfaced and volume corrected to 55 cc. Pistons were cut 0.060 on the intake relief and 0.025 on the exhaust. With all this work done, the car clocked a 14.02 elapsed time.

To take things a bit further, a Schiefer aluminum flywheel was installed. The Cyclone headers were removed and a pair of individual 1⅜ inch equal-length four-tube headers with thirty-inch collectors (shortened to twenty inches) was installed. The car now ran a 13.90 second elapsed time at 98 mph.

The Rogue proved to be a formidable foe as it earned over a dozen class win trophies at Irwindale Raceway, shut them down at Orange County International Raceway's weekly grudge races and won eliminator brackets at Lions Dragstrip.

As suggested by the logo on both sides of the little two-tone red-and-white hardtop, the car was indeed a *Rogue Runner*. (Incidentally, the logo was a road runner illustrated in motion—watch out Plymouth!)

1967-68 Grant Rambler Rebel SST

The 1967 Grant Rambler Rebel SST was AMC's first serious attempt to assault the quarter-mile and one-eighth-mile tracks. With the introduction of the all-new and biggest-yet 343 V-8 along with a nice clean body style for the 1967 model year, AMC, for the first time in its history, had something that just might be competitive on the track with the Big Three.

The Grant Rambler Rebel SST was engineered and built for AMC by Grant Industries in Los Angeles. It was campaigned by Hayden Proffitt and driven by Bill Hayes for the 1967 season, and Proffitt himself drove for the 1968 season. The crew included Gary Ferguson and Les Shockley.

From its first race in June 1967 to the end of the year, the Grant Rebel SST toured and raced in nineteen cities, setting a national speed record and six track records.

The racer's first impressive accomplishment was at the NHRA Summernationals in Indianapolis, where it ran 172 mph to make the top ten qualifiers.

It then set a new national speed record for one-eighth-mile tracks at Saint Louis International Raceway with an incredible 136 mph pass backed by a 156 mph run. This also set a new speed record for the track.

It was then off to Vargo Dragway in Allentown, Pennsylvania, where another track speed record was set. During its tour of Florida, new track speed and elapsed time records were set at Tampa Dragway and Central Florida Raceway in Orlando. At Tampa the Rebel defeated *The Penetration*, a Dodge Charger, with a speed of 180.85 mph at an 8.11 elapsed time.

The car was exhibited in AMC/Rambler showrooms for two or three days before each race, and it attracted an average of 850 visitors to each showroom. Numerous stick-on patches, giant buttons, radio antenna pennants, bumper stickers, jackets, T-shirts, drivers photos and posters of the car were available at the dealer to further promote the Rebel's racing program. The dealers agreed that this was a successful campaign by American Motors.

How could this new car be so successful in its first year of racing? It was not an easy task, but Grant Industries president Grant MacCoon and Hayden Proffitt could handle it. They went out of their way to prove the competitiveness of AMC's new image cars, dubbed the Giant Killers by American Motors marketing advertisers.

Proffitt, a four-time National Drag Racing champion, parked a Chevrolet racer to drive the Rebel. Grant had over twenty years of experience with automotive speciality equipment manufacturing in piston rings and ignition systems, and had campaigned and run Indy cars called the Grant Piston Ring Specials at the brickyard in the late 1940s and early 1950s. The two proved to be an almost unbeatable combination.

Chassis builder Dave Jeffers started out using a special 1.25 inch x 0.065 inch chromemoly tubular steel frame with a fiberglass shell body resembling the new 1967 Rebel two-door hardtop with a six-inch extended nose. The car was set up to run in NHRA's X/S (Experimental/Stock) class and SX/S (Super Experimental/Stock class, better known as the funny car class.

The wheelbase was set at 122 inches, and it had a front tread of fifty-eight inches and a rear tread of fifty-six inches. Goodyear tires were used all around, with the rears being 419-E 11.00x16 inch slicks set at 12 psi. Wheels were American Racing magnesium type with the fronts measuring 8x16 inches. There were no front brakes, but the rear was equipped with heavy-duty Airheart double spot discs, with steel brackets substituted for the aluminum ones, assisted by a fourteen-foot parachute for safe and controlled stopping. Adjustable coil shocks front and rear suspended the car. A three-inch dropped-tube axle with Ford Econoline spindles in front along with crossbraces and a bell crank were all engineered to make takeoff handling and high-speed motoring as effortless as possible. A Corvair steering assembly was used.

The cockpit was nicely finished with lightweight polished aluminum paneling. The transmission control, fuel lever and chute release were all within easy reach. The driver's bucket seat was constructed so that it sealed the driver off from any danger when the body was lowered into position. A thirteen-inch Grant woodgrain steering wheel topped things off. An escape hatch was also incorporated for the driver, just in case

of disaster, and a superthick rollover bar gave him further protection.

The rear of the car held the battery, the water tank and two sets of wheelie casters or bars. The power plug-in for starting had an oil pressure gauge nearby so a crewmember could shut the engine off before any damage was done. All aluminum panels were fastened with quick-disconnect clips.

The fiberglass replica 1967 Rebel body also received its share of modifications. Front and rear aerodynamic spoilers were molded in, along with air ducting on the forward hood surface. Grant Rambler Rebel SST was painted on both doors with National Speed Record Holder on each quarter panel. Grant Rebel SST also appeared on the front spoiler. The complete body was painted Candy Apple Red, and a blue stripe on top ran the length of the car from hood to rear spoiler, with white stars painted inside. There was also a liberal dose of chrome and polished aluminum outside to give the body that extra touch.

The body was hinged at the rear for easy entry and exit, and contained a hatch section in the roof for emergency situations. All glass used was General Electric Lexan which was bulletproof and did not shatter on impact.

The heart of the entire car was the new and extensively modified AMC 343 V-8 bored to $4^3/_{16}$ and stroked to $3^3/_8$ to produce a whopping 438 ci. The stroker crank was welded up, shot peened, microfinished and center counterweighted. The rod bearing journals were widened for more bearing area and the mains were grooved for additional lubrication. Special custom forged aluminum rods were made, forcing the bottoms of the cylinders to be clearanced $3/_8$x$3/_8$. The stock soft bearings were retained. The stock pistons were replaced with Grant aluminum forgings containing Dykes-type stainless top rings and moly steel second and third oil control rings. The pistons also had to be reverse-dished to form a slight Hemi-chambered dome to drop the compression ratio, which was set at 7.8:1. Nylon buttons on the piston's sides stabilized them in the cylinders. A dry-sump oil pump system containing a $2\frac{1}{2}$ gallon aluminum tank was designed for the engine. An experimental roller tappet cam was made, with a 0.540 inch lift and 340 degree duration. Late-model 426 Hemi Chrysler lifters were used with Chevy-length hardened chromemoly pushrods.

Rogers Porting had a tough job on its hands making the stock head handle a blown supercharged, prepped block. The heads were ported, polished, studded and O-ringed. Valves used were stainless steel billets measuring $1^{15}/_{16}$ inches for the intakes and $1\frac{3}{4}$ inches for the exhausts. The combustion chambers were reworked to displace 72 cc, and special half-inch head bolts and washers had to be fabricated to help keep the heads glued to the block. To finish off the heads, Chevy-size Vasco jet springs, titanium retainers, hardened keepers and modified aluminum wide roller rockers were installed.

For the crankshaft to accept a blower drive pulley, its nose was modified with a one-quarter-inch keyway.

The induction system consisted of Enderle Bug Catcher injectors topping a 6-71 GMC blower with anodized case and rotors turning seventeen percent overdrive with boost set at 19 to 20 psi. The manifold pop-off valve was set at 21 psi.

The Gilmer-style drive and ball-bearing end plates were supplied by Cragar. A special front cover drive unit built by Grant spun the Flamethrower dual-point magneto, oil pump and Rolls-Royce aircraft fuel pump. The ignition system was made up of dual-capacitive discharge units, also by Flamethrower, with ignition lead locked in at thirty-five degrees. This whole combination produced 1,200 hp at 9000 rpm.

The engine burned alcohol and nitromethane, blended at various percentages, and was set back forty percent in the chassis for maximum traction. Exhaust headers were also by Grant.

The drivetrain consisted of an AMC Borg-Warner automatic three-speed transmission extensively modified by B&M. The converter and valve body were reworked, line pressures were altered and the stall speed was set at 2500 rpm. A flex-blanket shield and cable control were added. The stock AMC rear end was used but with important changes. Heavy-duty Hy-Tuff steel billet axle shafts were used with heavy-duty 4.1:1 gears and a twenty-nine-inch open driveshaft. The entire car weighed only 2,145 pounds.

After a full season of racing, the 1967 Grant Rambler Rebel SST was retired from the track. It put on an auto show tour involving numerous cities and Rambler dealers while the new 1968 Grant Rebel SST took to the drag strip circuit. The Rambler name was dropped, as it was on the production Rebel SST for 1968, and the new car received the familiar red-white-blue American Motors paint scheme from front to rear. A host of other detail improvements were incorporated into the new racer.

The 1968 Grant Rebel SST followed in the footsteps of its 1967 predecessor. It went on tour to Rambler dealerships across the country, where it was displayed for one or two days before each race. It ran more or less the same speeds and elapsed times as the 1967 racer did.

At Greenvalley Raceway in Texas, it went 181.25 mph at an elapsed time of 8.41 seconds. It also set a new elapsed time record for the Greater Evansville Raceway in Indiana. The new Grant Rebel SST set records at six different drag strips for 1968.

All in all, the 1967 and 1968 racers did an excellent job.

1968 Doug Thorley Javelin 1 funny car

Right on the heels of the Grant Rebel SST came the Doug Thorley Javelin 1 funny car. This was also a joint venture, but this time it was with American Motors and header manufacturer Doug Thorley of Los Angeles. Thorley was famous for the designing and engineering of some of the best headers in the

Hayden Proffitt stands next to the newer 1968 version, called the Grant Rebel SST since the Rambler name was dropped.

The car also sported the corporate red-white-blue paint scheme that became an AMC trademark.

industry. He was also active on the drag strip, capturing the NHRA Nationals funny car championship in 1967 with his Chevy-powered Corvair racer. He decided to abandon that project and sign up with AMC to campaign the new Javelin funny car.

The American Motors Dealer Association backed this car. The association was run under the West Coast dealers banner by Clyde Morgan from Garden Grove, California. Thorley also designed headers for all AMC V-8s that were sold over the counter at the dealers.

Although the initial intended purpose of the Javelin funny car was to defend Thorley's title as funny car champion, the project ended up being an exhibition-only race car because of its low overall weight of 1,665 pounds. This was 480 pounds lighter than its forerunner, the Grant Rebel SST.

One of the first things Thorley did was to ask Woody Gilmore of Gilmore's race car engineering in Downing, California, to build the frame. Gilmore's was known for its dragster chassis construction. Thorley's head wrenchman, Gary Slusser, would build the blown fuel-burning mill.

To obtain maximum traction, a rear engine location was decided upon, thus eliminating the transmission and necessitating direct drive.

The chassis was constructed of 4130 moly steel with 1.25 inch x 0.058 inch wall main tubes. Struts were 4130 moly with a 0.049 inch wall, with diameters ranging from one-half to one inch. The chassis was built on a go-cart principle, and the design really did work on the strip.

The front suspension consisted of Pirelli tires on Halibrand wheels, two-inch axle by Gilmore, P&S spindles and a unique double-arm torsion bar setup leading back to P&S steering. There was only a single center-mounted shock attached to the torsion-bar-suspended RCE dropped axle. A stabilizing link coupled the axle to the frame. The car had a 122 inch wheelbase, and it had the upper main rails of the frame set wider apart than the lowers to allow torsional flex for better bite. The complete frame was painted with gold Sperex VHT spray.

There was no rear suspension, as the 1965 Chrysler third-member was solidly mounted. The rear housing was fabricated by Woody Gilmore of 4130 moly holding M/T magnesium third-member Mopar gears. Rear-end ratios were either 3.60:1 or 4.11:1. Henry's axles were used, transmitting the power to locked gears. Dual Airheart discs were fitted inside ten-inch-wide Halibrand wheels that carried 12.60x16 M&H heavy wall slicks. A rear aluminum pan was designed to keep the rear wheels on the ground at speed and also to aid in opening the twelve-foot Tri-Form drag chute. The car also sported a full belly pan for added streamlining.

Inside the cockpit, Thorley made sure it would be functional as well as safe. A cable-throttle Airheart brake pedal and a Gilmore master cylinder with a long-handled chute popper were controls vital to any funny car. The bucket seat was made out of hand-formed aluminum and held secure by Simpson harnesses. A padded roll cage with strong gussets and bracing protected the driver, who sat out front with the engine behind him. The brake lever was the between-the-knees type.

The fiberglass replica 1968 Javelin body made by Berry Plasti Glass was thirteen inches longer than stock, and again carried the familiar red-white-blue front-to-rear AMC paint scheme. The body incorporated an attached, honeycombed aluminum bulkhead that separated the engine from the driver's compartment. Also unique was the windshield, which was hinged at the top to act as an emergency exit in case of a crash or explosion. Driver entry was from the rear, and the complete body pivoted at the front, allowing free access to the engine. With the body down, the Javelin funny car looked long, low and aerodynamic.

The mighty AMC 390 V-8 was a work of art. It was bored to 4.25 inches and stroked to 3.875 inches to produce a displacement of 449 cubic inches. The crank was a beefed and counterweighted Reath Automotive

Doug Thorley teamed with AMC to produce the Javelin 1 funny car. The car's chassis was built on a go-kart principle and used a 449 ci highly modified AMC V-8.

unit holding Howard rods and Venolia 8:1 pistons, pins and rings. Reath Automotive handled all the crank work, including stroking, grooving the mains, adding the counterweights and turning down the rod throws to accept 427 Chevy bearings. Milodon billet main caps were used on the bottom and with stock AMC high-performance main bearings. The bumpstick was by Sig Erson, sporting a 0.550 inch lift and 340 degree duration along with same-brand pushrods. Sharp 289 Ford needle-bearing-roller-tipped rocker arms fit nicely.

The heads were ported by Joe Mondello and O-ringed, with studs and stock valves by Donovan, and solid copper head gaskets milled to 0.049 inch were used.

The blower was by Hampton, with Delta drive spinning it at eighteen percent over crankshaft speed. An Enderle Bug Catcher, with no provision for port injection in the Sharp manifold, shot loads of up to forty percent nitromethane straight to the huffer.

A front-cover-mounted Mallory ignition fired Autolite plugs. A semi-dry-sump oil system carrying Penzoil sixty-weight was used with a stock Fram filter. Headers were built by Thorley, of course.

Transmitting all this power to the rear end was a special high-gear-only B&M Torkmaster fluid coupling in-and-out box, since there was no driveshaft. With this setup conventional burnouts were not possible, so the Javelin had to heat up its tires on the way to the line.

What kind of performance was this car capable of? On its first full pass down the quarter-mile it cut an 8.53 elapsed time at 182.54 mph. It made believers of all the former Thorley Chevy fans and others.

For 1969 the car received a few changes and improvements as experienced from one full year of racing. The original 1968 car finally attained a top speed of 186 mph at an elapsed time of 8.13 seconds.

The new car hoped to top the 200 mph barrier and cut into the mid-seven-second bracket.

Innovations for the new car included an experimental set of heads, a slipping clutch in place of the automatic direct drive and a reduction in overall weight.

The new Javelin 1 racer never did reach the magic 200 mph mark, nor did it dip into the sevens. Doug Thorley did prove the competitiveness of AMC on the drag strip, however, with an unusual and uniquely designed funny car.

1968 Craig Breedlove AMX

Before the paint was dry on the new 1968½ AMX and even before the car's official dealer and public introductions, it managed to shatter 106 records at the hands of Craig and Lee Breedlove and their assistant Ron Dykes. In a series of spectacular high-speed runs, eight international, sixteen national, sixty-six American closed car, fourteen American unlimited and two national unlimited records were broken.

It all started on December 1, 1967, when Craig Breedlove was contacted by AMC performance activities manager Carl Chakmakian to discuss putting the AMX through its paces. What better way to promote the car than to have it attempt to set new speed and endurance records before it even hit the streets, and at the hands of such a speed expert as Craig Breedlove.

The deal was finalized and Breedlove received two cars at his Torrance, California, shop on December 17. He had less than six weeks to prepare the cars. The normal preparation for such a car was more like six months, but Breedlove decided to take the challenge nonetheless.

Breedlove was intrigued with the AMX from the moment he saw it. He praised its crisp, clean lines and overall styling. He even compared it with his record-

Craig Breedlove in motion during one of his record-setting runs in the 390-powered AMX Class B car.

setting *Spirit of America* racer, describing the AMX as sleek and sure-footed, with supersensitive handling characteristics.

After a trip around the American Motors test track, he was convinced. Later, after his record-setting experiences, he was quoted as saying: "Driving the AMX was really like a dream. In fact, I'd never driven a car quite like it. The steering and roll-resistance were excellent and it ran and felt about perfect."

The two cars delivered were identical AMXs with the exception of the engines. One was a 290 V-8 for Class C, and the other a 390 V-8 for Class B.

The engines were immediately pulled and sent to Traco Engineering for expert blueprinting. All pieces were x-rayed and all tolerances and clearances were checked for proper specifications. Both engines received a slight overbore for added speed and endurance. The 290 now displaced 304 cubic inches, and the 390 was punched out to 397 cubic inches. The cars were equipped with exhaust headers, enlarged baffled eight-quart oil pans, engine oil coolers, aluminum hi-rise intake manifolds and racing camshafts with solid lifters and stronger springs. The 304 used a Holley four-barrel and the 397 used a larger Holley three-barrel carburetor.

The chassis was just as critically prepped as the engine, having all the parts Magnafluxed for cracks. Mag racing wheels were used with wide Goodyear racing tires equipped with safety innerliners. Heavy-duty front and rear springs from the factory's optional handling package were installed, combined with rear spring traction control arms, heavy-duty shock absorbers, rear axle oil coolers and a panhard-type track bar in the rear to eliminate side sway.

A full roll bar cage, complete set of engine instruments and modified bucket seats to give extra body support rounded out the interior modifications. A thirty-seven-gallon cell-type safety gas tank for the sustained twenty-four-hour speed runs was installed in both cars.

To keep the cars from becoming airborne at such high speeds, the front ends were lowered, the hoods were slanted down and spoilers were put on just below the front bumpers. All times would be supervised and sanctioned by a crew of the USAC (United States Auto Club). This crew also inspected the cars thoroughly and set up their timing equipment.

The cars were ready, but the weather was not. Rain, sleet and snow kept on coming down.

AMC performance activities manager Carl Chakmakian and Breedlove took one car out on the highway for a quick spin during the bad weather. When the weather finally broke, the 304 car was the first to run. This car would be shooting to run over 150 mph, and the 397 car would attempt in excess of 175 mph.

The 304 car started off good, but little things began to happen. It lost a fan belt, which required a ten-minute fix in the pits. While Lee Breedlove was driving at 156 mph she complained the car wasn't handling as smoothly as it should, but that it was nothing to worry about. When she came in for her normal pit stop it was found that she had been running on a flat tire and that only the safety innerliner had kept the car from spinning out. This was a tribute to the AMX's excellent handling characteristics.

During Craig Breedlove's portion of the run with the 304 Class C car the alternator failed, dimming the headlights while the engine started missing. All this after sundown, and with only one hour to go for the twelve-hour record! He decided to go on because pitting would have cost him the record.

To avoid hitting the guardrail at the outside of the track, he came down on the inside. Every 500 feet kerosene-burning lights were placed, and cars parked at points along the track to help illuminate his way while traveling over 150 mph. The twelve-hour record was broken. At each pit stop through the night, the batteries were changed instead of the alternator, which meant slower speeds. In the end it did not matter because Breedlove still averaged 140.790 mph, covered 3,380 miles and established ninety new records with the C car.

Several days later it was time for the larger-engined Class B car to take to the track. As with the C car things started off good, but shortly after the eight-hour mark the car was burdened with transmission troubles.

The higher 175 plus mph speeds combined with a bumpy track made the wheels go airborne every time they hit a bump. The added load when the wheels came back down was too much for the transmission to

Craig and Lee Breedlove stand proudly next to one of the winning AMXs that shattered 106 speed and endurance records. Magnificent for a first-year model.

The American Spirit *was never able to get a chance at a record run. A flood shattered any hope of what could have* been one of the most significant achievements in AMC racing history.

take. By the time it was changed, bad weather had set in again.

Both cars were destined for the February 23, 1968, Chicago Auto Show, so the rest of the test had to be aborted.

Even in the abbreviated eight-hour test the Class B car set sixteen records, and the C car set ninety new records. In all, 106 speed and endurance records were recorded by the AMX before it had even run on the street as a production car for sale to the public.

1968 Craig Breedlove *American Spirit*

American Motors was so pleased with the record-setting 1968 AMXs driven by Craig Breedlove and his wife Lee that it decided to pull out all stops and go all out with an attempt on the land speed record at the Bonneville Salt Flats in Utah, to be run between November 3 and November 17 in 1968.

The vehicle constructed for the attempt was to be virtually a scaled-down version with the same cylindrical fuselage concept as the original *Spirit of America* jet-powered car Breedlove drove to a world record speed of 492.488 mph back in 1964.

Three different class records and one unlimited speed mark would be the goals of the AMC-powered streamliner. The three class records governed by engine size limitations were as follows:

Class B—305 to 488 cubic inches, record 345.755 mph set November 2, 1967, by Bob Herda, in the Autolite 999 Special

Class C—183 to 304.9 cubic inches, record 298.359 mph set November 8, 1967, by Bob Herda, in the Herda-Knapp streamliner

Class D—122 to 182.9 cubic inches, record 275.103 mph set October 30, 1967, by Fred Larsen in Larsen-Cummins' 115 D streamliner

Craig Breedlove had hoped to beat the Class B record by enough so that he could also take the

unlimited record of 409.277 mph set three years earlier by Bob Summers in his Goldenrod racer powered by four modified Chrysler Hemi engines mounted in tandem.

All three of the AMC engines used would be supercharged and fuel injected. For Class B the 390 was underbored to 373.5 ci, the 290 was bored to 294.5 ci and the 199 six-cylinder was underbored to 182.8 ci. All runs were to be timed two ways for a mile each, with flying starts, and averaged for record purposes.

The *American Spirit* was one of the smallest vehicles to ever attempt the unlimited speed record for wheel-driven cars. It measured only twenty feet in length (twelve feet shorter than the *Goldenrod*) and twenty-four inches in diameter and weighed only 2,000 pounds including 150 pound Breedlove, or about one-fourth the weight of the *Goldenrod*.

The chassis had an aluminum monocoque cockpit section, with the rest constructed of chromemoly-steel tubing. The body was made of stressed aluminum and fiberglass. Water tanks and fourteen-gallon fuel tanks as well as the parachute housing and dual tail section were also made of aluminum.

Some of the unique features of the car were laminar flow airfoils to streamline the rear wheels, with wing sections enclosing the rear axle housing which applied an aerodynamic downforce to the rear wheels, thus stabilizing the vehicle at high speeds. Two small wings were mounted behind the front wheels to adjust lift characteristics of the nose. An NACA flush duct was used when running the V-8 engines, and a conventional air scoop with boundary layer airbleed was used when running the six-cylinder.

A Halibrand two-speed rear end was redesigned by Bill Kharilla, Lamar Engineering and Margie Smith to accept an extra-large ring and pinion gear set and special bearings. The rear axle housing was made of chromemoly heat-treated steel sheet to withstand the load, but still remained lightweight.

Rear wheels were made by Goodyear and originally used on Breedlove's *Spirit of America, Sonic One* from 1965. Fronts were machined by Fan Steel from a solid block of Harvey aluminum alloy. The Timken Roller Bearing Company supplied the special wheel bearings.

The Goodyear tires measured 3.50x19 for the fronts and 8.00x25 for the rears. The tires were tested at speeds of up to 525 mph by Goodyear representatives. The front tires were twenty-five inches in diameter, and the rears were thirty-six inches. The rear suspension was solidly mounted, and the front utilized Monroe shocks with coil springs. The steering ratio was 15:1 with a six-degree turn capability each way. All four brakes were American Motors discs.

All fluid lines (water, hydraulic and fuel) were flexible stainless-steel-covered Teflon tubing designed and installed by Auto Flight Company. The clutch and flywheel were made of aluminum and supplied by Schiefer. The transmission was an American Motors Borg-Warner 2.23:1 first-gear close-ratio T-10 V four-speed without reverse gears and with modified oil-jet lubrication system, specially made gears, and larger input and output shafts to withstand the 400 plus mph capabilities of the car.

An eight-foot ribbon-type parachute was used, and a 16 mm motion picture camera was mounted in the rear wheel pants. Instrumentation was supplied by three manufacturers. Microdot supplied and installed the rear axle housing strain gauges, Lamar Engineering designed and installed the equipment for measuring the aerodynamic lift forces, and Stewart-Warner Corporation built and supplied the cockpit gauges.

The three engines used were extensively modified versions of the 199 six-cylinder and 290 and 390 V-8 engines. The 390 was reported to be producing over 1,000 hp. The six-cylinder engine used an Airesearch turbocharger and the V-8s used GMC 6-71 blowers. Fuel used was menthanol for the six and a mixture of nitromethane and methanol for the V-8s.

Some of the speciality parts and equipment used in the build-up of the engines came from Carillo, Armco, Forgedtrue, M/T, Reath, Crower, Harlan Sharp, Donovan, Navarro Engineering, Pesco, Delta Machine, Cummings, Grant Industries, Hilborne, Joe Hunt and Champion. American Motors was joined by four other primary sponsors in the Breedlove project. Goodyear supplied the tires, Borg-Warner the transmission, Champion the spark plugs, and Shell the lubricants and greases.

Breedlove, the car, the crew and the sponsors were all ready and waiting to assault Bonneville with the mighty *American Spirit*. Everything was going smoothly in the construction of the car and its

The *American Spirit's* highly modified 390 cubic inch AMX V-8 engine produced over 1,000 hp. The engine was an engineering work of art. Note the unique distributor front drive system.

powerplants, and most deadlines were being met. But then things began to go wrong.

Breedlove's wife Lee left him and filed for divorce. His managers mismanaged his business affairs and caused him to lose his tire store in Torrance, California, and then they too left him.

To top everything off, a brutal storm roared across southern California, flooding streets and wrecking homes. One of those homes was Breedlove's headquarters, which contained the *American Spirit*, both record-setting 1968 AMXs, various AMC engines and parts, and several lathes and milling machines. The building was not insured against floods, and the water rose four feet, wiping out everything and plunging Breedlove into bankruptcy with a loss of over $100,000. Breedlove lost interest in racing after all of this, and his sponsorship was withdrawn.

The *American Spirit* was never reconstructed to attempt a world land speed record.

1968-72 Trans-Am and NASCAR Javelins

SCCA Trans-Am racing was a twelve-race series for the manufacturers championship in large- and small-engined production sedans, where maximum engine size was 305 cubic inches (five liters) and a wheelbase of 116 inches or less. The Javelin was not, as many believe, the last of the American pony cars to enter this series; the Dodge Challenger arrived roughly two years later. But AMC was the last of the American auto manufacturers to enter such racing, and it was also the last to offer factory support to anyone who was willing to endorse its products through racing.

In the Javelin's first season of Trans-Am racing in 1968, George Folmer and Peter Revson were assigned the task of attempting to bring a victory to AMC. Skip

The first Trans-Am racing Javelins were prepared by Ronnie Kaplan of Kaplan Engineering. The cars were competitive in their first year of racing, completing every race entered in the 1968 season.

Scott and Jerry Grant were also team drivers of the Javelins, and Jim Jeffords was team manager for the Javelin racing team.

The Javelins were laboratories on wheels, with the team tuning their suspensions, carburetors, manifolds, airfoils and other related components according to how the cars performed in actual competition. It was not that the cars were unprofessionally or improperly prepared, but the new AMC thin-wall-design V-8 was just two years old and the cars were going up against seasoned competition that had had a two- or three-year headstart on debugging their cars.

The Javelins were prepared by Ron Kaplan Engineering. They had Traco-built 290 cubic inch V-8 engines and all the latest state-of-the-art components and techniques to produce the most competitive car

possible to do battle with the seasoned heavyweights. To keep under the five-liter (305 cubic inch) limit, the engines were bored out to 304.3 cubic inches and produced over 400 hp. Initially, the Javelins were running with a single four-barrel to the competition's dual setups. A couple of months into the season, the SCCA allowed the Javelin its own version of a dual cross-ram four-barrel intake manifold.

In retrospect, the AMC factory team effort should receive the golden award because in its first year against fierce competition, the Javelin managed to finish every race it entered even though a victory was not registered. AMC finished third in manufacturers standings behind Chevy and Ford.

For a brief period during the season, after seven races, AMC held second place. It was leading Ford thirty-four to thirty-three points, and Ford could not believe it was behind American Motors which was racing a virtually untested car.

1968

The Javelin made its debut in March 1968 at the Sebring twelve-hour race. It finished twelfth overall and fifth in the Trans-Am group. It was one of thirty-six finishers from a starting field of sixty-eight cars.

The War Bonnet was a significant achievement of the Javelin's early Trans-Am history. It was only the second Trans-Am race the Javelins ever entered and they were able to finish second and fourth at the expert hands of George Folmer and Peter Revson. Parnelli Jones, driving a Mustang, managed to come in third, and Mark Donohue, piloting a Roger Penske-prepared Camaro, took the checkered flag and the overall season's manufacturers standings.

A 1968 Trans-Am Javelin rounds a corner on its way to successfully completing another race.

Throughout the season, AMC recorded five second-place finishes in ten starts. After the rain, smoke, accidents, protests and what-have-you cleared for 1968, Chevy came out victorious, winning the manufacturers title and accumulating 105 points to Ford's sixty-three. AMC finished with fifty-one points. (Trans-Am points are awarded on a nine-six-four-three-two-one basis for the first six places.)

AMC realized that it was going to be a long, tough uphill road to victory for 1969 and beyond, but it was not afraid to continue the battle. With one full season of racing experience under its belt, improvements and debugging were accomplished for 1969.

Keeping everything within the legal bounds of the SCCA, Kaplan Engineering coaxed more horsepower out of the new-design small-block V-8. The car was able to do 0-60 in less than five seconds, and the quarter-mile in less than eleven seconds with a top speed of over 175 mph.

AMC was so confident that in the early spring of 1969 it announced it would also be fielding two Javelins in the NASCAR GT (Grand Touring) or Baby Grand Nationals, sponsored by Hurst Performance Research and Huggins Tire Sales. Bob Tullius would pilot the Hurst car under team manager Bob Tarozzi. The Huggins Javelin would have Jim Paschal as its driver. The engine used would be a 343 V-8 destroked to 305 cubic inches using an Edelbrock intake manifold with twin Holley four-barrel carburetors and Warren Prout's own headers (Prout owned and prepared the car).

1969

For the 1969 Trans-Am season, Kaplan Engineering once again prepared the cars. Ron Grable and John Martin were the team drivers. Martin had entered the AMC picture back in 1967, winning three divisional SCCA national races in a 1967 Rambler American two-door sedan.

One of the 1968 Javelin's major mechanical problems had been the valvetrain; that problem was taken care of for 1969. Although the 1969 cars were better prepared than earlier cars, they still had their share of problems.

Early in the season in a race at Bridgehampton, Grable broke a rear axle and Martin retired with a blown engine. At about mid-season, Martin suffered a broken arm in a garage accident and Lothar Motschenbacher substituted. This did not discourage AMC or anyone in the team. They pressed on.

AMC was quite competitive for only its second season, but its improvements in lap times still were not as good as Chevy's and Ford's. AMC performance marketing engineer John Voelpel sought rule changes for the 1970 season to make the cars more showroom stock, rather than all-out racing oriented. His suggestions were taken lightly by all parties concerned.

Most of the focus was on the Javelin, so little was known about the two-seater 1969 AMX that was run in SCCA's B/Production category by a dedicated group of twenty AMC employees. This car was not sponsored by American Motors Corporation. Driven by Dwight "Ike" Knupp, electrical laboratory supervisor for AMC in Detroit, this mildly modified 343 V-8 sleeper managed three straight national points races against the seasoned and well-prepared Corvette of Al Barker. This little AMX was indeed a Giant Killer. The twenty-man team even called itself Team Racing, a nonprofit organization.

During the entire season the Javelin was once again going against the toughest competition around. There was just no stopping the Penske racing team with Mark Donohue driving the winning Camaro, George Folmer and Parnelli Jones in the Mustangs, and Jerry Titus in the Firebird. (Somehow, the Firebird was allowed in Trans-Am racing with its Chevy 302 V-8.)

The final 1969 standings in points tallied as follows: Camaro, seventy-eight; Mustang, sixty-four; Firebird, thirty-two; and Javelin, fourteen.

In their first season of NASCAR GT racing, the Javelins achieved victories at the Greenville 100, Baton Rouge 200, Columbia 100, Charlotte 500 and Oxford 100. Pretty good for a company and a car that had been in heavyweight competition for only two years, finishing third in the GT's manufacturers championship standings, and still good enough to win the Northern Tour Championship.

1970

The year 1970 proved to be the turning point for American Motors. Early in the year, AMC signed a three-year contract with the Penske racing team to prepare and race the Javelins. A better winning combination than boss Roger Penske and driver Mark Donohue could not be found. There was no stopping American Motors now.

AMC and the Roger Penske team made sure they were starting off on the right foot. They were the first of the Trans-Am competitors to receive a stamp of approval from the SCCA and ACCUS (Automobile Competition Committee of the United States).

Each manufacturer had to meet the minimum production of 2,500 units available to the public for homologation purposes. The minimum production deadline date was extended to April 8 for the remaining competitors because of the early start of that year's Trans-Am series. It was extended further to the second week of May to better verify manufacturers' production quantities.

New rule changes by the SCCA for the 1970 season allowed any block to be used as long as the final displacement was under 305 cubic inches, and this led to the new AMC 360 block being used. Engine internals did not have to be stock production items, which opened up all avenues for improved rods, cranks, pistons and valvetrains. This flexibility also extended to allowing different suspension pivot points and brakes, and even quick-change differentials.

AMC and Donohue were ready. Ted Roberts would be driving another 1970 Javelin, called the Fyr-Fytr, sponsored by Pyrene C-O Two, and there were two new entries—Sam Posey's Dodge Challenger and Swede Savage's Plymouth Barracuda.

In the season's opening race at Laguna Seca, teammate Peter Revson's Javelin was plagued by brake problems and retired early. Even before the race, in the practice runs, an engine change was made because of problems. Donohue managed to finish second in that race, while the victory went to Parnelli Jones in a Bud Moore Mustang.

Donohue retired at about midpoint in the Lime Rock race with no oil pressure. Later on, Revson spun out in his own oil when the engine blew entering the pits. Parnelli Jones once again won in the Mustang.

At the Loudon race, Donohue and Revson managed second and third, although Donohue was temporarily sidelined with tire problems. What car won? You guessed it, a Bud Moore Mustang driven by Folmer.

The Lexington race was a little better for Donohue. During the morning warm-up the oil pump gave way and the engine was replaced. Donohue went on to finish third while the mighty Mustangs of Jones and Folmer finished first and second. Revson went out with a bad electrical system.

Bridgehampton brought AMC and the Javelin their first Trans-Am victory. Revson went out during practice with no oil pressure. Although Donohue had transmission problems, a quick fix worked and he took the victory. This time the mighty Mustangs of Folmer and Jones had to eat the Javelin's dust, coming in second and third. It was the first Trans-Am race in history to be won by a Javelin.

Engine problems arose again at Brainerd, with Donohue suffering a broken engine. He borrowed Revson's Javelin, but did not finish because its engine blew. Milt Minter's 1969 Camaro finally broke the Mustang victory string, but Folmer came in second and set a new lap record.

The tide finally turned at Elkhart Lake, where Donohue took the victory. Revson broke a driveshaft one lap before the finish line.

Mount Tremblant saw another victory for the Javelin. The Mustang came in second. Up to this point, the Javelin was second only to the Mustang in overall season points total.

At Watkins Glen, the Javelin almost scored its fourth victory. Due to what was believed to be an error in timing in the pits, Revson misjudged the time it would take Donohue's car to get a tire change, and

Mark Donohue and the Penske team signed on with AMC for the 1970 season and the next three years. Donohue posed with his new 1970 Trans-Am Javelin racer.

both cars ended up in the pits at the same time. Revson was immediately waved off and was brought back in one lap later. This lost time cost the Penske team its victory; the 1970 Camaro driven by Vic Elford took the checkered flag.

The Kent race could have once again spelled victory for the Javelin, but Donohue's last pit stop for fuel and tires gave Parnelli Jones, driving the Mustang, the victory.

The last race of the season at Riverside was all Jones and Folmer. Donohue came in third, and the Penske team was dissatisfied. Revson retired early with another seized engine.

How can the 1970 Trans-Am season be summed up? The Mustang finished with seventy-two points; Javelin, fifty-nine; Camaro, forty; Challenger, eighteen; and Barracuda, fifteen. Penske was quoted as saying: "We'll be back stronger next time." And he was right, because 1971 would be the banner year for American Motors.

In the NASCAR Grand American series (previously known as the Grand Touring series), Warren Prout and Jim Paschal attacked the 1970 season with their own company called American Performance Center, with a new 7,200 square foot facility in High Point, North Carolina. They were serious about winning.

On May 31, 1970, Paschal set the world one-mile closed-circuit speed record for a NASCAR Grand American Challenge series sedan by recording a 27.60 second 130.434 mph lap time and speed around the Dover Downs International Speedway in Dover, Delaware. Paschal scored victories at Bridgehampton, Daytona, Blue Hen, Raleigh and Henry County, to name a few, and accumulated a point total of 179 behind the Camaro's 248. A total of ten victories were racked up for the 1970 season. Another magnificent achievement for a corporation known for years for only its economy cars.

1971

The 1971 Trans-Am season was probably the highest point American Motors had reached since it started its racing program in 1967. By this time, AMC was the only car company sponsoring its Trans-Am racers. All the other racers were now racing on their own or had found outside sponsorship. Jim Paschal still ran at NASCAR, but without AMC support.

The 1970 winning Bud Moore Mustangs were now owned by Troy Promotions, with team drivers Tony Delorenzo and Terry Thompson. George Folmer and Peter Gregg also piloted Mustangs in 1971, with outside sponsorship from New York and Connecticut Ford dealers and Florida-based company builders. Bob Tullius raced a 1964 Pontiac Tempest. There were also 1968-70 Camaros running again, all on their own or with a little help from any outside sponsor they could find.

There were two Roy Woods American Racing Associates (ARA) yellow Javelins running without AMC sponsorship, but with all the help the Penske racing team could give them. The ARA cars were 1970 Penske cars updated mechanically and appearance-wise to look like the 1971 models.

What plagued the Penske cars in 1970 was not going to bother them in 1971. Remember all those blown and seized engines? SCCA rule changes allowing the dry-sump oil system greatly alleviated a chronic AMC V-8 oil circulation problem when it came to racing.

The engines were improved by Traco Engineering, generating between 440 and 460 hp from the destroked and highly modified AMC 360 block. The chassis was gone over completely, sporting important changes to the suspension points for better handling.

Donohue ran away with the season's rainy opening race at Lime Rock. He attributed a good part of his victory to the excellent rain tires used on his car and developed by Goodyear. Those coupled to an excellently prepared and debugged car produced the winning combination. Donohue's input in the design of the flush grille, front and rear spoilers, roof spoilerette, cowl-induction hood and overall body design also helped. Bob Tullius in his 1964 Pontiac Tempest stayed right behind Donohue until four laps from the finish, when he retired with an overheated engine.

The Loudon race looked like the old days of Ford sponsorship and factory teams. Folmer and Gregg fin-

Roger Penske brought AMC to its first Trans-Am victory in 1971, after finishing second in 1970.

177

ished first and second. Revson in the ARA Javelin finished third, and Tullius finished fourth. Donohue retired with carburetor float problems after only thirty-five laps.

At Lexington, Donohue's Javelin was again plagued with trouble, although he did finish second. This time he lost his front brakes early in the day and was forced to run the rest on rear brakes only. The two ARA Javelins driven by Revson and Adamowicz both retired early with blown engines. The victory? George Folmer and the mighty Mustang. It certainly looked as though it were going to be 1970 all over again.

Edmonton gave the Penske team the shot in the arm needed after the last two races. Donohue's Javelin coughed and sputtered across the finish line with more carburetor problems, but Folmer's Mustang did the same with a bad valve and Gregg's Mustang broke a crankshaft. Donohue managed to win while Folmer came in second.

Brainerd was the first race after Lime Rock in which there were no mechanical problems. Donohue came in first, Revson came in second, Delorenzo came in third and Thompson came in fourth.

For the next four races, Elkhart Lake, Mount Tremblant, Watkins Glen and Brooklyn, the red-white-blue Sunoco Javelin took the checkered flags at the hands of Donohue.

The new-bodied 1971 Trans-Am Javelin combined with Donohue's driving skills and Penske's pit crew skills produced the winning combination for the title of Trans-Am champion for AMC for the 1971 season.

Folmer was quoted as saying this about his Mustang: "It just doesn't go fast enough. We have last year's stuff and last year's speed." The Javelin proved unbeatable while the Mustang was plagued with problem after problem—a reversal of the 1970 season.

The race at Kent was canceled because track officials felt there would be no stiff competition and because Moore was having sponsorship problems bringing his team out West.

After the Brooklyn, Michigan, race, Donohue and Penske were contractually free to pursue other avenues. They chose Formula One racing instead of the last two SCCA races at Kent and Riverside.

In the last race at Riverside, Mustang drivers Folmer and Elford both switched and drove ARA Javelins. If you can't beat them, join them.

Jackie Oliver substituted and drove the Penske Javelin. He was a little shaky because it was his first Trans-Am start, but the Javelins took a one-two-three victory. It was Folmer, Elford and Oliver all the way.

The final point tally for the 1971 season was Javelin, seventy-two; Mustang, fifty-four; Camaro, seventeen; and Pontiac, seven. This was the year American Motors had been waiting for, the year it finally achieved the title of Trans-Am Champion.

1972

The 1972 Trans-Am season was a lean, confusing one. Penske and Donohue concentrated their efforts in NASCAR racing with the Matador. Roy Woods and the ARA, backed by AMC dealers, campaigned the Javelins. George Folmer was at the wheel and the back-up car was used only in an emergency. The 1972 ARA Javelins were painted red-white-blue, like Penske's Javelin, instead of yellow and black as they had been in 1971.

Peter Gregg again drove the Bud Moore Mustang, probably under Jacobs Company Sponsorship. Delorenzo ended up driving a 1972 Firebird, one of the newest models on the circuit. Marshall Robbins bought both the 1971 Moore cars and had them updated. John McComb drove the Sam Posey Challenger. Mo Carter and Warren Agor piloted 1970 and 1971 Camaros.

The Mark Donohue Javelin was sold to the University of Pittsburgh's racing team and driven by rookie Bob Fryer. The second Penske Javelin was sold to Bill Collins of Collins Racing, St. Paul, Minnesota. At first it was decided not to enter the car in the Trans-Am season for 1972, but later Collins did enter and race the car.

In the opening race at Lime Rock, Folmer led the race from flag to flag. Yet the challenge was there; Folmer in the Javelin and Warren Tope in the Moore Mustang were running neck-and-neck during the race. Agor finished second, and Tony Delorenzo finished third. Roy Woods driving his own RWR Javelin finished fourth while Tope finished fifth.

At the Loudon race, Folmer had to start in last place in teammate Woods' car because his own car would not turn over, but it took him only seven laps to take the lead, and he kept it till the end of the race. He even maintained the lead during the two routine pit stops for gas and tires. Milt Minter in the 1972 Firebird finished second.

The Lexington race finally ended the year-long victory of the Javelin. Milt Minter finished first, fifty-four seconds ahead of Folmer. Agor finished third, and Bill Collins and Roy Woods finished fourth and fifth, both driving Javelins. Folmer started from the back of the field and tried to do what he had done at Loudon, but it was just a day of bad luck, with flat tires, spin-outs; a bent front end and other problems. This did not, however, spell the end for the Javelin.

The next race at Watkins Glen was once again all Javelin and Folmer. Early in the race, the lead was exchanged six times between Folmer's car and the Mustangs of Thompson and Tope. Minter's Firebird followed close behind, waiting for an opening. Thompson finished second and Woods finished third; Folmer had won.

The Donnybrooke race was almost disastrous for the Javelin, but Folmer once again came out victorious. His car suffered a chronic engine miss, a broken suspension and repeated blistering of left front tires, necessitating four, rather than two, pit stops. In addition, the four-speed transmission stayed locked in fourth. Despite all those problems, Folmer set a new lap record, breaking Donohue's year-old record. All day, Minter gave the Javelins a run for their money. Thompson came in second, Woods third and Minter fourth.

Folmer's last 1972 Trans-Am race was at Elkhart Lake (he could not make the season's last race, the Sanair Trans-Am in Quebec on July 30). He led much of the race, but his engine went slightly bad, got worse and finally quit. Warren Tope's Mustang got the lead, followed by Minter's Firebird and Collins' Javelin. The race finally finished in that order, with the three winners just seconds behind each other.

The last race of the season at Sanair saw Roy Woods pack up his own Javelin and the car of substitute driver Bob Gerro because he felt the track was unsafe for Trans-Am racing, mainly the pit area. This feeling was shared by many drivers and teams at the track that day. Bill Collins, driving the number six Javelin, was the only AMC representative in the race. Extra precautions were taken in the pits and on the track, but a bad accident on the second lap sent Mo Carter to the hospital and eliminated both Carter's and Walter Perkins' Camaros.

Despite all this, the race went on, with Collins and Tope swapping positions for first place right up to the finish line. Collins was ahead, but Tope managed to pull alongside him in the straightaway and was able to slip inside him at turn one, taking the checkered flag.

The 1972 season was AMC's second victory in a row for the Trans-Am championship. It was also the first year the Trans-Am had a drivers championship, which went to George Folmer.

Penske concentrated his efforts with the Matador on the NASCAR tracks for 1972-75. The Javelin was run in various SCCA and IMSA events in 1973 and 1974 under independent teams and drivers. Jim Paschal in his 1970 Warren Prout Javelin raced in NASCAR events for the 1973 season and scored victories at Westchester, Ohio; Ona, West Virginia; and Heidelberg, Pennsylvania.

American Motors had proven that it could be more than competitive on the Trans-Am and NASCAR racing circuits with its red-white-blue Javelins.

1969 S/S AMX

AMC got together with Hurst Research in late 1968 to produce a fleet of fifty-three extensively modified 1969 AMXs to run in super stock competition. Fifty-two units had to be built for the car to be classified as a legal factory-prepared super stock race car.

Known as the S/S AMXs, these cars ran in S/SC, S/SD, S/SE and S/SG NHRA classes for the most part. AHRA classified the car in Formula One C/Stock. All fifty-three cars were sold. The last one was reserved as a spare in case of any mishap on delivery of the first fifty-two units.

All S/S AMXs had dashboard ID number plaques, as did all stock AMX models, and all had sequential vehicle identification numbers from A9M397X213560 to A9M397X21613, suggesting the fifty-three car production run. The dash plaque numbers ran from 12,567 to 12,620.

These torrid AMXs were made strictly for racing and were not able to be licensed for the street. As the window sticker said, "This vehicle is sold as is and the twelve month or 12,000 mile vehicle warranty coverage and five year or 50,000 mile power train warranty coverage does not apply to this vehicle." Factory list price was $5,979, and the manufacturer's suggested retail price was $5,994 plus tax, title, shipping, dealer prep. The cars were going out of the showrooms for over $6,000.

Shirley Shahan and her husband H. L. Shanan received the first one that was built. Shirley Shahan was also known as the drag-on-lady who helped propel AMC into third place in the National Hot Rod Association standings for 1969. She was so popular that a poster of her and her S/S AMX car was offered by Fram Filters (the S/S engines used Fram filters).

The cars were extensively modified by Hurst under direct AMC supervision. They came painted two ways: completely frost white, or red-white-blue in that order from front to back. The shade of colors differed slightly from the Trans-Am Javelin's.

The bodies were completely gutted and void of all sound insulation and undercoating. The rear wheelwells were opened up and the battery was relocated to the trunk. No comfort or power options appeared on this racer. The car did have carpeting, however, and a set of two stock AMX bucket seats (no rear seat, as on any stock 1969 AMX). Various supports, brackets, latches and hinges were deleted, as were the front sway bar and rocker panel moldings. Only one horn came with the car as opposed to the normal two units. The hood, fenders, doors and trunk lid were acid-dipped by the factory to reduce overall vehicle weight. A gigantic steel dual-inlet hood scoop fed fresh cold air to the dual Holley 650 cfm carburetors on an Edelbrock cross-ram aluminum intake manifold.

The stock 390 AMC V-8 engine was worked over for its intended purpose. The heads were opened up from 50 to 60 cc and redesigned by Hurst, but all head modifications were done by Crane Engineering. Pistons were JE 12.3:1 compression ratio, pushing up toward larger-than-stock valves measuring 2.065 inches for the intakes and 1.74 inches for the exhausts. Initially, the engine was also equipped with a stock cam; Mallory tach-drive distributor and ignition system; and Doug Thorley exhaust headers. The engine intentionally was not blueprinted or overbored, leaving those tasks to the personal preference and manner of the customer. The engine was equipped with the stock cam and valvetrain for the same reason.

With all these modifications the rated output of the engine was 340 hp, which was only 25 hp over a stock 390 AMX V-8. The engine was probably pumping

The BP 60 1969 AMX racer was campaigned by a dedicated group of 20 AMC employees. The car was a class Corvette beater.

out over 400 hp, but the factory commonly underrated its engines for racing. NHRA first factored the horsepower to be 405 hp and later changed it to 420 hp.

The transmission was a stock AMX Borg-Warner T-10 close-ratio 2.23:1 first gear four-speed engaged to a Schiefer clutch and flywheel assembly protected by a Lakewood bell housing. Hurst also installed a trick front cross-member, allowing removal of the oil pan to inspect rods and main and lower end without removing the engine. A Hurst shifter stirred the gears.

The rear end had a ratio of 4.44:1 and had super-tough Henry's Hi-Tuf forged axle shafts. The ratio was later changed by H. L. Shahan to 5.1:1. Some S/S AMXs were even equipped with heavy-duty Ford nine-inch rear axle assemblies. The rear suspension used special Rockwell springs and Monroe shocks with the standard AMX Torque Links. No other rear modifications were necessary or recommended by the factory, not even traction or snubber bars.

Cragar SS wheels were used all around, with Goodyear 10.00x15 slicks launching the car. Front tires were super stock skinnies at 7.00x15.

At time of delivery, two carburetor velocity stacks, a Hurst T-handle and various decals from the companies whose items were used on the vehicle were locked in the trunk. The complete AMX S/S racer, ready to run, weighed in at 3,050 pounds.

Shirley Shahan was a popular S/S AMX racing figure. Here she shows how it's done by pulling the front wheels off the ground.

This package was good enough for Shirley Shahan to knock off a 10.97 second elapsed time at 125.69 mph at the 1969 Orange County International Raceway Super Stock meet. At the same meet, Dave Kempton driving an SS/FA AMX did not fare too well, with a final elapsed time of 12.41 at 112.50 mph.

Shirley and H. L. Shahan also ran a Javelin stocker locally, and both cars were sponsored by the Southern California American Motors Dealer Association. There were also super stock Javelins running at various strips across the country. At OCIR, NHRA's car club director Ron Root in an SS/F Javelin scored low elapsed time in his class with a 12.08 elapsed time. Ben Carco of Bonanza Rambler in North Hollywood, California, campaigned an SS/JA Javelin with much success. This dealer also sponsored a club for Javelin and AMX owners, to keep its customers tuned in on the latest tricks.

Walt Czarnecki of AMC, along with Hurst Engineering, kept S/S AMX owners abreast of all technical developments in the areas of tires, suspensions, engine, performance at the drag strip, experiences of other owners, what to do, what was working, what was not working, problem solvers, suggestions and whatever else was of importance. These things were done through telegrams, personal phone calls and even special handling of needed parts.

Car Craft magazine built a project S/S AMX in 1969. It went over the entire car with a fine-toothed comb, changing over fifty percent of the car's original mechanical components, doing a complete engine blueprinting and new chassis setup. The resulting horsepower was around 460 at 6000 rpm with a strong torque curve throughout the 5000 to 7000 rpm range.

During the project, numerous problems with the AMC 390 engine were discovered and solved. The car had a tendency of blowing head gaskets because there was insufficient support on the lower edge of the head near the water jacket. This was solved by O-ringing the heads, which was done by Valley Head Service. The same problem was cured by H. L. Shahan by drilling, tapping and installing four extra studs and nuts on each head, lined up with each spark plug hole. AMC cured the problem by installing half-inch instead of $\frac{7}{16}$ shank diameter bolts on all 1970 and later V-8 engines.

The oiling system was inadequate because the oil supply was pumped out of the sump faster than it could return there. The flutter valves were replaced in the lifters and the 0.050 metering holes were enlarged to 0.063 to solve the problem.

When every bearing in the crankshaft was wiped out, AMC remedied the situation by offering a set of high-performance Clevite 77 bearing inserts for the mighty 390 V-8.

At the rear axle, the tubes had a tendency of twisting inside the pumpkin housing. A quick 360 degree Heli-Arc weld put the problem to bed.

All this fine-tuning to the S/S AMX produced a machine breaking into the low tens at over 130 mph. What a difference a little massaging could do.

Hurst Research also built and campaigned its own version of the S/S AMX. What better way to make sure a new part or assembly would stand up to the punishment of drag racing than to test it right on the car, on the track and in actual competition.

Like the *Car Craft* project car, the Hurst vehicle was gone over completely, with most of the original components being modified or changed with other brands or types.

Extensive modifications and changes went into the engine block, heads, intake and exhaust manifolds, carburetors, ignition system and a host of other detailed items. The Borg-Warner T-10 transmission was reworked for cleaner and smoother shifts, as was the Hurst linkage. The rear suspension setup was changed, and the rear axle housing and shafts were made bulletproof using one-piece billet units with flanged hubs instead of the stock keyway pressed-on-hub types, which tended to shear off the axle shafts at every other shift. Different-size wheels and tire combinations were also tried.

Throughout the project, assistance came from such noted people as H. L. Shahan and Dave Phelps (who helped build the Hemi-under-glass Barracuda and hairy Olds F-85). Chief Engineer Bob Tarozzi of Hurst Engineering designed many of the pieces from scratch. Tarozzi was also team manager for the Hurst 1969 NASCAR GT Javelin.

S&K Performance Combine of North Lindenhurst, New York, and Westbury Rambler built and raced a record-setting AMX. Brian Higgins built the car and Fred Dellis did the driving. This car too was gone over completely, being blueprinted, massaged and tricked up within the legal specifications of the classes it was run in. It held the AHRA world record with an 11.08 elapsed time at 127.11 mph. It also won the AHRA Summernationals running in C/Stock class Formula One, and was runner-up for the stock eliminator position.

Probably one of the quickest, meanest and most successful of all S/S AMXs was that of Pete Peterson's, named *Pete's Patriot*. The car was driven by Lou Downing, who was a member of the AMX racing team car club in Kearny, Nebraska. This car and driver were Division V S/S champions in 1969 and again in 1970. They held both ends of the record and held the speed record at 126.96 mph, and were runners up in S/S eliminator at the 1970 Nationals. This car was by far the most popular S/S AMX in the Midwest.

Other S/S AMXs were being run and were breaking class records at drag strips across the United States. John Beachy drove an AMX from Ray Wells Motors of Kokomo, Indiana, and Chuck Miller owned a racer out of Port Rambler in Shreveport, Louisiana, which was driven by Wayne Nissen. Rick Venol and his *Mr. AMX* car were a favorite in the Midwest. Bud Gregson driving *The Revenge* was another favorite. Dave Kempton was a West Coast racer rivaling the Shahans. Margo and Bob Smith from Kansas City, Missouri, were another well-known Midwestern team. Bob Bundy was still another respected name in the S/S AMX crowd.

There was even an effort in England. In 1971, the Mattel toy company supported British drag racing with a three-car Hot Wheels drag team and a sizeable cash purse. These helped subsidize a national point series

covering events organized by BDR, HRA and the NDRAC.

The finals were to be scheduled at Santa Pod Raceway, only five miles from Mattel's factory at Wellingborough. One of the cars entered was an S/S AMX painted blue and yellow. The car was also sponsored by John Wolfe Racing, hence its colors. It was driven by Ed Shaver, and run in the B/MP class.

AMC did not want the 1969 S/S AMX's reign to end, so it attempted to qualify them as current cars for the 1970 season, by converting them cosmetically and mechanically to 1970 models. This would permit AMC to mechanically update and improve the car from the lessons learned after one full season of racing. The company began shipping the appropriate sheet metal, interior and mechanical parts to all S/S owners, and many did receive the pieces and perform all the needed modifications for the changeover.

At the last minute the conversions were not allowed by the NHRA and AHRA, and the cars were not permitted to run on any sanctioned tracks as new 1970 models. Thus, they were forced to run as original 1969 cars with original 1969 mechanical and cosmetic configurations.

But the mighty S/S AMXs had proven their point. They could not only run with, but could win against, such veteran superstars as Ronnie Sox and Buddy Martin, Dick Landy and Bill "Grumpy" Jenkins.

The American Revolution *was just one of the fleet of 53 S/S AMXs that terrorized drag strips across the country.*

The modified off-road version of the SC/Rambler won the 1969 Baja 500 at the hands of the Jim Garner racing team. The Baja 500 was the car's most grueling test of endurance, performance and reliability.

1969 SC/Rambler off-road

The SC/Rambler was assigned an unusual task almost immediately after its initial introduction, that of off-roading. American Motors signed a three-year contract with actor James Garner and his American International Racers (AIR) to field ten modified SC/Ramblers to do battle in the Sedan class of the June 10, 1969, Baja 500 and most other major off-road events. Garner and AIR president John Crean formerly raced Ford Broncos in various off-road events. The Baja 500 was the SC/Ramblers peak off-road performance showing, an outing that covered 558 miles from Ensenada to La Paz in Baja, California, with rules requiring it to be completed in just thirty hours.

This type of racing was not new to AMC; two years earlier, a 1967 Rambler American driven by Spencer Murray and Ralph Poole had set a thirty-one-hour record between Tijuana and La Paz. A 1966 Rambler Rebel had also finished that race satisfactorily, thus promoting the 1967 Rambler American effort. For the 1968 season a new 1968 American was entered, but problems in navigation and battered roads delayed its arrival to ten hours over the passenger car record.

Of the ten cars prepared for Garner and AIR, four were to be converted to four-wheel drive, but only two cars actually received the conversion. The two-wheel-drive SCs would compete in Class I (production two-wheel-drive passenger vehicles) and the four-wheel-drive cars would compete in Class VI (nonproduction four-wheel-drive vehicles).

In the four-wheel-drive cars, Spicer front-end-drive units were used along with Spicer transfer cases behind the regular transmission. The engine had to be raised about four inches to permit the front propeller shaft to span the distance between the transfer case and the forward differential.

Seven of the eight two-wheel-drive SC/Ramblers used the stock Borg-Warner T-10 four-speed, and one used AMC's three-speed automatic. All cars used the stock 390 V-8 equipped with exhaust headers.

The task of prepping the cars was accomplished by Bill Rohrbacher of Hemet, California, who also prepped the winning and record-holding Garner-driven Broncos.

All cars were given additional ground clearance and carried divided forty-four-gallon fuel tanks mounted in the middle with dual quick-fill spouts allowing refueling in less than ten seconds. The cars were completely gutted, all glass was removed, and a 1¾ inch chromemoly roll cage was installed. The engines and drivetrains were completely disassembled and blueprinted. Engine output was now up to 410 hp, and tests showed the cars could do 140 mph at 7000 rpm in high gear on the straightaways! The bodies were then repainted the familiar red-white-blue paint scheme, as on the Trans-Am Javelins and other AMC cars in racing.

On race day of the 1969 Baja 500, the drivers for the ten cars included Bob Bondurant, Davey Jordan, Carl Jackson, Rodney Hall, Hunter Floyd, Ed Orr, two

wally Booth's pro stock Gremlin was quite a competitive machine on the strip. The car could pull wheelies with ease, thanks to its 600 plus hp.

Jim Wrights and *Rod and Custom* magazine editor Spencer Murray. Because of a movie commitment in Spain, Garner himself was unable to attend. Other team drivers were Jim Fricker, Eck Tur, Tony Murphy, Eltrick, Hansen, Fox and Crean. AMC entered the race with its own version of a 1969 Rambler, number 188, painted red-white-blue and driven by the team of Samida and Henderson.

As is any off-road race, the Baja was a spectacular, dirty, grimy, gruesome and tiring event. There were quite a few close calls between the SC/Ramblers and the other racers, which included two- and four-wheel-drive vehicles, pickups, buggies, passenger cars, utility vehicles and motorcycles. Even before the race, ten-penny nails were found wedged between the rear tire tread and the ground on nine of the ten AIR cars and on various other vehicles. The sabotage was found before any of the cars moved, preventing a bunch of punctured tires. During the race, a protest was lodged against the Bondurant and Murphy car (number 100) by a Jeepster driver who claimed damages done to his vehicle were caused by Bondurant's reckless driving while both cars tried to avoid an oncoming hay truck.

Seven of the ten Garner cars managed to finish the race. In the Sedan class, the SC/Ramblers swept three of the first five places. The Bondurant and Murphy two-wheel-drive car placed first in Class I and finished thirtieth overall. The Jackson and Fricker four-wheel-drive car placed fourth in Class VI and finished fourteenth overall. Also finishing in the production two-wheel-drive Sedan class were the Ed Orr and J. W. Wright car, placing third, and the Simpson and Evans car, placing fifth.

1972-73 Gremlin X and Hornet X

American Motors assaulted the pro stock division of drag racing with a 1972 Gremlin X in the spring of 1972. Wally Booth and partner Dick Arons prepared the car from the ground up along with crew Gordy Foust, Dave Tratechaud and Dave Gostenick. Booth was one of the sport's top competitors, having been runner-up five times in major national events driving Chevrolets.

The car was built by Booth-Arons Racing Enterprises, a Detroit-based firm engaged in the building of engines and related race car components for super stock and pro stock applications.

The car was to make its debut at the Gatornationals March 18 and 19, but because of problems it instead made its debut at the NHRA World Championship series point meet in Indianapolis, Indiana, on April 30, 1972, where Booth won pro stock eliminator honors.

The car was equipped with a destroked 340 ci version of the AMC 360 V-8. Its competition had nearly 100 more cubic inches, but new rules permitted small-block engines to have a weight advantage, which made up for this.

Cars like the Gremlin with stock block inline valve engines had to weigh 6.75 pounds per cubic inch of displacement and have a wheelbase of 100 inches or less. Cars with staggered valve engines needed seven pounds per cubic inch, and exotic engines such as the Chrysler Hemi had to carry 7.25 pounds per cubic inch. This put the Gremlin at 2,300 pounds with 550 to 570 hp available. A Plymouth Hemi was at 3,000 pounds with 720 hp.

The Gremlin went up against seasoned competition such as Sox and Martin, Grumpy Jenkins and Don Nicholson running Plymouth Crickets, Chevy Vegas and Ford Pintos, respectively.

The car was professionally prepared. Before modifications, the team started with a 506 pound body; after completion it had a legal acid-dipped 208 pounder as a starting point. Many body panels were replaced with ten-gauge aluminum, and the full floor pan was replaced with a thinner metal. To prevent frame twisting, cross-members were added front and rear. A 360 degree roll cage was welded onto the frame rails for strength and rigidity.

The V-8 engine had to be in its same stock location, so no firewall modifications were permitted. The Pinto, Vega and Cricket were allowed these modifications because they were not available with factory-installed V-8s.

The engine was modified by Booth. Bore and stroke were 4.175x3.250 for a final displacement of 355 cubic inches. Redline was 9000 rpm. Intake and

Wally Booth raced Chevrolets before coming over to AMC.

exhaust ports were huge. The intake manifold was specially designed by Booth and was made available to the general public for sale. It carried two Holley four-barrel 4500 series carburetors. The engine used Stahl headers, JE pistons, 332 degree 0.605 inch lift General Kinetics cam, Manley lightweight steel valves, Holley electric fuel pump and Cragar CD ignition.

The clutch was a Booth modified 10.5 inch 3,200 pound Borg and Beck. It was tied to a Borg-Warner super T-10 four-speed transmission with a Hurst ram rod and 2.65:1 low gear. The flywheel used was a forty-pound Schiefer aluminum. The rear was a Dana 5.57:1.

A Pinto rack-and-pinion steering system was added. Front wheels were 3.5x15 inches and carried 7.10x15 tires, and rear wheels were twelve inches wide with Firestone slicks that were fourteen inches wide and thirty-one inches tall. Front coil springs were stock light-tension AMC units, and the rear leaf springs were stock heavy-duty AMC pieces.

The car ran consistent 9.40s at 142 mph, and it beat Sox and Martin as well as Nicholson.

In 1972, Booth managed to win the NHRA Division III championship. Throughout the 1973 season he was competitive, but not enough so to score any significant victories.

Even in the quarter-mile, aerodynamics can play a big role, and the boxy Gremlin was not aerodynamic at all. But the new 1973 Hornet hatchback looked like a much smoother design. Two veteran drag specialists, Dick Maskin and David Kanners, decided to build a new pro stock racer based on its body style to run in the same NHRA pro stock category as Wally Booth. Their goal was to break the 9.01 second 150.50 mph record for the pro stock class, a new class formed by NHRA in 1970.

Booth and his partner Arons prepared and built a new 370 ci version of the AMC 360 engine for the new car. Extensive head work was required to make the engine competitive. The team improved its elapsed times throughout the season, beginning with its initial run at the NHRA Gatornationals in Gainesville, Florida, where it made a pass clocking an elapsed time of 9.33 seconds at 146.50 mph, equaling the existing national record.

Financial backing by AMC ended in 1974, three weeks before Wally Booth's first major win at the 1974 Gatornationals. Booth consistently outpowered and outraced all comers, recording an 8.97 elapsed time at 152.80 mph to take his first NHRA National title.

Booth, Arons, Maskin and Kanners pressed on and raced their AMC models into the 1975 season, still waving the red, white and blue colors. In that year, Booth's time of 8.75 seconds made him the lone qualifier at the nationals. He completely dominated the Springnationals at Columbus, Ohio, where he was again the low qualifier and took his second championship. His final round time of 8.74 seconds was 0.22 seconds under the old event record and 0.06 under the current record.

After AMC withdrew its factory support of the car, Booth entered the 1976 season with a Chevrolet Vega in which he qualified for the season-opening Winternationals at Pomona, California. After totaling the Vega on his second time out, he went back to the Hornet at the Gatornationals and was promptly disqualified for a technical violation.

Booth was determined, however, and he came back strong by taking runner-up honors at the Inaugural Cajun Nationals at New Orleans. His win at the Springnationals put him back into the Winston World Championship standings.

During the 1976 season, Booth was right on the heels of such notable veterans as Warren Johnson of Fridley, Minnesota; Lombardo and Roy Hill of High Point, North Carolina, driving the Jenkins Vega; Win-

The pro stock Hornet X of Richard Maskin and David Kanners was another superperformer. Wally Booth's pro stock Hornet X looked practically the same, and both cars were prepared in a similar fashion since Booth worked closely with the team.

ston World Champ Bob Glidden of Beech Grove, Indiana; defending Summernationals champion Wayne Gapp of Livonia, Michigan; and Ally Dave Kanners of Troy, Michigan, driving the only other competitive Hornet in which he finished third in the world in 1975.

Since Booth built the engine for the Maskin and Kanners Hornet X, both cars were constructed and prepared in more or less the same basic manner. Such cooperation between teams is not as uncommon as one may think. In the long run, both teams benefit.

Maskin was not new to AMC vehicles. He had raced and campaigned the most successful independent Gremlin pro stocker in 1972, leading to his factory sponsorship in 1973. In that Gremlin, he qualified at every major meet he attended and came within two-tenths of a second of the national record with a season's best clocking of 9.60. The total cost of that car was about $25,000, so without factory sponsorship it was an expensive hobby.

The Hornet X sat on a larger wheelbase of 108 inches and weighed 2,308 pounds, just over the 2,300 pound weight minimum for NHRA pro stockers for 100 inch wheelbase or greater cars. For match races, the car was stripped down to a mere 2,150 pounds.

The Booth-Arons modified AMC 360 V-8 engine pushed out between 580 and 590 hp.

The basic steel body was retained but was acid-dipped to reduce skin thickness and weight. Front and rear longitudinal frame rails were connected to the unibody with square tubing. They were then reinforced with a 360 degree roll cage of 1.750x0.125 chromemoly-steel tubing that also acted as mounting points for the rear suspension components, steering column, and clutch and throttle linkages.

The front and rear suspensions were basically stock, with Monroe shocks to provide the necessary limited front-end travel. Titanium spindles were supplied by Apollo Welding, and a compact rack-and-pinion steering system was installed to further lighten the front end. Apollo also supplied titanium clutch and throttle linkage components.

A Hays clutch and flywheel combination was used with a Borg-Warner super T-10 four-speed transmission with a Mr Gasket straight-line shifter. Liberty transmission gears were substituted for the stock gears because of their strength and durability. On occasion, Maskin and Kanners even substituted a funny car/dragster-type two-speed Lenco automatic transmission bolted together with a reverser. The clutch was used only off the line, and the three gear changes in a run were made by pulling one of the three levers.

Because the engine was set farther back than stock, a shortened driveshaft was made that hooked up to a narrowed Dana rear end, housing Schiefer 5.57:1 ring and pinion gears.

An ATA fiberglass front-facing snorkle-type hood scoop fed air into a pair of Holley four-barrel carburetors mounted on an Edelbrock tunnel-ram intake

Richard Maskin had been active with his 1972 Gremlin pro stocker before the Hornet X project.

David Kanners worked closely with his teammate. With the combined skills of the two men, another victory was chalked up to AMC.

187

manifold. A General Kinetics roller cam was used, assisted by needle bearing rocker arms held in place with a Jomar rocker arm girdle. Aluminum pistons, forged steel rods from Mr. Rod and a 3,400 inch stroker AMC forged steel crankshaft completed the internals.

Outside, BW ignition, Hooker headers, Champion spark plugs and a Lee high-performance oil filter were used. Lee also supplied a heavy-duty battery that was mounted in the rear portion of the car for better weight transfer. Kendall racing oil was used for lubrication.

The car sported Cragar Super Trick spun aluminum wheels all around, with the fronts measuring 4x15 inches and the rears 13x15 inches. Low-profile funny car tires were used in front, and the rear had fourteen-inch slicks mounted on the wheels. Autometer supplied the tachometer and all other cockpit engine gauges.

Other notable Gremlins were raced and campaigned by a host of colorful drivers. The *Gruntin Gremlin* started off as a stock 390 V-8 1970 Gremlin and was sponsored by the Southern California American Motors Dealers. It was later acquired by Jim Johnston and Steve Kathary of Reseda, California.

The 390 was replaced with a modified 401 featuring an Edelbrock cross-ram manifold and dual 660 cfm Holleys. It also sported Donovan big steel valves, Norris cam and spring kit and Sharp needle rockers. Rods and crank were modified AMC. The block was a four-bolt main with a host of aftermarket speed equipment such as Mason, Mallory, Doug Thorley and Schiefer.

The car was built and run roughly two years before the more publicized 1972 Wally Booth Gremlin. Its best elapsed time was around 11.17 at 129 plus mph.

Other Gremlin pro stockers in the spotlight were the Jim Gilbert and Dick Maskin effort using an engine built and prepared by Booth and Arons.

Another venture was that of former Ford racers Rich Lamont and Bob Heiser teaming with Philadelphia radio entrepreneur Rick Buckley. This Gremlin had a chassis built by Hollman and Moody and an engine supplied by Traco, the same people who built the NASCAR Matador and Trans-Am Javelins with the winning engines.

Noted more for their roles in the record-setting S/S AMX, Shirley and H. L. Shahan successfully raced pro stock Gremlins and Hornets in 1971 and 1972, with a lot of help from AMC. The cars were prepared by H. L. Shahan himself, and were used for numerous exhibition and special showcase match drag racers.

The cars used were equipped with AMC 360 V-8s featuring nonfactory bores and strokes. Bore was at 4.187 inches, an increase of 0.107 inch, and the stroke was reduced by 0.18 inch to 3.260 inches. Cranks were modified 401 steel forgings, cross-drilled and using Federal-Mogul F77 bearings. The bottom ends were reinforced with Milodon 392 Chrysler four-bolt-style main bearing girdles modified to fit. Carillo rods were

modified to use Chevy 302 bearings. A Crane roller cam was used with a 0.628 inch lift and 324 degree duration. The cars were prepped with an array of other namebrand heavy-duty equipment. The Gremlin could muster an elapsed time of 10.01 seconds at 137.20 mph.

The Hornet's longer wheelbase and greater rear overhang contributed to better and more weight transfer off the line, enabling it to turn a 9.89 elapsed time at 139.52 mph. Although the Hornet was a bigger car than the Gremlin, it weighed ten pounds less in race-prepped form. This was the result of a lot of metal thinning through acid-dipping the entire body. The Gremlin came in at a weight of 2,220 pounds, which was 300 pounds under the legal NHRA weight limit for both cars, explaining their exhibition- and match-race-only duties.

1972-75 NASCAR Matador hardtop and coupe

Just before Christmas 1971, AMC and the Penske team announced they would be entering NASCAR racing for the 1972 season with a Matador two-door hardtop. They would run one car and possibly two later in the season. Donohue would be the main driver with teammate Gary Bettenhausen substituting if NASCAR and Can Am (Canadian American) races conflicted.

Hollman and Moody would build the chassis and body. For the first time in a stock car, they would incorporate power steering from the Trans-Am Javelins. Chuck Cantwell would be project chief and Jim Travers of Traco would build the engine. Eddie Pagan and Dick Hutcherson of Pagan Industries would manage the pit crew and direct the race operations during the 1972 season. The car would attempt to enter twelve races in the season.

The first NASCAR Matador prototype was run at Charlotte Motor Speedway and was equipped with a Trans-Am 305 V-8 built by Traco. The actual racer used a stroked version of that engine having a displacement of 366 cubic inches and producing over 500 hp. Because of its small displacement, its engine was allowed to run with no carburetor restriction. The engine had a bore of 4.10 inches and a stroke of 3.44 inches. It was stuffed with such heavy-duty equipment as a Moldex crank, Carillo modified AMC rods, TRW pistons, Traco valvetrain and four-bolt main bearing caps. The car also featured Hedman headers, dry-sump oil system, eleven-inch four-wheel Girling disc brakes, Borg-Warner T-10 close-ratio four-speed transmission and 3.31:1 heavy-duty rear axle assembly.

1972

The Matador made its debut at the January 23, 1972, Riverside International 500 mile race, where it finished thirty-ninth. In a practice run at Daytona Beach, Florida, the car cruised effortlessly at 170 mph. At the February 12 qualifying runs for the February 22 Daytona race, the Matador hit 173.808 mph. The average speed for the rest of the cars was around 180 mph, and Donohue qualified for twelfth position.

The high-speed NASCAR tracks proved to be no good for the Matador, as it had undesirable aerodynamics. At the race, the car broke a pushrod after only eleven laps and placed thirty-fifth. Richard Petty, driving a Woods Brothers Mercury, took an easy win for the Daytona race.

Pete Hamilton observed the Matador's action and became quite interested. He told the Penske team he would like to race the car and substitute for Donohue if other race dates conflicted.

Veteran stock car mechanic J. C. Elder had spent many years with Petty Engineering and also with Hollman and Moody. He commented that AMC needed to build a better and more aerodynamic body style to compete with the others on the track. Elder said the Matador's front end was too square: its roofline was two inches higher than that of the other cars and its windshield stood almost straight up and down instead of being slanted back as on the other cars.

At the start of the 1972 season, the Matador ran on the short tracks of Riverside and Daytona. At those short tracks aerodynamics did not play too big a role, and to win, drafting was almost always necessary. The Matador did not do too badly at either track, but Donohue did receive a lot of harassment and snide remarks at the Daytona race, which was won by A. J. Foyt.

At the race at Riverside the Matador almost managed to capture the Winston Grand National victory. Donnie Allison was substituting for Donohue. Penske's strategy was to pit only four times to everyone else's five, but things did not go as planned. There was confusion as to what tires needed changing and one pit stop extended to almost two minutes. As the race progressed, Bobby Isaac's Dodge was leading, Ray Elder's Dodge was second and Donnie Allison was third. Isaac pitted, leaving the lead to Elder and second to Allison, and Isaac remained twenty-five seconds behind. Suddenly Allison got sideways, went off course and stalled, and could not get restarted until four laps later. A brake imbalance caused a lockup and the spin-out. This killed a chance for a possible victory or maybe even second place. Ray Elder went on to win.

The Matador was called a shoe box by NASCAR people at Ontario, but it managed to stay running in seventh position. By the fortieth lap Donohue was running third, and going into turn one he led Bobby Isaac driving a 1972 Dodge. Isaac got underneath Donohue and hit his rear end, turning the Matador and causing its tail to hit the wall. Isaac then hit the wall nose first. Both drivers were shaken but unhurt. Foyt went on to run the race.

At the Atlanta 500, the Matador completed 314 laps and finished fifteenth. A fifth-lap spin-out and wreck against the front stretch pit rail cost the team a

lot of time. Bobby Allison driving a 1971 Monte Carlo took the victory.

The Matador did not even finish the Pocono 500, but a 1970 Javelin driven by Ken McEldonney finished thirty-third.

In the Irish Hills, Michigan, race, Dave Marcis was able to complete 194 laps safely and finished ninth. At the Southern 500 Marcis came in seventh, completing 348 laps. After only seventy laps at Dover, engine trouble sidelined his victory attempt, and differential trouble after 108 laps held him back at the Old Dominion 500. He did manage to finish 246 laps at Charlotte, placing twenty-sixth, and completed 475 laps at the American 500, finishing seventh.

The 1972 season was long, difficult and frustrating for the Penske team. A Matador that seemed promising on short tracks where aerodynamics were not that demanding proved to be disastrous on the superspeedways where aerodynamics were the most important aspect of winning. Meanwhile, if it wasn't one mechanical failure, it was another. And things did not change for the 1973 season, except for the first race.

1973

Donohue roared to AMC's first Grand National victory at the January 21, 1973, season's opening race, the Winston Western 500 in Riverside, California. It was Donohue and the red-white-blue Matador all the way. A number of top stars dropped out owing to mechanical failure. Petty suffered a blown engine, Pearson had clutch problems, Yarborough's transmission gave out, Isaac blew a head gasket, Baker broke a timing chain and a host of problems plagued other drivers.

Bobby Allison in a 1973 Chevelle was about the only one who was giving Donohue a run for his money. Donohue was running away from Allison and the rest of the pack at such a fast rate that at one point he was almost a full lap ahead of Allison. Of the 191 laps the Matador led 141 laps, and it made the 500

Dave Marcis also drove for the Penske racing team. The old-bodied Matador needed help aerodynamically to enable it to be more competitive on the track.

189

miles in a time of 4.48.33 hours at an average speed of 104.056 mph.

Donohue was driving an updated 1973 Matador with over 525 hp, a little more horsepower than the 1972 racer had had. The car had better disc brakes all around, and the chassis and suspension were fine-tuned. Penske was able to get American Motors to stamp part numbers on water-cooled brakes off a Porche 917/30 racer, thus enabling them to be used on the NASCAR Matador. This was the first time any car in NASCAR history was equipped with four-wheel disc brakes.

Donohue did not expect a streak of wins for the Matador in the upcoming races, but he was confident that he could run with the best of them. At the next Daytona 500 race, however, Marcis was once again at the wheel, and he retired after 125 laps with rear end trouble. Donohue was able to drive in the Atlanta 500 race, but was not a threat to anyone that day. Marcis drove again for the Alamo 500, but wrecked his car on the fifteenth lap.

The last race of the season that the Matador entered was the American 500. This time Marcis was able to complete 484 laps with no mechanical mishaps, and finished sixth.

During the 1973 season, Penske tried a 428 ci version of the present 366 AMC V-8, which had to run with a carburetor restrictor plate because of rule changes. It was felt that the additional torque at low rpm would help the car get around the racetrack. But from the start, the 428 was plagued with problems. It was a case of too big an engine in too little a block. Some of the problems encountered were excessive temperatures, piston failures, hot spots from poor manifolding and cracking of component parts from too much stress. The 428 produced less power than the 366, and was practically a total failure. It did not even finish one race it entered. The switch was made back to the tried and proven 366 version for the 1974 season.

1974

With two seasons of stock car racing, AMC was now ready to taste victory, but the old Matador body style was just not aerodynamic. This led to the new frog-eyed 1974 Matador coupe. It is said that Penske had quite a bit to do with its design; it is also said that this new coupe was introduced for the sole purpose of making AMC more competitive on the track.

The car looked aerodynamically sleek and proved to be so on the track. It rode on a four-inch-shorter wheelbase than the 1973 Matador's, and was about

Donohue passes Richard Petty driving the number 43 STP Dodge to AMC's first Grand National victory at the Winston Western 500 in Riverside, California, on January 21, 1973.

three inches lower. The car was available only in a two-door sport coupe.

The suspension was changed slightly, as was the rear sway bar arrangement. A hydraulic clutch instead of a manual linkage clutch was used to ease operation and save fifteen pounds at the same time. Numerous other small details in overall packaging were also changed.

John Woodard was signed on as a mechanic and Karl Kainhofer, who had been chief mechanic on the Penske Indy cars, worked on the gearboxes and differentials. Don Kean and Harold Fagan performed most of the fabrication and arranging of the sheet metal, with the help of Nick Olilla from Formula A Racing. Jay Signure handled the chores of general manager.

At the 1974 season's opening race at Riverside, Gary Bettenhausen drove the new coupe with Donohue as a team manager. Many drivers were discontented and annoyed by the so-called fuel shortage, and attendance was affected.

Rain halted the race after sixty-three laps. Bobby Allison was in fifth place, followed by Richard Petty and David Pearson. Bettenhausen was in eighth place. When the race was resumed the following week Cale Yarborough in a 1973 Monte Carlo came out victorious, and the newly designed Matador came in seventh, finishing 185 laps.

At the Daytona 500 race, Bettenhausen was able to finish twelfth and completed 196 laps out of a possible 200.

The Atlanta 500 race looked promising for the Penske team. During much of the race the Matador ran second, but it dropped back to ninth after some sloppy pit stops and finished in that position, completing 322 laps. Dave Marcis drove in the Rebel 500 and completed 327 laps, coming in sixth.

The Winston 500 at Talladega could have been the 1974 Matador's first victory, if it had not been for a pit stop accident on lap 105. It had been raining on and off all day, and Bettenhausen was leading the race when a yellow flag came out. The pit area was slick with water and oil. Bettenhausen went past his station and had to go around one more lap to come back in. The pit crew was working on the car routinely when Grant Adcox had to pit in the station behind them. He slid right into the back of the Matador, and the pit crew went flying. Four Penske crew men were injured, one seriously (Don Miller, sales manager for the Penske products line of Sears Automotive Accessories). All four crew members eventually recovered, but Pearson in the Mercury went on to win the race, and Benny Parsons in a Chevy came in second.

The Motor State 400 was one of the Matador's better races of the season. Bettenhausen kept his car in

The new 1974 Matador coupe gave AMC the edge it needed on the superspeedways. Victory came at the Los Angeles

Times 500 in Ontario, California, the 1974 season's closing race.

191

contention and finished fourth, completing 178 laps. The Matador was coming on strong.

At the Firecracker 400, Bobby Allison signed on to drive with the Penske team, and with him he brought his Coca-Cola sponsorship. The car became known as the number sixteen Coca-Cola Matador, although the Penske crew was still running the show. Coca-Cola's advertising theme of "Look Up America" was painted on the hood of the Matador. At the Firecracker race, the Matador had the second-fastest qualifying time behind Pearson's Mercury; it was Bobby Allison's lap time of 49.791 seconds at 180.755 mph to David Pearson's 49.790 seconds at 180.759 mph. A reporter calculated that if both drivers maintained their exact qualifying times and ran a lap around the track side by side, Pearson would get to the line three inches ahead of Allison. As it turned out, Pearson won and Allison came in fifth, completing 159 laps.

The Dixie 500 was thumbs down for the Matador again. After Allison completed 101 laps a piston ring broke. Richard Petty and the STP Dodge took the checkered flag.

At the Purolator 500 Allison again retired after 154 laps, dropping a valve, and Petty roared to win his second straight 500 miler.

But at the Talladega 500, the Matador once again bounced back to a good race day. Allison led the race in the early stages but lost a couple of laps when a windshield had to be replaced. He came back from more than two laps down to finish third, one lap off the race, and completed 187 laps. Petty and Pearson came in first and second.

Then came the Yankee 400 and another disappointment. Allison finished fifth and completed 198 laps; brake troubles kept him from any attempt at victory.

And the beat went on at the Southern 500. In a slight spin-out with other cars in lap eighty the Matador's steering was damaged, ending that day's race. Yarborough took the win.

For the Matador, the Tuborg 400 at Riverside ended almost as soon as it began. Gary Bettenhausen was committed to drive in the Milwaukee USAC race. Enter George Folmer, who left the Bud Moore team and was now signed up to run the Riverside race. He set the fastest qualifying lap and was the odds-on favorite to win. But after only one lap of racing, Bobby Allison passed him on the outside of turn one. Folmer had missed a shift at 9000 rpm, which was enough to stretch the timing chain and end the day for the Penske effort. Yarborough finished first and Allison came in second, both driving Chevrolets.

Allison finished thirteenth at the Delaware 500 in the Matador, completing 468 laps, and Petty again won.

The National 500 at Charlotte was a somewhat close race for the Matador. Bobby Allison once again showed he could stay right up there with the tough guys. During most of the race he was in the same lap with brother Donnie, Richard Petty, David Pearson and Darrel Waltrip. All five were having a great time swapping positions. But Bobby Allison had to pit on lap 278 for tires, and this cost him a chance to win. By the time he came back out, the Big Four were on his tail end and he went down on lap 283 and was not able to come back within striking distance thereafter. He was able to finish the race in fifth place, completing 333 of the 334 laps. Pearson and Petty came in first and second.

At the American 500, it was just another day cruising around the track for Bobby Allison. The Matador did not break or suffer any problems that day and it managed to finish fourth, completing 487 of the 492 laps. Once again, David Pearson was the victor, capturing his thirteenth superspeedway win. Cale Yarborough came in second, and Richard Petty placed third.

Victory finally came to Allison and the new-bodied Matador at the Los Angeles Times 500 in Ontario, California, the closing race of the season. The win backfired for Allison and Penske, however. In a post-race teardown of the Matador at the speedway itself, valve lifters were found in the 355 ci V-8 that did not comply with NASCAR specifications. Since there was no provision in NASCAR rules for disqualification of a winner, Allison was fined $9,100 for the infraction, which was his share of the first-place purse. Penske refused any comment or discussion on the matter. But Allison did set a new record for the 500 miler in a time of 3.42:11 hours for an average speed of 134.963 mph. Pearson came in second, and Yarborough finished third.

It was a long uphill battle for the Penske team. In three years its only victories were the first race of the 1973 season and the last one of the 1974 season. The 1975 season was a little better.

1975

For the 1975 season, the Matador was well prepared. It included the latest in stock car techniques and was built up by famed chassis builder Banjo Matthews. It also sported a new 357 ci engine producing 520 hp at 7000 rpm. Chief mechanic John "Woody" Woodard was pleased with the preparation of the new car.

At the 1975 season's opening race, the Winston Western 500 in Riverside, California, the mighty Matador took the win and easily outdistanced David Pearson in several head-to-head confrontations. The previous day in the Sportsman Race, Allison had been leading when his engine blew three laps from the end. Bobby Allison had put the Matador on the pole for race day, and it was only a shade faster than Pearson's Purolator Mercury.

The Matador's careful preparation showed in the Riverside race as Allison pulled away from the competition at the drop of the green flag, leaving Pearson and Petty behind. Even the numerous yellow caution flags that came out during the race, allowing the field to bunch up, posed no problem for Allison. Pearson was constantly at his rear bumper, but it took Allison only a few laps after each yellow to open up his lead and dispose of the Mercury. At the finish line, Allison was a half of a lap ahead of the second-place Pearson. Cecil Gordon in a Chevrolet came in third, and Petty placed seventh.

Things were certainly looking good for the Penske team and the new Matdor when Bobby Allison scored a third victory at the first 125 mile qualifying race for the Daytona 500 at Daytona Beach, Florida. Although he qualified third behind first qualifier, brother Donnie, and second qualifier Buddy Baker, Allison's driving experience coupled to an excellently prepared car turned the trick for the Penske team.

Allison was quoted as saying, "The car was just about perfect. I could take it anywhere on the track I wanted to and I could run it as hard as I needed to. If it runs this well on Sunday, we'll be in pretty good shape."

Team captain Donohue was then quoted as saying, "Three years ago when we came here with the Matador we took a lot of ribbing about our little box. We knew it was a little box and American Motors knew it was a little box. The little box even knew it was a little box. But we've come a long way with our little box since then. I think our track record in the past three races proves that."

Richard Brooks in a Ford placed second and Lennie Pond in a Chevrolet came in third.

At the Daytona 500 mile race, Bobby Allison and the Matador almost did it. They came in second and completed 199 of the 200 laps, all the while running on seven cylinders since a rocker arm broke early in the race. A dramatic dual causing a spin-out took place between Pearson, Petty and Parsons during the closing laps of the race. Yarborough and Richie Panch, who both were out of the race victorywise at that point, got tangled up in the shuffle. When it was all over two laps

later, Parsons, who had started thirty-second in a field of forty, took the checkered flag. Yarborough came in third, and a furious Pearson came in fourth. Petty was way down in seventh place.

The Matador's last three victories placed Bobby Allison ahead in the Winston Cup standings with 355 points, ten more than Pearson, forty-five more than Marcis in a Dodge, fifty-three ahead of Petty and seventy-one ahead of James Hylton driving a Chevrolet.

The Atlanta 500 race was a big disappointment for Bobby Allison and the Penske crew. Allison started on the outside pole and led the race for two laps, but on lap sixteen he pitted for gas and tires and fell a lap behind. Six laps later he spun out when he locked the brakes because he was completely engulfed in smoke from rookie Ricky Rudd's tire blowout. Allison skidded backwards for 200 feet along the inside guardrail, which flat-spotted his tires, so again he had to come in. A broken valve finally sidelined the Matador, making the engine miss severely, so Allison just parked it for

Driver Bobby Allison and chief mechanic John Woodard were excited and confident over the newly designed and improved 1974 Matador coupe for the 1975 racing season.

Coca-Cola sponsorship was introduced to AMC and the Matador coupe for the 1975 racing season. At the season's opening race, the Winston Western 500 in Riverside, Califor- *nia, Bobby Allison and the mighty Matador took the victory once again for AMC.*

the remainder of the day. It was a fairly easy victory for Petty, and Baker and Pearson came in second and third.

The Rebel 500 at good old Darlington International Raceway in South Carolina was described as a miracle win for the Matador and the Penske crew. One mishap after another dropped out some of the heavy favorites, including Yarborough with an engine blowup and Petty with a blown tire that put him into the wall. Dick Brooks went out with overheating problems, Donnie Allison and Cecil Gordon crashed into each other putting themselves out for the rest of the day, Baker went out with engine trouble, and Pearson and Parsons crashed together and both went into the wall. Bobby Allison was running two laps behind, one as a result of being penalized by NASCAR for passing the pace car under a yellow caution flag and the other as a result of having to make an unscheduled pit stop for a cut tire, but all the other racer's mishaps worked in his favor. Through Allison's skill and experience combined with the finely running Matador, he was able to achieve the winning combinations once again for AMC. At the closing eight laps it was neck-and-neck with brother Donnie and Waltrip. Bobby Allison was able to edge both out at the finish line, with Waltrip coming in second and Donnie Allison third.

This was the next-to-the-last victory race for the Matador under the Penske team. Their last victory took place at the same Darlington International Speedway for the running of the Southern 500. It was also the last year the Matador was entered in the NASCAR racing or in any other race with AMC sponsorship, as Penske's contract with AMC ended after 1975 and was not renewed.

Penske was so enthused he was quoted as saying, "To win on a road course in January (as Allison did in the Western Winston 500) is one thing. But to win one at Darlington in front of the Southern fans is something you can't match. Boy, it's super, isn't it? Did you see that car run?"

The Winston 500 at Talladega, Alabama, was another big thumbs down for the Matador early in the race. On lap forty-eight the engine blew. The car fishtailed three times and then hit the outside wall almost head on in front of the flagman's stand at the start-finish line. It spun backwards off the track and through the infield grass for almost 800 feet before coming to rest near the apron of the first and second turn. Allison was not hurt, but it was all over for the rest of the day for the Penske crew. Buddy Baker won in a Ford and Pearson came in second in the Purolator Mercury.

The Tuborg 400 at Riverside, California, was again an almost victory for the Matador. Allison had the fastest qualifying time and sat on the pole with Petty. A last-minute gamble by the Penske crew to change four tires instead of two late in the race cost Allison a chance to race Petty for the win. At the finish line Petty was less than ten seconds ahead of Allison,

just about the extra time it took to change those right-side tires. When Petty pitted, only the left-side tires were replaced, accounting for a quicker pit stop thus giving him the winning edge. Parsons and Elder came in third and fourth a full lap behind Petty and Allison.

The Motor State 400 in Michigan was not a good one for Allison. Although he remained competitive from the start, his engine failed when he was only fifty-six miles from the finish line. Once again Pearson and Petty came in first and second.

The Firecracker 400 was just another disappointing race, as the Matador dropped out after only sixty-seven laps because of engine trouble again. Petty and Baker took the first- and second-place wins.

It looked as though the Matador would come roaring back, as Allison had the fastest qualifying time and sat on the pole for the Purolator 500 at the Pocono International Raceway in Pennsylvania. Everything worked and looked fine, until after only twenty-two laps the engine once again went sour. Pearson and Petty repeated their first- and second-place victories, with Baker and Parsons right behind them.

At the Talladega 500 the Matador once again suffered a blown engine, this time on lap 128 after leading four times for nine laps, the last lap led being lap ninety-eight. Buddy Baker won with his Ford, and Petty came in second with the STP Dodge.

The Dixie 500 at Hampton, Georgia, was another disaster, with Allison losing oil pressure on lap 196. It was a fight to the finish, with Baker, Marcis and Petty finishing in the top three spots.

The Los Angeles Times 500 saw the Matador running and finishing its last race. Although Allison put the right side of the car into the wall early in the race, he was still able to continue. Allison managed to finish fifth. He could have finished fourth had it not been for an incident in the pits, where a NASCAR official cited the Penske team for having too many people over the wall. This held up Allison for about twenty-five seconds in the pits. Yarborough came in fourth, with Baker winning and Pearson and Marcis coming in second and third.

The Matador and the Penske team had an uphill battle from the start, and they knew it, but Penske was not one to turn down such a big challenge. With his past success in Trans-Am racing, he knew he could turn the trick for AMC in NASCAR racing. Although it did not record as many wins as the Javelin did, the Matador did show that with the proper preparation and skillful driving, it could run right up there with the best of them.

Bobby Allison was voted most popular driver in both the Winston Cup Grand National and Grand National East divisions by the NASCAR membership for three straight years (1971, 1972 and 1973). He raced the Matador again roughly two years later without AMC backing for about two seasons, but was not as successful as when he was racing it with the Penske team.

An AMC-backed NASCAR-type prepared 1978 Concord hatchback complete with NASCAR-race-proven 355 cubic inch engine was raced in 1978 and 1979 on some of the shorter USAC tracks and was to follow in the footsteps of the Coca-Cola Penske Matador coupe. Driven by Roger McCluskey and owned by Warner Hodgedon of Hodgedon National Engineering Research and Development Group, the car saw limited success. This ended the project, as well as any other NASCAR attempt by AMC.

1971-81 IMSA Gremlin, Hornet, Pacer and Spirit

Although they were not as popular as the Javelin in Trans-Am events and the Matador in NASCAR events, the Gremlin, Hornet, Pacer and Spirit were raced in IMSA, in the Goodrich Radial Challenge or Baby Grand Races.

1971-74

In 1971, Amos Johnson bought, modified and raced a Gremlin on his own in the first race of the season at Daytona Beach in Florida. He finished third his first time out and then drove the car home. He later wrote an engineering paper on the car and forwarded it to AMC, explaining what he had done and what else he could do. AMC officials were impressed and almost immediately signed him on as their IMSA race car driver, thus starting a relationship that lasted almost ten years.

The AMC drivers that most stood out in 1972 and 1973 were Amos Johnson and Whit Diggett, known as the Highball Team. George Alderman, Dennis Shaw and Brett Lunger also drove Gremlins at one time or another. Their cars were all backed by AMC and Levi's Jeans. The Levi's Gremlin Xs were equipped with 232 ci six-cylinder engines mated to standard three-speed manual transmissions.

At the end of the 1972 season, Diggett and Johnson came out as winners of Class B honors against such cars as the Capri, Pinto, Opel, Datsun, BMW and others. The two-car Gremlin team also finished third and fourth in the IMSA series.

The first Gremlin road racing victory came in Brainerd, Minnesota, in 1973, and the car placed first at Daytona Beach, Florida, during the seven-race season. Johnson placed first and Diggett fourth in series during the 1973 events, driving their Gremlins to three first places at Daytona Beach.

During the 1974 season Dennis Shaw joined the Gremlin team. Shaw started out as a mechanic with the Highball Team and wound up becoming a co-driver with Johnson. Johnson finished third and Shaw finished fifth in points.

During the entire seasons of 1972, 1973 and 1974, if the Gremlins did not come in first, they were almost always close behind in either second, third, fourth or fifth positions. Two Hornet hatchbacks driven by Bob Hennig and Charles Cook, known as Team 21, were not as successful as the Gremlins.

The Gremlin was the first AMC subcompact to be used by the Highball Team in IMSA racing. The car saw tremendous success during the 1972-76 racing seasons. Shown is a later 1977-78 model.

Warner Hodgedon and his firm, along with driver Roger McCluskey, tried a 1978 Concord hatchback on a few short USAC tracks with limited success.

195

1975

For the 1975 season, the Gremlin and Hornet once again raced, and the Pacer was introduced in the last race of the season. Johnson and Shaw, both of Raleigh, North Carolina, piloted the vehicles, since they both had brought AMC the IMSA Manufacturers title with their Gremlins, finishing second and third, respectively, in the drivers standings the year before.

At the January 31, 1975, B.F. Goodrich Radial Challenge race at Daytona, Johnson and Shaw took first and second places using the old Gremlins. To prove the ruggedness of the Gremlin, the Johnson team entered the car in the twenty-four-hour Daytona race the next day. The car came in seventeenth and was the first American car to finish.

There were even Gremlins entered in NASCAR racing in 1975, namely in the Dogwood 500 National Championship modified race. Seven Gremlins were entered and were driven by such notable drivers as Harry Gant, Don Maclaren, Donald "Satch" Worley, John Bryant, Don Dionne, Gary Cornelius and Dean Hoag. This race was probably the most disappointing one for AMC enthusiasts, as not one Gremlin finished. All were either wrecked in accidents or sidelined with mechanical failures.

The field was made up mostly of Vegas, Pintos and Capris, with a Mustang II and Monza thrown in for good measure, and even an old Chevy II. Carl "Bugs" Stevens won in a Vega, with Ron Bouchard coming in second driving a Pinto.

During the beginning of the 1975 season, the Gremlins were winning so many races that IMSA changed the rules during their West Coast victories and required them to run with carburetor restrictor plates. Johnson and Shaw sportingly accepted the new rules, and even with this handicap they managed to compete throughout the season. Once again, if they did not finish first or second they were close behind, finishing in the top five spots in almost every race.

After the rule changes, a lot of the cars on the field suddenly became competitive. The AMC six-cylinders were way ahead of their direct competition in efficiency. IMSA based all the competition on the AMC's performance, and then went on to handicap the AMC engine.

At the final race of the 1975 season, Nick Craw drove a Pinto to take the checkered flag, winning the B.F. Goodrich Radial Challenge series championship title. But Johnson and Shaw took the IMSA Manufacturers first-place title with the Gremlins. A close contender was Carson Baird driving a Colt.

The Pacer made its debut at this last race of 1975, at Daytona International Speedway. It showed its competitive road racing abilities by finishing seventh in a forty-car field in the 250-mile race. It also had qualified as the fourth fastest the previous day. The Pacer was

Amos Johnson started racing with the new Pacer beginning at the end of the 1975 season. It was not as successful as the first Gremlins that were used.

allowed to run without the carburetor restrictor plate that IMSA required on the Gremlin since the Pacer weighed 250 pounds more than the Gremlin.

With their Gremlin entries, Johnson and Shaw ended second and third in points after the eleven-race IMSA season for 1975, scoring four first-place finishes. Some of the other notable AMC drivers that year were Joe Amato, Gene Felton, Byron Wever, Steve Coleman, Tom Waugh and Lee Brantley.

1976

For the 1976 season Johnson and Shaw again campaigned the Gremlins, and others drove the Hornet, but really started to push the Pacers. Gene Felton came on as another AMC driver and proved to be a formidable foe on the racecourse.

To start the season, the Pacer was chosen to be the official pace car for the 1976 IMSA races. The B.F. Goodrich Company, which sponsored the Radial Challenge series, equipped the Pacer with a turbo-supercharged 258 ci six-cylinder engine. The transmission and differential were also modified to withstand the additional power increase. According to a Goodrich spokesman, the Pacer was able to "light up" its rear tires in high gear at 45 mph.

The Gremlins and Hornets were still forced to run with the restrictor plates, and now the Pacers were, too, owing to IMSA rule changes. Through other modifications, the cars managed to remain competitive—too competitive as far as IMSA officials were concerned, which prompted close inspection during postrace teardowns. Some Gremlins were found to be running illegal carburetors and were thus disqualified for the races in which they had just run.

The Pacers experienced bugs early in the season. The brakes were inadequate, and a fuel feed problem caused the engine to cut out in left-hand turns. Howdy Holmes was now driving a Pacer, and he found it almost impossible to keep the car running on the track at times.

The problems were overcome during the season, and the Gremlins and Hornets won some races, but the cars were still not as competitive as they had been two years before when they practically dominated the radial series. Those dreaded carburetor restrictor plates were choking the engines.

At about midseason, IMSA rule changes again allowed the removal of the restrictors. At the Pacers' first race without the restrictors, the Radial 100 at Alabama International Speedway in Talladega, Alabama, Amos Johnson in the number seven Pacer roared to an easy victory over the rest of the field. The little AMC 232 ci six-cylinder came back to life when allowed to breathe properly.

AMC captured the 1976 Manufacturers Championship title with the Gremlin. Colt came in second, Datsun third, Mazda fourth and BMW fifth. Johnson and Shaw were not able to recapture the B.F. Goodrich Challenge Series Championship title for 1976, how-ever. Carson Baird won the series championship with his Colt, Gene Felton came in second with his Gremlin, Don Devendorf third with his Datsun and Amos Johnson a disappointing seventh in his Gremlin. Defending 1975 series champion Nick Craw came in sixth.

1977-78

The 1977 season was not a good one for the Highball Team. Although the team was quite competitive, it did not come anywhere near its racing success of previous years.

In the 1978 season the team sprang back to life. Driving the Pacer, Johnson placed second at Daytona, third at Sebring and Talladega, fourth at Portland and in the Daytona Pepsi six-hour challenge with Dick Barbour. Shaw earned a fourth place at Daytona in February, a fifth at Daytona in November and a fifth at Road Atlanta with the Pacer, as well as scoring second in the Pepsi Challenge.

Hornets were also raced in every season, but they did not share the successes of the Gremlins and Pacers.

1979-81

For the 1979 season the new AMC Spirit was prepared to do battle on the IMSA circuit. Once again Johnson and Shaw campaigned two cars. Scott and Irv Hoerr, Joe Amato, Robert Wood, Joe Varde and Joe Llauget also drove AMC products.

Dennis Shaw was Johnson's teammate driver, having started out first as one of his mechanics. Shaw's driving skills were immediately apparent on the track, as evidenced by his numerous victories driving the AMC vehicles.

The Spirit was aerodynamically improved over the Gremlin and produced less drag. Wind tunnel tests showed that the Spirit had eight percent less drag than the Pacers, and the slope of the liftback was much more gradual than that of the Pacer hatchback or Gremlin squareback. The Spirit had less frontal area and its weight was distributed closer to the ground, thus providing better ballast on the racetrack. With the Spirit's overall improved aerodynamics, top speed was increased about 5 mph; in other words, it took less power to go as fast or faster.

The first Spirit made its debut at the final race of the 1978 season in November, at Daytona, where it had the fifth-fastest qualifying time at 100.177 mph. It managed to place sixth, losing fifth to teammate Shaw's Pacer "by a headlight" in a dramatic duel to the finish line.

Compared with the first Gremlins that raced in 1971 and 1972, the Spirits were the highpoint of all AMC IMSA-prepared vehicles. The first Gremlins and Hornets had a top speed of 119 mph. The 232 six was now belting out 245 hp at 5400 rpm, enabling the Spirit to exceed speeds of 150 mph. The 1978 Pacers were able to travel 152 mph.

IMSA rule changes in 1977 and 1978 had just about killed the competitiveness of the AMC cars on the track. The imports such as Mazda, Datsun, BMW, Colt and others started to come on strong with their new designs. Even Buick and Olds got into the picture, becoming competitive foes with their compact Skyhawks and Sunbirds.

For the 1979 season, IMSA rule changes again reduced the power of those vehicles, enabling the Spirit to become competitive on the track, as had been done with the Gremlins and Pacers in 1975 and 1976.

The new AMC Spirit raced during the 1979-80 racing season at the hands of Johnson, Shaw and Irv Hoerr. The Spirit's success was nowhere near that of the Gremlin, even though the new car's body style was aerodynamically better.

Johnson completed the 1979 racing season with no significant victories, contrary to what was anticipated at the beginning of the year with the new Spirit. The drivers point standings for Johnson and Shaw at the end of the 1979 season were not as good as in previous years. Johnson ended up in fifth place, and Shaw did a little better, placing third.

Both Johnson and Shaw pressed on into the 1980 season. Irv Hoerr, who started running with AMC in late 1979, came on board for the 1980 season. He started off with a bang by winning the first race of the year at Daytona and running second at the second race at Sebring. For the remainder of the season victories were scored here and there. Hoerr came in second at Road America in Elkhart Lake and again at Daytona Beach. Johnson, Shaw and Hoerr did not do too well in the other races they entered, finishing usually in third, fourth or lower positions. At the end of the season Johnson placed fourth with 110 points, Hoerr fifth with ninety-three points and Shaw seventh with sixty-six points.

Things appeared to pick up for 1981, the final season for AMC involvement in IMSA racing. Hoerr managed to score a victory in the first race at Daytona Beach and came in second at the Sebring event. Johnson placed sixth and third in those races, respectively. But it was almost all downhill from there. Shaw did not race in the 1981 season, and more IMSA rule changes, this time favoring the new front-wheel-drive cars, drove the final nails into the AMC coffin.

Javelin Speed Spectacular

AMC has been involved in just about all types of motorsports. This chapter has highlighted some of the most famous models, sponsors, drivers and racing teams, but these were not the only ones.

In 1968 AMC launched the Javelin Speed Spectacular Contest, consisting of three equally prepared Javelins supported by three individual teams at the Bonneville Salt Flats in Utah. These cars were equipped with 343 V-8s and four-speed manual transmissions.

Roscoe Turner from Cragar Industries and Craig Breedlove picked the teams. Each team was to individualize and finely tune its own car for the three-way shoot-out. Breedlove was to drive the three cars to determine which was the best prepared vehicle.

The victor would get to take all three cars home, and the second and third winners would receive tools, parts, racing jackets or gift certificates from Proto Tool Company, Edelbrock Industries, Venolia pistons, Cure-Ride shocks, Schiefer Manufacturing Company and various others whose parts and pieces went into the cars during their basic build-up and preparation.

The contest was originally scheduled for August, but it was rained out and was run on a limited basis in November. Breedlove was able to reach a speed of 161 mph in a two-way, one-mile run over the salt flats. He did it in the car prepared by Matthew J. Strong, Jr., of St.

Louis, Missouri; Charles F. Seabrook II of Bridgeton, New Jersey; and Private, First Class David E. Darnell of Louisville, Kentucky.

Between runs with the Javelins, Breedlove made several passes with a specially prepared AMX powered by the same fuel-injected and supercharged 390 V-8 that he was to run in the *American Spirit* streamliner. Even with bad weather and slippery salt, the AMX was timed at a peak speed of 189 mph and was still accelerating. Breedlove's average two-way speed for the mile was 182 mph. He hit 176 with a two-mile approach to the timing traps going in one direction, and 187 with a three-mile approach headed the other way. Both the Javelin and AMX runs were made on pump gasoline and were timed and certified by USAC.

Magazine project cars

Several magazines built up AMC project cars or used their engines, drivetrains and chassis components to prove that they were just as worthy and adaptable in the hot rod industry as the more popular Chevy and Ford units. *Motor Trend* built up a 1967 Rambler American Rogue, and *Car Craft* built up an S/S AMX. Both were successful project cars.

Hi-Performance Cars magazine along with editor Martin L. Schorr decided to prove the competitiveness of the 1968 Javelin 390 as a hot street contender. The car used was originally red but was repainted black for a racy look. An AMX grille and hood were substituted, with flush-mounted key-operated locks. The large SST stripes were removed in favor of two fine-line chrome stripes running the length of the hood and deck lid. The black vinyl top was retained. A set of Goodyear raised-white-letter wide-tread GT tires was installed on Cragar SS chrome mags. To finish the body off, a set of Corvette finned aluminum side exhausts was installed.

The 390 V-8 was reworked, with the addition of the optional factory hi-po hydraulic cam and kit of 302 degree duration and 0.477 inch lift. An Edelbrock aluminum hi-rise intake manifold and a 780 cfm Holley carburetor were used with an M/P Mallory dual-point ignition and Ramcharger wiring. The heads were completely blueprinted using Chevy valves. Exhaust was by a pair of Jardine tuned four-port headers dumping into Douglas fifty-inch piggyback mufflers hidden by the Corvette aluminum shields.

M/P Cure-Ride superbit shocks and AMX traction bars were all that were needed for the suspension. The stock 3.90:1 gears were replaced with 4.44s at the track with Goodyear 8.50x14 inch cheater slicks. The stock Borg-Warner three-speed automatic transmission was retained.

Also at the track an Offenhauser 360 manifold and Holley 950 cfm three-barrel carburetor along with a Grant dual-coil, dual-point Flamethrower ignition were used.

The completed car weighed 3,100 pounds. It was able to do 0-60 in 6.5 to 7.0 seconds, and the quarter-mile in the high twelves and low thirteens. The car was a hot street contender.

In 1969, *Rod and Custom* magazine contracted with Dave Puhl's House of Kustoms to produce a mid-engined pickup to compete in the Oakland Roadster Show. The car was to be made more or less to the dimensions of the AMX/2 show car, and was to look like a street version of a McLaren Can Am race car. It

The three pit crews who participated in the Javelin Speed Spectacular Super-Tuner Contest pose with their cars and driver Craig Breedlove (in background). They are, from left, front row, Bill Tinker, Larry Lechner, Jim Riley; PFC David E.

"Pete" Darnell, Matt Strong, Jr., Charles Seabrook II; Bruce Nottingham II, Alynn Luessen and Carl Tracer. The crew of Darnell, Strong and Seabrook won the contest and the three Javelins.

was to be called Phase II, and was scheduled to be completed in one year.

The wheelbase was 107 inches, height thirty-six inches, width seventy inches and length 195 inches. For comparison, the AMX/2 had a wheelbase of 105 inches, height forty-three inches, width 70.40 inches and length 171.50 inches.

Stylist Harry Bradley, who met Puhl during the running of the 1969 Grand National Roadster Show, drew the preliminary proposals. It would use numerous stock AMX chassis, suspension and disc brake components or units, slightly modified, for the upcoming 1970 and 1971 AMC models! Vice-president in charge of styling Dick Teague was happy to supply the parts directly to Dave Puhl, along with a pretested and run stock 343 four-barrel V-8 engine.

The engine used a slightly modified 1963 Pontiac Tempest automatic transaxle since no other tried, proven, usable or affordable unit was available at the time. The engine was centered between the front and rear wheels, providing space for the driver and single passenger ahead, and for a small pickup box behind.

Eck Tur of Burbank, California, was flown into the Wisconsin area to take charge of the chassis building. He was a well-known dune buggy and off-road vehicle fabricator. Traylor Engineering, of drag racing fame, next door to the House of Kustoms, handled all the special machinery, the flame cutting of heavy steel plate and other related operations. Jim Slobodnik and Steve Donato were also involved in the building of the car.

The chassis was made up of 1¾ inch outside diameter, 0.083 inch wall thickness, cold-drawn, butt-welded mild steel. Throughout the chassis, high-tensile braze was used to keep the car as light as possible. The stock AMC coil spring suspension and steering system could not be used, so instead torsion bars and a rack-and-pinion steering system from a 1958 Morris Minor were used.

Puhl had specially made fifteen-inch rims all around, with the rears being ten inches wide and the fronts being eight inches. The five-slot-type centers were welded as far inboard as possible, and were then covered with original Bonneville Moon disc-type hubcaps, inverted so the concave side faced outward and then painted flat-black for a nice contrast with the chrome deep-dish. Tires used were Goodyear ten-inch-wide tread for the rear and eight-inch-wide tread for the front.

The car contained two five-gallon hand-fabricated sheet metal fuel tanks which were mounted on the engine side of the firewall.

The tubing used for the all-steel body was electrician's galvanized ⅝ inch diameter, 0.0625 inch wall thickness mild steel for corrosion protection. This type of tubing was also chosen because of its bending qualities and ease of brazing without eliminating the galvanize.

The body panels were made of low-carbon-content special killed cold-rolled twenty-gauge sheet steel, which was almost as easily bendable as aluminum. It was the type of metal that did not age harden or become brittle, and it was also easily brazed thus keeping warpage to an absolute minimum.

The body of the car was made up of roughly forty-eight individual pieces of the sheet metal brazed and welded together, and weighed a total of 400 pounds. The car was topless, with a small Plexiglas windscreen coming up at about neck level with manually operated wipers. Recessed rectangular Cibie headlights were turned on their sides and sported clear Plexiglas covers with chrome band retainers. Two vertical taillights were divided into three sections for tail, stop and directional light operation. Lens covers were red Plexiglas and also used chrome band retainers.

Before the body was mated to the chassis, the chassis was disassembled, blasted and painted with black wrinkle paint, and then dusted with gold flake, resulting in a dazzling Kandygold. Some pieces were even chrome plated.

The engine and transaxle were rebuilt by Kaplan Engineering. For added power it installed a Trans-Am Edelbrock cross-ram dual four-barrel intake manifold with twin Holley 650s. It also handled the chassis wiring and instrumentation. The car had no doors; entry was by stepping over. A mere twenty-six inches to the top of the windscreen made this easy.

A diamond-tufted interior contained Stewart-Warner gauges and a raised padded console. The completed car weighed 1,940 pounds and had a five-inch ground clearance.

A matching Kandygold-painted 1968 El Camino shop truck towed the trailer carrying the car. The car also sported quad chrome-plated exhaust pipes on the bottom of the pickup bed, exiting to the rear of the car and terminating into a rectangular housing. Two small lift-up lids covered the engine compartment.

The completed car cost over $20,000. It made its debut at the Chicago Rod and Custom Show at the Downtown Navy Pier. The big show Puhl was aiming for was the Oakland Roadster in California. He wanted the nine-foot trophy that was given out every year for America's Most Beautiful Roadster.

For the eleven-day run of the Oakland show, the Phase II was entered as a roadster. Without telling Puhl, judges reclassified his car to compete in the experimental class. When Master of Ceremonies LeRoy "Tex" Smith announced that a kit car had won the award of America's Most Beautiful Roadster and the Phase II had won the less significant experimental class award, Puhl was stunned. He never built another car from scratch again. His AMC-based car was one of the last fully operational vehicles of its kind.

Rod and Custom magazine simultaneously ran a 1936 Ford Roadster project car using an American Motors 343 four-barrel V-8 backed by a Borg-Warner

T-10 four-speed transmission. The compact dimensions of the AMC V-8 were becoming popular with the high-performance crowd, so *Rod and Custom* magazine was out to shout its adaptability to street rods. The project was a complete success. The AMC V-8 proved to be just as good as, if not better than, the more popular Chevy and Ford small-block V-8s.

Astro-Spiral Javelin

AMC was determined to cover all aspect of high-performance, so it even went one step further by getting involved in thrill shows, doing stunt driving and ramp jumps.

It all started in CAL (Cornell Aeronautical Laboratory) in Buffalo, New York, around 1968. Ray McHenry and William F. Milliken were conducting tests to investigate the causes and effects of single-car accidents. For instance, what happens to one car when it goes off the road? Was there any way to redirect it or absorb its energy harmlessly by changing the design of the car or roadway?

Instead of crashing countless cars, CAL programmed theoretical cars and roadways inside the memory of a computer. An infinite number of situations were possible. Everything could be proven theoretically with the computer, but the US Bureau of Public Roads wanted to know if actual cars and roads would behave in the same manner. This led to the CAL team setting up ramps and having professional drivers pilot the cars over them, thus causing the driver to react to unsafe conditions. When McHenry saw some of the cars flying through the air, he got the idea of putting on a thrill show.

In the spring of 1971, McHenry contacted W. Jay Milligan, Jr., of J.M. Productions in Orchard Park, New York, who was promoting the All American Hell Drivers stunt car team. Milligan immediately liked the idea, and groundwork was set. The initial speed would be no more than 40 mph because of the small tracks and arenas where the shows were put on. The ramps could

not be too large because of transportation problems from town to town, and the cars had to be basically stock to impress the audience.

McHenry, Milligan and the computer determined that it was theoretically possible for an automobile to corkscrew its way through the air in a full 360 degree roll as it flew from one ramp to the other. Milligan decided to build his 1972 thrill show on AMC cars, calling it the American Thrill Show, and to use Gremlins, Hornets, Matadors and a 1972 Javelin for the Astro-Spiral jump. The car became known as the Astro-Spiral Javelin, having that logo painted on both doors in big letters.

To minimize front-end weight, the car had a six-cylinder engine. It was also equipped with a NASCAR-type roll cage with some added bracing and a central driving seat for better driver protection and aim at the ramp. The car weighed 3,216 pounds. It would be airborne for about 1½ seconds, according to the computer.

Numerous tests were conducted using electronically controlled driverless junk cars before stunt driver Chick Galiano actually performed the test. The first actual driver jump was made on December 22, 1972. Galiano executed it quite well, but some fine-tuning to the equipment and the car were in order.

The left-hand surface of the takeoff ramp was made to automatically flop down after the front wheel passed over it. This allowed enough room for the left rear wheel to clear the ramp as the car began its roll to the left. The computer model showed that there was no way to pitch up the rear end of the car hard enough to complete the jump relying on the car's rear tires alone. Thus, a small steel-rimmed wheel was attached to the rear axle, slightly left of center, and matched to a steel strip on the takeoff ramp. This began the kick-up after the car had rolled some forty-five degrees to the left.

A few jumps made with these modifications were satisfactory, but still not good enough for a safe landing. New guardrails were installed to control the right

The Astro-Spiral Javelin thrilled audiences throughout the United States. Here the American Thrill Show with driver

Chick Galiano makes it look easy. Countless hours of engineering and testing produced the winning stunt jump.

front wheel as the car went up the takeoff ramp. The rails did not work properly and the car ended up on its roof. Galiano was unhurt.

Despite all the difficulties, the first official jump at the Houston Astrodome in Texas went perfectly. This was only the fourth jump with a human driver. A few front suspension parts broke but were quickly repaired. One jump almost ended in disaster when the engine started missing on its run approaching the ramp and then quit altogether just before hitting the ramp. The car coasted up the ramp at about 35 mph and was just able to complete the jump, landing on the other ramp with its tail dragging. The crowd loved it.

The Astro-Spiral Javelin went on tour throughout the United States for the next few years, and drew crowds wherever it performed. To get an idea of what it was like, you could watch the Astro-Spiral jump performed by a 1974 Hornet X hatchback in the 1974 James Bond movie, *The Man with the Golden Gun.* (Also worth watching in the same movie is the thrilling car chase scene that took place between the Hornet and a 1974 Cassini Matador.)

Drag AMCs

There were a few attempts with rail dragsters using AMC six-cylinder and V-8 engines. One of the most notable attempts was by the team of Roger Allred and Marvin Clarke. Their initial car was a twin six-cylinder 199 ci rail that held the NHRA D/D record on and off from 1968 to 1972. This car held the D/D track record at every track it had ever run in the Amarillo, Texas, area. It received factory support and captured the competition eliminator runner-up spot at three major meets. The rail was able to turn 8.60s at over 165 mph.

Kay Sissell of six-cylinder fame in California was co-builder of the record setter that sported a thirty-eight-inch rear tread and fifty-inch front tread. It had Goodyear 7.50-14.40x15 slicks, and its 218 inch chassis was by Jerry Norman/Motor Parts, which also did the steering and suspension. The rear end carried Summers axles, 4.88 gears, Hurst brakes and a P&G chute. The beautiful body was painted red, white and blue by Mark Moreland.

The two engines used were works of art. Both were bored to 3⅞ inches and had a three-inch stroke, producing a final displacement of 212 cubic inches. Venolia pistons with moly rings attached to Super Rod custom aluminum rods. Heads, cam and valvetrain were modified by Sissel, sporting 390 V-8 valves and 13:1 compression. Ignition was by a pair of Vertex mags, and the fuel system was made up of Enderle injectors modified by Clarke, using Clifford bases. Kustom headers were 1⅝x22 inch tubes. The rear engine was modified to accept a coupler, and both engines were mated at the cranks, held together by common angle iron.

The team of Allred and Clarke broke up. Allred campaigned the twin six rail, and Clarke went on his own and built a destroked 360 V-8 powered racer to run in C/D. Clarke built the 210 inch chassis himself. He used quarter-elliptic leaf springs with Ford Anglia spindles and a 1959 Renault rack-and-pinion steering system. Bob Elliott built the body, and Jean Buchanan and Ted Fancher did the red, white and blue paint job. Clarke's wife, Jennifer, stitched up the black Naugahyde driver's seat.

The car had a forty-two-inch front tread and a thirty-four-inch rear tread with a lightweight aluminum body. Rubber was Goodyear 10.75x15 slicks and bicycle wheels up front. A P&G fourteen-foot Tri-Form chute stopped the car, which weighed a mere 1,320 pounds.

The 360 block was destroked to 3.10 inches with a 4.08 inch bore for 320 cubic inches using a Moldex crank. TRW pistons from the AMC Trans-Am engines, Ramco rings, Super Rod aluminum rods and 11.5:1 compression Sissell heads were used. A Crane R-275 roller cam and kit operated stock-size 2.0 inch intake and 1.625 inch exhaust valves. The engine was also built up with a Vertex mag, Enderle injection, Milodon shutoff, special flywheel adapter with a ball-bearing pilot using a Savage clutch, M&M Clutchflite and a special adapter for the Lakewood Chevy housing that was two inches shorter than the AMC bellhousing to provide more engine setback.

Exhaust was by a set of Clarke's own headers. The hydraulic clutch was actuated by twin Girling master cylinders to engage an eleven-inch Savage single-disc slider, spinning back to a narrowed Pontiac rear with stock drum brakes.

Although the car proved to be competitive in a class dominated by Chevies, it was not as successful as the Allred twin six dragster.

Indy car

After the Navarro Indianapolis effort in the mid-to-late sixties, AMC decided to give it one more try from 1976 to 1981. This time it was with Warner Hodgedon of National Engineering, the same firm that briefly campaigned the NASCAR-type 1978 Concord hatchback.

Instead of using a six-cylinder engine as Navarro did, Hodgedon used the tried and proven AMC 360 V-8, which was classified by Indy rules as a stock block. This was theoretically the racing version of the same engine that powered the AMC family car. Realistically, the engine was far from being just a mildly modified stock version.

The block was cast by hand instead of being made by the normal production method. It utilized special heads and internal pieces machined to racing tolerances—in other words, larger clearances for sustained high-rpm use. The engine was less expensive and theoretically more durable than a specially built racing engine.

The idea was not new (Eddie Rickenbacker introduced stock blocks back in 1930, called semistock formula), but in the history of the Indy 500, no car with a stock block had ever managed to win the famed brickyard race, and the AMC effort was no exception. Dan Gurney came close, scoring back-to-back seconds in 1968 and 1969 with his stock block Ford Eagle racer.

To make the stock turbocharged blocks competitive with the more exotic racing turbocharged engines, rules were made to regulate manifold pressures on all engines. One big disadvantage the stock blocks had was their weight. Whereas a racing engine weighed about 400 pounds, the best the stock block could do was almost 600 pounds. Even with an aluminum block and heads, only about 100 pounds were shed.

Since the stock blocks were also bigger than the race blocks and had a higher center of gravity, it was not possible to just yank out a racing engine from a mated chassis and drop in the stock block. It was necessary to design a new chassis and to some extent a new aerodynamic body. The chassis used was an Eagle unit.

Hodgedon was determined to try to win the Indy 500 and make racing history with the AMC stock block. Bobby Allison of NASCAR fame also worked with Warner beginning in 1977.

In 1976, Jerry Grant qualified his racer at 183.617 mph. Jim McElreath qualified at 187.715 mph in 1977. Roger McCluskey qualified at 192.256 mph in 1978, but had to drop out with transmission trouble after eighty-one laps. Until that point he was running strong. All those times were with a cast-iron engine.

For the 1979 season Hodgedon had a slightly lighter cast-iron version, saving about sixty pounds. The big news was that also for 1979 he had a complete 209 ci aluminum version that was almost 200 pounds lighter, putting the car right in the league with the lightweight turbocharged Cosworth, Offenhauser and Drake racers!

Crew chief Jack McCormick and driver Roger McCluskey were confident with the new racer for the 1979 season. The crew's optimism was at an all-time high, what with the new engine and other positive factors, but the cars did not perform up to their expectations.

Although the cars easily qualified for the brickyard, they experienced oil problems early in the race and entered the pits in a blaze of black smoke. It is the opinion of Larry Daum, AMC authority and historian, that the failures experienced by the new aluminum-block engines could have been caused by the different expansion and flexing properties of aluminum versus cast iron, where the oil supply of the engine inside the galleries was cut off, resulting in almost immediate engine seize-up.

The cars did run in the 1980 and 1981 Indy 500 classics, but they did not finish because of mechanical failures.

Stock car driver Neil Bonnett tested the car before the 1980 race and clocked speeds in excess of 170 mph, but that was nowhere near competitive enough to become a threat on race day. Bonnett opted not to drive for Hodgedon, instead sticking to what he knew best, stock car racing.

And so, the AMC Indy effort ended, but AMC gave it its best shot.

Endurance racing

One of the last AMC factory-backed V-8 racing efforts was the two 1979 Spirit AMXs that raced in the twenty-four-hour Group One endurance race at West Germany's Nurburgring racetrack in October 1979. The B.F. Goodrich Company sponsored the two cars because it was going to make a promotional movie about the car racing for twenty-four hours on a set of radial T/A tires.

For the 1979 season, an all-aluminum version of the AMC 360 V-8 block was tried to save weight. Although the engine showed initial promise, the cars were not able to finish the races entered because of engineering and mechanical problems.

The last Indy effort using an AMC 360 V-8 was by Warner Hodgedon and his firm. Jerry Grant, Jim McElreath and Roger McCluskey were the most noted drivers who almost were able to score victories during the 1976-81 period.

The two cars were prepared by Amos Johnson and his Team Highball of IMSA racing fame. The first car was tested briefly at Mid-Ohio, and a few days later both cars and the B.F. Goodrich tractor-trailer rig were sent overseas.

On arrival in Germany the crew and cars were held up by German customs officials. After getting everything settled with the officials, the team was finally able to move on. The crew familiarized themselves with the course using rental cars, and were confident they could tackle the mission.

On race day German technical officials objected to the location of the master electrical cutoff switches, but Jeremy Nightingale, a British AMC racer, convinced them the switches were correct according to the Highball Team's English interpretation of the German rules.

Drivers for the number one car were Amos Johnson, Dennis Shaw (also of IMSA racing) and actor James Brolin. For car number two it was Jim Downing (also an IMSA driver with a Mazda), Lyn St. James (a Florida businesswoman) and Gary Witzenburg. Also in attendance to lend a helping hand were Goodrich Tire Division communications manager Athene Karis and advertising representative Bruce Butzier.

The number one car was made to go faster than the number two one in hopes of winning the race overall. As long as the second car finished it would be good enough. The cars qualified twentieth and twenty-first in a field of 120 foreign makes. The AMXs had times of 10:26, compared with 9:38 for an English Ford Escort and 14:10 for a one-liter Mini.

Throughout the entire race both team AMXs had bad brakes. The cars were also plagued by quite a few mishaps.

Johnson's throttle cable slipped out of place. Later on, Shaw experienced clutch slippage. Downing's car started to go off the roadcourse any time he took a left turn. The right front camber adjustment had loosened, snapping the wheel out in left turns. Before that was found, the right front spring and shock unit were replaced and some loose rear spring bracket bolts were tightened. Finally the bracket broke in the number one car, necessitating weld repair and the loss of an hour's time. St. James ran out of gas but was able to nurse the car to the pumps for a fill-up.

With about five hours to go the number one car was in bad shape. Both front shocks were gone, the clutch was slipping badly and the engine was using a lot of oil. The brakes were just about all gone. Some parts were even pirated off Nightingale's street AMX, as all spare parts had been used.

The race was grueling, and rainy weather almost throughout didn't help. B.F. Goodrich certainly proved the ruggedness of its street radials. The tires went well over eight hours between routine changes without a single failure.

And how did the two AMXs do? Although they did not win the race, they did manage to finish twenty-fifth and forty-third overall, which amounted to first and second in class. It was a remarkable feat for a first effort by an American car.

AMX Spirit Turbo

Probably the last authentic AMC high-performance racer was the 1981 factory experimental AMX Spirit Turbo pace car, designed by Richard Teague. Pittsburgh Paint & Glass Industries (PPG) initiated a pace car program to prove that American automotive technology was fully capable of producing cars that could handle and perform just as good as, if not better than, exotic high-priced foreign performance cars.

PPG approached the four major automobile manufacturers—GM, Ford, Chrysler and AMC—and asked each to produce a car based on an existing model incorporating special engineering features regarding design, styling, aerodynamics, engine, drivetrain, suspension and handling characteristics. PPG would assume an active role in cooperation with the car manufacturers, and all four cars would pace the 1981 CART (Championship Automobile Racing Team) races for Indy-type cars on a rotating basis, thus giving them plenty of public exposure. The cars were to be a glimpse at what the 1983 or 1984 production models could be.

Each manufacturer went about the task in a slightly different manner. GM built a Chevrolet Cavalier Type-10, Ford a Mercury LN-7 and Chrysler a Dodge Charger 024. AMC decided to base its car on the existing Spirit model and to resurrect the AMX designation. The AMX Spirit was the only car with rear-wheel drive and sported the largest engine of the four. The entire project was supervised by Dick Teague, for this would be his last baby.

The AMX Spirit Turbo measured 164 inches long overall, fifty inches high and seventy-two inches wide, and sat on the production Spirit's ninety-six-inch wheelbase. The unique two-passenger sculpted body was built by Autodynamics of Madison Heights, Michigan, under contract from PPG, and was finished in silver blue. The fuel-injected and turbocharged 258 cubic inch AMC six-cylinder engine was built by Turbo-Systems of Akron, Ohio, which also fabricated the custom dashboard with special instrumentation.

The heart of the car was the sophisticated powerplant. The engine incorporated extensive cylinder head modifications, electronic controls and special valve timing, and produced 18 psi boost. The engine did not use any wastegates or water injection, and was capable of running up to 7000 rpm on pump gasoline. The engine also sported 7.3:1 compression pistons, special high-rpm valve gear, a high-volume and high-pressure (60 psi) oiling system, and AMC electronic ignition with modified mechanical and electrical advance-retard curves.

Another special item that was needed and fabricated by Turbo-Systems was a special exhaust manifold and induction system, which incorporated an air-to-air aftercooler, which in turn allowed high boost without detonation. Castrol GTX20W-50 weight oil was used.

Estimated gross horsepower was said to be about 450, and the AMX Spirit Turbo could light the rear tires at will.

The rest of the car was considerably beefed to handle the engine's tremendous power. The subframe was reinforced, and the rear suspension utilized special traction devices and special leaf springs. Custom competition Bilstein shocks were used all around, and a large one-inch-thick sway bar was used up front.

The heavy-duty police and taxi 727 Torque Flite transmission was used along with heavy-duty U-joints and drive shaft terminating in a 3.54:1 ratio Powerlok rear end.

The interior received special custom seats and a massive three-inch roll bar tied into the subframe to provide rear suspension attachment points in traditional race car form. Two fire extinguishers were provided for safety.

The low-profile Goodyear Eagle GT 24x50x16 raised-white-letter tires were mounted on custom 16x8 inch Gotti aluminum wheels.

The body design of the car was superb. It sported fender flares, air dams, headlight covers, competition fuel filler, large rear spoiler, flush-fit rear window, rear roll bar diagonals, wind vents behind the front and rear wheelwells, and special four-lock tie-down fiberglass hood.

AMC turbo in large red-white-blue letters was placed on each door, with small 1981 Official Pace Car lettering just above. On the front air dam two checkerboard-square designs were placed at each end, plus PPG on the right and Indy Car World Series in a red background on the left side.

The hood contained eight slanted horizontal cooling slots, four on each side, and cooling slots were incorporated into the body for the front and rear brakes. Smoke Black tinted headlight covers and windows finished off the exterior.

The AMX Spirit Turbo is currently owned by Ray and Lynn Pinto, owners of American Performance Products located in Cocoa, Florida, where it is on display in the showroom. The unique AMX tours the car show circuit and collected two first-place trophies in its first two shows ever entered. The car is truly a tribute to the superb styling talents of Dick Teague.

In the late seventies, the Renault/Jeep Sport Incorporated Program took over AMC racing, just as Renault took over American Motors Corporation. AMC's involvement in racing had been spectacular, although small in scale. Hats off to AMC's racing efforts!

The AMX turbo was a tribute to the designing talents of vice-president of styling Dick Teague. The car was unique and innovative in almost every aspect.

Specifications

The following is an abbreviated guide to the 1968-74 American Motors muscle cars. The 1968-74 period is generally considered to be the height of AMC's involvement in high-performance supercars. The 1966-67 years are also covered for the Rambler American series, since that was the first of the AMC models to receive the new-design V-8 engine.

It is impractical to list or mention all options for each model and year, but most of the performance and popular or sporty options that really stood out are covered. Even some dealer-installed options are mentioned, but only those buyers were really interested in purchasing to further enhance the performance capabilities of their AMC underdogs.

With group options or packages, individual item substitutions could almost always be made, such as ordering FR78x14 steel-belted radial tires in place of the E60x15 Polyglas tires on the Javelin/AMX Go Package options.

Midyear changes have also been noted where applicable, or when pertaining to certain engines or performance models and equipment.

Prices listed for the popular and performance options are those in effect at the time of model introduction, whether in the fall or at midyear. Price changes during the model year are not covered. Prices did vary for both new cars and options in certain areas of the country for certain years.

All engine, transmission and rear axle ratio specifications are listed as advertised. Changes and variations occurred throughout the 1968-74 period, and conflicting information or specifications occasionally existed. When discrepancies appeared, the most likely information was used.

Engine codes appeared in the vehicle identification number, usually located on the left top portion of the dashboard, as opposed to the under-the-hood fenderwell location used on 1967 and older models.

Abbreviations

BRGM	Brougham
CONV	Convertible
CPE	Coupe
CR	Compression ratio
FSBK	Fastback
FT	Front tread width
HBK	Hatchback
HDTP	Hardtop
Hp	Advertised horsepower
HT	Height
NA	Not available
OL	Overall length
OW	Overall width
RT	Rear tread width
SED	Sedan
SPT	Sport
SW	Station wagon
Tq	Advertised torque in lb/ft
WB	Wheelbase
2-Dr	Two-door
2P	Two-passenger
4-Dr	Four-door
4P	Four-passenger
5P	Five-passenger
6P	Six-passenger

Low-compression engines

During the 1970-73 model years some six-cylinder and V-8 engines were available in low-compression-ratio versions mainly for export cars. These low-compression engines could also be ordered on certain domestic models. The 304 four-barrel V-8 with code M was still available in 1972-73, although it was a low-compression version in 1972. The following is a list of the codes for these specific engines:

1970: Code B, 199 1-bbl; code F, 232 1-bbl; code Q, 232 2-bbl; code I, 304 2-bbl.

1971: Code F, 232 1-bbl; code B, 258 1-bbl; code I, 304 2-bbl.

1972-73: Code F, 232 1-bbl; code B, 258 1-bbl.

1968 AMX

Model	Body style	Series	Model no.	Price
AMX	2-Dr FSBK 2P	30	6839-7	$3,245

Dimensions

WB: 97"	FT: 58.36"
OL: 177.22"	RT: 57"
OW: 71.57"	HT: 51.73"

Engines

Code	Type	CID	B×S	Hp @ Rpm	Tq @ Rpm	CR	Carb.
N	V-8	290	3.75x3.28	225 @ 4700	300 @ 3200	10.0	4-bbl
(T,W)[1]	V-8	343	4.08x3.28	280 @ 4800	365 @ 3000	10.2	4-bbl
(W,X)[2]	V-8	390	4.17x3.57	315 @ 4600	425 @ 3200	10.2	4-bbl

[1]T code in VIN. W code in engine valve cover tag denoted leftover 1967 Rambler Marlin 343 V-8.
[2]X code in VIN. W code in engine valve cover tag denoted Canadian 390 two-barrel V-8 used in some 1968 AMXs converted to four-barrel models.

Transmissions	Rear axle ratios
	(Optional ratios at no extra cost)
4-speed (std.)	290 V-8: 3.54 (3.15)[1]
	390 V-8: 3.15 (3.54)
Shift-Command cons. (opt.)	290 V-8: 3.15 (2.87)
	343 V-8 & 390 V-8: 2.87[2] (3.15)

[1]3.73, 3.91, 4.10 and 4.44 dealer kits at extra cost.
[2]3.15 is standard with Go Packages.

Popular and performance options

343 V-8, $45.35; 390 V-8, $123.05; Go Package for 343, $233.15, for 390, $310.85, included engine, power front disc brakes, E70x14 redline wide-profile fiberglass-belted tires, higher-rate front and rear springs, 1³/₁₆ inch piston diameter heavy-duty front and rear shock absorbers, Twin-Grip rear axle, heavy-duty engine cooling system consisting of heavy-duty radiator, seven-blade Power-Flex fan and shroud and over-the-top racing stripe; automatic transmission with floor shift and console, $95; quick-ratio manual steering, $16; power steering, $84; power brakes, $42; power front disc brakes, $97; Twin-Grip rear axle, $42; Adjust-O-Tilt steering wheel, $42; all-season air conditioning (included 60 amp battery, 40 amp alternator and heavy-duty engine cooling), $356; Special-duty handling package (standard with Go Package), $17, included higher-rate front and rear springs, 1³/₁₆ inch piston diameter heavy-duty front and rear shock absorbers.

Note: Specific prices for the AMX options are not available. Prices given are for the Javelin, which were more or less the same.

Engine CID emblems
(On rear portion of quarter panels)
290 V-8 Small chrome *V* with black numerals set in silver background above
343 V-8 Small chrome *V* set in red background with chrome numerals side-by-side
390 V-8 Large chrome *V* with red and blue rectangles side-by-side and chrome numerals above

1969 AMX

Model	Body style	Series	Model no.	Price
AMX	2-Dr FSBK 2P	30	6939-7	$3,297

Dimensions

WB: 97"	FT: 58.36"
OL: 177.22"	RT: 57"
OW: 71.57"	HT: 51.73"

Engines

Code	Type	CID	B×S	Hp @ Rpm	Tq @ Rpm	CR	Carb.
N	V-8	290	3.75x3.28	225 @ 4700	300 @ 3200	10.0	4-bbl
T	V-8	343	4.08x3.28	280 @ 4800	365 @ 3000	10.2	4-bbl
(W,X)[1]	V-8	390	4.17x3.57	315 @ 4600	425 @ 3200	10.2	4-bbl
Y[2]	V-8	390	4.17x3.57	340 @ NA	NA	12.3	2x4-bbl

[1]X code in VIN. W code in engine valve cover tag denoted Canadian 390 two-barrel V-8 used in some 1969 AMXs converted to four-barrel models.
[2]S/S AMX only.

Transmissions	
4-speed (std.)	
Shift-Command cons. (opt.)	

Rear axle ratios
(Optional ratios at no extra cost)
290 V-8: 3.54
343 V-8 & 390 V-8: 3.54 (3.15)
290 V-8: 287 (3.15)
343 V-8 & 3.90 V-8: 2.87[1] (3.15)

[1]3.15 is standard with Go Packages.
Note: 3.73, 3.91, 4.10, 4.44 and 5.00 dealer kits at extra cost available with any V-8 transmission combination.

Popular and performance options

343 V-8, $45; 390 V-8, $123; Go Package for 343, $233.15, for 390, $310.85, included engine, power front disc brakes, E70x14 redline wide-profile fiberglass-belted tires, 14x6 styled steel wheels, handling package, Twin-Grip rear, heavy-duty cooling and over-the-top racing stripe; automatic transmission with floor shift and console, $95; quick-ratio manual steering, $16; power steering, $95; power brakes, $42; power front disc brakes, $97; Twin-Grip rear axle, $42; Adjust-O-Tilt steering wheel, $42; all-season air conditioning, $369; heavy-duty cooling (standard with air conditioning), $53; handling package, $19; 70 amp battery, $8; 70 amp battery and 55 amp alternator, $26; midyear Big Bad Orange-Blue-Green exterior paint with color-keyed front and rear bumpers, $34; rear bumper guards, $12.65; E70x14 redline tires, $34.

Engine CID emblems
(On rear portion of quarter panels)
290 V-8 Small chrome *V* with black numerals set in silver background above
343 V-8 Small chrome *V* set in red background with chrome numerals side-by-side
390 V-8 Large chrome *V* with red and blue rectangles side-by-side and chrome numerals above

1970 AMX

Model	Body style	Series	Model no.	Price
AMX	2-Dr FSBK 2P	30	7039-7	$3,395

Dimensions

WB: 97"	FT: 59.7"
OL: 179"	RT: 57"
OW: 71.6"	HT: 51.73"

Engines

Code	Type	CID	B×S	Hp @ Rpm	Tq @ Rpm	CR	Carb.
P	V-8	360	4.08x3.44	290 @ 4800	395 @ 3200	10.0	4-bbl
X,S	V-8	390	4.17x3.57	325 @ 5000	420 @ 3200	10.0	4-bbl

Transmissions	Rear axle ratios
	(Optional ratios at extra cost)
4-speed (std.)	360 V-8 & 390 V-8: 3.54 (3.15 & 3.91)
Shift-Command cons. (opt.)	360 V-8 & 390 V-8: 2.87 (3.15 & 3.54)

Note: 360 & 390 Go Packages with automatic transmission, 3.15 standard with 2.87 and 3.54 optional; Twin-Grip optional with all axle ratios and mandatory with 3.91 ratio; 3.73, 3.91 (also factory option), 4.10, 4.44 and 5.00 dealer kits at extra cost.

Popular and performance options

390 V-8, $11; Go Package for 360, $298.85, for 390, $383.90, included engine, power front disc brakes, F70x14 tires with raised white letters, handling package, Twin-Grip rear axle, heavy-duty cooling and Ram-Air hood; automatic transmission with floor shift and console, $117.85; quick-ratio manual steering, $16; power steering, $102; power brakes, $43; power front disc brakes, $84; Twin-Grip rear axle, $43; Adjust-O-Tilt steering wheel, $49; all-season air conditioning consisting of heavy-duty cooling, 50 amp battery and 55 amp alternator, $380; heavy-duty cooling, $16; handling package, $23; 70 amp battery, $13; Shadow Black paint scheme, $51.80; axle ratios, $10; leather-trimmed bucket seats, $84; rally side stripes, $32.

Engine CID emblems
(On rear portion of fenders)
360 V-8 Large chrome numerals against black background with blue painted insert
390 V-8 Large chrome numerals against black background with red painted insert and two rows of black-and-white checkerboard-square pattern below

1968 Javelin

Model	Body style	Series	Model no.	Price
Javelin	2-Dr FSBK 4P	70	6879-5	$2,482
Javelin SST	2-Dr FSBK 4P	70	6879-7	$2,587

Dimensions

WB: 109" FT: 57.92" (V-8 58.36")
OL: 189.22" RT: 57"
OW: 71.89" HT: 51.81"

Engines

Code	Type	CID	B×S	Hp @ Rpm	Tq @ Rpm	CR	Carb.
B	I-6	232	3.75x3.50	145 @ 4300	215 @ 1600	8.5	1-bbl
M	V-8	290	3.75x3.28	200 @ 4600	285 @ 2800	9.0	2-bbl
N	V-8	290	3.75x3.28	225 @ 4700	300 @ 3200	10.0	4-bbl
(T,W)[2]	V-8	343	4.08x3.28	280 @ 4800	365 @ 3000	10.2	4-bbl
(W,X)[3]	V-8	390[1]	4.17x3.57	315 @ 4600	425 @ 3200	10.2	4-bbl

[1]Midyear.
[2]T code in VIN. W code in engine valve cover tag denoted leftover 1967 Rambler Marlin 343 V-8.
[3]X code in VIN. W code in engine valve cover tag denoted Canadian 390 two-barrel V-8 used in some 1968 Javelins converted to four-barrel models.
Note: 390 V-8 NA on base Javelin, although twelve were built on special order.

Transmissions / Rear axle ratios

Transmissions	Rear axle ratios (Optional ratios at no extra cost)
3-speed, all-sync., col. shift (145 hp) (std.)	3.08 (3.31)
Shift-Command, col. shift (145 hp) (opt.)	3.08 (2.73 & 3.31)
3-speed, all-sync., col. shift (200 hp) (std.)	3.15
Shift-Command, col. shift (200 & 280 hp) (opt.)	200 hp: 3.15 (2.87)
	280 hp: 2.87[1] (3.15)
Shift-Command, cons. shift (200, 280 & 315 hp)(opt.)	200 hp: 3.15 (2.87)
	280 & 315 hp: 2.87[1] (3.15)
4-speed, all-sync., floor shift (all V-8s) (opt.)	290 V-8: 3.54 (3.15)[2]
	343 V-8 & 390 V-8: 3.15 (3.54)[2]

[1]3.15 is standard with Go Packages.
[2]3.73, 3.91, 4.10 and 4.44 dealer kits at extra cost.

Popular and performance options

200 hp V-8, $116; 225 hp V-8, $45; 280 hp V-8, $91; 315 hp V-8, $168; Go Package for 343 V-8, $265.50; Go Package for 390 V-8, $343.25; automatic transmission with floor shift and console, $269; quick-ratio manual steering, $16; power steering, $85; power brakes, $42; power front disc brakes, $97; Twin-Grip rear axle, $42; Adjust-O-Tilt steering wheel, $42; all-season air conditioning, $356; handling package, $17; four-speed manual transmission with floor shift, $184; dual exhausts, $21; handling package and rally stripes, $266; turbo-cast wheel covers for SST, $51, for base model, $65; visibility group package, $27; AM/FM multiplex stereo push-button radio, $134.

Engine CID emblems
(On rear portion of quarter panels)

232 I-6 None
290 V-8 Small chrome V with black numerals set in silver background above
343 V-8 Small chrome V set in red background with chrome numerals side-by-side
390 V-8 Large chrome V with red and blue rectangles side-by-side and chrome numerals above

1969 Javelin

Model	Body style	Series	Model no.	Price
Javelin	2-Dr FSBK 4P	70	6979-5	$2,512
Javelin SST	2-Dr FSBK 4P	70	6979-7	$2,633

Dimensions

WB: 109" FT: 57.92" (V-8 58.36")
OL: 189.22" RT: 57"
OW: 71.89" HT: 51.81"

Engines

Code	Type	CID	B×S	Hp @ Rpm	Tq @ Rpm	CR	Carb.
B	I-6	232	3.75x3.50	145 @ 4300	215 @ 1600	8.5	1-bbl
M	V-8	290	3.75x3.28	200 @ 4600	285 @ 2800	9.0	2-bbl
N	V-8	290	3.75x3.28	225 @ 4700	300 @ 3200	10.0	4-bbl
T	V-8	343	4.08x3.28	280 @ 4800	365 @ 3000	10.2	4-bbl
(W,X)*	V-8	390	4.17x3.57	315 @ 4600	425 @ 3200	10.2	4-bbl

*X code in VIN. W code in engine valve cover tag denoted Canadian 390 2-bbl V-8 used in some 1969 Javelins converted to 4-bbl models.
Note: 390 V-8 NA on base Javelin, although a limited amount were probably built.

Transmissions / Rear axle ratios

Transmissions	Rear axle ratios (Optional ratios at no extra cost)
3-speed, all-sync., floor shift (145 hp) (std.)	3.08 (3.31)
Shift-Command, col. shift (145 hp) (opt.)	3.08 (3.31)
3-speed, all-sync., floor shift (200 hp) (std.)	3.15
Shift-Command, col. shift (200 & 280 hp) (opt.)	200 hp: 2.87 (3.15)
	280 hp: 2.87[1] (3.15)
Shift-Command, cons. shift (200 & 280 hp) (opt.)	200 hp: 2.87 (3.15)
	280 hp: 2.87[1] (3.15)
4-speed, all-sync., floor shift (all V-8s exc. 200 hp) (opt.)	225 hp: 3.54
	280 & 315 hp: 3.54 (3.15)

[1]3.15 is standard with Go Packages.
Note: 3.73, 3.91, 4.10, 4.44 and 5.00 dealer kits at extra cost available with any V-8 transmission combination.

Popular and performance options

200 hp V-8, $116; 225 hp V-8, $45; 280 hp V-8, $91; 315 hp V-8, $168; Go Package for 343 V-8, $265.50; Go Package for 390 V-8, $343.25; automatic transmission with floor shift and console for 200 and 280 hp V-8s, $287; quick-ratio manual steering, $16; power steering, $95; power brakes, $42; power front disc brakes, $97; Twin-Grip rear axle, $42; Adjust-O-Tilt steering wheel, $42; all-season air conditioning, $369; handling package, $19; four-speed manual transmission with floor shift, $205; dual exhausts, $31; electric clock plus visibility package group, $43; Solex glass, all windows, $32; E70x14 redline tires, $75; heavy-duty clutch for 200 hp V-8, $11; 70 amp battery, $8; 70 amp battery and 55 amp alternator, $26; heavy-duty cooling, $53; console with column Shift-Command, $53; instrument cluster with tachometer and 140 mph speedometer, $50; rally side stripes, $27; 14x6 inch wheel rims, $72; wire wheel covers for base model, $72, for SST, $51; midyear Big Bad Orange-Blue-Green exterior paint with color-keyed front and rear bumpers, $34; rear bumper guards, $12.65.

Engine CID emblems
(On rear portion of quarter panels)

232 I-6 None
290 V-8 Small chrome V with black numerals set in silver background above
343 V-8 Small chrome V set in red background with chrome numerals side-by-side
390 V-8 Large chrome V with red and blue rectangles side-by-side and chrome numerals above

1970 Javelin

Model	Body style	Series	Model no.	Price
Javelin	2-Dr FSBK 4P	70	7079-5	$2,720
Javelin SST	2-Dr FSBK 4P	70	7079-7	$2,848
Javelin SST Trans-Am	2-Dr FSBK 4P	70	7079-7	$3,995
Javelin SST Mark Donohue[1]	2-Dr FSBK 4P	70	7079-7	—

[1]Midyear.

Dimensions

WB: 109" FT: 59.3" (V-8 59.7")
OL: 191" RT: 57"
OW: 71.9" HT: 51.60"

Engines

Code	Type	CID	B×S	Hp @ Rpm	Tq @ Rpm	CR	Carb.
E	I-6	232	3.75x3.50	145 @ 4300	215 @ 1600	8.5	1-bbl
H*	V-8	304	3.75x3.44	210 @ 4400	305 @ 2800	9.0	2-bbl
N	V-8	360	4.08x3.44	245 @ 4400	365 @ 2400	9.0	2-bbl
P	V-8	360	4.08x3.44	290 @ 4800	395 @ 3200	10.0	4-bbl
X	V-8	390	4.17x3.75	325 @ 5000	420 @ 3200	10.0	4-bbl

*A limited number of 304 4-bbl engines with code M were produced for export.

Transmissions / Rear axle ratios

Transmissions	Rear axle ratios (Optional ratios at extra cost)
3-speed, all-sync., floor shift (145 hp) (std.)	3.08 (3.31)
Shift-Command, col. shift (145 hp) (opt.)	3.08 (3.31)
3-speed, all-sync., floor shift (210 hp) (std.)	3.15 (3.54)
Shift-Command, col. shift (all V-8s exc. 325 hp) (opt.)	2.87 (3.15 & 3.54[1])
Shift-Command, cons. shift (all V-8s) (opt.)	2.87 (3.15 & 3.54[2])
4-speed, all-sync., floor shift (290 & 325 hp) (opt.)	3.54 (3.15 & 3.91)

[1]290 Hp only.
[2]290 and 325 Hp only.
Note: 360 & 390 Go Packages with automatic transmission, 3.15 standard with 2.87 and 3.54 optional; Twin-Grip optional with all axle ratios and mandatory with 3.91 ratio; 3.73, 3.91 (also factory option), 4.10, 4.44 and 5.00 dealer kits at extra cost.

Popular and performance options

210 hp V-8, $99; 245 hp V-8, $41; 290 hp V-8, $80; 325 hp V-8, $168; Go Package for 290 hp V-8, $321.65, for 325 hp V-8, $409.75, included engine, power front disc brakes, E70x14 redline tires, six-inch wheel rims, dual exhausts, handling package and AMX functional Ram-Air hood; automatic transmission with floor shift and console for 304 and 360 V-8s, $264 and $287; automatic transmission with column shift for 232, 304 and 360 engines, $195, $200 and $233; quick-ratio manual steering, $16; power steering, $102; power brakes, $43; power front disc brakes, $84; Twin-Grip rear axle, $43; Adjust-O-Tilt steering wheel, $49; all-season air conditioning, $380; handling package, $23; four-speed manual transmission with floor shift for 290 and 325 hp V-8s, $205; dual exhausts, $31; heavy-duty cooling, standard with air conditioning, $16; heavy-duty 70 amp battery, $13; console with column Shift-Command, $53; instrument cluster with tachometer and 140 mph speedometer, $50; rally side stripes, $32; 14x6 styled steel wheels for base model, $98, for SST, $72; simulated exhaust-type rocker panel moldings for base model, $50, for SST, $32; corduroy fabric for bucket seats, SST only, $50; leather-trimmed bucket seats, SST only, $127; rear bumper guards, $13; roof spoiler (NA with vinyl top), $33; black, white or blue vinyl roof, $84.

Engine CID emblems
(On rear portion of fenders)

232 I-6 None
304 V-8 Large dull smooth machined and bright rough finished numerals against black background with red-and-silver checkerboard-square pattern inside O
360 V-8 Large chrome numerals against black background with blue painted insert
390 V-8 Large chrome numerals against black background with red painted insert and two rows of black-and-white checkerboard-square pattern below

Performance models

Trans-Am SST
Model included red-white-blue exterior paint scheme from front to back, black vinyl interior, 390 ci 325 hp V-8, four-speed close-ratio transmission with Hurst shifter, 3.91 Twin-Grip rear, functional AMX Ram-Air hood, dual exhaust system, heavy-duty cooling system, power steering, power front disc brakes, handling package, 14x6 mag-styled wheels, F70x14 raised-white-letter Goodyear Polyglas tires, 140 mph speedometer and 8000 rpm tachometer, front and rear body spoilers, visibility group, light group, AM push-button radio, Space Saver spare tire plus all the standard SST equipment minus the sill moldings and paint stripes.

Mark Donohue SST
Model included 360 or 390 4-bbl V-8, Pistol Grip console-shift automatic or four-speed manual transmission with Hurst shifter, dual exhaust system, functional AMX Ram-Air hood, power front disc brakes, handling package, 14x6 mag-styled wheels, E70x14 raised-white-letter Goodyear Polyglas tires, rear-deck-mounted spoiler with Mark Donohue signature plus all the standard SST equipment. Any Javelin exterior color could be ordered, including the Big Bad colors, plus any SST option. Some Mark Donohue 360 models were equipped with a special thick-walled 360 ci V-8 that could be overbored 0.1075 inches to a maximum bore diameter of 4.1875 inches. The block also had provisions for four-bolt main bearing caps.

1971 Javelin

Model	Body style	Series	Model no.	Price
Javelin	2-Dr FSBK 4P	70	7179-5	$2,879
Javelin SST	2-Dr FSBK 4P	70	7179-7	$2,999
Javelin AMX	2-Dr FSBK 4P	70	7179-8	$3,432

Dimensions

WB: 110" FT: 59.3" (V-8 59.7")
OL: 191.77" RT: 60"
OW: 75.2" HT: 50.9"

Engines

Code	Type	CID	B×S	Hp @ Rpm	Tq @ Rpm	CR	Carb.
E	I-6	232	3.75x3.50	135 @ 4000	210 @ 1600	8.0	1-bbl
A	I-6	258	3.75x3.90	150 @ 3800	240 @ 1800	8.0	1-bbl
H[1]	V-8	304	3.75x3.44	210 @ 4400	300 @ 2600	8.4	2-bbl
N	V-8	360	4.08x3.44	245 @ 4400	365 @ 2600	8.5	2-bbl
P	V-8	360	4.08x3.44	285 @ 4800	390 @ 3200	8.5	4-bbl
Z	V-8	401	4.17x3.68	330 @ 5000	430 @ 3400	9.5[2]	4-bbl

[1]A limited number of 304 4-bbl engines with code M were produced for export.
[2]10.2 on early 1971.
Note: 245 Hp V-8 standard on AMX.

Transmissions

Transmissions	Rear axle ratios (Optional ratios at extra cost)
3-speed, all-sync., floor shift (135 hp) (std.)	3.08 (3.31 & 3.58)
Shift-Command, col. shift (135 & 150 hp) (opt.)	3.08 (3.31)
3-speed, all-sync., floor shift (all V-8s exc. 330 hp) (std.)	3.15 (3.54)
Shift-Command, col. shift (all V-8s exc. 330 hp) (opt.)	2.87 (3.15)[1]
Shift-Command, cons. shift (all V-8s) (opt.)	2.87 (3.15 & 3.54[2])[1]
4-speed, all-sync., floor shift (285 & 330 hp) (opt.)	3.54 (3.15 & 3.91)

[1]For Javelin AMX with combination of automatic transmission and Go Package: 360 4-bbl, 3.15 standard, 2.87 optional; 401 4-bbl, 3.15 standard, 2.87 and 3.54 optional.
[2]330 Hp only.
Note: Column-Shift NA on AMX; Twin-Grip optional with all axle ratios and mandatory with 3.91 ratio; 3.73, 3.91 (also factory option), 4.10, 4.44 and 5.00 dealer kits at extra cost.

Popular and performance options

150 hp I-6, $50; 210 hp V-8, $104; 245 hp V-8, $48; 285 hp V-8 for Javelin, $97, for AMX, $49; 330 hp V-8 for Javelin & AMX, $137; Go Package for AMX 285 hp V-8, $410.90, for AMX 330 hp V-8, $498.95, included engine, dual exhausts, hood T-stripe, blacked-out rear panel, Rally-Pak instruments, handling package, fiberglass cowl-induction hood, heavy-duty cooling system, Twin-Grip rear, power front disc brakes, E60x15 raised-white-letter Goodyear Polyglas tires, 15x7 styled steel wheels and Space Saver spare; automatic transmission with column shift for 232 & 258 sixes, $217; 304 V-8, $223; 360 V-8 except AMX, $246; automatic transmission with floor shift and console for 304 V-8, $279, for Javelin 360 V-8, $302, for AMX 360 V-8, $246, for Javelin 401 V-8, $312, for AMX 401 V-8, $256; console only, $56; four-speed transmission for Javelin with 285 or 330 hp engines, $209; power steering, $111; power brakes, $46; power front disc brakes, $89; Twin-Grip rear, $47; Adjust-O-Tilt steering, $49; all-season air conditioning, $399; handling package, $28.35; dual exhausts for 360 4-bbl V-8, $31; heavy-duty cooling, $16; heavy-duty 70 amp battery, $14; rally side stripes exc. AMX, $37; cold start package, $18; front manual disc brakes, $40; AM/FM multiplex stereo radio, $224; leather bucket seats for SST and AMX, $84; corduroy fabric bucket seats for SST & AMX, $52; electric wiper/washers, $22; center armrest and cushion, Javelin without console, $51; black, white, blue or green vinyl roof, $89; front and rear bumper guards, $32.

Engine CID emblems
(On front portion of fenders)

232 I-6 None
258 I-6 None
304 V-8 Large dull smooth machined and bright rough finished numerals against black background with red-and-silver checkerboard-square pattern inside O
360 V-8 Large chrome numerals against black background with blue painted insert
401 V-8 Large chrome numerals with red painted insert

1972 Javelin

Model	Body style	Series	Model no.	Price
Javelin SST	2-Dr FSBK 4P	70	7279-7	$2,807
Javelin AMX	2-Dr FSBK 4P	70	7279-8	$3,109

Dimensions

WB: 110" FT: 59.3" (V-8 59.7")
OL: 191.77" RT: 60"
OW: 75.2" HT: 50.9"

Engines

Code	Type	CID	B×S	Hp @ Rpm	Tq @ Rpm	CR	Carb.
E	I-6	232[1]	3.75x3.50	100 @ 3600	185 @ 1800	8.0	1-bbl
A	I-6	258[1]	3.75x3.90	110 @ 3500	195 @ 2000	8.0	1-bbl
H	V-8	304[2]	3.75x3.44	150 @ 4200	245 @ 2500	8.4	2-bbl
N	V-8	360	4.08x3.44	175 @ 4000	285 @ 2400	8.5	2-bbl
P	V-8	360	4.08x3.44	195 @ 4400[3]	295 @ 2900[4]	8.5	4-bbl
Z	V-8	401	4.17x3.68	255 @ 4600	345 @ 3300	8.5	4-bbl

[1]Low-compression six-cylinder engine available in these horsepower ratings.
[2]150 Hp V-8 standard on AMX.
[3]220 @ 4400 with dual exhaust.
[4]315 @ 3100 with dual exhaust.
Note: Horsepower and torque ratings are SAE net.

209

<table>
<tr><td colspan="2">Transmissions</td><td colspan="2">Rear axle ratios
(Optional ratios at extra cost)</td></tr>
</table>

Transmissions / **Rear axle ratios** *(Optional ratios at extra cost)*

Transmissions	Rear axle ratios
3-speed, all-sync., floor shift (100 hp) (std.)	3.08 (3.31 & 3.58)
Torque Command, col. shift (100 & 110 hp) (opt.)	3.08 (3.31)
3-speed, all-sync., floor shift (150 hp) (std. or opt. cons.)	3.54 (3.15)
Torque Command, col. shift (all V-8s exc. 255 hp) (opt.)	2.87 (3.15)
Torque Command, cons. shift (all V-8s) (opt.)	2.87 (3.15 & 3.54[1])[2]
4-speed, all-sync., floor shift (195, 220 & 255 hp) (opt.)	3.54 (3.15 & 3.91)

[1]255 hp only.
[2]For Javelin AMX with combination of automatic transmission and Go Package: 360 4-bbl, 3.15 std., 2.87 opt.; 401 4-bbl, 3.15 std., 2.87 & 3.54 opt.
Note: Column shift NA on AMX; Twin-Grip optional with all axle ratios and mandatory with 3.91 ratio; 3.73, 3.91 (also factory option), 4.10, 4.44 and 5.00 dealer kits at extra cost.

Popular and performance options

110 hp I-6, $43; 150 hp V-8, $94; 175 hp V-8, $42; 195 hp V-8, $85; 255 hp V-8, $162; Go Package for 220 hp V-8 AMX, $428, for 255 hp V-8 AMX, $505, included engine, dual exhausts, hood T-stripe, blacked-out rear panel, Rally-Pak instruments, handling package, fiberglass cowl-induction hood, heavy-duty cooling, Twin-Grip rear, power front disc brakes, E60x15 raised-white-letter Goodyear Polyglas tires, 15x7 slot-styled wheels and Space Saver spare; automatic transmission with floor shift and console for 304 V-8, $282; for 360 V-8, $293; for 401 V-8, $305; four-speed transmission for Javelin with 195, 220 or 255 hp V-8 engine, $188; power steering, $106; power brakes, $44; power front disc brakes, $77; Twin-Grip rear, $43.45; Adjust-O-Tilt steering, $43; all-season air conditioning, $377; handling package, $28.35; dual exhausts for 360 4-bbl V-8, $31; heavy-duty cooling, $16; heavy-duty 70 amp battery, $14; rally side stripes exc. AMX, $39; hood T-stripe AMX, $39; front manual disc brakes, $47; quick-ratio manual steering, $15; front spoiler for AMX with disc brakes, $31; three-spoke sports steering wheel for Javelin, standard on AMX, $19; remote mirror, clock and three-speed wipers, $46; center armrest and cushion, Javelin without console, $54; rear deck luggage rack, Javelin SST, $32; AM/FM multiplex stereo radio, $196; 8-track tape player with manual AM radio, $190; Cardin trim package for Javelin SST, $85; black, white, blue or green vinyl top, $88; front and rear bumper guards, $29; E60x15 RWL Polyglas tires, $205; Solex glass, $40; light group, $32; insulation, $22; floor mats, $12.

Engine CID emblems
(On front portion of fenders)

232 I-6 None
258 I-6 None
304 V-8 None
360 V-8 None
401 V-8 Large chrome numerals with red painted insert

1973 Javelin

Model	Body style	Series	Model no.	Price
Javelin	2-Dr FSBK 4P	70	7379-7	$2,889
Javelin AMX	2-Dr FSBK 4P	70	7379-8	$3,191

Dimensions

WB: 110" FT: 59.3" (V-8 59.1")
OL: 192.31" RT: 60"
OW: 75.2" HT: 50.5"

Engines

Code	Type	CID	B×S	Hp @ Rpm	Tq @ Rpm	CR	Carb.
E	I-6	232[1]	3.75x3.50	100 @ 3600	185 @ 1800	8.0	1-bbl
A	I-6	258[1]	3.75x3.90	110 @ 3500	195 @ 2000	8.0	1-bbl
H	V-8	304[2]	3.75x3.44	150 @ 4200	245 @ 2500	8.4	2-bbl
N	V-8	360	4.08x3.44	175 @ 4000	285 @ 2400	8.5	2-bbl
P	V-8	360	4.08x3.44	195 @ 4400[3]	295 @ 2900[4]	8.5	4-bbl
Z	V-8	401	4.17x3.68	255 @ 4600	345 @ 3300	8.5	4-bbl

[1]Low-compression six-cylinder engine available in these horsepower ratings. Code F for 232, code B for 258.
[2]150 hp V-8 standard on AMX.
[3]220 @ 4400 with dual exhaust.
[4]315 @ 3100 with dual exhaust.
Note: Horsepower and torque ratings are SAE net.

Transmissions / **Rear axle ratios** *(Optional ratios at extra cost)*

Transmissions	Rear axle ratios
3-speed, all-sync., floor shift (100 hp) (std.)	3.08 (3.31 & 3.58)
Torque Command, col. shift (100 & 110 hp) (opt.)	3.08 (3.31)
3-speed, all-sync., floor shift (150 hp) (std. or opt. cons.)	3.54 (3.91)
Torque Command, col. shift (all V-8s exc. 255 hp) (opt.)	2.87 (3.15)
Torque Command, cons. shift (all V-8s) (opt.)	2.87 (3.15 & 3.54[1])[2]
4-speed, all-sync., floor shift (195, 220 & 255 hp) (opt.)	3.54 (3.91)

[1]255 hp only.
[2]For Javelin AMX with combination of automatic transmission and Go Package: 360 4-bbl, 2.87 std., 3.15 opt.; 401 4-bbl, 2.87 std., 3.15 and 3.54 opt.
Note: Column shift NA on AMX.

Popular and performance options

150 hp V-8, $94; Go Package for 220 hp V-8 AMX, $428, for 255 hp V-8 AMX, $476; four-speed transmission, $188; power brakes, $44; power disc brakes, $79; manual disc brakes, $47; power steering, $106; front spoiler, $31; all-season air conditioning, $377; AM Radio, $66; AM/FM stereo multiplex radio, $196; protection group, $19; insulation group, $22; Cardin interior package, $85; vinyl roof, $88; light group, $32; visibility group, $24; Solex glass, $40; interior map pockets, $6.

Note: Prices for additional options are not available, but they were similar to those in 1972.

Engine CID emblems
(On front portion of fenders)

232 I-6 None
258 I-6 None
304 V-8 None
360 V-8 None
401 V-8 Large chrome numerals with red painted insert

1974 Javelin

Model	Body style	Series	Model no.	Price
Javelin	2-Dr FSBK 4P	70	7479-7	$2,999
Javelin AMX	2-Dr FSBK 4P	70	7479-8	$3,299

Dimensions

WB: 110" FT: 59.3" (V-8 59.1")
OL: 192.31" RT: 60"
OW: 75.2" HT: 50.5"

Engines

Code	Type	CID	B×S	Hp @ Rpm	Tq @ Rpm	CR	Carb.
E	I-6	232	3.75x3.50	100 @ 3600	185 @ 1800	8.0	1-bbl
A	I-6	258	3.75x3.90	110 @ 3500	195 @ 2000	8.0	1-bbl
H	V-8	304[1]	3.75x3.44	150 @ 4200	245 @ 2500	8.4	2-bbl
N	V-8	360	4.08x3.44	175 @ 4000	285 @ 2400	8.25	2-bbl
P	V-8	360	4.08x3.44	195 @ 4400[2]	295 @ 2900[3]	8.25	4-bbl
Z	V-8	401	4.17x3.68	255 @ 4600[4]	345 @ 3300[5]	8.5[6]	4-bbl

[1]150 hp V-8 standard on AMX.
[2]220 @ 4400 with dual exhaust.
[3]315 @ 3100 with dual exhaust.
[4]Changed shortly after introduction to 235 @ 4600.
[5]Changed shortly after introduction to 335 @ 3300 or 335 @ 3200.
[6]Changed shortly after introduction to 8.25.
Note: 401 V-8 in aftermarket charts was sometimes rated at 225 hp; horsepower and torque ratings are SAE net.

Transmissions / **Rear axle ratios** *(Optional ratios at extra cost)[1]*

Transmissions	Rear axle ratios
3-speed, all-sync., floor shift (100 hp) (std.)	3.08 (3.31)
Torque Command, col. shift (100 & 110 hp) (opt.)	3.08 (3.31)
3-speed, all-sync., floor shift (150 hp) (std. or opt. cons.)	3.54
Torque Command, col. shift (all V-8s exc. 255 hp) (opt.)	304 V-8: 287 (3.15) 360 V-8: 3.15 (3.54)
Torque Command, cons. shift (all V-8s) (opt.)	304 V-8: 2.87 (3.15) 360 & 401 V-8: 3.15 (3.54)
4-speed, all-sync., floor shift (195, 220 & 255 hp) (opt.)	3.54

[1]Many standard and optional axle ratios were either changed or deleted early in the model year shortly after model introduction.
Note: Column shift NA on AMX; four-speed transmission NA in California.

Popular and performance options

Automatic transmission with floor shift and console for Javelin, $280; four-speed manual transmission for Javelin 304 V-8, $188; all-season air conditioning, $400; rally side stripes for Javelin, $38; hood T-stripe for AMX without Go Package, $39; power front disc brakes, $81; power steering, $111; AM/FM multiplex stereo radio with four speakers, $230; 8-track tape player with manual AM radio, $190; Adjust-O-Tilt steering, $46; Domino fabric trim for Javelin, $47; aluminum trim rings and hubcaps for Javelin, $33; custom wheel covers, $50; 15x7 slot-style wheels, $205; handling package, $23; Rally-Pak instruments for Javelin, $77.

Engine CID emblems

232 I-6 None
258 I-6 None
304 V-8 None
360 V-8 None
401 V-8 None

1966 American

Model	Body style	Series	Model no.	Price
American 220	4-Dr SED 6P	01	6605	$2,086
American 220	2-Dr SED 6P	01	6606	$2,017
American 220	4-Dr SW 6P	01	6608	$2,369
American 440	4-Dr SED 6P	01	6605-5	$2,203
American 440	2-Dr SED 6P	01	6606-5	$2,134
American 440	2-Dr CONV 6P	01	6607-5	$2,486
American 440	4-Dr SW 6P	01	6608-5	$2,477
American 440	2-Dr HDTP 6P	01	6609-5	$2,227
American Rogue	2-Dr HDTP 5P	01	6609-7	$2,370

Dimensions

WB: 106" FT: 56"
OL: 181" RT: 55"
OW: 69.5" HT: SED and SW six 54.5", SED and SW V-8 54.8", HDTP six 53.4", HDTP V-8 53.7", CONV six 54.4", CONV V-8 54.7"

Engines

Code	Type	CID	B×S	Hp @ Rpm	Tq @ Rpm	CR	Carb.
A	I-6	199	3.75x3.00	128 @ 4400	182 @ 1600	8.5	1-bbl
B	I-6	232	3.75x3.50	155 @ 4400	222 @ 1600	8.5	2-bbl
C	V-8	290*	3.75x3.28	200 @ 4600	285 @ 2800	9.0	2-bbl
D	V-8	290*	3.75x3.28	225 @ 4700	300 @ 3200	10.0	4-bbl

*Midyear.

Transmissions

3-speed, 2-3 sync., col. shift (199 SED & HDTP without AC) (std.)

3-speed, 2-3 sync., overdrive col. shift (199 SED & HDTP without AC) (Opt)

Flash-O-Matic, col. shift (199 SED & HDTP without AC) (opt.)

Shift-Command, cons. shift (All with 232) (opt.)

Flash-O-Matic, col. shift (All with 200) (opt.)

Shift-Command, console shift (All with 200) (opt.)

4-speed, all-sync., floor shift (All with 290) (opt.)*

Rear axle ratios
(Optional ratios at no extra cost)

3.08 (3.31) (199 SW & CONV and all with AC or all with 232: 3.31)

3.08 (3.31) (199 SW & CONV and all with AC or all with 232: 3.58)

2.73 (3.08) (199 SW & CONV and all with AC or all with 232: 3.31)

3.31

3.15 (2.87)

3.15 (2.87)

3.15 (3.54)

*Midyear.

Popular and performance options

232 six, $51; 200 hp V-8, $114; 225 hp V-8, $32; 4-speed manual transmission, $184; automatic transmission, $187; power steering, $84; power brakes, $42; all-season air conditioning, $303; power front disc brakes, $91.

Engine CID emblems
(On rear portion of quarter panels)

199 I-6 None
232 I-6 Rectangular with chrome numerals and chrome letters set in red-and-black background
290 V-8 Small chrome V with chrome numerals set in silver background above

1967 American

Model	Body style	Series	Model no.	Price
American 220	4-Dr SED 6P	01	6705	$2,142
American 220	2-Dr SED 6P	01	6706	$2,073
American 220	4-Dr SW 6P	01	6708	$2,425
American 440	4-Dr SED 6P	01	6705-5	$2,259
American 440	2-Dr SED 6P	01	6706-5	$2,191
American 440	2-Dr HDTP 6P	01	6709-5	$2,283
American 440	4-Dr SW 6P	01	6708-5	$2,533
American Rogue	2-Dr HDTP 5P	01	6709-7	$2,426
American Rogue	2-Dr CONV 6P	01	6707-7	$2,611

Dimensions

WB: 106" FT: 56"
OL: 181" RT: 55"
OW: 70.84" HT: SED and SW six 54.5", SED and SW V-8, 54.8", HDTP six 53.4", HDTP V-8 53.7", CONV six 54.4", CONV V-8 54.7"

Engines

Code	Type	CID	B×S	Hp @ Rpm	Tq @ Rpm	CR	Carb.
A	I-6	199	3.75x3.00	128 @ 4400	182 @ 1600	8.5	1-bbl
E	I-6	232	3.75x3.50	145 @ 4300	215 @ 1600	8.5	1-bbl
B	I-6	232	3.75x3.50	155 @ 4400	222 @ 1600	8.5	2-bbl
C	V-8	290	3.75x3.28	200 @ 4600	285 @ 2800	9.0	2-bbl
D	V-8	290	3.75x3.28	225 @ 4700	300 @ 3200	10.0	4-bbl
X	V-8	343[1]	4.08x3.28	280 @ 4800	365 @ 3000	10.2	4-bbl

[1]Midyear.
Note: 343 NA on station wagons.

Transmissions

3-speed, 2-3 sync., col. shift (199 SED & HDTP without AC) (std.)

3-speed, 2-3 sync., overdrive col. shift (199 SED & HDTP without AC) (opt.)

Flash-O-Matic, col. shift [199 SED & HDTP without AC) (opt.)

3-speed, all-sync., col. shift (all with 290 V-8) (std.)

Shift-Command, cons. shift (all with 200 hp) (opt.)

Flash-O-Matic, col. shift (all with 200 hp) (opt.)

4-speed, all-sync., floor shift (all with 290 and 343 V-8) (opt.)

Rear axle ratios
(Optional ratios at no extra cost)

3.08 (3.31) [199 SW & CONV and all with AC or all with 232: 3.08 (3.31)]

3.31 (3.08) [199 SW & CONV and all with AC or all with 232: 3.31 (3.08)]

2.73 (3.08 & 3.31) [(199 SW & CONV and all with AC or all with 232: 308 (2.73 & 3.31)]

3.15

3.15 (2.87)

3.15 (2.87)

3.15 (3.54)

Note: 4.44 dealer-installed option for V-8s.

Popular and performance options

145 hp I-6, $39; 155 hp I-6, $51; 200 hp V-8, $119; 225 hp V-8, $32; 280 hp V-8, $90.65; four-speed manual transmission, $184.25; Twin-Grip rear, $36.85; power steering, $84.40; power front disc brakes, $90.60; power brakes, $42; V-8 handling package, $15.20; heavy-duty cooling system, $16.05; heavy-duty battery, $7.40; heavy-duty alternator, $10.10; Firestone wide-oval tires, $64.15; sport steering wheel, $15.55; visibility group, $26.80; light group, $15.55; overdrive transmission, $109; automatic transmission, $174; Shift-Command automatic transmission with floor shift and console in Rogue with bucket seats, $192; heavy-duty clutch for V-8, $5; all-season air conditioning, $311; Solex glass, all, $28.70; exterior appearance group, included rocker moldings and wheel covers, $77; wheel covers on 220/440, $21; turbo-cast wheel covers, $61; vinyl roof for hardtops, $75; reclining seats for 220/440, $25; reclining bucket seats with center armrest and cushion for Rogue convertible, standard on Rogue hardtop, $98; custom steering wheel for 220, $8; safety headrests, $15. Dealer-installed items: high-performance camshaft kit, $200; traction bars, $20; tachometer, $48; seatbelt retractors, $9.45; all-transistor manual radio, $49; all-transistor push-button radio, $57.

Engine CID emblems
(On rear portion of quarter panels)

199 I-6 None
232 I-6 Rectangular with chrome numerals and chrome letters set in red-and-black background
290 V-8 Small chrome *V* with chrome numerals set in silver background above
343 V-8 Small chrome *V* with chrome numerals set in red background above

1968 American

Model	Body style	Series	Model no.	Price
American 220	4-Dr SED 6P	01	6805	$2,024
American 220	2-Dr SED 6P	01	6806	$1,946
American 440	4-Dr SED 6P	01	6805-5	$2,166
American 440	4-Dr SW 6P	01	6808-5	$2,426
American Rogue	2-Dr HDTP 6P	01	6809-7	$2,244

Dimensions
WB: 106" FT: 56" (V-8 56.40")
OL: 181" RT: 55" (V-8 55.27")
OW: 70.84" HT: SED six 54.24", SED V-8 54.48", SW six and V-8 55.24", HDTP V-8 53.60", HDTP six 53.36"

Engines

Code	Type	CID	B×S	Hp @ Rpm	Tq @ Rpm	CR	Carb.
A	I-6	199	3.75x3.00	128 @ 4400	182 @ 1600	8.5	1-bbl
B	I-6	232	3.75x3.50	145 @ 4300	215 @ 1600	8.5	1-bbl
M	V-8	290	3.75x3.28	200 @ 4600	285 @ 2800	9.0	2-bbl
N	V-8	290	3.75x3.28	225 @ 4700	300 @ 3200	10.0	4-bbl

Transmissions
3-speed, all-sync.,[1] col. shift (199 SED less AC) (std.)
3-speed, overdrive col. shift (199 SED less AC) (opt.)
Shift-Command, col. shift (199 SED less AC) (opt.)

3-speed, all-sync., col. shift (200 hp) (std.)
Shift-Command, col. shift (200 hp) (opt.)
4-speed, all-sync., floor shift (290 V-8) (opt.)

Rear axle ratios
(Optional ratios at no extra cost)
3.08 (3.31) [199 SW & SED with AC or all with 232: 3.08 (3.31)]
3.31 (3.08) [199 SW & SED with AC 3.31 (3.08)]
2.73 (3.08 & 3.31) [199 SW & SED with AC or all with 232: 3.08 (2.73 & 3.31)[2]]
3.15
3.15 (2.87)
3.54 (3.15)[3]

[1]199 six, sync. on 2-3 only.
[2]Rogue 232 HDTP; 2.37 std. (2.73 & 3.08 opt.)
[3]3.73, 3.91, 4.10 and 4.44 dealer kits at extra cost.

Popular and performance options
145 hp I-6, $45; 200 hp V-8, $119; 225 hp V-8, $45; all-season air conditioning, $311; power steering, $84; power brakes, $42; power front disc brakes, $97; four-speed manual transmission, $184; tachometer for V-8, $48; Firestone wide-oval tires, $64; Solex glass, all, $29, windshield only, $16; vinyl roof for hardtops, $79; sport steering wheel, $21; custom steering wheel for 220, $9; column-shift automatic transmission, $174; vinyl seat upholstery, standard on SW, $24; front and rear bumper guards, $23; front bumper guards only, $12; individually reclining seats, $49; electric windshield wipers, $12; all-transistor push-button radio, $61; safety head-rests, $35; special paint colors, $28; full wheel discs, $21; wire wheel covers, $66; turbo-cast wheel covers, $61.

Engine CID emblems
(On rear portion of fenders)

199 I-6 None
232 I-6 Rectangular with chrome numerals and chrome letters set in red-and-black background
290 V-8 Small chrome *V* with black numerals set in silver background above

1969 Rambler

Model	Body style	Series	Model no.	Price
Rambler	4-Dr SED 6P	01	6905	$2,076
Rambler	2-Dr SED 6P	01	6906	$1,998
Rambler 440	4-Dr SED 6P	01	6905-5	$2,218
Rambler 440	2-Dr SED 6P	01	6908-5	$2,478
Rambler Rogue	2-Dr HDTP 6P	01	6909-7	$2,296
SC/Rambler Hurst	2-Dr HDTP 6P	01	6909-7	$2,998

Dimensions
WB: 106" FT: 56" (V-8 56.4")
OL: 181" RT: 55" (V-8 55.3")
OW: 70.84" HT: SED 54.2", SW 55.2", HDTP 53.4"

Engines

Code	Type	CID	B×S	Hp at Rpm	Tq at Rpm	CR	Carb.
A	I-6	199	3.75x3.00	128 @ 4400	182 @ 1600	8.5	1-bbl
B	I-6	232[1]	3.75x3.50	145 @ 4300	215 @ 1600	8.5	1-bbl
M	V-8	290	3.75x3.28	200 @ 4600	285 @ 2800	9.0	2-bbl
N	V-8	290	3.75x3.28	225 @ 4700	300 @ 3200	10.0	4-bbl
X	V-8	390[2]	4.17x3.57	315 @ 4600	425 @ 3200	10.2	4-bbl

[1]Low-compression 7.7 six-cylinder engine available in this horsepower rating.
[2]SC/Rambler Hurst only introduced at mid-year.

Transmissions
3-speed, all-sync., col. shift (std.)

3-speed, overdrive col. shift (opt.)
Shift-Command, col. shift (opt.)

Shift-Command, col. shift (200 hp) (opt.)
4-speed, all-sync., floor shift (225 hp) (opt.)[3]

Rear axle ratios
(Optional ratios at no extra cost)
199 I-6: 3.08
232 I-6: 3.08 (3.31)
199 I-6: 3.31
199 I-6:[1] 2.73 (3.08)
232 I-6:[2] 3.08 (3.31)
2.87 (3.15)
3.54[3]

[1]Only for sedans and hardtops without air conditioning; sedans and hardtops with air conditioning and all wagons got 3.08 (2.73).
[2]Rogue with automatic transmission got 2.37 (3.08).
[3]Standard on SC/Rambler Hurst.
Note: 3.73, 3.91, 4.10, 4.44 and 5.00 dealer kits at extra cost available with any V-8 transmission combination.

Popular and performance options
145 hp I-6, $45; 200 hp V-8, $116; 225 hp V-8, $45; overdrive transmission, $116; automatic transmission for six, $171; four-speed manual transmission, $193; column-shift automatic transmission in 440 for V-8, $190; automatic transmission oil cooler, $18; heavy-duty 70 amp battery, $8; heavy-duty battery and 55 amp alternator, $26; heavy-duty cooling system, $53; dealer-installed dual exhaust, $31; Twin-Grip rear, $42; heavy-duty clutch with three-speed transmission, $5; power brakes, $42; power steering, $90; all-season air conditioning, $324; handling package, $17; two-tone paint in standard colors, $24; special paint color application, $39; Solex glass, all windows, $32, windshield only, $23; custom steering wheel for base Rambler, $12; sports steering wheel for Rogue, $30; individually reclining bench seats, $52; undercoating and underhood insulation pad, $21; electric windshield wipers, $15; black or white vinyl roof for Rogue, $79; all-transistor push-button radio, $61; full wheel discs, $21; light group, $23; visibility group, $29; 6.45x14 WW tires, $32; 6.95x14 WW tires, $32; air conditioning package, included Solex glass and power steering, $387.

Engine CID emblems
(On rear portion of fenders)

199 I-6 None
232 I-6 Rectangular with chrome numerals and chrome letters set in red-and-black background
290 V-8 Small chrome *V* with black numerals set in silver background above
390 V-8 Large chrome *V* with red and blue rectangles side-by-side and chrome numerals above; SC/Rambler Hurst on front portion of fenders

Performance models
SC/Rambler Hurst
Model included 390 cubic inch 315 hp AMX V-8 engine; Borg-Warner close-ratio all-synchromesh four-speed manual transmission; 3.54:1 Twin-Grip rear with AMX Torque Links and staggered shocks; heavy-duty U-joints; heavy-duty 10.5 inch clutch disc; handling package consisting of heavy-duty springs, shocks and large-diameter front sway bar; heavy-duty cooling system consisting of heavy-duty radiator, Power-Flex fan and fan shroud; AMX 11.2 inch diameter power front disc brakes; AMX-type 20:1 quick-ratio manual steering; special Hurst four-speed shift linkage with T-handle; Sun tachometer on steering column; dual exhaust system with special-tone Thrush Glasspac mufflers and chrome tailpipe extensions; mailbox-type functional cold-air induction hood scoop; five E70x14 Goodyear Polyglas redline tires mounted on 14x6 specially painted blue five-spoke Magnum 500 mag-styled steel wheels with trim rings; two chrome hood tie-downs with locking safety pins and cables; right and left outside custom teardrop rearview mirrors; custom blacked-out grille, flat-black-finished taillight bezels and rear deck treatment; wood-grain-look sports steering wheel; individually adjustable reclining seats; all-vinyl

charcoal seat upholstery with full carpeting; front seat headrests in matching red-white-blue vinyl upholstery; special SC/Rambler Hurst emblems on fenders and rear panel; and the special application of red, white and blue exterior colors; all the regular Rogue safety and comfort equipment including the Weather-Eye heating and ventilation system, plus electric windshield wipers.

1968 Rebel

Model	Body style	Series	Model no.	Price
Rebel 550	4-Dr SED 6P	10	6815	$2,443
Rebel 550	2-Dr CONV 6P	10	6817	$2,736
Rebel 550	4-Dr SW 6P	10	6818	$2,729
Rebel 550	2-Dr HDTP 6P	10	6819	$2,454
Rebel 770	4-Dr SED 6P	10	6815-5	$2,542
Rebel 770	4-Dr SW 6P	10	6818-5	$2,854
Rebel 770	2-Dr HDTP 6P	10	6819-5	$2,556
Rebel SST	2-Dr CONV 6P	10	6817-7	$2,999
Rebel SST	2-Dr HDTP 6P	10	6819-7	$2,775

Dimensions

WB: 114"   FT: 58.20"
OL: 197" (SW 198")   RT: 58.50"
OW: 77.24"   HT: SED 54.61", SW 55.06", HDTP 53.49", CONV 54.79"

Engines

Code	Type	CID	B×S	Hp @ Rpm	Tq @ Rpm	CR	Carb.
B	I-6	232	3.75x3.50	145 @ 4300	215 @ 1600	8.5	1-bbl
C	I-6	232	3.75x3.50	155 @ 4400	222 @ 1600	8.5	2-bbl
M	V-8	290[1]	3.75x3.28	200 @ 4600	285 @ 2800	9.0	2-bbl
S	V-8	343	4.08x3.28	235 @ 4400	345 @ 2600	9.0	2-bbl
T	V-8	343	4.08x3.28	280 @ 4800	365 @ 3000	10.2	4-bbl
(W,X)[2]	V-8	390[3]	4.17x3.57	315 @ 4600	425 @ 3200	10.2	4-bbl

[1]Standard on SST.
[2]X code in VIN, W code in engine valve cover tag denoted Canadian 390 2-bbl V-8 used in some 1968 Rebels converted to 4-bbl models.
[3]Midyear.

Transmissions	Rear axle ratios (Optional ratios at no extra cost)
3-speed, all-sync., col. shift (232) (std.)	3.15
3-speed, all-sync., overdrive col. shift (145 hp) (opt.)	3.54
Shift-Command, col. shift (232) (opt.)	3.15
3-speed, all-sync., col. shift (200 hp) (std.)	3.15 (3.54)
3-speed, all-sync., overdrive column shift (200 hp) (opt.)	3.54
Shift-Command, col. shift (all V-8s) (opt.)	290 V-8: 3.15 (2.87) 343 & 390 V-8: 2.87 (3.15)
Shift-Command, cons. shift (all V-8s) (opt.)	290 V-8: 3.15 (2.87) 343 & 390 V-8: 2.87 (3.15)
4-speed, all-sync., floor shift (200, 280 & 315 hp) (opt.)	290 V-8: 3.54 (315)[1] 343 & 390 V-8: 3.15 (3.54)[1]

[1]3.73, 3.91, 4.10 and 4.44 dealer kits at extra cost.
Note: Console shift available on SST only.

Popular and performance options

200 hp V-8, $106; 235 hp V-8, $45; 280 hp V-8, $76; 315 hp V-8, $168; SST Shift-Command console with V-8, $249; four-speed manual transmission, $184; tachometer with V-8, $48; power brakes, $42; power front disc brakes, $97; power steering, $84; all-season air conditioning, $356; Solex glass, all windows, $34, windshield only, $21; bucket seats, $49; bench seat headrests, $35; two-tone paint, $32; SST exterior paint stripe, $14; AM/FM all-transistor push-button radio, $134; SST reclining bucket seats with center armrest, $91; vinyl roof, $79; 8-track tape player with two rear speakers, $134; Adjust-O-Tilt steering, $42; sports steering wheel, $21; turbo-cast wheel covers, SST, $40, 550 and 770, $51; wire wheel covers, SST, $45, 550 and 770, $66; power windows, SST, $100.

Engine CID emblems
(On rear portion of quarter panels)

232 I-6 None
290 V-8 Small chrome V with black numerals set in silver background above
343 V-8 Small chrome V set in red background with chrome numerals side-by-side
390 V-8 Large chrome V with red and blue rectangles side-by-side and chrome numerals above

1969 Rebel

Model	Body style	Series	Model no.	Price
Rebel	4-Dr SED 6P	10	6915	$2,484
Rebel	2-Dr HDTP 6P	10	6919	$2,496
Rebel	4-Dr SW 6P	10	6918	$2,817
Rebel SST	4-Dr SED 6P	10	6915-7	$2,584
Rebel SST	2-Dr HDTP 6P	10	6919-7	$2,598
Rebel SST	4-Dr SW 6P	10	6918-7	$2,947

Dimensions

WB: 114"   FT: 60"
OL: 197" (SW 198")   RT: 60"
OW: 77.2"   HT: SED 54.6", SW 55.1", HDTP 53.5"

Engines

Code	Type	CID	B×S	Hp @ Rpm	Tq @ Rpm	CR	Carb.
B	I-6	232	3.75x3.50	145 @ 4300	215 @ 1600	8.5	1-bbl
C	I-6	232	3.75x3.50	155 @ 4400	222 @ 1600	8.5	2-bbl
M	V-8	290	3.75x3.28	200 @ 4600	285 @ 2800	9.0	2-bbl
S	V-8	343	4.08x3.28	235 @ 4400	345 @ 2600	9.0	2-bbl
T	V-8	343	4.08x3.28	280 @ 4800	365 @ 2600	10.2	4-bbl

Transmissions	Rear axle ratios (Optional ratios at no extra cost)
3-speed, all-sync., col. shift (145 hp) (std.)	3.15
3-speed, all-sync., overdrive col. shift (145 hp) (opt.)	3.54
Shift-Command, col. shift (232) (opt.)	3.15
Shift-Command, col. shift (290 & 343) (opt.)	2.87 (3.15)
Shift-Command, cons. shift (290 & 343) (opt.)	2.87 (3.15)

Note: Console shift available on SST hardtop only; 3.73, 3.91, 4.10, 4.44 and 5.00 dealer kits at extra cost available with any V-8 transmission combination.

Popular and performance options

155 hp I-6, $16; 200 hp V-8, $116; 235 hp V-8, $52; 280 hp V-8, $80; overdrive transmission, $116; automatic transmission, $201; automatic transmission for SST, $280; automatic transmission oil cooler, $18; Shift-Command column shift for 343 V-8, $223; Shift-Command with floor control for SST, $280; power steering, $100; power brakes, $42; all-season air conditioning, $376; heavy-duty 70 amp battery, $8; heavy-duty battery and 55 amp alternator, $26; heavy-duty cooling, $53; dual exhausts, $31; Twin-Grip rear, $42; exterior paint stripe, except SST, $14; individually reclining seats, $58; reclining bucket seats with front armrest and center cushion, SST only, $111; 8-track tape player with manual radio for sedans and hardtops, $134; Adjust-O-Tilt steering, $45; custom steering wheel, standard in SST, $13; sport steering wheel for SST, $30; wire wheel covers, base model, $72, SST, $51; turbo-cast wheel covers, base model, $67, SST, $46; visibility group with electric clock, $43.

Engine CID emblems
(On rear portion of quarter panels)

232 I-6 None
290 V-8 Small chrome V with black numerals set in silver background above
343 V-8 Small chrome V set in red background with chrome numerals side-by-side

1970 Rebel

Model	Body style	Series	Model no.	Price
Rebel	4-Dr SED 6P	10	7015-0	$2,626
Rebel	2-Dr HDTP 6P	10	7019-0	$2,660
Rebel	4-Dr SW 6P	10	7018-0	$2,766
Rebel SST	4-Dr SED 6P	10	7015-7	$2,684
Rebel SST	2-Dr HDTP 6P	10	7019-7	$2,718
Rebel SST	4-Dr SW 6P	10	7018-7	$3,072
Rebel Machine	2-Dr HDTP 6P	10	7019-7	$3,475

Dimensions

WB: 114"   FT: 60"
OL: 199" (SW 198")   RT: 60"
OW: 77.2"   HT: SED 54.6", SW 55.1", HDTP 53.5", Machine 54.4"

Engines

Code	Type	CID	B×S	Hp @ Rpm	Tq @ Rpm	CR	Carb.
E	I-6	232	3.75x3.50	145 @ 4300	215 @ 1600	8.5	1-bbl

Code	Type	CID	B×S	Hp @ Rpm	Tq @ Rpm	CR	Carb.
G	I-6	232	3.75x3.50	155 @ 4400	222 @ 1600	8.5	2-bbl
H[1]	V-8	304	3.75x3.44	210 @ 4400	305 @ 2800	9.0	2-bbl
N	V-8	360	4.08x3.44	245 @ 4400	365 @ 2400	9.0	2-bbl
P	V-8	360	4.08x3.44	290 @ 4800	395 @ 3200	10.0	4-bbl
X	V-8	390[2]	4.17x3.57	325 @ 5000	420 @ 3200	10.0	4-bbl
Y	V-8	390[3]	4.17x3.57	340 @ 5100	430 @ 3600	10.0	4-bbl

[1]A Limited number of 304 4-bbl engines with code M were produced for export.
[2]NA on base Rebel.
[3]Rebel Machine only.

Transmissions
3-speed, all-sync., col. shift (145 hp) (std.)
Shift-Command, col. shift (232) (opt.)
Shift-Command, col. shift (all V-8s exc. 340 hp) (opt.)
Shift-Command, cons. shift (all V-8s) (opt.)

4-speed, all-sync., floor shift (340 hp only) (std.)

Rear axle ratios
(Optional ratios at extra cost)
3.15 (3.54)
3.15
2-bbl V-8s: 2.87 (3.15)
4-bbl V-8s: 2.87 (3.15 & 3.54)
2-bbl V-8s: 2.87 (3.15)
4-bbl V-8s exc. 340 hp: 2.87 (3.15 & 3.54)
340 hp: 3.54 (3.15)

3.54 (3.91)

Note: Twin-Grip optional with all axle ratios and mandatory with 3.91 ratio; 3.73, 3.91 (also factory option), 4.10, 4.44 and 5.00 dealer kits at extra cost; console shift available on hardtop only with bucket seats.

Popular and performance options
155 hp I-6, $19; 210 hp V-8, $94; 245 hp V-8, $41; 290 hp V-8, $80; 325 hp V-8, $168; Shift-Command with floor shift for Rebel Machine, $188; power steering, $105; power brakes, $43; all-season air conditioning group, $380; tinted glass, all windows, $37, windshield only, $30; two-tone paint, $27; special paint, $39; AM push-button radio, $62; AM/FM multiplex stereo radio, $134; individual seat, fabric, except Machine, $64; bucket seats, fabric or vinyl, for SST hardtop, $123; sports steering wheel with Rim-Blow for SST, $37; Adjust-O-Tilt steering, $45; black or white vinyl roof for SST sedan and hardtop, $95; heavy-duty cooling, $16; dual exhausts, $31; Twin-Grip rear, $43; heavy-duty 70 amp battery, $13; axle ratios, $10; wire wheel covers except Machine, $74; turbo-cast wheel covers except Machine, $74.

Engine CID emblems
(On rear portion of fenders)
232 I-6 None
304 V-8 Large dull smooth machined and bright rough finished numerals against black background with red-and-silver checkerboard-square pattern inside *O*
360 V-8 Large chrome numerals against black background with blue painted insert
390 V-8 Large chrome numerals against black background with red painted insert and two rows of black-and-white checkerboard-square pattern below

Note: 390 V-8 not designated on Rebel Machine.

Performance models
Rebel Machine
Model included choice of any of the sixteen Rebel exterior factory colors; Shadow Black paint on major portion of hood, hood scoop and fresh air cowl panel; silver paint accent on front opening hood scoop and silver pinstripe over center rib on hood and hood scoop; The Machine decals on rear portions of fenders and on right-side bottom corner of deck lid; venturi grille with blacked-out rear panel and headlight bezels; Rebel and 390 V-8 emblems on fenders along with fender and door ribbed side moldings and SST emblems on quarter panels deleted; high-back bucket seats upholstered in Ventilair vinyl with matching rear seats minus center cushion and fold-down armrest available in black, blue or brown; rear armrests and ashtrays deleted; full carpeting; base-line door and rear side interior panels; Javelin/AMX two-spoke Rim-Blow steering wheel; The Machine emblem on glovebox; dual horns; special 390 ci 340 hp V-8 with modified intake and exhaust manifolds; 680 cfm 4-bbl carburetor; removal of heat-riser control valve; 2.23 close-ratio four-speed manual transmission with Hurst linkage; 3.54 non-Twin-Grip rear; dual exhaust system with special-tone low-restriction mufflers and larger 2.5 inch exhaust pipes; handling package consisting of heavy-duty springs, shock absorbers and rear sway bar; heavy-duty engine cooling system consisting of high-capacity radiator, shroud and Power-Flex fan; power front disc brakes; functional Ram-Air fiberglass hood scoop with vacuum-operated flapper valve and integrated 8000 rpm lighted tachometer; Space Saver spare mounted on regular fourteen-inch orange painted wheel; E60x15 Goodyear Polyglas raised-white-letter tires mounted on 15x7 Kelsey-Hayes styled steel wheels with trim rings. The car used heavy-duty Rebel station wagon rear

coil springs that raised the rear two inches for a special raked look. The car also included most of the standard Rebel SST equipment and could be ordered with just about any regular Rebel SST option.

1971 Matador

Model	Body style	Series	Model no.	Price
Matador	4-Dr SED 6P	10	7115-7	$2,770
Matador	2-Dr HDTP 6P	10	7119-7	$2,799
Matador	4-Dr SW 6P	10	7118-7	$3,163

Dimensions
WB: 118" FT: 60"
OL: 206" (SW 205") RT: 60"
OW: 77.24" HT: 55.4"

Engines
Code	Type	CID	B×S	Hp @ Rpm	Tq @ Rpm	CR	Carb.
E	I-6	232	3.75x3.50	135 @ 4000	210 @ 1600	8.0	1-bbl
A	I-6	258	3.75x3.90	150 @ 3800	240 @ 1800	8.0	1-bbl
H[1]	V-8	304	3.75x3.44	210 @ 4400	300 @ 2600	8.4	2-bbl
N	V-8	360	4.08x3.44	245 @ 4400	365 @ 2600	8.5	2-bbl
P	V-8	360	4.08x3.44	285 @ 4800	390 @ 3200	8.5	4-bbl
Z	V-8	401	4.17x3.68	330 @ 5000	430 @ 3400	9.5[2]	4-bbl

[1]A limited number of 304 4-bbl engines with code M were produced for export.
[2]10.2 on early 1971.

Transmissions
3-speed, all-sync., col. shift (232) (std.)
Shift-Command, col. shift (232 & 258) (opt.)
Shift-Command, col. shift (all V-8s) (opt.)
Shift-Command, cons. shift (all V-8s) (opt.)
4-speed, all-sync., floor shift (285 & 330 hp) (opt.)

Rear axle ratios
(Optional ratios at extra cost)
3.15 (3.54)
3.15 (3.54)
2.87 (3.15)
2.87 (3.15 & 3.54[1])
3.54 (3.15 & 3.91)

[1]401 V-8 only.
Note: Console shift available on hardtop only with bucket seats; four-speed available with Machine Go Package only; Twin-Grip optional with all axle ratios and mandatory with 3.91 ratio; 3.73, 3.91 (also factory option), 4.10, 4.44 and 5.00 dealer kits at extra cost.

Popular and performance options
150 hp I-6, $50; 210 hp V-8, $99; 245 hp V-8, $48; 285 hp V-8, $97; 330 hp V-8, $137; Shift-Command column shift for 232 and 258, $217, for 304, $223, for 360, $246, for 401, $256; Shift-Command floor shift with console for 304, $279, for 360, $302, for 401, $312; four-speed manual transmission with Go Package, $209; dual exhausts for 285 hp V-8, $31; heavy-duty cooling, $16; axle ratios, $14; Twin-Grip rear, $47; heavy-duty 70 amp battery, $15; cold start package, $19; power brakes, $49; power front disc brakes, $89; power steering, $111; all-season air conditioning, $399; Adjust-O-Tilt steering, $49; Solex glass, all windows, $44, windshield only, $36; two-tone paint for sedans, $31; AM/FM push-button radio, $143; 8-track stereo radio with two speakers, $140; Serape fabric reclining seats for hardtop, $71; vinyl center armrest with bucket seats, $136; sports steering wheel with Rim-Blow, $40; air-adjustable rear suspension, $42; black, white, blue or green vinyl top, $97; styled steel wheels, $108; electric wiper/washers, $22; engine block heater, $12.

Engine CID emblems
(On rear portion of fenders)
232 I-6 None
258 I-6 None
304 V-8 Large dull smooth machined and bright rough finished numerals against black background with red-and-silver checkerboard-square pattern inside *O*
360 V-8 Large chrome numerals against black background with blue painted insert
401 V-8 Large chrome numerals with red painted insert

1972 Matador

Model	Body style	Series	Model no.	Price
Matador	4-Dr SED 6P	10	7215-7	$2,784
Matador	2-Dr HDTP 6P	10	7219-7	$2,818
Matador	4-Dr SW 6P	10	7218-7	$3,140

Dimensions

WB: 118"		FT: 60"	
OL: 206" (SW 205")		RT: 60"	
OW: 77.24"		HT: 55.4"	

Engines

Code	Type	CID	B×S	Hp @ Rpm	Tq @ Rpm	CR	Carb.
E	I-6	232[1]	3.75x3.50	100 @ 3600	185 @ 1800	8.0	1-bbl
A	I-6	258[2]	3.75x3.90	110 @ 3500	195 @ 2000	8.0	1-bbl
H	V-8	304	3.75x3.44	150 @ 4200	245 @ 2500	8.4	2-bbl
N	V-8	360	4.08x3.44	175 @ 4000	285 @ 2400	8.5	2-bbl
P	V-8	360	4.08x3.44	195 @ 4400[3]	295 @ 2900[4]	8.5	4-bbl
Z	V-8	401	4.17x3.68	255 @ 4600	345 @ 3300	8.5	4-bbl

[1]Standard sedan and hardtop only.
[2]Station wagon, optional sedan and hardtop.
[3]220 @ 4400 with dual exhaust.
[4]315 @ 3100 with dual exhaust.
Note: Horsepower and torque ratings are SAE net.

Transmissions	Rear axle ratios (Optional ratios at extra cost)
3-speed, all-sync., col. shift (232) (std.)[1]	3.15 (3.54)[2]
3-speed, all-sync., col. shift (258) (std.)[3]	3.54
Torque Command, col. shift (232 & 258) (opt.)	3.15 (3.54)
Torque Command, col. shift (all V-8s) (opt.)	2.87 (3.15)

[1]Standard sedan and hardtop only.
[2]3.54 std. ratio for California cars, no options permitted.
[3]3-speed transmission with 258 available on station wagon only.
Note: Twin-Grip optional with all axle ratios; 3.73, 3.91, 4.10, 4.44 and 5.00 dealer kits at extra cost.

Popular and performance options

110 hp I-6, $46; 150 hp V-8, $99; 175 hp V-8, $42; 255 hp V-8, $170; Torque Command for 401 V-8, $257; dual exhausts for 175 hp V-8, $31; axle ratios, $14; Twin-Grip rear, $46; heavy-duty cooling, $16; heavy-duty 70 amp battery, $15; all-season air conditioning, $377; front manual disc brakes, $50; Solex glass, all windows, $42, windshield only, $35; power brakes, $47; power front disc brakes, $81; power steering, $111; AM/FM multiplex stereo radio with two speakers, $230; air-adjustable rear suspension, $40; Adjust-O-Tilt steering, $46; power windows, $123; three-spoke sports steering wheel, $20; black, white, blue, green or brown vinyl top, $91; turbo-cast wheel covers, $78; front and rear bumper guards, $31.

Engine CID emblems
(On rear portion of fenders)

232 I-6 None
258 I-6 None
304 V-8 None
360 V-8 None
401 V-8 Large chrome numerals with red painted insert

1973 Matador

Model	Body style	Series	Model no.	Price
Matador	4-Dr SED 6P	10	7315-7	$2,814
Matador	2-Dr HDTP 6P	10	7319-7	$2,887
Matador	4-Dr SW 6P	10	7318-7	$3,197

Dimensions

WB: 118"		FT: 60"	
OL: 208.48" (SW 207.66")		RT: 60"	
OW: 77.28"		HT: 55.4"	

Engines

Code	Type	CID	B×S	Hp @ Rpm	Tq @ Rpm	CR	Carb.
E	I-6	232[1,2]	3.75x3.50	100 @ 3600	185 @ 1800	8.0	1-bbl
A	I-6	258[1,3]	3.75x3.90	110 @ 3500	195 @ 2000	8.0	1-bbl
H	V-8	304	3.75x3.44	150 @ 4200	245 @ 2500	8.4	2-bbl
N	V-8	360	4.08x3.44	175 @ 4000	285 @ 2400	8.5	2-bbl
P	V-8	360	4.08x3.44	195 @ 4400[4]	295 @ 2900[5]	8.5	4-bbl
Z	V-8	401	4.17x3.68	255 @ 4600	345 @ 3300	8.5	4-bbl

[1]Low-compression six-cylinder engine available in these horsepower ratings.
[2]Standard sedan and hardtop only.
[3]Station wagon, optional sedan and hardtop.

[4]220 @ 4400 with dual exhaust.
[5]315 @ 3100 with dual exhaust.
Note: Horsepower and torque ratings are SAE net.

Transmissions	Rear axle ratios (Optional ratios at extra cost)
3-speed, all-sync., col. shift (232) (std.)[1]	3.15 (3.54)
3-speed, all-sync., col. shift (258) (std.)[2]	3.54 (3.15)
Torque Command, col. shift (232 & 258) (opt.)	3.15 (3.54)
Torque Command, col. shift (all V-8s) (opt.)	3.15 (3.54)

[1]Standard sedan and hardtop only.
[2]3-speed transmission with 258 available on station wagon only.

Popular and performance options

150 hp V-8, $138; power brakes, $44; power front disc brakes, $79; vinyl-covered top, $91; reclining seats, $80; AM/FM multiplex stereo radio, $230; power windows, $123.

Note: Prices for additional options are not available, but they were similar to those in 1972.

Engine CID emblems
(On rear portion of fenders)

232 I-6 None
258 I-6 None
304 V-8 None
360 V-8 None
401 V-8 Large chrome numerals with red painted insert

1974 Matador

Model	Body style	Series	Model no.	Price
Matador	4-Dr SED 6P	10	7415-7	$3,052
Matador	2-Dr CPE 6P	10	7416-7	$3,096
Matador	2-Dr BRGM CPE 6P	10	7416-9	$3,249
Matador	4-Dr SW 6P	10	7418-7	$3,378
Matador X	2-Dr CPE 6P	10	7416-8	$3,699

Dimensions

WB: CPE 114" (SED & SW 118")	FT: 60"
OL: CPE 209.4" (SED & SW 216")	RT: 60"
OW: CPE 77.4" (SED & SW 76.7")	HT: CPE 51.8" (SED & SW 55.4")

Engines

Code	Type	CID	B×S	Hp @ Rpm	Tq @ Rpm	CR	Carb.
E	I-6	232[1]	3.75x3.50	100 @ 3600	185 @ 1800	8.0	1-bbl
A	I-6	258[2]	3.75x3.90	110 @ 3500	195 @ 2000	8.0	1-bbl
H	V-8	304[3]	3.75x3.44	150 @ 4200	245 @ 2500	8.4	2-bbl
N	V-8	360	4.08x3.44	175 @ 4000	285 @ 2400	8.25	2-bbl
P	V-8	360	4.08x3.44	195 @ 4400[4]	295 @ 2900[5]	8.25	4-bbl
Z	V-8	401	4.17x3.68	255 @ 4600[6]	345 @ 3300[7]	8.5[8]	4-bbl

[1]Standard on 15-7, 16-7 and 16-9.
[2]Standard on 18-7 (opt. on 15-7, 16-7 and 16-9).
[3]Standard on 16-8 (opt. others).
[4]220 @ 4400 with dual exhaust.
[5]315 @ 3100 with dual exhaust.
[6]Changed shortly after introduction to 235 @ 4600.
[7]Changed shortly after introduction to 335 @ 3300 or 335 @ 3200.
[8]Changed shortly after introduction to 8.25.
Note: Horsepower and torque ratings are SAE net; 401 V-8 in aftermarket charts was sometimes rated at 225 hp; for state of California, 232 ci 1-bbl six NA; 360 ci 2-bbl minimum required engine size on Matador wagon.

Transmissions	Rear axle ratios (Optional ratios at extra cost)
3-speed, all-sync., col. shift (232) (std.)	3.15[1] (3.54)
3-speed, all-sync., col. shift (258) (NA CPE) (std.)	3.54
Torque Command, col. shift (232 & 258) (opt.)	3.15 (3.54)
Torque Command, col. shift (all V-8s) (std. 16-8 with 304 V-8) (opt. others)	3.15 (3.54)
Torque Command, cons. shift (all V-8s) (CPE only) (opt.)	3.15 (3.54)

[1]Standard ratio changed to 3.54 with no optional ratio available early in the model year shortly after model introduction.
Note: 3.54 ratio required on six-cylinder Matador coupes and four-door sedans.

Popular and performance options

Torque Command with floor shift and console for Matador, $291 to $316, for Matador X, $59 to $84; 150 hp V-8, standard in Matador X, $99; all-season air conditioning, $400; two-tone paint, $37; special paint application, $69; power steering, $111; power front disc brakes, $81; AM/FM push-button radio, $179; AM/FM multiplex stereo radio with four speakers, $230; Adjust-O-Tilt steering, $46; black, white, blue, green or brown vinyl top, $91; spoke-style wheels for Matador X, $49; 51 amp alternator, $13; 62 amp alternator, $48; 80 amp battery, $21; heavy-duty cooling, $17; heavy-duty clutch for Matador six, $12; 4-bbl 360 or 401 V-8, $32; handling package for Matador X, $30.

Engine CID emblems

232 I-6 None
258 I-6 None
304 V-8 None
360 V-8 None
401 V-8 None

1968 Ambassador

Model	Body style	Series	Model no.	Price
Ambassador	4-Dr SED 6P	80	6885-2	$2,820
Ambassador	2-Dr HDTP 6P	80	6889-2	$2,842
Ambassador DPL	4-Dr SED 6P	80	6885-5	$2,920
Ambassador DPL	2-Dr HDTP 6P	80	6889-5	$2,941
Ambassador DPL	4-Dr SW 6P	80	6888-5	$3,207
Ambassador SST	4-Dr SED 6P	80	6885-7	$3,151
Ambassador SST	2-Dr HDTP 6P	80	6889-7	$3,172

Dimensions

WB: 118"
OL: 202.50" (SW 203")
OW: 77.24"
FT: 58.58"
RT: 58.50"
HT: SED six 54.69", SW six 55.41", HDTP six 53.57", SED V-8 55.06", SW V-8 55.78", HDTP V-8 53.94"

Engines

Code	Type	CID	B×S	Hp @ Rpm	Tq @ Rpm	CR	Carb.
B	I-6	232	3.75x3.50	145 @ 4300	215 @ 1600	8.5	1-bbl
C	I-6	232	3.75x3.50	155 @ 4400	222 @ 1600	8.5	2-bbl
M	V-8	290[1]	3.75x3.28	200 @ 4600	285 @ 2800	9.0	2-bbl
S	V-8	343	4.08x3.28	235 @ 4400	345 @ 2600	9.0	2-bbl
T	V-8	343	4.08x3.28	280 @ 4800	365 @ 3000	10.2	4-bbl
(W,X)[2]	V-8	390[3]	4.17x3.57	315 @ 4600	425 @ 3200	10.2	4-bbl

[1]Standard on SST.
[2]X code in VIN, W code in engine valve cover tag denoted Canadian 390 2-bbl V-8 used in some 1968 Ambassadors converted to 4-bbl models.
[3]Midyear.

Transmissions	Rear axle ratios (Optional ratios at no extra cost)
3-speed, all-sync., col. shift (232) (std.)	3.15
3-speed, all-sync., overdrive col. shift (145 hp) (opt.)	3.54
Shift-Command, col. shift (232) (opt.)	3.15
3-speed, all-sync., col. shift (200 hp) (std.)	3.15 (3.54)
3-speed, all-sync., overdrive col. shift (200 hp) (opt.)	3.54
Shift-Command, col. shift (all V-8) (opt.)	290 V-8: 3.15 (2.87) 343 & 390 V-8: 2.87 (3.15)
Shift-Command, cons. shift (all V-8s) (opt.)	290 V-8: 3.15 (2.87) 343 & 390 V-8: 2.87 (3.15)
4-speed, all-sync., floor shift (200, 280 & 315 hp) (opt.)	290 V-8: 3.54 (3.15)[1] 343 & 390 V-8: 315 (3.54)[1]

[1]3.73, 3.91, 4.10 and 4.44 dealer kits at extra cost.
Note: Console shift available on SST only.

Popular and performance options

200 hp V-8, $16; 235 hp V-8, $58; 280 hp V-8, $91; 315 V-8, $168; Shift-Command console for V-8, SST only, $250; four-speed manual transmission, $184; tachometer with V-8, $48; power brakes, $43; power front disc brakes, $97; power steering, $95;

Twin-Grip rear, $42; two-tone paint, $32; DPL special paint with painted side panel and accent trim, $45; exterior paint stripe, SST only, $14; vinyl top, $79; reclining bucket seats with center armrest cushion, $91; AM/FM push-button radio, $58; 8-track tape player with two rear speakers, $134; sports steering wheel, $21; turbo-cast wheel covers, SST/DPL, $40, others, $61; wire wheel covers, SST/DPL, $45, others, $66; power windows, SST/DPL, $100; heavy-duty cooling, $16; handling package, $10; visibility group, $41; light group, $22.

Engine CID emblems

(On rear portion of quarter panels)

232 I-6 None
290 V-8 Small chrome *V* with black numerals set in silver background above
343 V-8 Small chrome *V* set in red background with chrome numerals side-by-side
390 V-8 Large chrome *V* with red and blue rectangles side-by-side and chrome numerals above

1969 Ambassador

Model	Body style	Series	Model no.	Price
Ambassador	4-Dr SED 6P	80	6985-2	$2,914
Ambassador DPL	4-Dr SED 6P	80	6985-5	$3,265
Ambassador DPL	4-Dr SW 6P	80	6988-5	$3,504
Ambassador DPL	2-Dr HDTP 6P	80	6989-5	$3,182
Ambassador SST	4-Dr SED 6P	80	6985-7	$3,605
Ambassador SST	4-Dr SW 6P	80	6988-7	$3,998
Ambassador SST	2-Dr HDTP 6P	80	6989-7	$3,622

Dimensions

WB: 122"
OL: 206.5" (SW 207")
OW: 77.2"
FT: 60"
RT: 60"
HT: SED 54.7", SW 55.4", HDTP 53.6"

Engines

Code	Type	CID	B×S	Hp @ Rpm	Tq @ Rpm	CR	Carb.
C	I-6	232	3.75x3.50	155 @ 4400	222 @ 1600	8.5	2-bbl
M	V-8	290[1]	3.75x3.28	200 @ 4600	285 @ 2800	9.0	2-bbl
S	V-8	343	4.08x3.28	235 @ 4400	345 @ 2600	9.0	2-bbl
T	V-8	343	4.08x3.28	280 @ 4800	365 @ 3000	10.2	4-bbl
(W,X)*	V-8	390[2]	4.17x3.57	315 @ 4600	425 @ 3200	10.2	4-bbl

[1]Standard on SST.
[2]NA on base and DPL.
*X code in VIN, W code in engine valve cover tag denoted Canadian 390 2-bbl V-8 used in some 1969 Ambassadors converted to 4-bbl models.

Transmissions	Rear axle ratios (Optional ratios at no extra cost)
3-speed, all-sync., col. shift (232) (std.)[1]	3.15
Shift-Command, col. shift (232) (opt.)	3.15
Shift-Command, col. shift (all V-8s) (opt.)[2]	2.87 (3.15)
Shift-Command, cons. shift (all V-8s exc. 235 hp) (opt.)[3]	2.87 (3.15)

[1]Standard on base and DPL.
[2]Standard on SST with 290 V-8.
[3]Console shift available on SST hardtop only.
Note: 3.73, 3.91, 4.10, 4.44 and 5.00 dealer kits at extra cost available with any V-8 transmission combination.

Popular and performance options

200 hp V-8, $16; 235 hp V-8, $52; 280 hp V-8, $80; 315 hp V-8, $168; Shift-Command for SST 343, $22, for SST 390, $37; Shift-Command column shift for base and DPL 343, $223; Shift-Command floor control for SST 343, $69, for SST 390, $79; power brakes, $43; power steering, $100; Solex glass, all windows, $39; exterior paint stripe for base model, $14; power windows for DPL and SST, $105; 8-track tape player, sedans and hardtops, $134; individually reclining seats, $58; reclining bucket seats with armrest and center cushion for SST, $111; Adjust-O-Tilt steering, $45; sport steering wheel, $30; custom velour trim for SST sedan including stainless steel trim insert, $68; black, white or blue vinyl top for DPL and SST, $100; wire wheel covers for DPL and SST, $51, for base model, $72; turbo-cast wheel covers for DPL and SST, $46, for base model, $67; visibility group with electric clock for SST, $29, for base and DPL, $43; heavy-duty 70 amp battery, $8; heavy-duty battery and 55 amp alternator, $26; dual exhausts, $31; Twin-Grip rear, $42.

Engine CID emblems
(On front portion of fenders)

232 I-6 None
290 V-8 Small chrome *V* with black numerals set in silver background above
343 V-8 Small chrome *V* set in red background with chrome numerals side-by-side
390 V-8 Large chrome *V* with red and blue rectangles side-by-side and chrome numerals above

1970 Ambassador

Model	Body style	Series	Model no.	Price
Ambassador	4-Dr SED 6P	80	7085-2	$3,020
Ambassador DPL	4-Dr SED 6P	80	7085-5	$3,588
Ambassador DPL	2-Dr HDTP 6P	80	7089-5	$3,605
Ambassador DPL	4-Dr SW 6P	80	7088-5	$3,946
Ambassador SST	4-Dr SED 6P	80	7085-7	$3,722
Ambassador SST	2-Dr HDTP 6P	80	7089-7	$3,739
Ambassador SST	4-Dr SW 6P	80	7088-7	$4,122

Dimensions

WB: 122"   FT: 60"
OL: 208" (SW 207")   RT: 60"
OW: 77.2"   HT: SED 54.7", SW 55.4", HDTP 53.6"

Engines

Code	Type	CID	B×S	Hp @ Rpm	Tq @ Rpm	CR	Carb.
G	I-6	232[1]	3.75x3.50	155 @ 4400	222 @ 1600	8.5	2-bbl
H[2]	V-8	304[3]	3.75x3.44	210 @ 4400	305 @ 2800	9.0	2-bbl
N	V-8	360	4.08x3.44	245 @ 4400	365 @ 2400	9.0	2-bbl
P	V-8	360	4.08x3.44	290 @ 4800	395 @ 3200	10.0	4-bbl
X	V-8	390[4]	4.17x3.57	325 @ 5000	420 @ 3200	10.0	4-bbl

[1]Standard on base model.
[2]A limited number of 304 4-bbl engines with code M were produced for export.
[3]Standard on DPL and SST.
[4]NA on base model.

Transmissions
3-speed, all-sync., col. shift (232) (std.)[1]
Shift-Command, col. shift (232) (opt.)
Shift-Command, col. shift (all V-8s) (opt.)[2]
Shift-Command, cons. shift (all V-8s) (opt.)[3]

Rear axle ratios
(Optional ratios at extra cost)
3.15 (3.54)
3.15
2.87 (3.15)
2.87 (3.15)

[1]Standard on base model only.
[2]Standard on DPL and SST with 304 V-8.
[3]Console shift available on SST hardtop only with bucket seats.
Note: Twin-Grip optional with all axle ratios; 3.73, 3.91, 4.10, 4.44 and 5.00 dealer kits at extra cost.

Popular and performance options
210 hp V-8, $94; 245 hp V-8, $41; 290 hp V-8, $80; 325 hp V-8, $168; power brakes, $43; power steering, $105; Solex glass, all windows, $42, windshield only, $32; two-tone paint, sedans and hardtops, $27; special paint, $39; power windows, DPL and SST, $105; AM push-button radio, $62; AM/FM mutliplex stereo radio, $134; 8-track tape player, $134; individual seat, fabric, standard SST, $64; velour individual cushion interior for SST sedan, $68; bucket seats, fabric, or vinyl for SST hardtop, $123; Adjust-O-Tilt steering, $45; heavy-duty 70 amp battery, $13; dual exhausts, $31; Twin-Grip rear, $43; axle ratios, $10; black, white or blue vinyl top, DPL/SST, $106; turbo-cast wheel covers, base model, $74, SST/DPL, $49; wire wheel covers, base model, $74, SST/DPL, $49; front and rear bumper guards, $32.

Engine CID emblems
(On rear portion of fenders)

232 I-6 None
304 V-8 Large dull smooth machined and bright rough finished numerals against black background with red-and-silver checkerboard-square pattern inside *O*
360 V-8 Large chrome numerals against black background with blue painted insert
390 V-8 Large chrome numerals against black background with red painted insert and two rows of black-and-white checkerboard-square pattern below

1971 Ambassador

Model	Body style	Series	Model no.	Price
Ambassador DPL	4-Dr SED 6P	80	7185-2	$3,616
Ambassador SST	4-Dr SED 6P	80	7185-5	$3,852
Ambassador SST	2-Dr HDTP 6P	80	7189-5	$3,870
Ambassador SST	4-Dr SW 6P	80	7188-5	$4,253
Ambassador BRGM	4-Dr SED 6P	80	7185-7	$3,983
Ambassador BRGM	2-Dr HDTP 6P	80	7189-7	$3,999
Ambassador BRGM	4-Dr SW 6P	80	7188-7	$4,430

Dimensions

WB: 122"   FT: 60"
OL: 210.8" (SW 209.8")   RT: 60"
OW: 77.2"   HT: 55.5"

Engines

Code	Type	CID	B×S	Hp @ Rpm	Tq @ Rpm	CR	Carb.
A	I-6	258[1]	3.75x3.90	150 @ 3800	240 @ 1800	8.0	1-bbl
H[2]	V-8	304[3]	3.75x3.44	210 @ 4400	300 @ 2600	8.4	2-bbl
N	V-8	360	4.08x3.44	245 @ 4400	365 @ 2600	8.5	2-bbl
P	V-8	360	4.08x3.44	285 @ 4800	390 @ 3200	8.5	4-bbl
Z	V-8	401[4]	4.17x3.68	330 @ 5000	430 @ 3400	9.5[5]	4-bbl

[1]Standard on DPL.
[2]A limited number of 304 4-bbl engines with code M were produced for export.
[3]Standard on SST and Brougham.
[4]NA on DPL.
[5]10.2 on early 1971.

Transmissions
Shift-Command, col. shift (258) (std.)[1]
Shift-Command, col. shift (all V-8s) (opt.)[2]
Shift-Command, cons. shift (all V-8s) (opt.)[3]

Rear axle ratios
(Optional ratios at extra cost)
3.15 (3.54)
2.87 (3.15)
2.87 (3.15 & 3.54[4])

[1]Standard on DPL only.
[2]Standard on SST and Brougham with 304 V-8.
[3]Console shift available on Brougham hardtop only with bucket seats.
[4]401 V-8 only.
Note: Twin-Grip optional with all axle ratios; 3.73, 3.91, 4.10, 4.44 and 5.00 dealer kits at extra cost.

Popular and performance options
210 hp V-8, $99; 245 hp V-8, $48; 285 hp V-8, $97; 330 hp V-8, $137; Shift-Command column shift for SST/Brougham 304 V-8, $6, for DPL 360 V-8, $29, for SST/Brougham 360 V-8, $23, for SST/Brougham 401 V-8, $33; Shift-Command console shift for Brougham 304 V-8, $56, for Brougham 360 V-8, $79, for Brougham 401 V-8, $89; Twin-Grip rear, $47; axle ratios, $14; dual exhausts for 285 hp V-8, $31; heavy-duty 70 amp battery, $15; cold start package, $19; power brakes, $49; power steering, $111; Solex glass, all windows, $47, windshield only, $38; electric rear window defogger, $52; two-tone paint, $31; bodyside scuff molding, $31; power windows, $120; AM push-button radio, $72; AM/FM multiplex stereo radio, $143; 8-track tape player with AM radio and two speakers, $140; vinyl center armrest with bucket seats for Brougham hardtop, $136; Harem fabric reclining seats for Brougham, $75; sports steering wheel with Rim-Blow, $40; Adjust-O-Tilt steering, $49; air-adjustable rear suspension, $42; black, white, blue or green vinyl top, $108; styled steel wheels, $108; custom wheel covers, $25; turbo-cast or wire wheel covers, $52; electric wiper/washers, $22.

Engine CID emblems
(On rear portion of fenders)

258 I-6 None
304 V-8 Large dull smooth machined and bright rough finished numerals against black background with red-and-silver checkerboard-square pattern inside *O*
360 V-8 Large chrome numerals against black background with blue painted insert
401 V-8 Large chrome numerals with red painted insert

1972 Ambassador

Model	Body style	Series	Model no.	Price
Ambassador SST	4-Dr SED 6P	80	7285-5	$3,885
Ambassador SST	2-Dr HDTP 6P	80	7289-5	$3,902
Ambassador SST	4-Dr SW 6P	80	7288-5	$4,270
Ambassador BRGM	4-Dr SED 6P	80	7285-7	$4,002
Ambassador BRGM	2-Dr HDTP 6P	80	7289-7	$4,018
Ambassador BRGM	4-Dr SW 6P	80	7288-7	$4,437

Dimensions

WB: 122"	FT: 60"
OL: 210.8" (SW 209.8")	RT: 60"
OW: 77.2"	HT: 55.5"

Engines

Code	Type	CID	B×S	Hp @ Rpm	Tq @ Rpm	CR	Carb.
H	V-8	304[1]	3.75x3.44	150 @ 4200	245 @ 2500	8.4	2-bbl
N	V-8	360	4.08x3.44	175 @ 4000	285 @ 2400	8.5	2-bbl
P	V-8	360	4.08x3.44	195 @ 4400[2]	295 @ 2900[3]	8.5	4-bbl
Z	V-8	401	4.17x3.68	255 @ 4600	345 @ 3300	8.5	4-bbl

[1]Standard on SST and Brougham.
[2]220 @ 4400 with dual exhaust.
[3]315 @ 3100 with dual exhaust.
Note: Horsepower and torque ratings are SAE net.

Transmissions
Torque Command, col. shift (all V-8s) (opt.)[1]

Rear axle ratios
(Optional ratios at extra cost)
2.87 (3.15)

[1]Standard on SST and Brougham with 304 V-8.
Note: Twin-Grip optional with all axle ratios; 3.73, 3.91, 4.10, 4.44 and 5.00 dealer kits at extra cost.

Popular and performance options
195 hp V-8, $89; 255 hp V-8, $170; Torque Command column shift for 360 V-8, $23, for 401 V-8, $35; front manual disc brakes, $50; power steering, $111; power front disc brakes, $50; power windows, $123; Solex glass, all windows, $49; Twin-Grip rear, $43; dual exhausts for 195 hp V-8, $28; axle ratios, $12; heavy-duty 70 amp battery, $14; front and rear bumper guards, $31; AM/FM multiplex stereo radio with two rear speakers, $230; Harem fabric trim for Brougham, $69; adjustable rear suspension, $40; Adjust-O-Tilt steering, $46; three-spoke sports steering wheel, $20; black, white, blue, green or brown vinyl top, $109; turbo-cast wheel covers for Brougham, $50.

Engine CID emblems
(On rear portion of fenders)

304 V-8 None
360 V-8 None
401 V-8 Large chrome numerals with red painted insert

1973 Ambassador

Model	Body style	Series	Model no.	Price
Ambassador BRGM	4-Dr SED 6P	80	7385-7	$4,461
Ambassador BRGM	2-Dr HDTP 6P	80	7389-7	$4,477
Ambassador BRGM	4-Dr SW 6P	80	7388-7	$4,861

Dimensions

WB: 122"	FT: 60"
OL: 212.86" (SW 212.04")	RT: 60"
OW: 77.2"	HT: 55.5"

Engines

Code	Type	CID	B×S	Hp @ Rpm	Tq @ Rpm	CR	Carb.
H	V-8	304	3.75x3.44	150 @ 4200	245 @ 2500	8.4	2-bbl
N	V-8	360	4.08x3.44	175 @ 4000	285 @ 2400	8.5	2-bbl
P	V-8	360	4.08x3.44	195 @ 4400[1]	295 @ 2900[2]	8.5	4-bbl
Z	V-8	401	4.17x3.68	255 @ 4600	345 @ 3300	8.5	4-bbl

[1]220 @ 4400 with dual exhaust.
[2]315 @ 3100 with dual exhaust.
Note: Horsepower and torque ratings are SAE net.

Transmissions
Torque Command, col. shift (all V-8s) (opt.)[1]

Rear axle ratios
(Optional ratios at extra cost)
3.15 (3.54)

[1]Standard with 304 V-8.

Popular and performance options
Bucket seats with center armrest and console, $131; power windows, $123; AM/FM multiplex stereo radio, $61; vinyl top, $109.

Note: Prices for additional options are not available, but they were similar to those in 1972.

Engine CID emblems
(On rear portion of fenders)

304 V-8 None
360 V-8 None
401 V-8 Large chrome numerals with red painted insert

1974 Ambassador

Model	Body style	Series	Model no.	Price
Ambassador BRGM	4-Dr SED 6P	80	7485-7	$4,559
Ambassador BRGM	4-Dr SW 6P	80	7488-7	$4,960

Dimensions

WB: 122"	FT: 60"
OL: 219.4" (SW 218.8")	RT: 60"
OW: 77.2"	HT: 55.5"

Engines

Code	Type	CID	B×S	Hp @ Rpm	Tq @ Rpm	CR	Carb.
H	V-8	304	3.75x3.44	150 @ 4200	245 @ 2500	8.4	2-bbl
N	V-8	360	4.08x3.44	175 @ 4000	285 @ 2400	8.5	2-bbl
P	V-8	360	4.08x3.44	195 @ 4400[1]	295 @ 2900[2]	8.5	4-bbl
Z	V-8	401	4.17x3.68	255 @ 4600[3]	345 @ 3300[4]	8.5[5]	4-bbl

[1]220 @ 4400 with dual exhaust.
[2]315 @ 3100 with dual exhaust.
[3]Changed shortly after introduction to 235 @ 4600.
[4]Changed shortly after introduction to 335 @ 3300 or 335 @ 3200.
[5]Changed shortly after introduction to 8.25.
Note: 401 V-8 in aftermarket charts was sometimes rated at 225 hp; for state of California, 360 V-8 2-bbl is minimum required engine size; horsepower and torque ratings are SAE net.

Transmissions
Torque Command, col. shift (all V-8s) (opt.)[1]

Rear axle ratios
(Optional ratios at extra cost)
3.15 (3.54)

[1]Standard with 304 V-8.

Popular and performance options
Torque Command column shift for 360 V-8, $13, for 401 V-8, $35; heavy-duty 80 amp battery, $21; coolant recovery system, $19; two-tone paint, $37; power windows, $123; AM push-button radio, $66; AM/FM push-button radio, $179; AM/FM multiplex stereo radio with four speakers, $161; 8-track stereo tape player, $190; Adjust-O-Tilt steering, $43; black, white, blue, green, brown or cinnamon vinyl top, $109; intermittent electric windshield wipers, $23.

Engine CID emblems

304 V-8 None
360 V-8 None
401 V-8 None

1970 Hornet

Model	Body style	Series	Model no.	Price
Hornet	4-Dr SED 6P	01	7005-0	$2,072
Hornet	2-Dr SED 6P	01	7006-0	$1,994
Hornet SST	4-Dr SED 6P	01	7005-7	$2,221
Hornet SST	2-Dr SED 6P	01	7006-7	$2,144

Dimensions

WB: 108"	FT: 57.5" (V-8 57.2")
OL: 179.3"	RT: 57" (V-8 56.6")
OW: 71.1"	HT: 52.4"

Engines

Code	Type	CID	B×S	Hp @ Rpm	Tq @ Rpm	CR	Carb.
A	I-6	199[1]	3.75x3.00	128 @ 4400	182 @ 1600	8.5	1-bbl
E	I-6	232[2]	3.75x3.50	145 @ 4300	215 @ 1600	8.5	1-bbl
G	I-6	232	3.75x3.50	155 @ 4400	222 @ 1600	8.5	2-bbl
H	V-8	304[3,4]	3.75x3.44	210 @ 4400	305 @ 2800	9.0	2-bbl

[1]Standard base model.
[2]Standard SST.
[3]Optional SST and special order on base model.
[4]A limited number of 304 four-barrel engines with code M were produced for export.

Transmissions
3-speed, 2-3 sync., col. shift (128 & 145 hp)
(std.)
Shift-Command, col. shift (all I-6s) (opt.)

Shift-Command, col. shift (304) (opt.)

Rear axle ratios
(Optional ratios at extra cost)
3.08 (3.31)

128 & 155 hp: 3.08 (3.31)
145 hp: 2.37 (2.73)
2.87 (3.15)

Note: Twin-Grip optional with all axle ratios; 3.73, 3.91, 4.10, 4.44 and 5.00 dealer kits at extra cost.

Popular and performance options
145 hp I-6, $45; 155 hp I-6, $19; 210 hp V-8, $116; Shift-Command automatic transmission, $201; power brakes, $43; power steering, $96; all-season air conditioning, $381; heavy-duty cooling, $16; axle ratios, $10; Twin-Grip rear, $43; heavy-duty 70 amp battery, $13; special application paint, $39; AM push-button radio, $62; Air-Command ventilation system, $41; Solex glass, all windows, $34, windshield only, $26; SST two-tone paint, $24; exterior body striping, $19; vinyl insert scuff side molding, $27; handling package, $23; front disc brakes for SST, $84; electric wipers/washers, $20; wheel disc covers, $25; electric clock for base model, $16; SST Caranaby plaid interior trim, $78; SST reclining individual seats, fabric trim, $52, vinyl trim, $71; SST bench seat, vinyl trim, standard base model, $20; base model bench seat, cloth trim, standard SST, $13; group Decor package with air, $34, without air, $58; light group package, $25; SST vinyl top, $84; front and rear bumper guards, $25.

Engine CID emblems
(On rear portion of quarter panels)
199 I-6 None
232 I-6 None
304 V-8 Large dull smooth machined and bright rough finished numerals against black background with red-and-silver checkerboard-square pattern inside O

1971 Hornet

Model	Body style	Series	Model no.	Price
Hornet	2-Dr SED 6P	01	7106-0	$2,174
Hornet	4-Dr SED 6P	01	7105-0	$2,234
Hornet SST	2-Dr SED 6P	01	7106-7	$2,324
Hornet SST	4-Dr SED 6P	01	7105-7	$2,274
Hornet SST	4-Dr SW 6P	01	7108-7	$2,594
Hornet SST SC/360	2-Dr SPT SED 6P	01	7106-1	$2,663

Dimensions
WB: 108″   FT: 57.5″ (V-8 57.2″)
OL: 179.3″   RT: 57″ (V-8 56.6″)
OW: 70.6″   HT: 52.4″

Engines

Code	Type	CID	B×S	Hp @ Rpm	Tq @ Rpm	CR	Carb.
E	I-6	232[1]	3.75x3.50	135 @ 4000	210 @ 1600	8.0	1-bbl
A	I-6	258	3.75x3.90	150 @ 3800	240 @ 1800	8.0	1-bbl
H	V-8	304[2,5]	3.75x3.44	210 @ 4400	300 @ 2600	8.4	2-bbl
N	V-8	360[3]	4.08x3.44	245 @ 4400	365 @ 2600	8.5	2-bbl
P	V-8	360[4]	4.08x3.44	285 @ 4800	390 @ 3200	8.5	4-bbl

[1]Standard base, SST and Sportabout station wagon.
[2]Optional SST and Sportabout station wagon and special order on base model.
[3]Standard SC/360, NA in other models.
[4]Optional SC/360 only.
[5]A limited number of 304 four-barrel engines with code M were produced for export.

Transmissions
3-speed, 2-3 sync., col. shift (232) (std.)
Shift-Command, col. shift (232) (opt.)

3-speed, all-sync., floor shift (258) (opt.)
Shift-Command, col. shift (258) (opt.)
Shift-Command, col. shift (304) (opt.)
3-speed, all-sync., floor shift (SC/360 2- & 4-bbl) (std.)
Shift-Command, col. shift (SC/360 2- & 4-bbl) (opt.)

4-speed, all-sync., floor shift (SC/360 4-bbl only) (opt.)

Rear axle ratios
(Optional ratios at extra cost)
3.08 (3.31)
Base & SST: 2.37 (2.73 & 3.08)[1]
Sportabout: 2.73 (3.08 & 3.31)
3.08 (3.31)
2.73 (3.08 & 3.31)
2.87 (3.15)
3.15 (3.54)

2-bbl: 2.87 (3.15)
4-bbl: 3.15 (3.54)
3.54 (3.15 & 3.91)

[1]With air conditioning, 2.73 standard (3.08 & 3.31 opt.).
Note: Twin-Grip optional with all axle ratios and mandatory with 3.91 ratio; 3.73, 3.91 (also factory option), 4.10, 4.44 and 5.00 dealer kits at extra cost.

Popular and Performance options
150 hp I-6, $54; 210 hp V-8, $125; Go Package, $199; Shift-Command column shift for six, $210, for 304 V-8, $216, for SC/360, $238; dual exhausts for 285 hp V-8, $31; Twin-Grip rear, $43; axle ratios, $14; heavy-duty cooling, $16; heavy-duty 70 amp battery, $15; cold start package, $19; power brakes, $49; power steering, $111; all-season air conditioning, $399; power front disc brakes for SC/360 and SST 304 V-8, $84; electric clock for base model, $17; Solex glass, all windows, $40, windshield only, $30; bodyside scuff molding, $27; SST two-tone paint, $28; exterior body striping for base model, standard SST, $10; AM push-button radio, $67; custom steering wheel, $14; sports steering wheel with Rim-Blow, $37; tachometer for SC/360 only, $50; undercoating for SC/360, $18; undercoating and hood insulation for other models, $22; styled steel wheels for SC/360, $46, for other models, $108; turbo-cast or wire wheel covers, $75; electric wiper/washers except SC/360, $21; black, white, blue or green vinyl top except SC/360, $88; front and rear bumper guards, $20.

Engine CID emblems
(On rear portion of quarter panels)
232 I-6 None
258 I-6 None
304 V-8 Large dull smooth machined and bright rough finished numerals against black background with red-and-silver checkerboard-square pattern inside O
SC/360 V-8 Die-cut into rally side stripes on rear portion of fenders

Performance models
Hornet SC/360
Model included 360 ci 245 hp 2-bbl V-8, full-synchromesh three-on-the-floor manual transmission, heavy-duty clutch, 14x6 eight-slot mag-style wheels without trim rings, D70x14 Goodyear Polyglas tires, Space Saver spare, individually reclining seats, lower rear deck red plastic reflective panel and unique SC/360 rally side and deck stripes. All the regular SST standard equipment was also included. The optional Go Package consisted of the 360 ci 285 hp 4-bbl V-8, Ram-Air induction with flat-black-finish hood scoop, tachometer, handling package, dual exhausts and D70x14 Goodyear Polyglas raised-white-letter tires. Optional transmission choices were either the full-synchromesh four-on-the-floor manual or the column-mounted Shift-Command automatic. No console-shift automatic transmission was available. Other optional equipment available was a Twin-Grip rear with ratios of up to 3.91, power steering, power brakes, power front disc brakes, air conditioning, light and visibility groups and most other regular SST options.

1972 Hornet

Model	Body style	Series	Model no.	Price
Hornet SST	2-Dr SED 6P	01	7206-7	$2,199
Hornet SST	4-Dr SED 6P	01	7205-7	$2,265
Hornet SST	4-Dr SW 6P	01	7208-7	$2,587

Dimensions
WB: 108″   FT: 57.5″ (V-8 57.2″)
OL: 179.3″   RT: 57″ (V-8 56.6″)
OW: 70.6″   HT: 52.4″

Engines

Code	Type	CID	B×S	Hp @ Rpm	Tq @ Rpm	CR	Carb.
E	I-6	232	3.75x3.50	100 @ 3600	185 @ 1800	8.0	1-bbl
A	I-6	258	3.75x3.90	110 @ 3500	195 @ 2000	8.0	1-bbl
H	V-8	304	3.75x3.44	150 @ 4200	245 @ 2500	8.4	2-bbl
N	V-8	360	4.08x3.44	175 @ 4000	285 @ 2400	8.5	2-bbl

Note: Horsepower and torque ratings are SAE net.

Transmissions
3-speed, 2-3 sync., col. shift (232) (std.)
Torque Command, col. shift (232) (opt.)
3-speed, all-sync., floor shift (232 & 258) (opt.)
Torque Command, col. shift (258) (opt.)
3-speed, all-sync., floor shift (304) (opt.)
Torque Command, col. shift (304 & 360) (opt.)

Rear axle ratios
(Optional ratios at extra cost)
3.08 (3.31)
2.37 (2.73 & 3.08)[1]
3.08 (3.31)
2.73 (3.08 & 3.31)
3.54 (3.15)
2.87 (3.15)

[1]Sedans with air conditioning and all Sportabouts, 2.73 standard (3.08 & 3.31 optional).
Note: Twin-Grip optional with all axle ratios; 3.73, 3.91, 4.10, 4.44 and 5.00 dealer kits at extra cost.

Popular and performance options

110 hp I-6, $51; 150 hp V-8, $138; 175 hp V-8, $42; Torque Command automatic transmission for six, $200; three-speed manual floor-shift transmission, $32; Twin-Grip rear, $46; axle ratios, $14; heavy-duty cooling, $16; heavy-duty 70 amp battery, $15; quick-ratio manual steering, $11; all-season air conditioning, $473; manual front disc brakes, $47; Solex glass, all windows, $40, windshield only, $30; power brakes, $44; power front disc brakes with Rallye package, $32, without Rallye package, $79; power steering, $99; AM push-button radio, $66; Scorpio fabric trim with reclining seats, $109; Adjust-O-Tilt steering, $43; three-spoke sports steering wheel, $19; sunroof for two-door sedan without vinyl top and Sportabout, $142; black, white, blue, green or brown vinyl top, $88; turbo-cast wheel covers for D/L, $25; front and rear bumper guards, $21; sedan Rallye package, $119; individual reclining seats with Sportabout Gucci trim, $142.

Engine CID emblems

232 I-6 None
258 I-6 None
304 V-8 None
360 V-8 None

1973 Hornet

Model	Body style	Series	Model no.	Price
Hornet	2-Dr SED 6P	01	7306-7	$2,298
Hornet	4-Dr SED 6P	01	7305-7	$2,343
Hornet	2-Dr HBK 6P	01	7303-7	$2,449
Hornet	4-Dr SW 6P	01	7308-7	$2,675

Dimensions

WB: 108"   FT: 56.44"
OL: 184.9"   RT: 57"
OW: 71"   HT: 52.4"

Engines

Code	Type	CID	B×S	Hp @ Rpm	Tq @ Rpm	CR	Carb.
E	I-6	232	3.75x3.50	100 @ 3600	185 @ 1800	8.0	1-bbl
A	I-6	258	3.75x3.90	110 @ 3500	195 @ 2000	8.0	1-bbl
H	V-8	304	3.75x3.44	150 @ 4200	245 @ 2500	8.4	2-bbl
N	V-8	360	4.08x3.44	175 @ 4000	285 @ 2400	8.5	2-bbl

Note: Horsepower and torque ratings are SAE net.

Transmissions	Rear axle ratios (Optional ratios at extra cost)
3-speed, 2-3 sync., col. shift (232) (std.)	2.73 (3.08 & 3.31)
Torque Command, col. shift (232 & 258) (opt.)	2.73 (3.08 & 3.31)
3-speed, all-sync., floor shift (232 & 258) (HBK only) (opt.)	2.73 (3.08 & 3.31)
Torque Command, floor shift (232 & 258) (HBK only) (opt.)	2.73 (3.08 & 3.31)
3-speed, all-sync., floor shift (304) (HBK only) (opt.)	3.54 (3.91)
Torque Command, col. shift (304 & 360) (opt.)	2.87 (3.15)
Torque Command, floor shift (304 & 360) (HBK only) (opt.)	2.87 (3.15)

Popular and performance options

Power brakes, $44; power front disc brakes, $79; manual front disc brakes, $47; bucket seats, $131; individual reclining seats, $80; vinyl top, $88; Sportabout D/L package, $284; Gucci vinyl interior, $142.

Note: Prices for additional options are not available, but they were similar to those in 1972.

Engine CID emblems

232 I-6 None
258 I-6 None
304 V-8 None
360 V-8 None

1974 Hornet

Model	Body style	Series	Model no.	Price
Hornet	2-Dr SED 6P	01	7406-7	$2,774
Hornet	4-Dr SED 6P	01	7405-7	$2,824
Hornet	2-Dr HBK 6P	01	7403-7	$2,849
Hornet	4-Dr SW 6P	01	7408-7	$3,049

Dimensions

WB: 108"   FT: 56.44"
OL: 187"   RT: 57"
OW: 70.6"   HT: 52.4"

Engines

Code	Type	CID	B×S	Hp @ Rpm	Tq @ Rpm	CR	Carb.
E	I-6	232	3.75x3.50	100 @ 3600	185 @ 1800	8.0	1-bbl
A	I-6	258	3.75x3.90	110 @ 3500	195 @ 2000	8.0	1-bbl
H	V-8	304	3.75x3.44	150 @ 4200	245 @ 2500	8.4	2-bbl
N	V-8	360	4.08x3.44	175 @ 4200	285 @ 2400	8.5	2-bbl

Note: Horsepower and torque ratings are SAE net.

Transmissions	Rear axle ratios (Optional ratios at extra cost)
3-speed, 2-3 sync., col. shift (232) (std.)	2.73 (3.08)[1]
Torque Command, col. shift (232 & 258) (opt.)	2.73 (3.08)[1]
3-speed, all-sync., floor shift (232 & 258) (HBK only) (opt.)	2.73 (3.08)[1]
Torque Command, floor shift (232 & 258) (HBK only) (opt.)	2.73 (3.08)[1]
3-speed, all-sync., floor shift (304) (HBK only) (opt.)	3.54
Torque Command, col. shift (304 & 360) (opt.)	304 V-8: 2.87 (3.15) 360 V-8: 3.15[2] (3.54)
Torque Command, floor shift (304 & 360) (HBK only) (opt.)	304 V-8: 3.15 360 V-8: 3.15[2] (3.54)

[1] 3.08 is the required axle ratio for the state of California on all six-cylinder Hornets.
[2] 2.87 standard and 3.15 optional on Hornet two-door sedan with 360 V-8.

Popular and performance options

150 hp V-8, $138; Torque Command with floor shift control for hatchback, $220 to $251; all-season air conditioning, $490; power steering, $111; power brakes, $44; power front disc brakes, $81; Sportabout D/L package with vinyl trim, $284, with custom fabric trim, $333; Sportabout X package, $139; two-tone paint for sedan and hatchback, $30; 51 amp alternator, $13; heavy-duty 10-inch clutch for six, $12; AM push-button radio, $70; AM/FM push-button radio, $179; Domino fabric for hatchback, $99, for hatchback X, $50; individually reclining seats with Venetian fabric, $109; Adjust-O-Tilt steering, $46; black, white, blue, green, brown or cinnamon vinyl top, $88; handling package, $30; hatchback X package, $207; Levi's trim package for hatchback, $150, for hatchback X, $101; hatchback Rallye X package with air conditioning, $100, without air, $199.

Engine CID emblems

232 I-6 None
258 I-6 None
304 V-8 None
360 V-8 None

1970 Gremlin

Model	Body style	Series	Model no.	Price
Gremlin	2-Dr SED 2P	40	7046-0	$1,879
Gremlin	2-Dr SED 4P	40	7046-5	$1,959

Dimensions

WB: 96"   FT: 57.46"
OL: 161.25"   RT: 57"
OW: 70.58"   HT: 51.80" (52.40" with opt. 14" tires)

Engines

Code	Type	CID	B×S	Hp @ Rpm	Tq @ Rpm	CR	Carb.
A	I-6	199	3.75x3.00	128 @ 4400	182 @ 1800	8.5	1-bbl
E	I-6	232	3.75x3.50	145 @ 4300	215 @ 1600	8.5	1-bbl

Transmissions / Rear axle ratios

Transmissions	Rear axle ratios *(Optional ratios at extra cost)*
3-speed, 2-3 sync, col. shift (199) (std.)	2.73 (3.08)
Shift-Command, col. shift (199) (opt.)	2.73 (3.08)
3-speed, 2-3 sync., floor shift (232) (std.)	3.08 (3.31)
Shift-Command, col. shift (232) (opt.)	2.37 (2.73)
Shift-Command, col. shift with air conditioning (232) (opt.)	2.73 (3.08)

Note: Twin-Grip optional with all axle ratios; 3.73, 3.91, 4.10, 4.44 and 5.00 dealer kits at extra cost.

Popular and performance options

145 hp I-6, $45; Shift-Command automatic transmission, $195; power steering, $96; power brakes, $43; Twin-Grip rear, $43; axle ratios, $10; heavy-duty cooling, $16; heavy-duty 70 amp battery, $13; all-season air conditioning, $381; special application paint, $39; AM push-button radio, $62; front and rear bumper guards, $25; locking gas cap, $6; custom steering wheel, $12; wheel covers, $25; electric wipers/washers, $20; Solex glass, all windows, $34, windshield only, $26; bucket seats and custom interior, $90; white-sidewall tires, $32; visibility group, $35; all-season air conditioning package (includes power steering, B78x14 tires and Solex glass) $461; white, black or red rally side stripes, $25; rooftop luggage rack, $39.

Engine CID emblems

199 I-6 None
232 I-6 None

1971 Gremlin

Model	Body style	Series	Model no.	Price
Gremlin	2-Dr SED 2P	40	7146-0	$1,899
Gremlin	2-Dr SED 4P	40	7146-5	$1,999

Dimensions

WB: 96″ FT: 57.46″
OL: 161.25″ RT: 57″
OW: 70.58″ HT: 51.80″ (52.40″ with opt. 14″ tires)

Engines

Code	Type	CID	B×S	Hp @ Rpm	Tq @ Rpm	CR	Carb.
E	I-6	232	3.75x3.50	135 @ 4000	210 @ 1600	8.0	1-bbl
A	I-6	258	3.75x3.90	150 @ 3800	240 @ 1800	8.0	1-bbl

Transmissions	Rear axle ratios *(Optional ratios at extra cost)*
3-speed, 2-3 sync., col. shift (232) (std.)	2.73 (3.08 & 3.31)
Shift-Command, col. shift (232) (opt.)	2.37 (2.73 & 3.08)[1]
3-speed, all-sync.,[2] floor shift (232 & 258) (opt.)[3]	2.73 (3.08 & 3.31)
Shift-Command, col. shift (258) (opt.)	2.73 (3.08 & 3.31)

[1]With air conditioning, 2.73 standard (3.08 and 3.31 optional).
[2]2-3 sync. on 232.
[3]Standard on 232, optional on 258.
Note: Twin-Grip optional with all axle ratios; 3.73, 3.91, 4.10, 4.44 and 5.00 dealer kits at extra cost.

Popular and performance options

150 hp I-6, $50; Shift-Command automatic transmission, $200; power steering, $100; power brakes, $45; Twin-Grip rear, $43; axle ratios, $12; heavy-duty cooling, $16; heavy-duty 70 amp battery, $14; cold start package, $18; all-season air conditioning, $399; front and rear bumper guards, $20; locking gas cap, $6; Solex glass, all windows, $37, windshield only, $30; rooftop luggage rack, $40; bodyside scuff molding, $27; white, black or red rally side stripes, $30; AM push-button radio, $67; custom steering wheel, $14; sports steering wheel with Rim-Blow, $37; tailgate air deflector, $49; undercoating and hood insulation, $22; styled steel wheels for Gremlin X, $34; electric wipers/washers, $21.

Engine CID emblems
(On right portion of rear deck panel)

232 I-6 None
258 I-6 None
232 I-6 X package "3.8 litre" die-cut into panel stripe
258 I-6 X package "4.2 litre" die-cut into panel stripe

1972 Gremlin

Model	Body style	Series	Model no.	Price
Gremlin	2-Dr SED 4P	40	7246-5	$1,999

Dimensions

WB: 96″ FT: 57.46″
OL: 161.25″ RT: 57″
OW: 70.58″ HT: 51.80″ (52.40″ with opt. 14″ tires)

Engines

Code	Type	CID	B×S	Hp @ Rpm	Tq @ Rpm	CR	Carb.
E	I-6	232	3.75x3.50	100 @ 3600	185 @ 1800	8.0	1-bbl
A	I-6	258	3.75x3.90	110 @ 3500	195 @ 2000	8.0	1-bbl
H	V-8	304	3.75x3.44	150 @ 4200	245 @ 2500	8.4	2-bbl

Note: Horsepower and torque ratings are SAE net.

Transmissions	Rear axle ratios *(Optional ratios at extra cost)*
3-speed, 2-3 sync., col. shift (232) (std.)	2.73 (3.08 & 3.31)
Torque Command, col. shift (232) (opt.)	2.37 (2.73 & 3.08)[1]
3-speed, all-sync.,[2] floor shift (232 & 258) (opt.)[2]	2.73 (3.08 & 3.31)
Torque Command, col. shift (258) (opt.)	2.73 (3.08 & 3.31)
3-speed, all-sync., floor shift (304) (opt.)	3.54 (3.15)
Torque Command, col. shift (304) (opt.)	2.87 (3.15)

[1]With air conditioning, 2.73 standard (3.08 & 3.31 optional).
[2]For 232: 2-3 sync. standard, all-sync. optional.
Note: Twin-Grip optional with all axle ratios; 3.73, 3.91, 4.10, 4.44 and 5.00 dealer kits at extra cost.

Popular and Performance Options

110 hp I-6, $51; 150 hp V-8, $154; three-speed manual floor-shift transmission, $32; Torque Command automatic transmission for six, $200; quick-ratio manual steering, $11; power steering, $99; power brakes, $44; power front disc brakes, $79; front manual disc brakes, $47; Twin-Grip rear, $46; axle ratios, $14; heavy-duty cooling, $16; heavy-duty 70 amp battery, $15; all-season air conditioning, $473; front and rear bumper guards, $21; Solex glass, all windows, $37, windshield only, $30; locking gas cap, $6; rally side stripes, $39; AM push-button radio, $66; bench seat with custom trim, $79; bucket seats with custom trim, $117; Adjust-O-Tilt steering, $43; three-spoke sports steering wheel, $33; sunroof, $142; custom wheel covers, $53; turbo-cast wheel covers, $78.

Engine CID emblems
(On right portion of rear deck panel)

232 I-6 None
258 I-6 None
304 V-8 None
232 I-6 X package "3.8 litre" die-cut into panel stripe
258 I-6 X package "4.2 litre" die-cut into panel stripe
304 V-8 X package "5 litre V/8" die-cut into panel stripe

1973 Gremlin

Model	Body style	Series	Model no.	Price
Gremlin	2-Dr SED 6P	40	7446-5	$2,481

Dimensions

WB: 96″ FT: 57.46″
OL: 166.2″ RT: 57″
OW: 70.58″ HT: 52.40″

Engines

Code	Type	CID	B×S	Hp @ Rpm	Tq @ Rpm	CR	Carb.
E	I-6	232	3.75x3.50	100 @ 3600	185 @ 1800	8.0	1-bbl
A	I-6	258	3.75x3.90	110 @ 3500	195 @ 2000	8.0	1-bbl
H	V-8	304	3.75x3.44	150 @ 4200	245 × 2500	8.4	2-bbl

Note: Horsepower and torque ratings are SAE net.

Transmissions	Rear axle ratios *(Optional ratios at extra cost)*
3-speed, all-sync., floor shift (232 & 258) (std.)	2.73 (3.08 & 3.31)
Torque Command, col. shift (232 & 258) (opt.)	2.73 (3.08 & 3.31)

Transmissions	Rear axle ratios *(Optional ratios at extra cost)*
Torque Command, floor shift (232 & 258) (opt.)	2.73 (3.08 & 3.31)
3-speed, all-sync., floor shift (304) (std.)	3.54 (3.91)
Torque Command, col. shift (304) (opt.)	2.87 (3.15)
Torque Command, floor shift (304) (opt.)	2.87 (3.15)

Popular and performance options

150 hp V-8, $154; X package, $285; power brakes, $44; power front disc brakes, $79; manual front disc brakes, $47; power steering, $99; all-season air conditioning, $377; bucket seats, $131.

Note: Prices for additional options are not available, but they were similar to those in 1972.

Engine CID emblems
(On right portion of rear deck panel)

232 I-6 None
258 I-6 None
304 V-8 None
232 I-6 X package "3.8 litre" die-cut into panel stripe
258 I-6 X package "4.2 litre" die-cut into panel stripe
304 V-8 X package "5 litre V/8" die-cut into panel stripe

1974 Gremlin

Model	Body style	Series	Model no.	Price
Gremlin	2-Dr SED 6P	40	7446-5	$2,481

Dimensions

WB: 96"	FT: 56.7"
OL: 170.3"	RT: 57"
OW: 70.58"	HT: 52.40"

Engines

Code	Type	CID	B×S	Hp @ Rpm	Tq @ Rpm	CR	Carb.
E	I-6	232	3.75x3.50	100 @ 3600	185 @ 1800	8.0	1-bbl
A	I-6	258	3.75x3.90	110 @ 3500	195 @ 2000	8.0	1-bbl
H	V-8	304	3.75x3.44	150 @ 4200	245 @ 2500	8.4	2-bbl

Note: Horsepower and torque ratings are SAE net.

Transmissions	Rear axle ratios *(Optional ratios at extra cost)*
3-speed, all-sync., floor shift (232 & 258) (std.)	2.73[1] (3.08)
Torque Command, col. shift (232 & 258) (opt.)	2.73[1] (3.08)
Torque Command, floor shift (232 & 258) (opt.)	2.73[1] (3.08)
3-speed, all-sync., floor shift (304) (std.)	3.54
Torque Command, col. shift (304) (opt.)	3.15
Torque Command, floor shift (304) (opt.)	3.15

[1]3.08 is the required axle ratio in the state of California on all six-cylinder Gremlins.

Popular and performance options

150 hp V-8, $154; Torque Command floor shift for six and V-8, $220 to $251; all-season air conditioning, $490; power brakes, $44; power front disc brakes, $81; power steering, $111; 51 amp alternator, $13; 10-inch heavy-duty clutch, $12; X package, $227; X package with Levi's trim, $298; rally side stripes, $33; AM push-button radio, $70; Adjust-O-Tilt steering, $46; sports steering wheel, $33; aluminum trim rings and hubcaps, $33; spoke-style wheels, $49; vent rear quarter windows, $28; custom trim package with bench seat, $109, with bucket seats, $147; Levi's trim package, $165, with X package, $50; Rallye X package with air conditioning, $100, without air conditioning, $199; handling package, $30.

Engine CID emblems
(On right portion of rear deck panel)

232 I-6 None
258 I-6 None
304 V-8 None
232 I-6 X package "3.8 litre" die-cut into panel stripe
258 I-6 X package "4.2 litre" die-cut into panel stripe
304 V-8 X package "5 litre V/8" die-cut into panel stripe

AMC clubs

The following AMC car clubs are dedicated to the promotion and preservation of AMC vehicles, and they can benefit the typical AMC enthusiast in all aspects. Write them for further details about membership application.

American Motors Owners
Association (AMO)
517 New Hampshire
Portage, MI 49081

National American
Motors Drivers and
Racers Association (NAMDRA)
923 Plainfield Road
Countryside, IL 60525

Total Performance
Independents (TPI)
P.O. Box 9307
Daytona Beach, FL 32020

American Motorsport
International (AMS) &
Classic AMX Club
International (CACI)
7963 Depew Street
Arvada, CO 80003

AMC Rambler Club
2645 Ashton Road
Cleveland Heights, OH 44118

Toyota Performance
AMC (TPA)
P.O. Box 29
Avon Park, FL 33825

Index